MW00763019

ADVANCES IN POSITIVE ORGANIZATIONAL PSYCHOLOGY

ADVANCES IN POSITIVE ORGANIZATIONAL PSYCHOLOGY

Series Editor: Arnold B. Bakker

ADVANCES IN POSITIVE ORGANIZATIONAL
PSYCHOLOGY   VOLUME 1

ADVANCES IN POSITIVE ORGANIZATIONAL PSYCHOLOGY

EDITED BY

ARNOLD B. BAKKER
Erasmus University, Rotterdam, Netherlands

United Kingdom – North America – Japan
India – Malaysia – China

Emerald Group Publishing Limited
Howard House, Wagon Lane, Bingley BD16 1WA, UK

First edition 2013

Reprints and permission service
Contact: permissions@emeraldinsight.com

British Library Cataloguing in Publication Data
A catalogue record for this book is available from the British Library

ISBN: 978-1-78052-000-1
ISSN: 2046-410X (Series)

Printed and bound by CPI Group (UK) Ltd, Croydon, CR0 4YY

ISOQAR certified
Management System,
awarded to Emerald
for adherence to
Environmental
standard
ISO 14001:2004.

Certificate Number 1985
ISO 14001

INVESTOR IN PEOPLE

CONTENTS

v

LIST OF CONTRIBUTORS

Simon L. Albrecht	School of Psychology, Deakin University, Melbourne, Australia
Arnold B. Bakker	Department of Work & Organizational Psychology, Erasmus University, Rotterdam, The Netherlands
Charlotte P. Barner	School of Education & Human Development, Southern Methodist University, Dallas, TX, USA
Robert W. Barner	School of Education & Human Development, Southern Methodist University, Dallas, TX, USA
Justin M. Berg	The Wharton School, University of Pennsylvania, Philadelphia, PA, USA
Uta K. Bindl	The UWA Business School, University of Western Australia, Crawley, Australia
Kim S. Cameron	Ross School of Business, University of Michigan, Ann Arbor, MI, USA
Tori L. Crain	Department of Psychology, Portland State University, Portland, OR, USA
Hans De Witte	Research Group Work, Organizational and Personnel Psychology, KU Leuven, Leuven, Belgium; Vanderbijlpark Campus, North-West University, South Africa
Maren Dollwet	School of Behavioral & Organizational Sciences, Claremont Graduate University, Claremont, CA, USA

Stewart I. Donaldson	Schools of Behavioral & Organizational Sciences; Politics & Economics, Claremont Graduate University, Claremont, CA, USA
Adrienne Dougherty	Department of Psychology, University of Michigan, Ann Arbor, MI, USA
Jane E. Dutton	Stephen M. Ross School of Business, University of Michigan, Ann Arbor, MI, USA
Taru Feldt	Department of Psychology, University of Jyväskylä, Jyväskylä, Finland
Barbara L. Fredrickson	Department of Psychology, University of North Carolina, Chapel Hill, NC, USA
Marylène Gagné	School of Psychology, University of Western Australia, Crawley, WA, Australia
Jamie A. Gruman	Department of Business, University of Guelph, Guelph, Canada
Leslie B. Hammer	Department of Psychology, Portland State University, Portland, OR, USA
Ulla Kinnunen	School of Social Sciences and Humanities, University of Tampere, Tampere, Finland
Ethan Kross	Department of Psychology, University of Michigan, Ann Arbor, MI, USA
David Seungjae Lee	Department of Psychology, University of Michigan, Ann Arbor, MI, USA
Nicholas LoBuglio	The Wharton School, University of Pennsylvania, Philadelphia, PA, USA
Fred Luthans	Department of Management, University of Nebraska, Lincoln, NE, USA
Anne Mäkikangas	Department of Psychology, University of Jyväskylä, Jyväskylä, Finland
Saija Mauno	Department of Psychology, University of Jyväskylä, Jyväskylä, Finland

Wido G.M. Oerlemans	Department of Work & Organizational Psychology, Erasmus University, Rotterdam, The Netherlands
Sharon K. Parker	The UWA Business School, University of Western Australia, Crawley, Australia
Alan M. Saks	Centre for Industrial Relations and Human Resources, University of Toronto, Toronto, Canada
Jeffrey Sanchez-Burks	Ross School of Business, University of Michigan, Ann Arbor, MI, USA
Tanya Vacharkulksemsuk	Department of Psychology, University of North Carolina, Chapel Hill, NC, USA
Anja Van den Broeck	Human Relations Research Group, HU Brussel, Brussels, Belgium; Research Group Work, Organizational and Personnel Psychology, KU Leuven, Leuven, Belgium
Joris van Ruysseveldt	Faculty of Psychology, Open University of the Netherlands, Heerlen, The Netherlands
Els Vanbelle	Research Group Work, Organizational and Personnel Psychology, KU Leuven, Leuven, Belgium
Maarten Vansteenkiste	Department of Developmental, Personality and Social Psychology, Ghent University, Ghent, Belgium
Amy Wrzesniewski	Yale School of Management, Yale University, New Haven, CT, USA
Chia-Huei Wu	The UWA Business School, University of Western Australia, Crawley, Australia
Oscar Ybarra	Department of Psychology, University of Michigan, Ann Arbor, MI, USA
Carolyn M. Youssef-Morgan	College of Business, Bellevue University, Bellevue, NE, USA
Yufang Zhao	Department of Psychology, Southwest University, Chongqing, P.R. China

TAMING THE WAVES AND WILD HORSES OF POSITIVE ORGANIZATIONAL PSYCHOLOGY

Stewart I. Donaldson and Maren Dollwet

Ruark (2009) described positive psychology as an intellectual movement for the masses. That is, she asserted while most scholars labor in obscurity, positive psychologist's ideas, concepts, theories, research findings, and applications are in incredibly high demand across the globe. The almost exclusive focus on pathology that has dominated traditional psychology for decades, has made some room for a new attempt to develop a science of optimal human and organizational functioning and flourishing, that has already ignited a substantial new generation of scholars and practitioners (Donaldson, Csikszentmihalyi, & Nakamura, 2011). This relatively new effort referred to as the science of positive psychology is committed to the prevention of pathologies that arise when life is barren and meaningless, and to understanding how best to improve quality of life and make life worth living (Seligman & Csikszentmihalyi, 2000).

THE TSUNAMI

During the past decade, the winds and raucous waves of positive psychology have altered the landscape and brought new life to the profession and

Advances in Positive Organizational Psychology, Volume 1, 1–21
Copyright © 2013 by Emerald Group Publishing Limited
All rights of reproduction in any form reserved
ISSN: 2046-410X/doi:10.1108/S2046-410X(2013)0000001003

discipline of psychology. Since Seligman and Csikszentmihalyi (2000) proffered the positive psychology manifesto at the turn of the century, an amazing plethora of books, articles, research investigations, grants, awards, and applications for improving human welfare and society at large have emerged (see Donaldson, 2011a). Sheldon, Kashdan, and Steger (2011) fully described this impressive groundswell of positive psychology activity in their recent edited volume on *Designing positive psychology: Taking stock and moving forward*. This rapid growth of scholarly activity has also spawned new professional societies such as the *International Association of Positive Psychology* (http://www.ippanetwork.org/Home/), scholarly journals includ-ing the *Journal of Positive Psychology* (http://www.tandf.co.uk/journals/titles/17439760.asp) and *Journal of Happiness Studies* (http://www.springer.com/social + sciences/well-being/journal/10902), and top tier graduate pro-grams such as the Masters of Applied Positive Psychology at the University of Pennsylvania and the MA and PhD programs in Positive Organizational Psychology and Positive Developmental Psychology at Claremont Graduate University. All of these efforts share the desire to better organize and foster the continued growth and impact of positive psychology.

Recently, Donaldson and Dollwet (under review) took stock on the field of positive psychology as a whole. Their analysis revealed that over 1,100 articles have been published on positive psychology in peer-reviewed academic journal articles from its birth in 1998 to 2012. This massive swell of positive psychology in the past 14 years includes both theoretical work (e.g., defining new concepts and theories, synthesizing existing literature) as well as rigorous empirical studies testing theoretically proposed concepts. The examined publications also reveal that positive psychology covers virtually all aspects and domains of human life and extends across the life span. Specifically, both theoretical and empirical work in positive psycho-logy includes children, adolescents, adults, and even reaches into late adul-thood with the study of positive aging.

Donaldson and Ko (2010) documented that the perspectives and concepts from positive psychology are now being applied to a wide range of profes-sions and disciplines at an accelerating rate. For example, research, scholar-ship, and applications drawing on the core concepts of positive psychology can now be found in education, public health, healthcare, social and human services, economics, political science, public policy, neuroscience, manage-ment, leadership, and the organizational sciences among others. Even Seligman and Csikszentmihalyi (2000) could not have imagined how far and wide across the land and sea the core ideas of positive psychology would travel in such a relatively short amount of time.

THE WORK HORSE

A detailed review of the impact of positive psychology across the professions and disciplines is beyond the scope of this chapter. Instead, this chapter takes on a more focused task of summarizing positive psychology's influence on the world of work and organizations (see Bakker & Schaufeli, 2008; Cameron & Spreitzer, 2012; Luthans & Youssef, 2007), and suggests new directions for research and application. Positive psychology has been defined as the science of positive subjective experience, positive individual traits, and positive institutions (Seligman & Csikszentmihalyi, 2000). Peterson (2006) elaborated on this definition and articulated the three pillars of positive psychology – (1) positive subjective experience, (2) positive traits, and (3) positive institutions. The third pillar, positive institutions, includes families, schools, businesses, communities, and societies, and is believed to facilitate the first two pillars to promote human flourishing. Organizations and work environments are viewed in the positive psychology literature as subset of the third pillar of positive institutions. This implies that organizations are considered institutions by Peterson (2006), but not necessarily vice versa. Therefore, positive organizational psychology has been defined as the scientific study of positive subjective experiences and traits in the workplace and positive organizations, and its application to improve the effectiveness and quality of life in organizations (Donaldson & Ko, 2010).

As positive psychology has grown up and found a job in the workplace, it has done so under several identities including positive psychology at work, positive workplace, positive organization, positive organizational behavior, positive organizational scholarship, positive occupational health psychology, and the like. In our view, each one of these identities has nuanced but highly interrelated definitions, concepts, and applications. For example,

Luthans (2002a) defines positive organizational behavior "as the study and application of positively oriented human resource strengths and psychological capacities that can be measured, developed and effectively managed for performance improvement in today's workplace." (p. 59)

Cameron and Spreitzer (2012) assert "positive organizational scholarship rigorously seeks to understand what represents the best of the human condition based on scholarly research and theory. Just as positive psychology focuses on exploring optimal individual psychological states rather than pathological ones, organizational scholarship focuses attention on the generative dynamics in organizations that lead to the development of human strengths, foster resiliency in employees, enable healing and restoration, and cultivate extraordinary individual and organizational performance." (p. 1)

Additionally, positive occupational health psychology (POHP) as discussed by Bakker and Derks (2010) refers to "... how work contexts (such as jobs, units, work groups, professions, and organizations) affect and are affected by positive relationships, positive emotions, and positive meanings (see Frederickson & Dutton, 2008). In sum, POHP is the study and application of optimal functioning in the workplace. It promotes occupational health and flourishing, and examines how positive phenomena (context, personal resources) can be used to protect against occupational risks." (p. 201)

While we acknowledge there are some differences in how these concepts and definitions have developed, most of the topics pursued under these definitions and identities fit within our broad definition of positive organizational psychology. It is important to acknowledge that many of the scholars pursuing topics in this broad area are not positive psychologists or psychologists in general, but have been influenced by the positive psychology movement to frame their scholarship in the work and organizational sciences using a positive perspective. In addition to those who identify themselves as positive psychologists, work and organizational psychologists, occupational health psychologists, and industrial/organizational psychologists, scholars working on this topic come from or identify with fields such as business administration, management, leadership, human resource management, organizational behavior, and the like. Our focus next is to summarize the literature that has been produced by this multidisciplinary collection of scholars applying the concepts and principles of positive psychology to improve organizations and the world of work.

Donaldson and Ko (2010) illustrated that applications of positive psychology in work and organizational settings have generally been classified under the headings or frameworks of positive organizational psychology, positive organizational behavior, and positive organizational scholarship. Therefore, they conducted a study to analyze the peer reviewed conceptual and empirical contributions that have been made in these areas between 2001 and 2009. They identified a total of 172 publications during this time period, and discovered that there has been steady increase in scholarly activity over time. For example, Fig. 1 shows a high of 35 publications (including 19 empirical studies) in 2008, compared to 3 publications (1 empirical study) in 2001.

The two most popular topics identified during this initial 9-year period were positive leadership (17 publications) and positive organizational development and change (16 publications). Taking together the findings from Donaldson and Ko and complementing them with the recent work by Donaldson and Dollwet (under review), we see that there are a number of ways positive psychology has infiltrated the workplace. Specifically, some of

Fig. 1. Positive Organizational Psychology Peer-Reviewed Journal Articles from 2001 to 2009. *Source:* Donaldson and Ko (2010).

Table 1. Key Topics in Positive Organizational Psychology.

Positive Leadership
Positive Organizational Development and Change
Positive Individual Attributes
Positive Emotions
Strengths and Virtues
Positive Relationships
Positive Human Resource Practices
Positive Organizational Processes
Psychological Capital
Flow
Organizational Virtuousness and Ethics
Employee Work Engagement
Workplace Well-Being

Source: Donaldson and Ko (2010); Donaldson and Dollwet (under review).

the key topics being addressed in positive organizational psychology are shown in Table 1.

Many of the key topics within positive organizational psychology that are outlined in the table above are concerned with when and how employees thrive at work. Thriving in general refers to a state in which humans feel vigorous and are functioning at their optimal level. While thriving or "blooming" has been studied more extensively in the domains of sports and educational psychology, the concept has also found a place at work. It appears that certain work conditions such as acquiring new and relevant knowledge on a daily basis and finding meaning in the work performed lead to higher levels of thriving at work (e.g., Niessen, Sonnentag, & Sach, 2012). Thus, we can see that workplace settings and contexts (e.g., job design) can have a positive impact on the employees' functioning at work.

Ko and Donaldson (2011) probed deeper to uncover the empirical findings in this literature that demonstrated the potential benefits of positive organizational psychology concepts. In particular, many of these concepts expand our understanding of traditional organizational psychology topics and provide implications for how they can be put to use to improve organizational effectiveness and the quality of work life. In addition, the current research by Donaldson and Dollwet (under review) extends these findings by showing how the work horse of positive psychology has left its footprints in the recent years of 2010 and 2012. Taking these findings together, we provide a high-level overview and sample of specific research studies that have linked positive organizational psychological concepts to desired organizational outcomes in Table 2.

Besides the above described effects that positive psychology concepts can have in the workplace, there are also a number of interventions embedded within the field of positive organizational psychology that have the goal of increasing employee and organizational effectiveness. These types of interventions use key principles of positive psychology (e.g., strengths, psychological capital, positive emotions, flow) to impact organizational outcomes.

In their recent review of the field of positive psychology, Donaldson and Dollwet (under review) found a number of positive psychology intervention types that are effective in the workplace. As an example, interventions using coaching principles that focus on identifying and using strengths, positive refraining, and building self-efficacy can have multiple positive outcomes for employees. In one study by Green, Oades, and Grant (2006), participants of a coaching program showed significant increases in goal striving, well-being, and hope after completing the program. These types of coaching interventions rooted in positive organizational psychology appear to be applicable to a large variety of job levels, employees, and organizations. For instance, executive leaders can benefit from coaching in that they are better able to attain their goals, have higher resilience, and workplace well-being,

Table 2. Examples of the Potential Benefits of Positive Organizational Psychology.

Strength-based approach

- Decreased turnover rate and increased employee engagement, state hope, and life satisfaction (Black, 2001; Hodges & Clifton, 2004)
- Increased employee engagement (Clifton & Harter, 2003)
- Increased employee and team productivity (Connelly, 2002)
- Progress toward goals and increased well-being (Linley, Nielsen, Gillett, & Biswas-Diener, 2010)

Positive leadership

- Higher OCB, higher organizational commitment, better organizational performance, higher follower satisfaction with supervisor, higher job satisfaction, and better job performance (Walumbwa et al., 2008)
- Increased employee work engagement (Tuckey et al., 2012)
- Higher levels of employee proactivity in terms of anticipating and solving problems as well as searching for ways to change work situations (Den Hartog & Belschak, 2012)

Positive organizational development and change

- Higher future success expectancy, better coping with stress, better job performance, and higher job satisfaction (Armstrong-Stassen & Schlosser, 2008)
- Increase in stock prices, better customer relations, better employee relations, higher quality product, and innovative union–management partnership (Cooperrider & Whitney, 1999; Whitney & Cooperrider, 2000)

Organizational virtuousness

- Better objective and perceived organizational performance: higher profit margin, innovation, customer retention, employee turnover, and quality (Cameron et al., 2004)
- Higher employee well-being and affective commitment (Rego, Ribeiro, Cunha, & Jesuino, 2011)

Psychological capital

- Better job performance, higher job satisfaction, and higher organizational commitment (Larson & Luthans, 2006; Luthans, Norman, Avolio, & Avey, 2008)
- More engagement, higher OCB, lower voluntary and involuntary absenteeism, and lower cynicism and deviance (Avey, Wernsing, & Luthans, 2008; Avey et al., 2010)

Flow

- Extra-role job performance (Eisenberger, Jones, Stinglhamber, Shanock, & Randall, 2005)
- Better in-role and extra-role job performance (Demerouti, 2006)
- More organizational and personal resources (Salanova, Bakker, & Llorens, 2006)
- Higher motivation, enjoyment, participation, aspirations, and buoyancy (Martin & Jackson, 2008)
- Absorption at work (Rodriguez-Sanchez, Schaufeli, Salanova, Cifre, & Sonnenschein, 2011)
- Higher intrinsic motivation (Keller, Ringelhan, & Blomann, 2011)

Table 2. (*Continued*)

Positive emotions

- Favorable evaluation of entrepreneurial opportunity (Grichnik et al., 2010)
- Higher job performance and mitigates the potential negative impact of role stressors (Wincent & Ortqvist, 2011)
- Increased authenticity and performance success as perceived by others (Van Gelderen, Konijn, & Bakker, 2011)
- Increases the effect of savoring on employee's task performance (Lin, Chen, & Wang, 2011)

Work engagement

- Increased business performance in terms of financial returns, customer service, and employee retention (Harter, 2000)
- Higher productivity, lower turnover, and higher customer loyalty at both employee and work unit levels (Harter et al., 2002)
- Higher task performance and more innovativeness (Gorgievski et al., 2010)

Source: Ko and Donaldson (2011); Donaldson and Dollwet (under review).

as well as reduced depression and stress after participating in such a program (Grant, Curtayne, & Burton, 2009). Furthermore, positive organizational psychology coaching interventions can also be useful to other types of jobs and professions including the teaching profession. Grant, Green, and Rynsaardt (2010) recently found that coaching can help high school teachers achieve their goals, reduce their stress levels, and have higher workplace well-being.

Another intervention type that can yield beneficial organizational and work outcomes is focused on building psychological capital (PsyCap). Luthans, Avey, and Patera (2008) conducted an intervention study and found that PsyCap can be increased through targeted exercises in just a 2-hour period of time. Increasing employees' PsyCap then has multiple positive implications for their behavior at work including higher performance and organizational commitment, and less counterproductive work behaviors (e.g., Avey, Luthans, & Youssef, 2010).

These are just two examples of types of positive psychology interventions that have found their way into the working world in order to achieve positive employee and organizational outcomes. There are many more types of interventions within the field of positive organizational psychology, yet their common goal is to better employees' worklife. While they each may differ in the concepts that are applied and the various outcomes gained, what these interventions all share is that they utilize approaches that are rooted within positive psychology and its theoretical frameworks in order to benefit individual employees and organizations at large.

With the above described empirical findings and interventions, we can begin to see the mere size, speed, and stamina of the positive psychology work horse. Just recently, Cameron and Spreitzer (2012) published a 79-chapter volume, *The Oxford handbook of positive organizational scholarship*, that comprehensively addresses positive psychology topics focused on the workplace and organizations, key concepts, theories, and research findings. In this volume, we see that positive organizational psychology has placed a new lens on already existing constructs, such as leadership, work engagement, and creativity. In addition, the swell of positive psychology into the workplace has introduced several new constructs, such as callings or peak performance, to the world of organizations. Table 3 highlights some of the constructs within positive psychology that "have been put to work."

With regards to positive individual attributes, studies show that certain characteristics within an employee (creativity, proactivity, curiosity) may be particularly beneficial in yielding exceptional work results. For example, a study by Valentine, Godkin, Fleischman, and Kidwell (2011) revealed that creativity within a work group was positively related with job satisfaction and negatively with turnover intentions. Furthermore, employees who experience a calling at work have higher career commitment, work meaning, and job satisfaction (Duffy, Bott, Allan, Torrey, & Dik, 2012). In a related vein, the construct of employee engagement also has various applications to the work world. Multiple studies have shown that engaged employees have higher job performance and productivity and also are less likely to leave the organization (e.g., Gorgievski, Bakker, & Schaufeli, 2010; Harter, Schmidt, & Hayes, 2002). Such findings therefore have practical implications for organizations as they can create work environments that foster creativity, engagement, and motivation in their employees (Zhou, Hirst, & Shipton, 2012).

Another topic area within positive psychology, namely positive emotions, also has important implications at the workplace. The impact of positive emotions at work becomes clear when we look at studies that show employees who experience more positive emotions are better able to translate job role stressors into high performance (Wincent & Ortqvist, 2011) and also perceive more entrepreneurial opportunities (Grichnik, Smeja, & Welpe, 2010). In a related vein, the authenticity of displayed positive emotions as well as the level of emotion regulation appear to be factors impacting these relationships. For example, Pisaniello, Winefield, and Delfabbro (2012) conducted a study on the impact of emotional labor and emotional work on

Table 3. Positive Organizational Psychology Topic Areas and
Constructs.

Topic Area	Construct
Positive Individual Attributes	• Prosocial motivation • Callings in work • Work engagement • Proactivity • Creativity • Curiosity • Positive traits
Positive Emotions	• Positive energy • Subjective well-being • Passion • Emotional intelligence
Strengths and Virtues	• Forgiveness • Compassion • Hope • Courage • Justice • Integrity • Positive ethics
Positive Relations	• High-quality connections • Reciprocity • Trust • Humor
Positive Human Resource Practices	• Career development • Mentoring • Diversity • Work–life dynamics
Positive Organizational Practices	• Collective efficacy • Work design • Mindful organizing • Innovation
Positive Leadership and Change	• Appreciative inquiry • Authentic leadership • Peak performance

Source: Cameron and Spreitzer (2012).

occupational health and found that being able to regulate your emotions at work as well as those of others may lead to lower levels of job burnout. Meanwhile, having to display emotions that are not actually felt (an aspect of emotional labor) may lead to increased levels of burnout. Furthermore, having more authentic emotional experiences at work may lead to higher job satisfaction, positive health, and well-being.

Likewise, strengths and virtues is another topic area that applies itself very well to the working world. There are a large number of strengths an employee may have as outlined by the Clifton Strengths Finder (Buckingham & Clifton, 2001) or the VIA Character Strengths (Peterson & Seligman, 2004). These strengths include characteristics such as forgiveness, compassion, courage, justice, integrity, and the like. Research within the field of positive organizational psychology has shown that these strengths may be applicable and useful in the workplace. For instance, employees who use and identify their strengths as relating to their job may be less likely to leave the job, have higher work engagement, and higher productivity (e.g., Black, 2001; Hodges & Clifton, 2004). It is also important to note that the character strengths can be redefined in order to match specific work environments (e.g., McGovern, 2011).

In today's fast-paced workplace, we are highly reliant on each other and often work in project teams that may be spread across different locations with team members communicating virtually. Thus, examining the effect of positive relations at work, such as trust, reciprocity, and humor is becoming more and more important for organizations. In 2006, an entire book was published that focused solely on the importance of positive relationships at work and how they impact various aspects of worklife including giving the employee a sense of attachment to the workplace and facilitating organizational and team-commitment (Dutton & Ragins, 2006).

Positive organizational psychology also includes topic areas that focus on positive human resources and organizational practices. These practices refer to the unit- or organizational-level initiatives, ways of organizing, and structuring that are based on principles within positive psychology. The idea behind these positive practices is to create a work environment that will allow employees to strive, self-actualize, and reach peak performance while maintaining a good quality of life. One example of these practices includes work–life balance initiatives, which can increase organizational commitment (Muse, Harris, Giles, & Feild, 2008). The importance of these types of initiatives also becomes apparent in research demonstrating the positive impact one's family life can have on work life and vice versa (e.g., Masuda, McNall, Allen, & Nicklin, 2012). Besides work–family initiatives, there are a number of other positive organizational practices that yield beneficial outcomes for the organization's employees. An example of this can be seen in a recent study by Cheung and Wu (2012). These authors investigated positive aging at work and found that organizational training and developmental initiatives were positively associated with employee growth, and that support from the organization was an important predictor of positive aging at the workplace. Thus, there are a number of ways organizations can implement practices and initiatives that are based in the positive psychology paradigm and enable their employees to blossom – across the lifespan and extending into their family life.

Finally, positive organizational psychology has also greatly influenced the study of leadership, as leaders often shape work environments, build an organizational culture, and can thereby impact their organizations and individual employees in a variety of different ways. Authentic virtuous leaders may have a particularly positive impact on the work environment they create. One recent example of the importance of putting a positive psychology lens on the study of leadership comes from Woolley, Caza, and Levy (2011). These authors found that an authentic leadership style was associated with followers' psychological capital and the creation of a positive work environment.

From the sample of topics and studies described above, we can see that there are many general topic areas within positive organizational behavior and their related constructs that have tangible impacts on employees, teams, and organizations as whole. Taking all these findings together, it appears that positive organizational psychology has been working very hard to infiltrate many aspects of organizational life by redefining existing organizational concepts and by developing new theories and constructs.

WAVES AND WILD HORSES

Since Seligman's 1998 APA Presidential address and subsequent *American Psychologist* volume on *Happiness, Excellence, and Optimal Human Functioning*, there has been a tsunami of new positive psychology research and scholarship focused on organizations and the workplace. Luthans and his colleagues began integrating positive psychology into organizational research in 1999, and positive organizational behavior research was born (Luthans, 2002b). In 2003, positive organizational scholarship was introduced as a new area of study in the organizational sciences (Cameron & Spreitzer, 2012). Just over a decade later, there is no shortage of boosterism and grand optimism for the future of positive psychology, and its potential application to organizations and the quality of work life.

However, there seems to be a growing number of prominent scholars and researchers raising serious questions and doubts about the legitimacy and value of the positive psychology movement. For example, Lazarus (2003) began by arguing that many of the claims of positive psychology are naïve and misleading. He asserted the field lacks conceptual clarity and that serious methodological problems with positive psychology research are not being faced. Essentially he suggested many enthusiasts are being taken on a wild horse ride that will eventually end in disappointment and injury.

Kashdan and Steger (2011), Miller (2008), and Wong (2011) have recently identified similar challenges and pitfalls. For example, Miller (2008) claims:

> The new science of positive psychology is founded on a whole series of fallacious arguments; these involve circular reasoning tautology, failure to clearly define or properly apply terms, the identification of casual relations where none exist, and unjustified generalization. Instead of demonstrating that positive attitudes explain achievement, success, well-being and happiness, positive psychology merely associates mental health with a particular personality type: a cheerful, outgoing, goal-driven, status-seeking extravert.

Wong (2011) provided a more measured critique and focused largely on the claim that positive psychology has ignored the reality and benefits of negative emotions and experiences. He goes on to claim that most psychological phenomena can't be properly understood without considering both positive and negative experiences, and proposes a more balanced interactive model which he calls "Positive Psychology 2.0." Kashdan and Steger (2011) deal with similar limitations but also raise a serious concern that many working in this area have taken positive psychology to market too soon.

More specific critiques and criticisms have been levied against those applying positive psychology principles to organizations and workplaces. For example, Hackman (2009) claimed that research in positive organizational psychology is accumulating so rapidly that the field is being built on a shaky foundation. He believes research in this area is surprisingly ahistorical, lacks evidence of validity, that too few methods are being used, and that this new research paradigm is seductive and needs to be critically examined. Fineman (2006) raised similar concerns and added there is an unarticulated dark side to positiveness at work. He asserted that promoting a social orthodoxy of positiveness can stigmatize employees and leaders who do not fit the template. Fineman also emphasized current conceptions of positive organizational psychology tend to be culturally constrictive, tied broadly to North American cultural norms of individualism, optimism, and self-confidence. In summary, despite the amazing energy and enthusiasm for positive psychology in the workplace, there are many challenges that must be thoughtfully tamed in order to achieve sound science and practice in this emerging discipline.

PROMISING FUTURE SWELLS AND RIDES

What lies ahead for positive organizational psychology? Is Lazarus (2003) right by claiming that positive psychology is just another fad here today but gone tomorrow? Will the energy fueling the current surge of positive organizational psychology research dissipate and give way to the next flavor of the month? Is it true that positive organizational psychology is built on a house of cards? Or will positive organizational psychology be one of the most powerful and productive innovations in the areas of human resource development and the organizational sciences to occur in decades? We believe the answers to these questions are up to us, including you the reader and the next generation of workplace and organizational researchers who try to realize the dream of establishing a rigorous science of positive organizational psychology.

Our review of literature on positive psychology and positive organizational psychology above was mainly limited to peer-reviewed publications. It is important to point out that many consider the rapid proliferation of trade books, magazine articles, newspaper coverage, blogs, and many other types of non-peer reviewed publications related to topics in positive psychology to be fair game in their critiques of the field. We reject that notion because most of these non-peer reviewed publications do not meet the most basic criteria specified for the science of positive psychology (Seligman & Csikszentmihalyi, 2000).

We believe the critiques of the peer-reviewed scientific articles in positive psychology are very useful for smoothing out and improving future rides of the epic waves and galloping stallions that await us on the horizon. However, a much more optimistic picture emerges when critical analyses of the evidence base are limited to the scientific literature. For example, Donaldson and Ko (2010) identified 172 peer-reviewed articles in positive organizational psychology published between 2001 and 2009, and the vast majority of these articles made it through some of the most rigorous peer-review processes in the behavioral and organizational sciences. That is, the positive organizational psychology research was published across 70 different scientific journals, with the most popular outlets being top scholarly journals such as *Journal of Organizational Behavior, Academy of Management Review, The Journal of Positive Psychology, The Journal of Organizational Behavior Management,* and *The Journal of Applied Behavioral Science.* It is highly unlikely that the reviewers and editors of these top journals would publish literature with the usually serious measurement and methodological flaws that some critics have asserted in broad strokes.

Support for the empirical rigor of positive organizational psychology also comes from the recent review by Donaldson and Dollwet (under review), which demonstrated that the majority of the empirical articles in this field are quantitative in nature. There are also a numerous rigorous mixed-method approaches that have furthered this new field by assessing both quantitative and qualitative measures (e.g., Cameron, Bright, & Caza, 2004; Walumbwa, Avolio, Gardner, Wernsing, & Peterson, 2008). For example, Yaun, Clifton, Stone, and Blumberg (2000) used a mixed-method approach in order to investigate leader talents and optimism as they relate to leader effectiveness. Another study investigated the impact of positive experiences in teachers using interviews, reflections, and questionnaires (Janssen, de Hullu, & Tigelaar, 2008).

Also, while the majority of studies use correlational methods, there are quite a few studies that make use of longitudinal designs, measuring the impact of positive organizational psychology constructs over time. Trougakos, Beal, Green, and Weiss (2008) made use of the experience-sampling method by assessing employees positive affectivity at multiple points in time and found that break activities (taking a break from work) was related to higher positive affectivity.

In addition, many of the interventions mentioned earlier in this chapter are grounded in research based on experimental or quasi-experimental designs, thereby lending strong empirical support for their findings (e.g., Luthans, Avey, et al., 2008a). Finally, there is evidence that especially in the more recent studies on positive organizational psychology, complex research designs and multilevel approaches are used to investigate important topics such as positive leadership and employee engagement (e.g., Tuckey, Bakker, & Dollard, 2012).

However, future research in positive organizational psychology (and most related fields of scientific inquiry) can be greatly improved by addressing the challenges raised by harsh critics. Moving forward, we think it is prudent to heed the advice of critics and better link positive organizational psychology research to previous research on topics of interest that have been conducted prior to or outside of the positive psychology movement (e.g., employee wellness, occupational health promotion, job and career satisfaction, motivation and high performance at work and the like). It is unfortunate that many positive psychology studies are currently viewed as ahistorical, and fail to give due credit to previous research related to topics of interest. Similarly, it is important to design future research in a way that clearly defines and properly applies terms and key constructs, and demonstrates the added value of the positive over and above the negative (Bakker & Schaufeli, 2008). Deliberate attempts should be made to integrate positive and negative emotions and experiences (Wong, 2011). A handful of studies within positive organizational psychology have done this already and can lead the way for future research by setting examples. For instance, rigorous studies investigating well-being conceptualize this construct as consisting of multiple aspects including not only the presence of positive emotions, but also assess negative emotions and cognitive components of well-being (e.g., Delle Fave, Brdar, Freire, Vella-Brodrick, & Wissing, 2011; Gallagher & Lopez, 2007). Furthermore, the seminal broaden-and-build theory of positive emotions by Fredrickson assumes that we have an optimal ratio of positive and negative emotions in order to achieve human flourishing (Fredrickson & Losada, 2005). Specifically, Fredrickson and Losada (2005) found a ratio of positive to negative affectivity of about 2.9 to be related to flourishing and high performance. The broaden-and-build theory of positive emotions has also been found to relate to organizational settings (e.g., Bakker & Bal, 2010). Additional work that provides a good example of balancing the positive and the negative when investigating concepts within positive organizational psychology stems from the work by Bakker and Demerouti (2008), who investigated the negative and positive impact of job demands and resources on employee engagement.

Thus, we see very promising swells on the horizon for positive organizational psychology. Yet some of the issues raised by critics such as moving away from self-report and mono-method studies should be addressed in future research when applying positive psychology to the workplace (Donaldson & Grant-Vallone, 2002). In line with this argument, researchers need to be careful not to claim causal relations or unjustified generalizations when rival explanations can't be ruled out. Framing future research studies in positive organizational psychology that are sensitive to and address diversity issues and cross-cultural differences will also be critical to the future development of the field. Finally, theory-driven evaluations of rigorous positive organizational psychology interventions hold great promise for determining what works, as well as developing a generalizable knowledge base for how to improve organizational effectiveness and quality of work life (Donaldson, 2007; Donaldson, 2011b; Mark, Donaldson, & Campbell, 2011).

CONCLUSION

The unusually rapid growth and development of the field of positive psychology in general, and positive organizational psychology in particular, offer great hope for advancing our understanding and ability to improve the quality of life and/or work life of millions of children, adolescents, and adults across developed and developing societies throughout the world. Advances in these areas also promise to facilitate the design of optimally functioning and flourishing organizations of all types, shapes, and sizes. It is our hope that the research summarized in this opening chapter combined with the research and issues raised throughout the chapters in this volume, will accelerated the rate at which we move toward an evidence-based positive organizational psychology that realizes great aspirations for human and social betterment.

REFERENCES

Armstrong-Stassen, M., & Schlosser, F. (2008). Taking a positive approach to organizational downsizing. *Canadian Journal of Administrative Sciences, 25*, 93–106.

Avey, J. B., Luthans, F., & Youssef, C. M. (2010). The additive value of positive psychological capital in predicting work attitudes and behaviors. *Journal of Management, 36*, 430–452.

Avey, J. B., Wernsing, T. S., & Luthans, F. (2008). Can positive employees help positive organizational change? Impact of psychological capital and emotions on relevant attitudes and behaviors. *The Journal of Applied Behavioral Science, 44*, 48–70.

Bakker, A. B., & Bal, M. P. (2010). Weekly work engagement and performance: A study among starting teachers. *Journal of Occupational and Organizational Psychology, 83*, 1189–206.

Bakker, A. B., & Demerouti, E. (2008). Towards a model of work engagement. *Career Development International, 13*, 209–223.

Bakker, A. B., & Derks, D. (2010). Positive occupational health psychology. In S. Leka & J. Houdmont (Eds.), *Occupational health psychology* (pp. 194–224). Oxford: Wiley-Blackwell.

Bakker, A. B., & Schaufeli, W. B. (2008). Positive organizational behavior: Engaged employees in flourishing organizations. *Journal of Organizational Behavior, 29*, 147–154.

Black, B. (2001). The road to recovery. *Gallup Management Journal, 1*, 10–12.

Buckingham, M., & Clifton, D. O. (2001). *Now, discover your strengths*. New York, NY: The Free Press.

Cameron, K. S., Bright, D., & Caza, A. (2004). Exploring the relationships between organizational virtuousness and performance. *American Behavioral Scientist, 47*, 766–790.

Cameron, K. S., & Spreitzer, G. M. (2012). *The Oxford handbook of positive organizational scholarship*. New York, NY: Oxford.

Cheung, F., & Wu, A. M. S. (2012). An investigation of predictors of successful aging in the workplace among Hong Kong Chinese older workers. *International Psychogeriatics, 24*, 449–464.

Clifton, D. O., & Harter, J. K. (2003). Investigating in strengths. In K. S. Cameron, J. E. Dutton & R. E. Quinn (Eds.), *Positive organizational scholarship* (pp. 111–121). San Francisco, CA: Berrett-Koehler.

Cooperrider, D. L., & Whitney, D. (1999). Appreciative Inquiry: A positive revolution in change. In P. Holan & T. Devane (Eds.), *The change handbook* (pp. 245–261). San Francisco, CA: Berrett-Koehler.

Connelly, J. (2002). All together now. *Gallup Management Journal, 2*, 13–18.

Delle Fave, A., Brdar, I., Freire, T., Vella-Brodrick, D., & Wissing, M. (2011). The eudaimonic and hedonic components of happiness: Qualitative and quantitative findings. *Social Indicators Research, 100*, 185–207.

Demerouti, E. (2006). Job characteristics, flow, and performance: The moderating role of conscientiousness. *Journal of Occupational Health Psychology, 11*, 266–280.

Den Hartog, D. N., & Belschak, F. D. (2012). When does transformational leadership enhance employee proactive behavior? The role of autonomy and role breadth self-efficacy. *Journal of Applied Psychology, 1*, 194–202.

Donaldson, S. I. (2007). *Program theory-driven evaluation science: Strategies and applications.* Mahwah, NJ: Erlbaum.

Donaldson, S. I. (2011a). Determining what works, if anything, in applied positive psychology. In S. I. Donaldson, M. Csikszentmihalyi & J. Nakamura (Eds.), *Applied positive psychology: Improving everyday life, health, schools, work, and society* (pp. 3–11). London: Routledge.

Donaldson, S. I. (2011b). A practitioner's guide for applying the science of positive psychology. In S. I. Donaldson, M. Csikszentmihalyi & J. Nakamura (Eds.), *Applied positive psychology: Improving everyday life, health, schools, work, and society*. London: Routledge.

Donaldson, S. I., Csikszentmihalyi, M., & Nakamura, J. (Eds.). (2011). *Applied positive psychology: Improving everyday life, health, schools, work, and society*. London: Routledge.

Donaldson, S. I., & Dollwet, M. (under review). Happiness, excellence, and optimal human functioning revisited: Evaluating the progress of positive psychology.

Donaldson, S. I., & Grant-Vallone, E. J. (2002). Understanding self-report bias in organizational behavior research. *Journal of Business and Psychology, 17*, 245–262.

Donaldson, S. I., & Ko, I. (2010). Positive organizational psychology, behavior, and scholarship: A review of the emerging literature and evidence base. *Journal of Positive Psychology, 5*, 177–191.

Duffy, R. D., Bott, E. M., Allan, B. A., Torrey, C. L., & Dik, B. J. (2012). Perceiving a calling, living a calling, and job satisfaction: Testing a moderated, multiple mediator model. *Journal of Counseling Psychology, 59*, 50–59.

Dutton, J. E., & Ragins, B. R. (2006). *Exploring positive relations at work: Building a theoretical and research foundation.* New York, NY: Psychology Press.

Eisenberger, R., Jones, J. R., Stinglhamber, F., Shanock, L., & Randall, A. T. (2005). Flow experience at work: For high need achievers alone? *Journal of Organizational Behavior, 26*, 755–775.

Fineman, S. (2006). On being positive: Concerns and counterpoints. *Academy of Management Review, 31*, 270–291.

Fredrickson, B. L., & Losada, M. F. (2005). Positive affect and the complex dynamics of human flourishing. *American Psychologist, 60*, 678–686.

Gallagher, M. W., & Lopez, S. J. (2007). Curiosity and well-being. *Journal of Positive Psychology, 2*, 236–248.

Gorgievski, M. J., Bakker, A. B., & Schaufeli, W. B. (2010). Work engagement and workaholism: Comparing the self-employed and salaried employees. *Journal of Positive Psychology*, *5*, 83–96.

Grant, A. M., Curtayne, L., & Burton, G. (2009). Executive coaching enhances goal attainment, resilience, and workplace well-being: A randomized control study. *Journal of Positive Psychology*, *4*, 396–407.

Grant, A. M., Green, L. S., & Rynsaardt, J. (2010). Developmental coaching for high school teachers: Executive coaching goes to school. *Consulting Psychology Journal: Practice and Research*, *62*, 151–168.

Green, L. S., Oades, L. G., & Grant, A. M. (2006). Cognitive-behavioral solution-focused life coaching: Enhancing goal striving, well-being and hope. *Journal of Positive Psychology*, *1*, 142–149.

Grichnik, D., Smeja, A., & Welpe, I. (2010). The importance of being emotional: How do emotions affect entrepreneurial opportunity evaluation and exploitation? *Journal of Economic Behavior & Organization*, *76*, 15–29.

Hackman, J. R. (2009). The perils of positivity. *Journal of Organizational Behavior*, *30*, 309–319.

Harter, J. K. (2000). Managerial talent, employee engagement, and business-unit performance. *Psychologist-Manager Journal*, *4*, 215–224.

Harter, J. K., Schmidt, F. L., & Hayes, T. L. (2002). Business-unit-level relationship between employee satisfaction, employee engagement, and business outcomes: A meta-analysis. *Journal of Applied Psychology*, *87*, 268–279.

Hodges, T. D., & Clifton, D. O. (2004). Strengths-based development in practice. In P. A. Linely & S. Joseph (Eds.), *Positive psychology in practice: From research to application* (pp. 256–268). Hoboken, NJ: Wiley.

Janssen, F., de Hullu, E., & Tigelaar, D. (2008). Positive experiences as input for reflection by student teachers. *Teachers and Teaching: Theory and Practice*, *14*, 115–127.

Kashdan, T. B., & Steger, M. F. (2011). Challenges, pitfalls, and aspirations for positive psychology. In K. M. Sheldon, T. B. Kashdan & M. F. Steger (Eds.), *Designing positive psychology: Taking stock and moving forward*. New York, NY: Oxford.

Keller, J., Ringelhan, S., & Blomann, F. (2011). Does skills–demands compatibility result in intrinsic motivation? Experimental test of a basic notion proposed in the theory of flow-experiences. *Journal of Positive Psychology*, *6*, 408–417.

Ko, I., & Donaldson, S. I. (2011). Applied positive organizational psychology: The state of the science and practice. In S. I. Donaldson, M. Csikszentmihalyi & J. Nakamura (Eds.), *Applied positive psychology: Improving everyday life, health, schools, work, and society*. London: Routledge.

Larson, M., & Luthans, F. (2006). Potential added value of psychological capital in predicting work attitudes. *Journal of Leadership and Organizational Studies*, *13*, 75–92.

Lazarus, R. S. (2003). Does the positive psychology movement have legs? *Psychological Inquiry*, *14*, 93–109.

Lin, C. W., Chen, S. L., & Wang, R. Y. (2011). Savoring and perceived job performance in positive psychology: Moderating role of positive affectivity. *Asian Journal of Social Psychology*, *14*, 165–175.

Linley, P., Nielsen, K. M., Gillett, R., & Biswas-Diener, R. (2010). Using signature strengths in pursuit of goals: Effects on goal progress, need satisfaction, and well-being, and implications for coaching psychologists. *International Coaching Psychology Review*, *5*, 6–15.

Luthans, F. (2002a). Positive organizational behavior: Developing and managing psychological strengths. *Academy of Management Executive, 16*, 57–72.

Luthans, F. (2002b). The need for and meaning of positive organizational behavior. *Journal of Organizational Behavior, 23*, 695–706.

Luthans, F., Avey, J., & Patera, J. (2008). Experimental analysis of a web-based training intervention to develop positive psychological capital. *Academy of Management Learning and Education, 7*, 209–221.

Luthans, F., Norman, S. M., Avolio, B. J., & Avey, J. B. (2008). The mediating role of psychological capital in the supportive organizational climate – Employee performance relationship. *Journal of Organizational Behavior, 29*, 219–238.

Luthans, F., & Youssef, C. M. (2007). Emerging positive organizational behavior. *Journal of Management, 33*, 321–349.

Mark, M. M., Donaldson, S. I., & Campbell, B. (2011). Social psychology and evaluation: Building a better future. In M. M. Mark, S. I. Donaldson & B. Campbell (Eds.), *Social psychology and evaluation*. New York, NY: Guilford.

Martin, A. J., & Jackson, S. A. (2008). Brief approaches to assessing task absorption and enhanced subjective experience: Examining 'short' and 'core' flow in diverse performance domains. *Motivation and Emotion, 32*, 141–157.

Masuda, A. D., McNall, L. A., Allen, T. D., & Nicklin, J. M. (2012). Examining the constructs of work-to-family enrichment and positive spillover. *Journal of Vocational Behavior, 80*, 197–2010.

McGovern, T. V. (2011). Virtues and character strengths for sustainable faculty development. *Journal of Positive Psychology, 6*, 446–450.

Miller, M. (2008). A critique of positive psychology – Or the new science of happiness. *Journal of Philosophy of Education, 42*, 591–608.

Muse, L., Harris, S. G., Giles, W. F., & Feild, H. S. (2008). Work-life benefits and positive organizational behavior: Is there a connection? *Journal of Organizational Behavior, 29*, 171–192.

Niessen, C., Sonnentag, S., & Sach, F. (2012). Thriving at work – A diary study. *Journal of Organizational Behavior, 33*, 468–487.

Peterson, C. (2006). *A primer in positive psychology*. New York, NY: Oxford University Press.

Peterson, C., & Seligman, M. E. P. (2004). *Character strengths and virtues: A handbook and classification*. Oxford: Oxford University Press.

Pisaniello, S. L., Winefield, H. R., & Delfabbro, P. H. (2012). The influence of emotional labor and emotional work on the occupational health and wellbeing of South Australian hospital nurses. *Journal of Vocational Behavior, 80*, 579–591.

Rego, A., Ribeiro, N., Cunha, M., & Jesuino, J. (2011). How happiness mediates organizational virtuousness and affective commitment relationship. *Journal of Business Research, 64*, 524–532.

Rodriguez-Sanchez, A. M., Schaufeli, W., Salanova, M., Cifre, E., & Sonnenschein, M. (2011). Enjoyment and absorption: An electronic diary study on daily flow patterns. *Work & Stress, 25*, 75–92.

Ruark, J. (2009, August 3). An intellectual movement for the masses: 10 years after its founding positive psychology, struggles with its own successes. *Chronicle of Higher Education*. Retrieved from http://chronicle.com/article/An-Intellectual-Movement-for/47500/. Accessed on April 24, 2012.

Salanova, M., Bakker, A. B., & Llorens, S. (2006). Flow at work: Evidence for an upward spiral of personal and organizational resources. *Journal of Happiness Studies, 7*, 1–22.

Seligman, M. E. P., & Csikszentmihalyi, M. (2000). Positive psychology: An introduction. *American Psychologist, 55*, 5–14.

Sheldon, K. M., Kashdan, T. B., & Steger, M. F. (2011). *Designing positive psychology: Taking stock and moving forward.* New York, NY: Oxford.

Tuckey, M. R., Bakker, A. B., & Dollard, M. F. (2012). Empowering leaders optimize working conditions for engagement: A multilevel study. *Journal of Occupational Health Psychology, 17*, 15–27.

Trougakos, J. P., Beal, D. J., Green, S. G., & Weiss, H. M. (2008). Making the break count: An episodic examination of recovery activities, emotional experiences, and positive affective displays. *Academy of Management Journal, 51*, 131–146.

Valentine, S., Godkin, L., Fleischman, G. M., & Kidwell, R. (2011). Corporate ethical values, group creativity, job satisfaction and turnover intention: The impact of work context and work response. *Journal of Business Ethics, 98*, 353–372.

Van Gelderen, B., Konijn, E. A., & Bakker, A. B. (2011). Emotional labor among police officers: The interpersonal role of positive emotions. *Journal of Positive Psychology, 6*, 163–172.

Walumbwa, F. O., Avolio, B. J., Gardner, W. L., Wernsing, T. S., & Peterson, S. J. (2008). Authentic leadership: Development and validation of a theory-based measure. *Journal of Management, 34*, 89–126.

Whitney, D., & Cooperrider, D. L. (2000). The appreciative inquiry summit: An emerging methodology for whole system positive change. *Journal of Organization Development Network, 32*, 13–26.

Wincent, J., & Ortqvist, D. (2011). Examining positive performance implications of role stressors by the indirect influence of positive affect: A study of new business managers. *Journal of Applied Social Psychology, 41*, 699–727.

Woolley, L., Caza, A., & Levy, L. (2011). Authentic leadership and follower development: Psychological capital, positive work climate, and gender. *Journal of Leadership Studies & Organizational Development, 18*, 438–448.

Wong, P. T. P. (2011). Positive psychology 2.0: Towards a balanced interactive model of the good life. *Canadian Psychology, 52*, 69–81.

Yaun, H., Clifton, D. O., Stone, P., & Blumberg, H. H. (2000). Positive and negative words: Their association with leadership talent and effectiveness. *Psychologist-Manager Journal, 4*, 199–213.

Zhou, Q., Hirst, G., & Shipton, H. (2012). Promoting creativity at work: The role of problem-solving demand. *Applied Psychology: An International Review, 61*, 56–80.

ADVANCES IN POSITIVE ORGANIZATIONAL SCHOLARSHIP

Kim S. Cameron

Positive organizational scholarship (POS) is an umbrella concept used to unify a variety of approaches in organizational studies, each of which incorporates the notion of "the positive."[1] In previously published work, POS has been associated with life-giving dynamics, optimal functioning, collective strengths, human flourishing, especially positive outcomes of organizations and their members, and concepts such as excellence, thriving, flourishing, abundance, resilience, and virtuousness in and through organizations (Cameron, Dutton, & Quinn, 2003; Dutton & Glynn, 2007; Roberts, 2006). All these descriptions emphasize terms that are associated with processes, dynamics, perspectives, and outcomes in organizations that are considered to be typical of "the positive."

KEY CONCEPTS

The three concepts that denote the focus of POS were deliberately selected and are important in elucidating the uniqueness of POS as a field of study. The "O" (organizational) and the "S" (scholarship) are relatively noncontroversial concepts. The "P" (positive), however, is more contentious and requires more explanation.

Advances in Positive Organizational Psychology, Volume 1, 23–44
Copyright © 2013 by Emerald Group Publishing Limited
All rights of reproduction in any form reserved
ISSN: 2046-410X/doi:10.1108/S2046-410X(2013)0000001004

Organizational

POS differs from the bulk of positive psychological research in that it explicitly focuses on *organizational* dynamics, or on the work context in which people operate. It examines positive phenomena within organizations as well as positive organizational contexts themselves. POS draws from the full spectrum of organizational theories to understand, explain, and predict the occurrence, causes, and consequences of positivity not so much within individuals' psyches as in the organizational milieu.

POS expands the boundaries of traditional organizational theories to make visible positive states, positive processes, and positive relationships that are typically ignored within organizational studies. For example, POS research spotlighted how the virtuousness of organizations is associated with financial performance in the context of downsizing, in contrast to a more typical focus on how organizations try to mitigate the harmful effects of downsizing (Cameron, Mora, Leutscher, & Calarco, 2011). POS research examined organizational practices that enable work meaningfulness through crafting a sense of calling in contrast to a more typical focus on employee productivity or morale (Berg, Wrzesniewski, & Dutton, 2010; Wrzesniewski, 2003). POS research identified how cascading empowerment processes created broader inclusion of stakeholders in public organizations, in contrast to a focus on the political dynamics of stakeholder demands (Feldman & Khademian, 2003). And, POS research highlighted how building collective efficacy accounts for more positive outcomes in educational institutions than do demographic, ethnic, or socioeconomic factors do (Goddard & Salloum, 2012).

As this sampling of studies implies, a POS lens exposes new or different mechanisms through which positive organizational dynamics and positive organizational processes produce extraordinarily positive or unexpected outcomes. At the same time, POS purposely illuminates how contexts and processes, and their interactions, are related to positive states in individuals, groups, and organizations.

Scholarship

There is no lack of self-help resources that advocate relatively simplistic and uncomplicated prescriptions for achieving happiness, fulfillment, or effectiveness. A variety of books describing parables, inspirational stories, personal experiences, and commonsense principles for success have become best sellers. What is lacking in most of these contributions, however, is empirical credibility and theoretical explanations for how and why the prescriptions work. Further, these more prescriptive accounts do not speak to the contingencies regarding when the directives will produce the desired results and when they won't. Having a foundation in the scientific method is the basis upon which most concepts, relationships, and prescriptions develop staying power. Intellectual fads come and go, and usually it is the scientific foundation that creates longevity and continuing impact.

POS does not stand in opposition to the array of self-help publications, but it extends beyond them in its desire to develop rigorous, systematic, and theory-based foundations for positive phenomena. POS requires careful definitions of terms, a rationale for prescriptions and recommendations, consistency with scientific procedures in drawing conclusions, and grounding in previous related work. It is also important to point out that an interest in POS implies a commitment to the full spectrum of activities involved in scholarship. This includes the practical application of this knowledge in organizations, interventions to help organizations achieve extraordinary success, and the dissemination of knowledge in classrooms and training facilities.

Positive

The most controversial concept associated with POS is the "P" – *positive*. Most of the misunderstandings and criticisms of POS have centered on this concept, creating controversy in organizational studies and spawning both skeptics and advocates. A review of dictionary definitions of "positive" reveals that the concept has such a wide range of connotations and so many applications that it defies establishing precise conceptual boundaries (e.g., *Webster's*, *Oxford*, *American Heritage*, *Dictionary.com*). Literally scores of meanings are offered. Experiencing the positive – like experiencing love or leadership – often serves as the basis for its meaning.

On the other hand, some convergence on the meaning of "positive" has begun to emerge as the term has been employed in organizational scholarship over the past decade. The convergence can be summarized in four approaches that help specify the domain of "positive" as applied to organizational phenomena. Identifying these themes helps provide a conceptual explanation of what "positive" means in the context of POS.

One approach to "positive" is adopting *a unique lens or an alternative perspective*. Adopting a POS lens means that the interpretation of

phenomena is altered. For example, challenges and obstacles are reinter-
preted as opportunities and strength-building experiences rather than as
tragedies or problems (Gittell, Cameron, Lim, & Rivas, 2006; Sutcliffe &
Vogus, 2003). Variables not previously recognized or seriously considered in
organizational scholarship become central, such as positive energy (Baker,
Cross, & Wooten, 2003); moral capital (Godfrey, 2003); flow (Quinn, 2002);
inspiration (Thrash & Elliott, 2003); compassion (Dutton, Worline, Frost, &
Lilius, 2006); elevation (Vianello, Galliani, & Haidt, 2010); and callings
(Wrzesniewski, 2003). Adopting a POS lens means that adversities and
difficulties reside as much in the domain of POS as do celebrations and
successes, but a positive lens focuses attention on the life-giving elements or
generative processes associated with these phenomena. It is the positive
perspective – not the nature of the phenomena – that draws an issue into the
POS domain.

A second consensual approach to the concept of "positive" is *a focus on
extraordinarily positive outcomes or positively deviant performance*. This
means that outcomes dramatically exceed common or expected performance.
Investigating spectacular results, surprising outcomes, and extraordinary
achievements have been the focus of several investigations (e.g., Gittell et al.,
2006; Hess & Cameron, 2006), with each treating "positive" as synonymous
with exceptional performance. Reaching a level of positive deviance, in other
words, extends beyond achieving effectiveness or ordinary success. For
example, the closure and clean-up of the Rocky Flats Nuclear arsenal
exceeded federal standards by a factor of 13, 60 years ahead of schedule, and
$30 billion under budget (Cameron & Lavine, 2006).

A third area of convergence regarding the term "positive" is its focus
on *an affirmative bias that fosters resourcefulness*. Positive organizational
scholarship accepts the premise that positivity unlocks and elevates
resources in individuals, groups, and organizations, so that capabilities are
broadened and capacity is built and strengthened (Fredrickson, 2009).
"Resourcefulness" means that individuals and organizations experience an
amplifying effect when exposed to positivity, such that resources and
capacity expand (Dutton & Sonenshein, 2009; Fredrickson & Joiner, 2002).
All living systems have a heliotropic inclination toward positive energy
(Cameron, 2008a), so that, indeed, positivity is life-giving (Cooperrider &
Srivastva, 1987). Adopting an affirmative bias, therefore, prioritizes positive
energy, positive climate, positive relationships, positive communication, and
positive meaning in organizations (Cameron, 2008b), as well as the value
embedded in difficult challenges or negative events (Clifton & Harter, 2003;
Losada & Heaphy, 2004).

Positive organizational scholarship is unapologetic in emphasizing affirmative attributes, capabilities, and possibilities more than problems, threats, and weakness, so that strengths-based activities and outcomes are highlighted (Clifton & Harter, 2003). Again, an affirmative approach does not exclude considering negative events. Rather, these are incorporated in accounting for life-giving dynamics, generating resources, and flourishing outcomes (e.g., Dutton et al., 2006; Dutton & Glynn, 2007; Weick, 2003).

A fourth area of convergence regarding the concept of the positive is *the examination of virtuousness or the best of the human condition*. POS is based on a eudaemonic assumption – that is, the postulation that an inclination exists in all human systems toward achieving the highest aspirations of humankind (Aristotle, *Metaphysics XII*; Dutton & Sonenshein, 2009). POS research examines the development of and the effects associated with virtuousness and eudaemonism (Bright, Cameron, & Caza, 2006; Cameron, 2003), or "that which is good in itself and is to be chosen for its own sake" (Aristotle, *Metaphysics XII*, p. 3). Studies of virtuousness *in* organizations focus, for example, on individuals' behaviors in organizational settings that help others flourish, including investigating character strengths, gratitude, wisdom, forgiveness, hope, and courage (Grant & Schwartz, 2011). Studies of virtuousness *through* organizations focus on practices and processes in organizations that represent and perpetuate what is good, right, and worthy of cultivation (Park & Peterson, 2003). This includes, for example, investigating profound purpose and transcendent objectives (Emmons, 1999); healing routines (Powley & Piderit, 2008); institutionalized forgiveness (Cameron & Caza, 2002); and human sustainability (Pfeffer, 2010).

These four convergent uses of the concept of "positive" – adopting a positive lens, investigating extraordinarily positive performance, espousing an affirmative bias, and exploring virtuousness – do not precisely *define* the term "positive" per se, but they do identify the scholarly domain that POS scholars are attempting to map. Similar to other concepts in organizational science that do not have precisely bounded definitions (e.g., culture, innovation, core competence), this mapping provides the conceptual boundaries required to locate POS as an area of inquiry.

EMERGENCE

Unlike positive psychology, POS did not emerge as an attempt to rebalance the prodigious emphasis on illness and languishing in organizations. Organizational research has not been focused overwhelmingly on failure, damage, and demise. In fact, studying organizational decline was first introduced in organizational studies in 1980 (Whetten, 1980), because most organizational theories focused almost exclusively on growth. Big was assumed to be better than small; getting more was preferable to getting less. Negative phenomena did not dominate organizational studies literature as it did in psychology, even though plenty of attention had been paid to alienation, stress, injustice, and the evils of bureaucracy in traditional organizational studies (e.g., Weber, 1997).

Rather, POS arose because an array of organizational phenomena was being ignored; consequently, such phenomena were neither systematically studied nor valued. It was usually not considered legitimate in scientific circles, for example, to discuss the effects of virtues in organizations or to use terms such as "flourishing" or "positive deviance" to describe outcomes. Studies of compassion and forgiveness – two of the early studies in the POS literature (Cameron & Caza, 2002; Dutton et al., 2006) – certainly diverged from the mainstream of organizational science. Similarly, certain kinds of organizational processes – for example, generative dynamics – remained largely uninvestigated, including high-quality connections (Dutton & Ragins, 2007); thriving (Spreitzer, Sutcliffe, Dutton, Sonenshein, & Grant, 2005); connectivity (Losada & Heaphy, 2004); and positive energy networks (Baker et al., 2003).

POS also arose because the outcome variables that dominated the organization literature focused mainly on profitability, competitive advantage, problem solving, and economic efficiency (Davis, 2009). Granted, outcomes such as job satisfaction, justice, and teamwork have appeared frequently in the organizational studies literature (Kramer, 1999), but alternative outcomes such as psychological, social, and eudaemonic well-being (Keyes, 2005) – including social integration, social contribution, social coherence, social actualization, and social acceptance – as well as human sustainability (Pfeffer, 2010) were largely outside the purview of mainline organizational science. The best of the human condition – what people care about deeply and profoundly – was almost invisible in organizational scholarship.

CRITICISMS

The legitimacy of POS as a field of scientific study is by no means universally accepted, and three primary criticisms of POS have been promoted: (a) POS ignores negative phenomena, (b) POS adopts an elitist (managerial) viewpoint, and (c) POS is not defined precisely. This third criticism notes that POS does not acknowledge that "positive" may not be the same for everyone, and the concepts and phenomena associated with POS are fuzzy terms that lack construct and discriminant validity and careful measurement.

The first criticism is that POS ignores issues such as conflict, poverty, exploitation, unemployment, war, and other negative circumstances that are typical of the human condition and are commonplace in organizational functioning. Positivity is equated with being Pollyannaish and simply "putting on a happy face" in the midst of serious problems and challenges. Some authors, such as Ehrenreich (2009), for example, find little that is positive in POS, claiming that positivity unrealistically assumes unremitting growth and guaranteed success in organizations, excuses excess and folly, denies reality, mitigates against hard work, implies pride and boastfulness, avoids difficult questions, invites unpreparedness, assumes that all success is deserved, and leads to "reckless optimism" and "delusional thinking" (Ehrenreich, 2009, p. 13). Little evidence exists, according to its critics, that positivity fosters success (Ehrenreich, 2009; Hackman, 2009).

To be sure, empirical evidence exists that bad is stronger than good (Baumeister, Bratslavsky, Finkenauer, & Vohs, 2001). That is, human beings react more strongly and more quickly to negative phenomena than to positive phenomena because existence is threatened. When equal measures of good and bad are present, the psychological effects of the bad outweigh those of the good. It is inaccurate, however, to argue that POS ignores negative phenomena inasmuch as some of the greatest triumphs, most noble virtues, and highest achievements have resulted from the presence of the negative (e.g., Cameron & Lavine, 2006). Common human experience and abundant scientific evidence supports the idea that negativity has an important place in investigating positive processes and outcomes. Developing positive identities in negative environments, organizational healing after trauma, and achieving virtuous outcomes in the face of trials exemplify cases in which negative conditions have been investigated with a POS lens (Dutton et al., 2006; Powley & Cameron, 2006; Weick, 2003). Positive organizational scholarship does not ignore the negative; instead, it seeks to investigate the positive processes, outcomes, and interpretations embedded in negative phenomena.

A second criticism of POS is that it adopts an elitist perspective. Critics claim that POS is oriented toward exploiting human beings in favor of corporate profits and productivity and maintaining power for the advantaged over the disadvantaged. Perpetuating the positive for the sake of organizational success, to make managers look good, to manipulate the workforce, or to reinforce unequal employment status are common criticisms (e.g., Ehrenreich, 2009; Fineman, 2006). These critiques fundamentally center on the claim that POS narrowly focuses on managers rather than on the exploited underclass. Detractors accuse POS of not asking the question, "Positive for whom?" and suggest that unexamined assumptions are biased toward Western philosophies and toward power elites.

On the other hand, this criticism seems to miss the unequivocally stated focus of POS on life-giving dynamics, generating resources, and flourishing outcomes whether for workers or managers, the underclass or the upper class, the individual or the organization (e.g., Cameron et al., 2003; Dutton & Sonenshein, 2009; Roberts, 2006). The fundamental assumption of POS is a eudaemonic one: all human systems are biased toward achieving the highest aspirations of humankind or excellence and goodness for its own sake. Adopting an affirmative bias prioritizes positive energy, positive climate, positive relationships, positive communication, and positive meaning for individuals and organizations. Indeed, exploitation that allows one party to achieve advantage over another is inconsistent with the fundamental assumptions of POS. Thus, the answer to "Positivity for whom?" is not exclusive.

Positive energy (Baker et al., 2003), flourishing relationships (Dutton & Heaphy, 2003), empowerment (Spreitzer & Quinn, 1996), and virtuousness (Cameron, 2003) all represent nonzero-sum dynamics that benefit all parties. Moreover, abundant research has examined cultural differences regarding positive phenomena, including employee well-being in more than 50 countries (Diener, 2009; Diener & Suh, 2000; Veenhoven, 1996, 2010) and has identified universal attributes and predictors, as well as unique cultural differences across a wide variety of cultures. Non-Western cultures are well-represented in POS research.

A third criticism of POS is that a precise definition of the term "positive" is lacking. Positive is experienced subjectively, such that what may be positive for one person is not necessarily positive for another. What is defined as "good" or "ennobling" may be individualistic. Imposing a definition of positive on others is an act of power and, therefore, is, by definition, nonpositive (Caza & Carroll, 2012). Moreover, other related terms used in POS research lack precise definition and scientific validity.

Of course, many core scientific terms are the subjects of investigation, measurement, and theory-building without precise definitions. Well-used and frequently discussed terms such as "life," "effectiveness," and "quality" are examples, none of which has been precisely and consensually defined. These terms are considered to be "constructs," meaning they are terms constructed to capture the meaning of something that is ambiguous and difficult to circumscribe precisely. In such circumstances, investigators artificially constrain the meaning or dimensions of the construct in order to examine certain aspects of it. The key is to be precise about what is and is not included in measuring the construct. Individualistic definitions are addressed, therefore, by defining the concept scientifically and precisely in scholarly investigations.

A variety of positively oriented constructs such as "thriving" (Spreitzer et al., 2005), "virtuousness" (Cameron, Bright, & Caza, 2004), "positive emotions" (Fredrickson, 1998), "meaningfulness" (Pratt & Ashforth, 2003), "energy" (Spreitzer, Lam, & Quinn, 2012), "best-self" (Roberts, Dutton, Spreitzer, Heaphy, & Quinn, 2005), "resilience" (Sutcliffe & Vogus, 2003), "positive deviance" (Spreitzer & Sonenshein, 2003), and others have been defined quite carefully in POS investigations. Mapping the conceptual terrain of "positive" is not so much an act of power, therefore, as a scientific necessity in order for cumulative work to be conducted and for the nomological network surrounding the constructs to expand. Some progress has been made in this regard, although much is left to be done.

ADVANCES

The progress or advancements in POS research can be highlighted by a review of a few empirical studies that have been published in the recent past. Of course, no summary of POS research can capture the breadth and core themes of all the work being done, but an examination of the empirical literature has uncovered a set of themes that describe several of the main thrusts.

The irony in many of these findings is that, by definition, positive practices do not need to produce traditionally pursued organizational outcomes in order to be of worth. An increase in profitability, for example, is not the criterion for determining the value of positivity in organizations. Positivity is inherently valued because it is eudaemonic. Nevertheless, studies have shown that organizations in several industries (including financial services, health care, manufacturing, education, and government) that implemented and improved their positive practices over time also increased their performance in desired outcomes such as profitability, productivity, quality, customer satisfaction, and employee retention. Positive practices that were institutionalized in organizations – including providing compassionate support for employees, forgiving mistakes and avoiding blame, fostering

the meaningfulness of work, expressing frequent gratitude, showing kindness, and caring for colleagues – led organizations to perform at significantly
higher levels on desired outcomes than most organizations (Cameron et al.,
2004, 2011; Gittell et al., 2006). Examples of these studies are briefly
summarized below.

Individual Virtue and Social Concern

A survey study of white-collar workers examined the relationship linking
hope, gratitude, and responsibility (Andersson, Giacalone, & Jurkiewicz,
2007). Hope was defined as a motivational state of felt agency, as the belief
that one could achieve a desirable effect. Gratitude was a moral affective
state, in which the individual feels motivated toward prosocial behavior, to
"give back" in return for whatever caused the feeling of gratitude. In this
study, the researchers found that gratitude led to greater feelings of
responsibility for employees and social issues if high hope was present. That
is, if individuals felt both grateful and hopeful, then they also felt greater
responsibility for other members of the organization and for extra-
organizational social matters.

Similar results were shown in two surveys that linked positive character
strengths to concern about corporate social performance (Giacalone,
Paul, & Jurkiewicz, 2005). In the first survey, consumers who scored high
on trait-based gratitude and hope were also more concerned that organizations serve multiple purposes so as to benefit society rather than simply
maximizing profits. The second survey linked similar concerns about
corporate social performance to the traits of spirituality (transcendent ideals
and a desire for meaning in community) and generativity (concern for future
generations). Together, these results suggest that individual virtue is an
important factor in understanding how individuals judge organizations.

Leadership

There have been several investigations of the role of POS phenomena in
explaining leadership. Bono and Ilies (2006) described a series of studies
showing that leaders who express more positive emotions engender the same
emotions in followers, who then perceive that leader as more charismatic
and effective. Similarly, another study found that Army leaders who
expressed more vision and love for their troops satisfied their followers'

needs for the same, fostering greater well-being, commitment, and productivity among followers (Fry, Vitucci, & Cedillo, 2005). In the fast food industry, leader hope has been linked to follower satisfaction and retention (Peterson & Luthans, 2003). Similarly, a simulation study showed that group members' assessment of an individual's leadership ability was influenced by that individual's displayed level of empathy (Kellett, Humphrey, & Sleeth, 2006). As a set, these studies indicate that POS phenomena can assist in predicting and explaining effective leadership.

Organizational Virtuousness

A number of studies have examined virtuousness as an organizational phenomenon. For example, one study described how members of a business school were able to redirect existing organizational systems to support compassionate responses to individual tragedy (Dutton et al., 2006). Similarly, O'Donohoe and Turley's (2006) interview study of newspaper staff dealing with bereaved clients found the staff engaging in "philanthropic emotion management," in which they made personal sacrifices for the sake of grieving clients, even though these sacrifices were neither required nor rewarded by the organization.

Several studies also link virtuousness to performance. One study within a health care network showed how units that were supportive of their members' spirituality produced higher levels of customer satisfaction (Duchon & Plowman, 2005). Another study, among Dutch sales staff, found that pride was a source of self-worth, motivation, creativity, and altruism, and thus led to higher levels of adaptive selling, individual effort, self-efficacy, and citizenship behavior (Verbeke, Belschak, & Bagozzi, 2004). Consistent with both of these studies, Cameron et al. (2004) used organizational forgiveness, trust, optimism, compassion, and integrity to predict measures of innovation, quality, turnover, customer retention, and profitability. In a related paper, Bright et al. (2006) found that leaders who took responsibility for the disruptive effects of downsizing received more forgiveness from followers, and this forgiveness reduced the performance losses usually created by downsizing.

More recently, Cameron et al. (2011) found that virtuous practices in two different industries – financial services firms and health care organizations – strongly predicted desired outcomes. In financial services, firms that improved the most in virtuous practices also achieved the highest levels of profitability, productivity, engagement, and employee and customer retention two years later compared to firms that did not improve or that improved the least. A similar result was detected among health care organizations. Double-digit improvement was produced on a dozen dimensions of health care effectiveness in units that scored highest in virtuous practices and that improved the most in implementing these practices.

One feature that all of these studies have in common is a consideration of the organizational nature of virtuousness. While it was obviously individuals experiencing or expressing virtuous behavior, these studies suggest that such expressions were also manifest as a collective, organizational phenomenon.

Positive Relationships and Performance

Relationships are another important source of potential performance benefits investigated by POS. A study of the airline industry found that carriers with better interpersonal relations showed greater resilience in the post-9/11 economy. Airlines with better internal relations had lower costs, fewer layoffs, and quicker recovery to pre-9/11 stock prices (Gittell et al., 2006). Similarly, an ethnographic study of a midwifery practice showed how that practice's emphasis on social relationships and humanistic values benefited patient service and staff development (Wooten & Crane, 2004). And in a study of management teams, Losada and Heaphy (2004) found that the highest performing teams on unit profitability, customer satisfaction, and 360-degree evaluations were characterized by more positive communication and interpersonal connection among members.

Psychological Capital

This is a second-order construct comprised of resilience, optimism, self-efficacy, and hope (Luthans, Youssef, & Avolio, 2007; see also Youssef & Luthans, this volume). Several studies have examined its effects in organizations. One study linked psychological capital to reduced absenteeism and found it was a better predictor of involuntary absenteeism than job satisfaction or organizational commitment (Avey, Patera, & West, 2006). In another study, nurses' psychological capital predicted their own intentions to stay in their job and their supervisors' ratings of their organizational commitment (Luthans & Jensen, 2005). A third study found that psychological capital predicted supervisory ratings of worker performance

(Luthans, Avolio, Walumbwa, & Li, 2005). As such, the positive individual state of psychological capital has been linked to improved health, motivation, commitment, and performance, suggesting its potentially broad importance in understanding organizational behavior.

Absence of Negativity

The importance of a POS perspective depends on positive phenomena involving more than the absence of negative ones (Cameron & Caza, 2004; Dutton & Glynn, 2007). Important differences exist between reducing the negative and increasing the positive (Roberts, 2006).

Britt and colleagues' (2007) results, for example, suggest that there is indeed a difference between that which is positive and an absence of that which is negative. Their survey study of soldiers deployed in Kosovo tested the idea that morale, defined as a positive construct of individual motivation and enthusiasm to accomplish the organizational mission, was distinct from depression. The authors challenged the prevailing view that morale and depression were opposing anchors of a single dimension and used their survey results to show that the two were distinct constructs. While both were influenced by individuals' confidence in their leaders, meaningful work was only important to morale, whereas stress was only a predictor of depression, implying that positivity is not simply an absence of negativity.

In a similar vein, Pittinsky and Shih (2004) presented indirect support for the value of a POS perspective. Their survey of Internet and software workers showed that, contrary to traditional expectations, job change did not reduce commitment to the organization during tenure. In an era of portfolio careers and high organizational mobility, most individuals can expect to work for multiple companies, and this would seem to reduce the potential for commitment to any particular organization, especially in contrast to an individual who has lifetime employment with one organization. However, Pittinsky and Shih (2004) showed that this is not necessarily true, and that commitment was possible even among highly mobile knowledge workers.

Energy

Owens, Baker, and Cameron (2012) investigated the positive energy displayed by unit leaders in a variety of business units. Several forms of energy exist, such as physical energy, emotional energy, and psychological energy. With each of these forms of energy, their use creates a diminishing of energy. People become exhausted after expending physical or emotional energy, for example. This study assessed relational energy, defined as the uplifting, motivational, and life-giving influence leaders have on employees. The study showed that positively energizing leaders had a significant, positive impact on individuals – including their performance, engagement, well-being, satisfaction, and even family life – as well as on the organization's perform-ance, teamwork, innovation, and learning orientation. Positive energy in leaders was a far more predictive factor than power position or information centrality in the organization.

APPLICATION

Practicing and applying POS in organizations has taken a variety of forms, including the writing of case studies to document especially positive organizational performance, developing specific tools and techniques for generating positive effects among workers, and designing university courses and executive education programs centered on POS knowledge. Examples include Hess and Cameron's (2006) case studies of the positive practices used in a variety of organizations. In addition, specific tools and techniques aimed at enhancing positive outcomes for individuals or organizations have been developed, such as the Reflected Best-Self Instrument (Quinn, Dutton, & Spreitzer, 2003; Roberts, Dutton, & Spreitzer, 2007), the Reciprocity Ring (Baker, 2007), Appreciative Inquiry Summits (Cooperrider & Whitney, 2005), supportive communication techniques (Cameron, 2011; Dutton, 2003), and Everest goals (Cameron & Plews, 2012).

These tools, and others, are being applied in a variety of organizational settings. Case studies of extraordinary leaders or organizations also have been developed for teaching purposes (e.g., Baker & Gunderson, 2005; Bek et al., 2007; Cameron & Plews, 2012; Dutton, Quinn, & Pasick, 2002). In addition, undergraduate and graduate courses based on POS have been designed and taught in several colleges and universities (syllabi for many of these courses are available at the Center for POS at http://www.bus.umich.edu/Positive).

Unfortunately, there has been relatively little formal study of the effect of POS interventions in organizations. This is primarily due to the constraints of detecting effects from planned organizational interventions while controlling for possible confounds. However, some reports have been made, with results suggesting that POS in practice is associated with higher levels of performance. For example, Cameron and Lavine (2006) studied the exceptional performance of a company that cleaned up and closed a nuclear production facility 60 years ahead of schedule, $30 billion under budget, and to standards 13 times greater than the federal standard. This was arguably the most remarkable example of organizational success in recent memory. More than 3 million square feet of buildings had to be decontaminated and removed, over 100 tons of plutonium residues had to be neutralized and disposed of, and numerous protesters had to be converted into supporters and advocates. During the cleanup, union members were motivated to work themselves out of a job as quickly as possible, an approach contradictory to traditional union priorities, while maintaining levels of morale and safety that exceeded industry averages by a factor of two. Cameron and Lavine (2006) explained this remarkable performance as a product of 21 different positive organizational practices.

Another intervention study was reported in which two different organizations, which had been suffering through periods of downsizing and deteriorating performance each implemented a new change agenda grounded in POS practices. In both of these organizations performance improvements were significant, and employees attributed the success to the implementation of POS principles (Cameron, 2003). Causality could not be determined in either of these two organizations because data were collected after the turnaround had begun to occur.

A third set of POS interventions is described in an interview with the CEO of one of the prudential financial services companies. This senior executive reported that his entire business strategy was driven by a reliance on the principles and practices associated with POS, and his business turned around from a $140 million loss to a $20 million profit in a period of just over a year (Cameron & Plews, 2012). Yet another study reported by Grant (2007) found that the perceived meaningfulness of work could be enhanced by personal interaction with recipients of services. Workers who had direct contact with the beneficiaries of their work subsequently displayed almost three times more task persistence. These workers also had significantly greater productivity in routine tasks, producing more than one and a half times the output of those who did not have contact with beneficiaries.

Baker et al. (2003) discovered that "positive energizers" (individuals who uplift and boost others) had higher performance than "negative energizers" (people who deplete the good feelings and enthusiasm of others). In fact, individuals who provided positive energy to many people were four times more likely to succeed than individuals who were at the center of information or influence networks. Moreover, the performance enhancement associated with positive energy was also conveyed to those interacting with the energizer. Baker, Cross, and Parker (2004) further reported that high performing organizations have three times as many positive energizers as average organizations. Because positive energy is not a personality trait, but rather a set of behavioral attributes, training in the enhancement of positive energy was reported to be part of an intervention agenda in some of these organizations.

This sample of applications provides support for the benefits of POS-related practices in real-world work settings. As yet, not enough is known to draw firm conclusions regarding the what, how, or when of such interventions, but there is growing evidence that practices based on POS benefit individuals and organizations.

WEAKNESSES

The studies described here represent a wide range of methods and contexts, and they cross multiple levels of analysis. This can be seen as a strength but also as a weakness. That is, certain issues and concerns arise as this array of studies is surveyed. For example, a large majority of the studies used distinctively POS phenomena to explain traditional outcomes, whereas only a few studied specifically POS outcomes (e.g., flourishing). Although POS emphasizes positive enablers, processes, and outcomes, much of the research conducted thus far has been primarily concerned with using POS to explain familiar outcomes such as firm profit and employee retention. This is mainly because of the need to establish the credibility and legitimacy of POS as a field of scholarly endeavor and as a useful set of tools to be used by leaders in organizations. But, it highlights the need to expand markedly the POS-related outcomes in future research.

Moreover, little work has examined questions of causality. Several time-lagged studies or longitudinal analyses are described in some of the more recent studies (e.g., Cameron et al., 2011), but the careful control of extraneous factors is largely absent in positive organizational scholarship. Positive psychology has a significant advantage in this regard because of the availability of controlled environments in experimental studies.

SUMMARY

Once again, POS is not value-neutral. It advocates the position that the desire to improve the human condition is universal and that the capacity to do so is latent in most systems. The means by which this latent capacity is unleashed and organized, the extent to which human possibilities are enabled, and the extent to which systems produce extraordinarily positive outcomes are of special interest. POS does not exclude phenomena that are typically labeled negative in organizational studies – such as competitive pressures, downsizing, stressful circumstances, or financial losses – but it has a bias toward life-giving, generative, and ennobling human conditions and addresses traditional negative phenomena with a positive lens.

POS offers a unique conceptual foundation for understanding how and why organizational strategies have their effects on human behavior in the workplace, and why some strategies and practices are more generative than others. An important function of POS, therefore, is to provide more attention to the processes and practices that unleash heliotropic effects and elevate resourcefulness. Empirical evidence suggests that when positive factors are given greater emphases than negative factors, individuals and organizations tend to flourish.

Research on POS has begun to explain variance that has largely been ignored in previous investigations of organizations. Processes and attributes are highlighted that have received little attention in previous organizational research – including virtuousness, positive energy networks, and high-quality connections. Adopting a positive lens illuminates research questions and relationships that have been under-investigated and frequently ignored. Thus, POS provides fertile territory for understanding the mechanisms and the outcomes associated with the naturally occurring but seldom examined inclination toward the positive in organizations.

NOTE

1. This chapter borrows from other works by the author, including Cameron and Winn (2012), Caza and Cameron (2008), and Cameron (2008).

REFERENCES

Andersson, L. M., Giacalone, R. A., & Jurkiewicz, C. L. (2007). On the relationship of hope and gratitude to corporate social responsibility. *Journal of Business Ethics, 70*, 401–409.
Aristotle (2009, Translation). *Metaphysics XII, 7*, 3–4.

Avey, J. B., Patera, J. K., & West, B. J. (2006). The implications of positive psychological capital on employee absenteeism. *Journal of Leadership and Organizational Studies, 13*, 42–60.

Baker, W. (2007). *The reciprocity ring*. Ann Arbor, MI: Center for Positive Organizational Scholarship, University of Michigan.

Baker, W., Cross, R., & Parker, A. (2004). What creates energy in organizations? *Sloan Management Review, 44*, 51–56.

Baker, W., Cross, R., & Wooten, L. (2003). Positive organizational network analysis and energizing relationships. In K. S. Cameron, J. E. Dutton & R. E. Quinn (Eds.), *Positive organizational scholarship: Foundations of a new discipline* (pp. 328–342). San Francisco, CA: Berrett-Koehler.

Baker, W., & Gunderson, R. (2005). *Zingerman's community of businesses*. Ann Arbor, MI: Center for Positive Organizational Scholarship, University of Michigan.

Baumeister, R. F., Bratslavsky, E., Finkenauer, C., & Vohs, K. D. (2001). Bad is stronger than good. *Review of General Psychology, 5*, 323–370.

Bek, J., Benedetto, K., Feldman, E., Goldenberg, S., Jaffe, A., Lavery, B., ... Russo, B. (2007). *A foundation of giving: How one company cares for its employees*. Ann Arbor, MI: Center for Positive Organizational Scholarship, University of Michigan.

Berg, J. M., Wrzesniewski, A., & Dutton, J. E. (2010). Perceiving and responding to challenges in job crafting at different ranks: When proactivity requires adaptivity. *Journal of Organizational Behavior, 31*, 158–186.

Bono, J. E., & Ilies, R. (2006). Charisma, positive emotion and mood contagion. *Leadership Quarterly, 17*, 317–334.

Bright, D. S., Cameron, K. S., & Caza, A. (2006). The amplifying and buffering effects of virtuousness in downsized organizations. *Journal of Business Ethics, 64*, 249–269.

Britt, T. W., Dickinson, J. M., Moore, D., Castro, C. A., & Adler, A. B. (2007). Correlates and consequences of moral versus depression under stressful conditions. *Journal of Occupational Health Psychology, 12*, 34–47.

Cameron, K. S. (2003). Organizational virtuousness and performance. In K. S. Cameron, J. Dutton & R. E. Quinn (Eds.), *Positive organizational scholarship* (pp. 48–65). San Francisco, CA: Berrett-Koehler.

Cameron, K. S. (2008a). Paradox in positive organizational change. *Journal of Applied Behavioral Science, 44*, 7–24.

Cameron, K. S. (2008b). *Positive leadership*. San Francisco, CA: Berrett Koehler.

Cameron, K. S. (2011). Building relationships by communicating supportively. In D. A. Whetten & K. S. Cameron (Eds.), *Developing management skills* (8th ed., pp. 233–278). Upper Saddle River, NJ: Prentice Hall.

Cameron, K. S., Bright, D. S., & Caza, A. (2004). Exploring the relationships between organizational virtuousness and performance. *American Behavioral Scientist, 47*, 766–790.

Cameron, K. S., & Caza, A. (2002). Organizational and leadership virtues and the role of forgiveness. *Journal of Leadership and Organizational Studies, 9*, 33–48.

Cameron, K. S., & Caza, A. (2004). Contributions to the discipline of positive organizational scholarship. *American Behavioral Scientist, 47*, 731–739.

Cameron, K. S., Dutton, J. E., & Quinn, R. E. (2003). *Positive organizational scholarship: Foundations of a new discipline*. San Francisco, CA: Berrett-Koehler.

Cameron, K. S., & Lavine, M. (2006). *Making the impossible possible: Leading extraordinary performance – The Rocky Flats story*. San Francisco, CA: Berrett-Koehler.

Cameron, K. S., Mora, C. E., Leutscher, T., & Calarco, M. (2011). Effects of positive practices on organizational effectiveness. *Journal of Applied Behavioral Science, 47,* 266–308.

Cameron, K. S., & Plews, E. (2012). Positive leadership in action: Applications of POS by Jim Mallozzi. *Organizational Dynamics, 41,* 99–105.

Cameron, K. S., & Winn, B. (2012). Virtuousness in organizations. In K. S. Cameron & G. M. Spreitzer (Eds.), *Oxford handbook of positive organizational scholarship* (pp. 231–243). New York, NY: Oxford University Press.

Caza, A., & Carroll, B. (2012). Critical theory and positive organizational scholarship. In K. S. Cameron & G. M. Spreitzer (Eds.), *Oxford handbook of positive organizational scholarship* (pp. 965–978). New York, NY: Oxford University Press.

Clifton, D. O., & Harter, J. K. (2003). Investing in strengths. In K. S. Cameron, J. E. Dutton & R. E. Quinn (Eds.), *Positive organizational scholarship: Foundations of a new discipline* (pp. 111–121). San Francisco, CA: Berrett-Koehler.

Cooperrider, D. L., & Srivastva, S. (1987). Appreciative inquiry in organizational life. In W. Pasmore & E. Woodman (Eds.), *Research in organization change and development* (Vol. 1). Greenwich, CT: JAI Press.

Cooperrider, D. L., & Whitney, D. (2005). *Appreciative inquiry: A positive revolution in change*. San Francisco, CA: Berrett-Koehler Publishers, Inc.

Davis, G. F. (2009). *Managed by the markets*. New York, NY: Oxford University Press.

Diener, E. (2009). *The science of well-being*. New York, NY: Springer.

Diener, E., & Suh, E. M. (2000). *Culture and subjective well-being*. Cambridge, MA: MIT Press.

Duchon, D., & Plowman, D. A. (2005). Nurturing the spirit at work: Impact on work unit performance. *Leadership Quarterly, 16,* 807–833.

Dutton, J. E. (2003). *Energizing your workplace: Building and sustaining high quality relationships at work*. San Francisco, CA: Jossey-Bass.

Dutton, J. E., & Glynn, M. (2007). Positive organizational scholarship. In C. Cooper & J. Barling (Eds.), *Handbook of organizational behavior*. Thousand Oaks, CA: Sage.

Dutton, J. E., & Heaphy, E. D. (2003). The power of high-quality connections. In K. S. Cameron, J. E. Dutton & R. E. Quinn (Eds.), *Positive organizational scholarship* (pp. 263–278). San Francisco, CA: Berrett Koehler.

Dutton, J. E., Quinn, R., & Pasick, R. (2002). *The heart of Reuters*. Ann Arbor, MI: Center for Positive Organizational Scholarship, University of Michigan.

Dutton, J. E., & Ragins, B. R. (2007). *Exploring positive relationships at work: Building a theoretical and research foundation*. Mahwah, NJ: Lawrence Erlbaum.

Dutton, J. E., & Sonenshein, S. (2007). Positive organizational scholarship. In S. Lopez & A. Beauchamps (Eds.), *Encyclopedia of positive psychology*. Malden, MA: Blackwell Publishing.

Dutton, J. E., Worline, M. C., Frost, P. J., & Lilius, J. M. (2006). Explaining compassion organizing. *Administrative Science Quarterly, 51,* 59–96.

Ehrenreich, B. (2009). *Bright-sided: How positive thinking is undermining America*. New York, NY: Henry Holt.

Emmons, R. A. (1999). *The psychology of ultimate concerns: Motivation and spirituality in personality*. New York, NY: Guilford Press.

Feldman, M. S., & Khademian, A. M. (2003). Empowerment and cascading vitality. In
    K. S. Cameron, J. E. Dutton & R. E. Quinn (Eds.), *Positive organizational scholarship:
    Foundations of a new discipline* (pp. 343–358). San Francisco, CA: Berrett-Koehler.
Fineman, S. (2006). On being positive: Concerns and counterpoints. *Academy of Management
    Review, 31,* 270–291.
Fredrickson, B. L. (1998). What good are positive emotions? *Review of General Psychology, 2,*
    300–319.
Fredrickson, B. L. (2009). *Positivity.* New York, NY: Crown.
Fredrickson, B. L., & Joiner, T. (2002). Positive emotions trigger upward spirals toward
    emotional well-being. *American Psychologist, 13,* 172–175.
Fry, L. W., Vitucci, S., & Cedillo, M. (2005). Spiritual leadership and army transformation:
    Theory, measurement, and establishing a baseline. *Leadership Quarterly, 16,* 835–862.
Giacalone, R. A., Paul, K., & Jurkiewicz, C. L. (2005). A preliminary investigation into the role
    of positive psychology in consumer sensitivity to corporate social performance. *Journal
    of Business Ethics, 58,* 295–305.
Gittell, J. H., Cameron, K., Lim, S., & Rivas, V. (2006). Relationships, layoffs, and
    organizational resilience: Airline industry responses to September 11. *The Journal of
    Applied Behavioral Science, 42,* 300–328.
Goddard, R. D., & Salloum, S. J. (2012). Collective efficacy beliefs, organizational excellence,
    and leadership. In K. S. Cameron & G. M. Spreitzer (Eds.), *Oxford handbook of positive
    organizational scholarship* (pp. 642–650). New York, NY: Oxford University Press.
Godfrey, P. C. (2003). The relationship between corporate philanthropy and shareholder
    wealth: A risk management perspective. *Academy of Management Review, 30,* 777–796.
Grant, A. M. (2007). Relational job design and the motivation to make a prosocial difference.
    Academy of Management Journal, 32, 393–417.
Grant, A. M., & Schwartz, B. (2011). Too much of a good thing: The challenges and
    opportunity of the Inverted-U. *Perspectives in Psychological Science, 6,* 61–76.
Hackman, J. R. (2009). The perils of positivity. *Journal of Organizational Behavior, 30,* 309–319.
Hess, E. D., & Cameron, K. S. (2006). *Leading with values: Positivity, virtue, and high
    performance.* Cambridge, MA: Cambridge University Press.
Kellett, J. B., Humphrey, R. H., & Sleeth, R. G. (2006). Empathy and the emergence of task
    and relations leaders. *Leadership Quarterly, 17,* 146–162.
Keyes, C. L. M. (2005). Mental illness and/or mental health? Investigating axioms of the com-
    plete state model of health. *Journal of Consulting and Clinical Psychology, 73,* 539–548.
Kramer, R. M. (1999). Trust and distrust in organizations: Emerging perspectives, enduring
    questions. *Annual Review of Psychology, 50,* 569–598.
Losada, M., & Heaphy, E. (2004). The role of positivity and connectivity in the performance
    of business teams: A nonlinear dynamics model. *American Behavioral Scientist, 47,*
    740–765.
Luthans, F., Avolio, B. J., Walumbwa, F. O., & Li, W. (2005). The psychological capital of
    Chinese workers: Exploring the relationship with performance. *Management and
    Organization Review, 1,* 249–271.
Luthans, F., Youssef, C. M., & Avolio, B. J. (2007). *Psychological capital.* Oxford, UK: Oxford
    University Press.
Luthans, K. W., & Jensen, S. M. (2005). The linkage between psychological capital and
    commitment to organizational mission: A study of nurses. *Journal of Nursing
    Administration, 35,* 304–310.

O'Donohoe, S., & Turley, D. (2006). Compassion at the counter: Service providers and bereaved consumers. *Human Relations, 59*, 1429–1448.

Owens, B., Baker, W., & Cameron, K. (2012). *Relational energy at work: Establishing construct, nomological, and predictive validity.* Working Paper, Ross School of Business, University of Michigan.

Park, N., & Peterson, C. M. (2003). Virtues and organizations. In K. S. Cameron, J. E. Dutton & R. E. Quinn (Eds.), *Positive organizational scholarship: Foundations of a new discipline* (pp. 33–47). San Francisco, CA: Berrett Koehler.

Peterson, S. J., & Luthans, F. (2003). The positive impact and development of hopeful leaders. *Leadership and Organization Development Journal, 24*, 26–31.

Pfeffer, J. (2010). Building sustainable organizations: The human factor. *Academy of Management Perspectives, 8*, 34–45.

Pittinsky, T. L., & Shih, M. J. (2004). Knowledge nomads: Organizational commitment and worker mobility in positive perspective. *American Behavioral Scientist, 46*, 791–807.

Powley, E. H., & Cameron, K. S. (2006). Organizational healing: Lived virtuousness amidst organizational crisis. *Journal of Management, Spirituality, and Religion, 3*, 13–33.

Powley, E. H., & Piderit, K. (2008). Tending wounds: Elements of the organizational healing process. *Journal of Applied Behavioral Science, 44*(1), 134–149.

Pratt, M. G., & Ashforth, B. E. (2003). Fostering meaningfulness in work and at work. In K. S. Cameron, J. E. Dutton & R. E. Quinn (Eds.), *Positive organizational scholarship: Foundations of a new discipline* (pp. 309–327). San Francisco, CA: Berrett-Koehler.

Quinn, R. E., Dutton, J. E., & Spreitzer, G. M. (2003). *Reflected best self exercise.* Ann Arbor, MI: Center for Positive Organizational Scholarship, University of Michigan.

Quinn, R. W. (2002). Flow in knowledge work: High performance experience in the design of national security technology. *Administrative Science Quarterly, 50*, 610–642.

Roberts, L. M. (2006). Shifting the lens on organizational life: The added value of positive scholarship. *Academy of Management Review, 31*, 292–305.

Roberts, L. M., Dutton, J. E., & Spreitzer, G. M. (2007). *Bringing my reflected best self to life.* Ann Arbor, MI: Center for Positive Organizational Scholarship, University of Michigan.

Roberts, L. M., Dutton, J. E., Spreitzer, G. M., Heaphy, E. D., & Quinn, R. E. (2005). Composing the reflected best-self-portrait: Building pathways for becoming extraordinary in work organizations. *Academy of Management Review, 30*, 712–736.

Spreitzer, G. M., Lam, C. F., & Quinn, R. W. (2012). Human energy in organizations: Implications for POS from six interdisciplinary streams. In K. S. Cameron & G. M. Spreitzer (Eds.), *Oxford handbook of positive organizational scholarship* (pp. 155–167). New York, NY: Oxford University Press.

Spreitzer, G., & Sonenshein, S. (2003). Positive deviance and extraordinary organizing. In K. S. Cameron, J. E. Dutton & R. E. Quinn (Eds.), *Positive organizational scholarship: Foundations of a new discipline* (pp. 207–226). San Francisco, CA: Berrett-Koehler.

Spreitzer, G., Sutcliffe, K., Dutton, J., Sonenshein, S., & Grant, A. (2005). A socially embedded model of thriving at work. *Organization Science, 16*, 537–549.

Spreitzer, G. M., & Quinn, R. E. (1996). Empowering middle managers to be transformational leaders. *Journal of Applied Behavioral Science, 32*, 237–261.

Sutcliffe, K. M., & Vogus, T. J. (2003). Organizing for resilience. In K. S. Cameron, J. E. Dutton & R. E. Quinn (Eds.), *Positive organizational scholarship: Foundations of a new discipline* (pp. 94–110). San Francisco, CA: Berrett-Koehler.

Thrash, T. M., & Elliott, A. J. (2003). Inspiration as a psychological construct. *Journal of Personality and Social Psychology, 84*, 871–889.

Veenhoven, R. (1996). Happy life-expectancy. A comprehensive measure of quality-of-life in nations. *Social Indicators Research, 39*, 1–58.

Veenhoven, R. (2010). *World databook on happiness (since 1984)*. Boston, MA: Dordrecht.

Verbeke, W., Belschak, F., & Bagozzi, R. P. (2004). The adaptive consequences of pride in personal selling. *Academy of Marketing Science Journal, 32*, 386–402.

Vianello, M., Galliani, E. M., & Haidt, J. (2010). Elevation at work: The effects of leaders' moral excellence. *Journal of Positive Psychology, 5*, 390–411.

Weber, M. (1997). *The theory of social and economic organization*. New York, NY: Free Press.

Weick, K. E. (2003). Positive organizing and organizational tragedy. In K. S. Cameron, J. E. Dutton & R. E. Quinn (Eds.), *Positive organizational scholarship: Foundations of a new discipline* (pp. 66–80). San Francisco, CA: Berrett-Koehler.

Whetten, D. A. (1980). Organizational decline. *Academy of Management Review, 5*, 577–588.

Wooten, L. P., & Crane, P. (2004). Generating dynamic capabilities through a humanistic work ideology: The case of a certified-nurse midwife practice in a professional bureaucracy. *American Behavioral Scientist, 47*, 848–866.

Wrzesniewski, A. (2003). Finding positive meaning in work. In K. S. Cameron, J. E. Dutton & R. E. Quinn (Eds.), *Positive organizational scholarship: Foundations of a new discipline* (pp. 296–308). San Francisco, CA: Berrett-Koehler.

LOOKING BACK AND GLIMPSING FORWARD: THE BROADEN-AND-BUILD THEORY OF POSITIVE EMOTIONS AS APPLIED TO ORGANIZATIONS

Tanya Vacharkulksemsuk and
Barbara L. Fredrickson

About 15 years ago, Fredrickson (1998) posed the question "What good are positive emotions?" challenging assumptions that only negative emotions (e.g., anger, fear, sadness) hold adaptive value for humans, in contrast to positive emotions (e.g., joy, gratitude, interest, serenity). Since then, a slew of laboratory and field research has addressed the timely and provocative question, with findings supporting the idea that experiencing positive emotions is indeed functional and valuable. Overall, findings support Fredrickson's *broaden-and-build theory of positive emotions* (1998, 2001, 2009), which explicates the adaptive significance of positive emotions for human ancestors and why they remain useful in the modern era. Specifically, the theory posits that positive emotions function in the short term to *broaden* one's attention and awareness in ways that, over the long term, *build* one's basin of survival-promoting personal resources. Such functionality is, of course, in contrast to negative emotions' attention-narrowing and

Advances in Positive Organizational Psychology, Volume 1, 45–60
Copyright © 2013 by Emerald Group Publishing Limited
ISSN: 2046-410X/doi:10.1108/S2046-410X(2013)0000001005

bodily-mobilizing effects that support quick, survival-promoting action (e.g., fight, flight). Play, for example, is an urge associated with joy. Specific forms of chasing play found in juveniles of a species – like running into a flexible sapling or branch and catapulting oneself in an unexpected direction – are seen in adults of that species during instances of predator avoidance (Dolhinow, 1987). That is, creative forms of chasing play *broadened* action repertoires and ultimately *built* the physical resource of speed and maneuverability that could be drawn on later in life to escape a dangerous situation.

Such short- and long-term outcomes can be quite beneficial in the workplace. That is, the seemingly inconsequential positive feelings that arise while at work – say, from a thank-you note, a congratulatory cheers from colleagues, or establishing a new productive collaboration – are associated with valuable workplace outcomes, such as prosociality, group development, established ethical cultures, and ongoing learning (Akrivou, Boyatzis, & McLeod, 2006; Arnaud & Sekerka, 2010; Luthans, Vogelgesang, & Lester, 2006; Triliva & Dafermos, 2008).

In this chapter, we review what experiencing felt positive emotions can offer workplaces. We begin with a review of recent and representative findings from social psychology validating the broaden-and-build theory, follow with consistent findings from organizational scholars, and conclude with promising future directions given the latest research.

EVIDENCE FOR THE BROADEN-AND-BUILD THEORY OF POSITIVE EMOTIONS

Positive Emotions Broaden

Experimental evidence for aspects of the broaden-and-build theory actually existed prior to the theory's introduction to the academic world. Generally speaking, laboratory studies showed a causal effect of positive feelings on thought processes. Across a host of studies, Isen and her colleagues demonstrated a wide range of cognitive outcomes resulting from induced positive emotions, including patterns of unusual thought (Isen, Johnson, Mertz, & Robinson, 1985), flexible thinking (Isen & Daubman, 1984), creativity (Isen, Daubman, & Nowicki, 1987), and receptivity to new information (Estrada, Isen, & Young, 1997).

Findings from subsequent social psychological investigations into positive emotions reflect positive emotions' ability to favorably alter people's cognitions and scope of attention. In a behavioral lab study, for example, Fredrickson and Branigan (2005) induced different emotions in people, then asked participants to list the things they felt like doing in that moment, given their current emotional state. Compared to participants induced with negative or no emotions, those who were induced to feel positive emotions listed a greater variety of potential activities. Similarly, studies using neuroimaging (Schmitz, DeRosa, & Anderson, 2009), eyetracking (Wadlinger & Isaacowitz, 2006), and autobiographical memory recall tasks (Talarico, Berntsen, & Rubin, 2009), support the broaden effects of positive emotions: that they shift participants' attention to perceive a wider scope.

Positive emotions have also been associated with enhanced attention to other people and reduced distinctions between one's self and others'. In other words, positive emotions evidently work to alter one's cognitions and scope of attention with respect to other people. In a study of college students during their first weeks of college, for example, those who experienced more positive emotions during that first week reported a greater sense of "oneness" between themselves and their newly assigned roommates. What's more, the positive students developed a deeper, more complex understanding of their roommate, demonstrating an influence of positive emotions on the affective and psychological processes underlying one's social world (Waugh & Fredrickson, 2006). Furthermore, positive emotions induced in the laboratory have been shown to increase trust between acquaintances (Dunn & Schweitzer, 2005), strengthen existing interpersonal relationships (Algoe, 2012; Algoe, Gable, & Maisel, 2010), and are foundational in creating bonds and opportunities for interdependence (Cohn & Fredrickson, 2006; Gable, Reis, Impett, & Asher, 2004). Together, these findings suggest broadening effects of positive emotions within interpersonal domains of one's life. The build hypothesis, as we discuss below, helps shed light on the benefits of experiencing positive emotions over the long term.

Positive Emotions Build

As suggested by the second corollary of Fredrickson's broaden-and-build theory, experiences of positive emotions *build* durable personal resources as well. In other words, the benefits of positive emotions extend beyond simply feeling good in a given moment. Resources that emerge as a result of experienced positive emotions can take a variety of forms, including cognitive (e.g., mindfulness skills or intellectual complexity); social (e.g., dense social networks and high-quality friendship bonds); psychological (e.g., resilience or optimism in the face of adversity); or physical (e.g., the ability to rebound from stress-induced cardiovascular activity or ward off the common cold).

In a recent field experiment, participants randomly assigned to a group that learned how to self-generate positive emotions (via loving–kindness meditation) reported greater levels of mindfulness, self-acceptance, positive relations with other people, better physical health, and fewer symptoms of depression up to eight weeks after beginning the study, compared to those who were in a wait-list control condition (Fredrickson, Cohn, Coffey, Pek, & Finkel, 2008). Strikingly, these effects were fully mediated by participants' increases in daily positive emotions. Again and again, studies show that positive emotions carry benefits, including improvements in problem-solving skills, interpersonal satisfaction, prosocial behavior, self-esteem, sociability, immune system functioning, and physical health (for a meta-analysis of nearly 300 studies, see Lyubomirsky, King, & Diener, 2005). Given that building resources is an inherently longitudinal process and thus difficult to capture in one-time laboratory studies, the list of empirical demonstrations supporting the build hypothesis is notably more sparse than that of the broaden hypothesis. Later in the chapter, we present a couple of findings from more recent years supporting the build hypothesis that can serve as a timely springboard for organizations.

Current Directions for the Broaden-and-Build Theory

More recently, social psychological investigations into the desirable effects of positive emotions have focused on mediators and moderators of the process: *how* and *when*, respectively, do positive emotions carry benefits for people? For example, in a study measuring students' daily emotions for a month, findings show that the link between positive emotions and increased life satisfaction is mediated by one's change in resilience – a psychological resource that helps people "bounce back" from stressful or challenging situations (Cohn, Fredrickson, Brown, Mikels, & Conway, 2009). That is, people who are happy are not simply experiencing more positivity, but are also developing a useful psychological resource that contributes to their wellness, which in turn contributes to their overall life satisfaction. Furthermore, the study suggests that the link between happiness and desirable life outcomes is not just a result of one holding positive evaluations about one's life, but rather, it is people's daily dose of in-the-moment, positive emotions underlying the process.

As for moderators, given that people differ on when they feel more alert and "on" throughout the day (i.e., feeling like a "morning person") versus tired (i.e., feeling the "afternoon slump"), a study recently demonstrated that during the times of day when one feels most cognitively depleted and more reliant on association-based processing, positive emotions are differentially effective (Cavanaugh, Cutright, Luce, & Bettman, 2011). Specifically, the authors find that feelings of hope, in contrast to pride, during one's *non*-preferred time of day facilitate fluid cognitive processing, such as value construction. Thus, not only do these results speak to the functions of different positive emotions (Griskevicius, Shiota, & Neufeld, 2010; Griskevicius, Shiota, & Nowlis, 2010), but also specific times of day when their benefit can be maximally extracted.

Another current direction that the broaden-and-build theory is trending toward intersects with theories of *embodied cognition*, the idea that information processing involves one's own motor experience (see Niedenthal, 2007; Havas, Glenberg, Gutowski, Lucarelli, & Davidson, 2010). That is, one's motor movements are implicated in the affective and psychological experience of a situation. For example, one's bodily expression when induced with feelings of joy and anger involve more shoulder, elbow, pelvis, and trunk motions, compared to feelings of sadness (Gross, Crane, & Fredrickson, 2012). As an interpersonal example, we turn to the concept of rapport, traditionally defined by interactants' perceptions of positivity and mutuality (Tickle-Degnen & Rosenthal, 1990). Yet recent findings on embodied cognition suggest that the bodily aspects of rapport have thus far gone underappreciated. Indeed, in a study of stranger–stranger dyads, greater degrees of nonverbal synchrony videocoded during a self-disclosing conversation emerged as a physical mediator that, in turn, predicted higher levels of rapport (Vacharkulksemsuk & Fredrickson, 2012). Notably, behavioral synchrony was a significant factor above and beyond self-reported positive emotions and psychological "oneness," lending support to the idea that rapport reflects interactants' physically shared motions, emotions, and vitality. In particular, beyond perceptions of positivity and mutuality, shared feelings of vitality and aliveness – bodily sensations theorized to stem from shared movements (McNeill, 1995) – are also key elements of rapport.

The intersection of the broaden-and-build theory with evidence on embodied cognition may point toward the crucial role of one's entire range of bodily motions – rather than just relying on facial expressions – in displaying emotions, which in turn affects how one experiences emotions as well. For dyads and groups, the latest findings on embodied emotion expression and perception are consistent with the effects of interpersonal emotions, such as gratitude and love, which are known to psychologically bring people closer to one another. Thus, it appears to be the case that physical movements do indeed play a role in directing one's cognitive and affective experiences, including degrees of broadening. In particular, given the interpersonal nature of concepts like behavioral synchrony, implications of embodied positive emotions may be greatest in one's building of social resources. Much of this research, of course, is in its infancy, but stands as a fruitful future direction of the broaden-and-build theory for psychologists and organizational scholars alike.

POSITIVE EMOTIONS IN THE WORKPLACE

Although much research on positive psychology has taken place among social psychologists, the benefits of positive emotions in work contexts have reliably captured the interest of management and organizational scholars and practitioners (e.g., *positive organizational scholarship*; Cameron, Dutton, & Quinn, 2003; Cameron & Spreitzer, 2012). Positive organizational scholarship arrived in tandem with the managerial shift of considering workers not just as automatons, but rather as social beings embedded within a socio-emotional network that is their workplace. Organizational research, in turn, notably began to focus on the role of emotions in the workplace (e.g., Ashkanasy & Ashton-James, 2005).

Since the introduction of the broaden-and-build theory, a host of revelations have emerged supporting the idea that positive emotions are valuable assets in the workplace. For example, beginning at the individual level of analysis, positive emotions are associated with greater levels of creativity (Amabile, Barsade, Mueller, & Staw, 2005); and the display of positive social self-conscious emotions, such as pride and empathy, show beneficial effects on personal accomplishment (Zapf & Holz, 2006), and can favorably impact customer relations (Bagozzi, 2006). Interestingly, an employee–customer experience can be driven by customers' behavior, such that when customers initiate an exchange, the employee's state positive affect increases, which in turn influences the customer's service experience as well (Zimmerman, Dormann, & Dollard, 2011). And, character strengths closely associated with positive emotions – such as optimism, hope, efficacy, and resilience – also impact employees' attitudes that support organizational change in a favorable manner. Such character strengths are found to play a more important role in individual success – beyond skill, education, and to a degree, even talent (Siegel, 2006). Experienced daily positive emotions have also been identified as the key process variable by which features of one's job environment (e.g., autonomy, psychological climate of warmth and cooperation) influence one's personal resources of optimism, self-efficacy, and self-esteem on a daily basis (Xanthopoulou, Bakker, Demerouti, & Schaufeli, 2012). Thus, similar to findings from social psychology demonstrating that people's daily dose of experiencing in-the-moment positive emotions underlie the path toward desirable life outcomes, research on optimal individual functioning in organizational contexts also speak to the power of positive emotions.

As discussed earlier, positive emotions experienced at the intrapersonal level can shift in-the-moment cognitive patterns interpersonally as well: positive emotions influence processing not just of information, but also of other people. We posit that positive emotions – following the course of broaden-and-build – can unlock beneficial ways of thinking to build relational capacity in the workplace. Beginning with findings that positive emotions generate more thought–action repertoires and less self–other distinctions, we see positive emotions as a powerful tool for leaders and work team members to foster leader–subordinate relationships and team-mate relationships, respectively. Then, fueled by strengths stemming from dyads and groups within the organization, positivity can spiral outward to a level that involves the entire organization and situated community (Vacharkulksemsuk, Sekerka, & Fredrickson, 2011). Importantly, positive emotions hold a distinctly social origin, such that interacting with others is a common platform for emotions to arise (Vittengl & Holt, 2000; Watson, Clark, McIntyre, & Hamaker, 1992). Leaders and team members can capitalize on this fact to extract not only the basic benefits of positive emotions, but also the power of strong, tensile dyads and groups. The trajectory of positive emotions when experienced among work groups, and how to most effectively enable them, however, is more complex (Rhee & Yoon, 2012). It is still unclear whether effects are additive or multiplicative, and where the tipping point of "too much" positive emotions is for organizations. Evidence is indeed, however, accumulating that suggests favorable trends for teams and leaders, which we briefly review next.

Implications of Positive Emotions for Teams and Leaders

Losada and Heaphy (2004) showed that a high degree of connectivity and positive-to-negative ratios within an organization correlated with higher levels of team performance. Not only did the researchers' mathematical models show that high-performing teams utilized a broader range of behavioral repertoires in the short term, but they also built greater amounts of psychological and social resources through durable connections with their fellow team members. In comparison, lower-performing teams had lower positive-to-negative ratios, which appeared to contribute to the teams' likelihood of getting "stuck" in situations due to a limited behavioral repertoire and weaker team member connectivity. This research on positivity ratios suggests that people simply perform better when their workday experiences include more positive emotions, adding to intrinsic motivation and more favorable perceptions of their work, team, leaders, and organizations (Amabile & Kramer, 2007). The positive-to-negative ratio within a team is also perhaps the driving force behind high-quality team member exchange and team-level productivity (Tse & Dasborough, 2008). What the studies suggest here is that positive emotions can indeed build relational resources, specifically in the context of teams. Stronger teams result from higher positivity ratios and there are hints that the process underlying the built social resource is broadened thinking extended toward others.

Moreover, as related to leaders, positive emotions are more closely associated with transformational leadership, rather than transactional leadership (Rowold & Rohmann, 2009). For example, a diary study by Tims, Bakker, and Xanthopoulou (2011) over five days revealed that daily transformational leadership predicts employees' daily engagement at work, an effect fully mediated by employees' daily levels of optimism. Positive emotions may be playing a role here, as leaders' expressivity of positive emotions in the workplace leads to more favorable perceptions among employees of leaders' effectiveness, and elevates employees' desire to work for them (Bono & Ilies, 2006). Moreover, because leaders often drive how employees feel at work (Sy, Cote, & Saavedra, 2005), emotions expressed from a hierarchical level above can truly make a difference for the entire organization's climate, which ultimately contributes to higher revenue and growth (Ozcelik, Langton, & Aldrich, 2008). Indeed, these findings linking positive emotions with leadership implications can be a product of emotional embodiment (Niedenthal, 2007; Niedenthal, Winkielman, Mondillon, & Vermeulen, 2009), emotional contagion (Hatfield, Cacioppo, & Rapson, 1994), mimicry (Chartrand & Bargh, 1999), or behavioral synchrony (Vacharkulksemsuk & Fredrickson, 2012). Similar to the findings reviewed for team implications, there is optimism for the potential downstream consequences of positive emotions when experienced at the group level. What appears to be a ripe topic of investigation for leadership scholars is the mechanisms of positive leadership, including the role of fostered emotions.

Evidence supports the idea that positive emotions can unlock individual-level thinking and build personal resources for the individual. But what about beneficial outcomes that extend beyond the individual to impact dyads and groups, and furthermore, thinking about dyads and groups as levels for change to occur? The studies reviewed suggest great potential for positive emotions to foster strong social resources (i.e., leadership and team relationships) at work. Once these social resources are formed, it begs the question of what strong, positive work *relationships* can unleash when positive emotions are experienced at the group level. What types of broadening outcomes will result? At what level will the built resources be benefitted?

Future Directions for Organizational Scholarship

Our review of the broaden-and-build theory of positive emotions, as presented within the organizational literature, shows very similar patterns of results to those within psychology, such that benefits of positive emotions are evident. The incorporation of positive emotions in the workplace is relatively nascent, however, we believe that a trove of positive benefits in the workplace remain to be demonstrated. For example, what can positive emotions do for newcomers to a team? Or when there is a transition in management? Do human motor movements stemming from felt positive emotions have similar effects on interpersonal relationships in organizational contexts, and if so, can such relationships be the lever for organizational level engagement and change? Moreover, there appears to be few studies within organizational research investigating process variables (i.e., mediators) and conditional variables (i.e., moderators) of positive emotions on workplace benefits, such as task type, team size, organizational climate, and leadership styles. Importantly, speaking from a scientific perspective, scholars will need to make a continued move from theoretical to empirical investigations to test the short- and long-term effects of positive emotions in organizations.

Much of the evidence reviewed in this chapter speaks to the broaden hypothesis; the build hypothesis is inherently more difficult to empirically support – especially in laboratory studies – given its longitudinal nature. The daily, routinized, and reoccurring nature of organizations, however, make them a fertile context for applying and testing the build hypothesis; moreover, organizations offer opportunities to examine emotions at various levels of analysis, both as a dynamic intra- and inter-individual process. We close this chapter by making one more bridge between social psychology and organizational studies: building upward spirals of positive emotions in organizations.

AN INTERDISCIPLINARY APPROACH TO BUILDING POSITIVITY SPIRALS IN ORGANIZATIONS

Inevitably, negativity arises in the workplace, and when it does, the negativity bias (Baumeister, Bratslavsky, Finkenauer, & Vohs, 2001) tends to dominate one's cognitive patterns. Thus, it would be advantageous for organizations to be equipped with positive emotions when faced with such situations in order to achieve, or maintain, an optimal positivity ratio. What amount of positivity, then, is necessary to balance out negativity? Fredrickson and Losada (2005) discovered that positive-to-negative ratios greater than 3:1 in daily life are a tipping point that predicts one's overall subjective well-being. Consistent with the 3:1 tipping point, a positivity ratio of 4:1 relates to optimal states of mind (Schwartz et al., 2002), and 5:1 describes profitable and well-regarded business teams (Losada, 1999). The good news based on the broaden-and-build theory is that, in addition to the short-term benefits of positive emotions, it is possible that steady, consistent experiences of positive emotions can compound over time to contribute to an upward spiral, ultimately potentially strengthening the entire collective.

In the spirit of interdisciplinary conversations, a good starting point for organizations is to serve as the applied setting of scientifically validated interventions shown to produce or maintain positive emotions. Loving–kindness meditation, for example, is an effective and durable intervention wherein participants are taught to self-generate positive emotions, specifically by focusing on interpersonal connections (Cohn & Fredrickson, 2010). As described earlier, social interactions and social relationships are empirically demonstrated to be highly associated with positive emotions (e.g., Vittengl & Holt, 2000); as such, loving–kindness meditation holds promise as a sustainable positive emotion intervention. Empirically based programs, such as the *REsilience and Activity for every DaY* (*READY*) program, are also good models for organizations to work from to generate positivity. The READY program is a psychosocial training program targeting five resilience protective factors, including positive emotions, cognitive flexibility, and social support (Burton, Pakenham, & Brown, 2010). In a pilot study of READY, clinically healthy employees at a large capital city university showed significant increase in acceptance of positive and negative experiences, environmental mastery, positive emotions, mindfulness, and personal growth, in addition to a reduction in stress, after 11 READY sessions over 13 weeks. It should be acknowledged, however, that sustaining the positive emotions and positivity more generally can of course be more difficult and more empirical examinations are necessary to establish further claims.

Evidence from laboratory studies of positive emotions and memory suggests promise for the possibility of building an upward spiral. If it is the case that stored memories are drawn upon in subsequent events, then the case should not be any different for memories and associations created as a result of broadened thinking. Consistent with the broaden hypothesis, studies demonstrate that positive emotions lead to a wider scope of attention and memory of peripheral (vs. central) details of events (Yegiyan & Yonelinas, 2011). What's more, and suggestive of the possibility of creating an upward spiral starting at the cognitive level, is that positive emotions increase the amount of incoming information that becomes stored as short-term visual memory, like a string of letters or numbers (Kuhbandner, Lichtenfeld, & Pekrun, 2011). Thus, positive emotions help people remember *more* of a given set of information for later recall of the whole set or subset, compared to negative emotions. Affect influences not just memory in-the-moment, but also the breadth of information as processed in its earliest stages (see also Schmitz et al., 2009). Drawing on such findings, organizations can develop strong, durable interventions that target fundamental levels of one's cognitions in order to foster positivity. It is perhaps the case that in order to alter and maintain people's affect and behavior, interventions need to target the earliest stages of thinking possible.

Indeed, especially when negativity strikes a workplace, implementing a positive emotion intervention to set off broadening-and-building effects is more than a matter of inducing positive emotions in people as if employees are lab participants. Rather, a more promising solution may be inducing the *climate* with positive emotions in order to unlock subsequent broadening-and-building. An *appreciative inquiry* summit, for example, is a platform for creating change within an organization by focusing generative efforts on positive aspects that already exist (Cooperrider & Srivastva, 1999). That is, collective explorations into what workers already appreciate and enjoy about their organization become the basis of cultivating whole-scale transformation. Appreciative inquiry has been notably implemented with successful results in an array of settings, including schools (Dickerson & Helm-Stevens, 2011; Kozik, Cooney, Vinciguerra, Gradel, & Black, 2009), the British Broadcasting Corporation (BBC; Mishra & Bhatnager, 2012), and even the United Nations (www.unglobalcompact.org, 2004).

These interventions and programs, of course, are just potential routes by which upward spirals can be fostered in real work settings. Ultimately, it will be necessary to determine the boundary conditions for each that guide where, when, with whom, and how they are most effective. Interdisciplinary conversations, wherein there is constant exchange of ideas and empirical examinations between basic and applied researchers will be key to determining effective and sustainable ways to extract short-term, long-term, and continued benefits of positive emotions.

CONCLUSION

A host of evidence from both social psychology and organizational research supports the broaden-and-build theory, validating the notion that positive emotions do indeed carry benefits for people's thoughts and behaviors at work. However, mechanisms and moderators remain open inquiries for both fields of research, in addition to the role of the human body and its movements. Basic findings are coming from psychology, and notably implicative results for teams, leaders, and workplace relationships are emerging from organizational research. The trajectory of broaden-and-build's impact on people's social worlds in the next 15 years remains to be determined, but certainly the forthcoming research can be strong and impactful by relying on an interdisciplinary approach wherein psychologists and organizational scholars continually exchange methods, findings, and ideas.

REFERENCES

Akrivou, K., Boyatzis, R. E., & McLeod, P. L. (2006). The evolving group: Towards a prescriptive theory of intentional group development. *The Journal of Management Development, 25*, 689–706.

Algoe, S. B. (2012). Find, remind, and bind: The functions of gratitude in everyday relationships. *Social and Personality Psychology Compass, 6*, 455–469.

Algoe, S. B., Gable, S. L., & Maisel, N. (2010). It's the little things: Everyday gratitude as a booster shot for romantic relationships. *Personal Relationships, 17*, 217–233.

Amabile, T. M., Barsade, S. G., Mueller, J. S., & Staw, B. M. (2005). Affect and creativity at work. *Administrative Science Quarterly, 50*, 367–403.

Amabile, T. M., & Kramer, S. J. (2007). Inner work life: Understanding the subtext of business performance. *Harvard Business Review, 85,* 72–86.

Arnaud, A., & Sekerka, L. E. (2010). Positively ethical: The establishment of innovation in support of sustainability. *International Journal of Sustainable Strategic Management, 2,* 121–137.

Ashkanasy, N. M., & Ashton-James, C. E. (2005). Emotion in organizations: A neglected topic in I/O Psychology, but with a bright future. In G. P. Hodgkinson & J. K. Ford (Eds.), *International review of industrial and organizational psychology* (Vol. 20, pp. 221–268). Chichester, UK: Wiley.

Bagozzi, R. E. (2006). The role of social and self-conscious emotions in the regulation of business-to-business relationships in salesperson-customer interactions. *The Journal of Business & Industrial Marketing, 21,* 453–457.

Baumeister, R., Bratslavsky, E., Finkenauer, C., & Vohs, K. (2001). Bad is stronger than good. *Review of General Psychology, 5,* 323–370.

Bono, J. E., & Ilies, R. (2006). Charisma, positive emotions and mood contagion. *Leadership Quarterly, 17,* 317–344.

Burton, N. W., Pakenham, K. I., & Brown, W. J. (2010). Feasibility and effectiveness of psychosocial resilience training: A pilot study of the READY program. *Psychology, Health, & Medicine, 15,* 266–277.

Cameron, K., Dutton, J. E., & Quinn, R. E. (Eds.). (2003). *Positive Organizational Scholarship: Foundations of a new discipline.* San Francisco, CA: Berett-Koehler Publishers.

Cameron, K., & Spreitzer, G. (Eds.). (2012). *Handbook of positive organizational scholarship.* New York, NY: Oxford University Press.

Cavanaugh, L. A., Cutright, K. M., Luce, M. F., & Bettman, J. R. (2011). Hope, pride, and processing during optimal and nonoptimal times of day. *Emotion, 11,* 38–46.

Chartrand, T. L., & Bargh, J. A. (1999). The chameleon effect: The perception-behavior link and social interaction. *Journal of Personality and Social Psychology, 76,* 893–910.

Cohn, M. A., & Fredrickson, B. L. (2006). Beyond the moment, beyond the self: Shared ground between selective investment theory and the broaden-and-build theory of positive emotions. *Psychological Inquiry, 17*(1), 39–44.

Cohn, M. A., & Fredrickson, B. L. (2010). In search of durable positive psychology interventions: Predictors and consequences of long-term positive behavior change. *The Journal of Positive Psychology, 5,* 355–366.

Cohn, M. A., Fredrickson, B. L., Brown, S. L., Mikels, J. A., & Conway, A. M. (2009). Happiness unpacked: Positive emotions increase life satisfaction by building resilience. *Emotion, 9,* 361–368.

Cooperrider, D. L., & Srivastva, S. (1999). Appreciative inquiry in organizational life. In S. Srivastva & D. L. Cooperrider (Eds.), *Appreciative management and leadership: The power of positive thought and action in organization* (Rev. ed., pp. 401–441). Cleveland, OH: Lakeshore Communications.

Dickerson, M. S., & Helm-Stevens, R. (2011). Reculturing schools for greater impact: Using appreciative inquiry as a non-coercive change process. *International Journal of Business and Management, 6,* 66–74.

Dolhinow, P. J. (1987). At play in the fields. In H. Topoff (Ed.), *The natural history reader in animal behavior* (pp. 229–237). New York, NY: Columbia University Press.

Dunn, J., & Schweitzer, M. (2005). Feeling and believing: The influence of emotion on trust. *Journal of Personality and Social Psychology, 88,* 736–748.

Estrada, C. A., Isen, A. M., & Young, M. J. (1997). Positive affect facilitates integration of information and decreases anchoring in reasoning among physicians. *Organizational Behavior and Human Decision Processes, 72,* 117–135.

Fairmount Minerals, Corporate Social Responsibility Report. (2011). *Inspiring innovation through our commitment to people, planet, & prosperity.* Retrieved from http://unglobal compact.org/COPs/detail/16371

Fredrickson, B. L. (1998). What good are positive emotions? *Review of General Psychology, 2,* 300–319.

Fredrickson, B. L. (2001). The role of positive emotions in positive psychology: The broaden-and-build theory of positive emotions. *American Psychologist, 56,* 218–226.

Fredrickson, B. L. (2009). *Positivity: Groundbreaking research reveals how to embrace the hidden strength of positive emotions, overcome negativity, and thrive.* New York, NY: Crown.

Fredrickson, B. L., & Branigan, C. (2005). Positive emotions broaden the scope of attention and thought-action repertoires. *Cognition and Emotion, 19,* 313–332.

Fredrickson, B. L., Cohn, M. A., Coffey, K. A., Pek, J., & Finkel, S. M. (2008). Open hearts build lives: Positive emotions, induced through loving-kindness meditation, build consequential personal resources. *Journal of Personality and Social Psychology, 95,* 1045–1062.

Fredrickson, B. L., & Losada, M. (2005). Positive affect and the complex dynamics of human flourishing. *American Psychologist, 60,* 678–686.

Gable, S. L., Reis, H. T., Impett, E. A., & Asher, E. R. (2004). What do you do when things go right? The intrapersonal and interpersonal benefits of sharing positive events. *Journal of Personality and Social Psychology, 87,* 228–245.

Griskevicius, V., Shiota, M. N., & Neufeld, S. L. (2010). Influence of different positive emotions on persuasion processing: A functional evolutionary approach. *Emotion, 10,* 190–206.

Griskevicius, V., Shiota, M. N., & Nowlis, S. M. (2010). The many shades of rose-colored glasses: An evolutionary approach to the influence of different positive emotions. *Journal of Consumer Research, 37,* 238–250.

Gross, M. M., Crane, E. A., & Fredrickson, B. L. (2012). Effort-shape and kinematic assessment of bodily expression of emotion during gait. *Human Movement Science, 31,* 202–221.

Hatfield, E., Cacioppo, J. T., & Rapson, R. L. (1994). *Emotional contagion.* New York, NY: Cambridge University Press.

Havas, D. A., Glenberg, A. M., Gutowski, K. A., Lucarelli, M. J., & Davidson, R. J. (2010). Cosmetic use of botulinum toxin-A affects processing of emotional language. *Psychological Science, 21,* 895–900.

Isen, A. M., & Daubman, K. A. (1984). The influence of affect on categorization. *Journal of Personality and Social Psychology, 47,* 1206–1217.

Isen, A. M., Daubman, K. A., & Nowicki, G. P. (1987). Positive affect facilitates creative problem solving. *Journal of Personality and Social Psychology, 52,* 1122–1131.

Isen, A. M., Johnson, M. M. S., Mertz, E., & Robinson, G. F. (1985). The influence of positive affect on the unusualness of word associations. *Journal of Personality and Social Psychology, 48,* 1413–1426.

Kozik, P. L., Cooney, B., Vinciguerra, S., Gradel, K., & Black, J. (2009). Promoting inclusion in secondary schools through appreciative inquiry. *American Secondary Education, 38,* 77–91.

Kuhbandner, C., Lichtenfeld, S., & Pekrun, R. (2011). Always look on the broad side of life: Happiness increases the breadth of sensory memory. *Emotion, 11*, 958–964.

Losada, M. (1999). The complex dynamics of high performance teams. *Mathematical and Computer Modeling, 30*, 179–192.

Losada, M., & Heaphy, E. (2004). The role of positivity and connectivity in the performance of business teams: A nonlinear dynamics model. *American Behavioral Scientist, 47*, 740–765.

Luthans, F., Vogelgesang, G. R., & Lester, P. B. (2006). Developing the psychological capital of resiliency. *Human Resource Development Review, 5*, 25–45.

Lyubomirsky, S., King, L. A., & Diener, E. (2005). The benefits of frequent positive affect. *Psychological Bulletin, 131*, 803–855.

McNeill, W. H. (1995). *Keeping together in time: Dance and drill in human history.* Cambridge, MA: Harvard University Press.

Mishra, P., & Bhatnager, J. (2012). Appreciative inquiry: Models & applications. *Indian Journal of Industrial Relations, 47*, 543–558.

Niedenthal, P. M. (2007). Embodying emotion. *Science, 316*, 1002–1005.

Niedenthal, P. M., Winkielman, P., Mondillon, L., & Vermeulen, N. (2009). Embodiment of emotion concepts. *Journal of Personality and Social Psychology, 96*, 1120–1136.

Ozcelik, H., Langton, N., & Aldrich, H. (2008). Doing well and doing good: The relationship between leadership practices that facilitate a positive emotional climate and organizational performance. *Journal of Managerial Psychology, 23*, 186–203.

Rhee, S. Y., & Yoon, H. J. (2012). Shared positive affect in workgroups. In K. S. Cameron & G. M. Sprietzer (Eds.), *Handbook of positive organizational scholarship* (pp. 215–227). Oxford University Press.

Rowold, J., & Rohmann, A. (2009). Transformational and transactional leadership styles, followers' positive and negative emotions, and performance in German nonprofit orchestras. *Nonprofit Management and Leadership, 20*, 41–59.

Schmitz, T. W., De Rosa, E., & Anderson, A. K. (2009). Opposing influences of affective state valence on visual cortical encoding. *Journal of Neuroscience, 3*, 7199–7207.

Schwartz, R. M., Reynolds, C. F., III., Thase, M. E., Frank, E., Fasiczka, A. L., & Haaga, D. A. F. (2002). Optimal and normal affect balance in psychotherapy of major depression: Evaluation of the balanced states of mind model. *Behavioral and Cognitive Psychotherapy, 30*, 439–450.

Siegel, L. (2006). *Suite success.* West Babylon, NY: AMACOM.

Sy, T., Cote, S., & Saavedra, R. (2005). The contagious leader: Impact of the leader's mood on the mood of group members, group affective tone, and group processes. *Journal of Applied Psychology, 90*, 295–305.

Talarico, J. M., Berntsen, D., & Rubin, D. C. (2009). Positive emotions enhance recall of peripheral details. *Cognition & Emotion, 23*, 380–398.

Tickle-Degnen, L., & Rosenthal, R. (1990). The nature of rapport and its nonverbal correlates. *Psychological Inquiry, 1*, 285–293.

Tims, M., Bakker, A. B., & Xanthopoulou, D. (2011). Do transformational leaders enhance their followers' daily work engagement? *The Leadership Quarterly, 22*, 121–131.

Triliva, S., & Dafermos, M. (2008). Philosophical dialogues as paths to a more positive psychology. *Journal of Community & Applied Social Psychology, 18*, 17–38.

Tse, H., & Dasborough, M. (2008). A study of exchange and emotions in team member relationships. *Group & Organization Management, 33*, 194–215.

Vacharkulksemsuk, T., & Fredrickson, B. L. (2012). Strangers in sync: Achieving embodied rapport through shared movements. *Journal of Experimental Social Psychology*, *48*, 399–402.

Vacharkulksemsuk, T., Sekerka, L. E., & Fredrickson, B. L. (2011). Establishing a positive emotional climate to create twenty-first century organizational change. In N. M. Ashkanasy, C. P. M. Wilderom & M. F. Peterson (Eds.), *Handbook of organizational culture and climate* (2nd ed., pp. 101–118). Thousand Oaks, CA: Sage.

Vittengl, J. R., & Holt, C. S. (2000). Getting acquainted: The relationship of self-disclosure and social attraction to positive affect. *Journal of Social and Personal Relationships*, *17*, 53–66.

Wadlinger, H. A., & Isaacowitz, D. M. (2006). Positive mood broadens visual attention to positive stimuli. *Motivation and Emotion*, *30*, 89–101.

Watson, D., Clark, L. A., McIntyre, C. W., & Hamaker, S. (1992). Affect, personality, and social activity. *Journal of Personality and Social Psychology*, *63*, 1011–1025.

Waugh, C. E., & Fredrickson, B. L. (2006). Nice to know you: Positive emotions, self-other overlap, and complex understanding in the formation of a new relationship. *The Journal of Positive Psychology*, *1*, 93–106.

Xanthopoulou, D., Bakker, A. B., Demerouti, E., & Schaufeli, W. B. (2012). A diary study on the happy worker: How job resources relate to positive emotions and personal resources. *European Journal of Work and Organizational Psychology*, *21*, 489–517.

Yegiyan, N. S., & Yonelinas, A. P. (2011). Encoding details: Positive emotion leads to memory broadening. *Cognition & Emotion*, *25*, 1255–1262.

Zapf, D., & Holz, M. (2006). On the positive and negative effects of emotion work in organizations. *European Journal of Work and Organizational Psychology*, *15*, 1–28.

Zimmerman, B. K., Dormann, C., & Dollard, M. F. (2011). On the positive aspects of customers: Customer-initiated support and affective cross-over in employee customer dyads. *Journal of Occupational and Organizational Psychology*, *84*, 31–57.

SELF-DETERMINATION THEORY'S CONTRIBUTION TO POSITIVE ORGANIZATIONAL PSYCHOLOGY

Marylène Gagné and Maarten Vansteenkiste

Self-determination theory (SDT; Deci & Ryan, 1985a), a theory of human motivation, developed by Edward L. Deci and Richard M. Ryan at the University of Rochester since the early 1970s, provides a rich theoretical platform to study a variety of positive outcomes in organizational psychology (Deci & Vansteenkiste, 2004; Sheldon & Ryan, 2011). This is because the assumptions regarding human nature articulated within SDT fit the broader agenda of the positive psychology movement. Just like the positive psychology movement is concerned with human flourishing and the way to promote such functioning (Gable & Haidt, 2005), SDT focuses on human strengths and well-being, as part of its dialectical character, and addresses the question of how the social environment fosters these positive outcomes. There are, however, three major differences between SDT and positive psychology that we discuss here.

First, positive psychology represents a scientific domain, while SDT is a theory that is made up of five interrelated mini-theories (Vansteenkiste, Niemiec, & Soenens, 2010). What characterizes the positive psychology movement is a shared focus on a variety of positive human experiences, including gratitude, prosocial behavior, engagement, and flow, among other things. As a result of this broad diversity of positive phenomena, the rapidly

Advances in Positive Organizational Psychology, Volume 1, 61–82
ISSN: 2046-410X/doi:10.1108/S2046-410X(2013)0000001006

growing field of positive psychology is rather heterogeneous and scattered. This stands in contrast to SDT, which represents a coherent body of work that has been steadily developed over the past five decades, starting from a number of critical meta-theoretical assumptions. Because of the lack of an overarching theoretical framework, such assumptions are not well-articulated within the domain of positive psychology.

Yet, as noted by Deci and Vansteenkiste (2004), the clarification of these basic assumptions is of critical importance for the positive psychology movement to evolve from a movement to a theory. The meta-theoretical assumptions outlined in SDT might, in that respect, be adopted by scholars in the field of positive psychology. According to SDT, human beings are not simply reacting to their environment, they have the capacity to proactively shape it. Further, throughout activity, they have a natural tendency to move toward increasing levels of growth and integrated functioning. However, the theory states that such movement should not be taken for granted. It needs to be supported by the social environment through the nurturing of basic psychological needs for autonomy, competence, and relatedness. Within SDT, psychological needs are assigned a key role, as they represent the "royal" road to optimal functioning and form the explanatory mechanism between the social environment and people's flourishing.

A third difference concerns the fact that, as the term "positive" in positive psychology suggests, this movement has so far been primarily concerned with fostering positive functioning. In contrast, SDT recognizes the fact that people are vulnerable to malfunctioning and even to pathology, and the thwarting of basic psychological needs plays a fundamental role in this process (Vansteenkiste & Ryan, in press). Indeed, to the extent that the needs are thwarted, especially on a more chronic basis, individuals find ways to cope at work that are sometimes maladaptive, such as developing obsessions (e.g., obsessive workaholism), and engaging in unethical (e.g., theft) and aggressive behaviors (e.g., bullying). What SDT brings to the positive psychology movement is the concept of psychological needs, which provides a parsimonious set of concepts to account for both the bright and dark side of human functioning (Ryan & Deci, 2000).

SDT is grounded in organismic and humanistic principles regarding human nature (Deci & Ryan, 1985a). The organismic principle stems from biological theories that have tried to account for the increasing complexity of biological organisms (Goldstein, 1934). The principle states that an organism grows by developing more complex and refined structures to deal flexibly with the challenges imposed by the environment, a process called differentiation. At the same time, these increasingly refined structures get steadily integrated into a coherent whole. The analog in psychology is to assume that human beings' psychological systems become increasingly complex and refined with life experiences, while becoming more strongly anchored into a coherent whole (von Bertalanffy, 1968). In SDT, the self is conceived of as the process that regulates behavior, the phenomenal center of personal experience and agency (Deci & Ryan, 2000). The self as a *process* differs from the notion of self-concept, which describes the way people view themselves as through a mirror. Indeed, these different self-concepts or identities can coexist in harmony but can also be more fragmented, suggesting that they are not fully integrated within one's sense of self (Ryan & Deci, 2003; Soenens & Vansteenkiste, 2011).

SDT is also consistent with humanistic theorizing, which emerged out of a need in clinical psychology to address the meaning of psychological health and growth, and to address the important role of human subjective experience (Rogers, 1951). In SDT, optimal functioning is the ultimate outcome, and is defined as a human being's maximal level of development, operationalized using behavioral and well-being indicators. As such, a person who is able to competently and consistently regulate her work behavior would be considered to be optimally functioning in this context. Optimal functioning would also mean that a person engages in an activity or behavior with volition, enthusiasm, positive affect, and energy. Therefore, behavioral engagement should be positively related to these experiences. Unlike some theories of positive psychology, SDT defines well-being in terms of eudaimonic factors, defined as the process of living well (Ryan, Huta, & Deci, 2008), and operationalized as the experience of vitality and serenity. This definition of well-being differs from hedonic viewpoints on well-being, defined as feeling good, and operationalized as the presence of positive affect and the absence of negative affect (Kahneman, Diener, & Schwartz, 1999; Ryan et al., 2008).

Like other humanistic theories, SDT relies on human experience as an important source of data to understand human motivation. Unlike other humanistic theories, including Rogers' (1951) person-centered approach and Maslow's (1954) hierarchy of needs, SDT is strongly empirically grounded (Sheldon, Joiner, Pettit, & Williams, 2003). That is, scholars working from the SDT perspective have attempted to gather empirical evidence for theoretical claims by relying on a variety of empirical methods, including the use of validated questionnaires (e.g., Gagné et al., 2010), experimental manipulations (e.g., Grolnick & Ryan, 1987), brain imaging (e.g., Murayama, Matsumoto, Izuma, & Matsumoto, 2010), the collection of biological markers (cortisol secretion; e.g., Reeve & Tseng, 2011), and implicit (unconscious) procedures (e.g., Lévesque & Pelletier, 2003).

The rest of this chapter provides a description of how SDT can contribute to positive organizational psychology, and explains how some of the central concepts and principles in SDT are (dis)similar with a variety of frameworks (e.g., psychological empowerment theory) and phenomena (e.g., engagement) that are often studied in the field of positive organizational psychology.

SELF-DETERMINATION THEORY: A BRIEF OVERVIEW

At the core of SDT is the postulation of three basic psychological needs, that is, the needs for autonomy, competence, and relatedness. The satisfaction of these three needs is said to be of utmost importance in its own right as it contributes to people's functioning. Moreover, need satisfaction forms the basis for the development of more optimal forms of motivation (i.e., intrinsic motivation, internalization) and contributes to individual differences in people's general motivational orientation, called general causality orientations, and differences in values that also affect how we live and thrive.

The Royal Road to Daily Well-being: The Role of Basic Psychological Need Satisfaction

The choice of basic psychological needs was determined through rigorous research, involving the consideration of many candidate needs across a wide range of cultures (Deci & Ryan, 2000; Sheldon, Elliot, Kim, & Kasser, 2001). The criterion used to determine whether a need is basic was whether its presence or absence was associated with increases and decreases in well-being, respectively. Three needs were retained: (1) the need to feel *competent* refers to the desire to master one's environment and to take on stimulating challenges, (2) the need to feel *autonomous* refers to the desire to feel like an agent of one's behavior and to experience a sense of psychological freedom, as opposed to feeling like a pawn and being pressured, and (3) the need to feel *related* to others is the desire to have meaningful social interactions.

A variety of studies have demonstrated that the satisfaction of these basic psychological needs relates to enhanced well-being, as indexed by higher vitality and life satisfaction, and less ill-being, as indexed by less anxiety and depressive symptoms (e.g., Vansteenkiste, Lens, Soenens, & Luyckx, 2006). Such findings have been observed at both the between-person and within-person levels, with more need satisfying days being associated with higher daily well-being and need frustrating days relating to drops in well-being (e.g., Reis, Sheldon, Gable, Roscoe, & Ryan 2000; Ryan, Bernstein, & Brown, 2010). More central to the field of organizational psychology, previous studies have shown that satisfaction of the needs in the workplace is key to promoting positive outcomes (Gagné & Deci, 2005), including better job performance (Baard, Deci, & Ryan, 2004), decreased risk of burnout (Fernet, Gagné, & Austin, 2010), higher commitment to the organization (Gagné, Chemolli, Forest, & Koestner, 2008), and lower turnover (Gagné, 2003). More recently, a well-validated need satisfaction at work scale was presented by Van den Broeck, Vansteenkiste, Lens, and De Witte (2010), who found, across four different samples, that need satisfaction at work was related to higher job-related (e.g., job satisfaction) and global (e.g., life satisfaction) well-being.

Motivation: From Intrinsic versus Extrinsic to Autonomous versus Controlled

The satisfaction of the basic psychological needs is not only essential for individuals' wellness, but also for the development of beneficial types of motivation, such as intrinsic motivation. Intrinsic motivation refers to doing an activity for its own sake, that is, out of inherent pleasure for the activity. Intrinsically motivated employees execute work tasks because they find them interesting, are passionate about the work, or are fascinated by the topic. Intrinsic motivation represents an important manifestation of people's growth-oriented nature, something that is readily observable in toddlers' interest in manipulating material objects and in exploring their environment. They are simply driven by curiosity, which forms the impetus for their intrinsic motivation to develop over time.

Numerous studies have demonstrated that the support of individuals' needs for autonomy and competence fosters interest in and liking of the activity at hand, while the undermining of these needs precludes the development of intrinsic motivation. Indeed, the most well-known finding emerging from the field of SDT probably concerns the empirical observation that external rewards can undermine intrinsic motivation under certain conditions (Deci, Koestner, & Ryan, 1999). Numerous laboratory studies have shown that to the extent that rewards put pressure on individuals to act and think in a certain way, they diminish their sense of autonomy, with resulting decreases in their interest and enjoyment of the task at hand. In effect, rewards can turn "play" into "work" (Lepper & Greene, 1975), because the motivational basis for doing the activity shifts from the sheer pleasure of doing the activity to doing the activity in order to obtain a separable outcome. Said differently, inducing an extrinsic motivational orientation has been shown to forestall a process-oriented approach, which is critical for a full absorption in, and true enjoyment of the activity at hand.

Notably, these autonomy-inhibiting effects of rewards can be offset in cases where rewards foster a sense of competence. At least some types of rewards (e.g., performance-contingent rewards) contain feedback, such that the informational rather than the evaluative character of rewards becomes more prominent, thereby increasing a sense of effectiveness among reward recipients. Other environmental events, which have been studied as part of a research program to test Cognitive Evaluation Theory, one of SDT's mini-theories (Deci & Ryan, 1985a), have also been shown to have this effect. These include pressuring deadlines, evaluative surveillance, and controlling competition (Deci & Ryan, 2000; Vansteenkiste, Niemiec, & Soenens, 2010). These findings have important implications for management, as workplaces are fraught with such means to control and evaluate behavior. To the extent these external events are perceived to be controlling, they would undermine subordinates' intrinsic motivation through forestalling their need for auto-nomy, while the informational value of these events would foster intrinsic motivation by supporting the need for competence (Deci & Ryan, 1985a). To sum up, the net effect on the needs for autonomy and competence determines the impact of an external event on subordinates' level of intrinsic motivation.

In some of the early work on intrinsic motivation, it was portrayed to be antagonistic to extrinsic motivation (Harter, 1981). This need not be the case, neither in theory, nor in practice. At a theoretical level, extrinsic motivation refers to doing something for an instrumental reason, that is, to obtain an outcome separable from the activity itself. This definition applies, evidently, to the classic examples of extrinsic motivation, such as doing something *to* obtain a reward or *to* avoid a punishment. Yet, this definition also applies to other types of motives, such as putting effort in one's work *to* avoid feelings of guilt, *to* boost one's self-esteem, or *to* reach a personally valued goal. These instrumental reasons differ in the extent to which they have been accepted and have become part of one's sense of self (i.e., internalized; Ryan & Connell, 1989). As a result, by specifying different types of extrinsic motivation that vary in their level of autonomy, the theory moved to a more differentiated perspective, such that the central distinction now concerns the difference between controlled and autonomous forms of motivation.

The differentiation of extrinsic motivation is also critical at a phenomenological level, as doing activities for these different extrinsic reasons engenders different affective experiences, ranging from feelings of coercion to internal conflict to inner harmony and peace. At a practical level, this more refined viewpoint has allowed us to understand how one could maintain a sense of autonomy when engaging in disliked activities, given that one has concurred with the reasons for doing so. Indeed, at work, various activities are far from interesting and enjoyable (e.g., doing administrative tasks), yet they are critical and must get done; to the extent that one personally values the accomplishment of these disliked activities, one would engage in them with a greater sense of willingness.

In light of these theoretical, experiential, and practical considerations, the distinction between different subtypes of extrinsic motivation goes as follows. When a behavior is completely externally determined and, therefore, not autonomously regulated at all, it is called *externally regulated extrinsic motivation*. This happens when an employee engages in a behavior to gain a valued reward or avoid an undesired punishment, which could both be either tangible or social. Tangible rewards and punishments include monetary rewards, medals, plaques, certificates, promotions, or job loss, demotion, monetary sanctions, etc. Social rewards and punishments include recognition from peers, approval, love contingent on one's behavior, rejection, criticism, etc. Thus, an employee who overworks to gain the appreciation of his manager or to get the extra bonus that was promised if the project is finished on time constitutes examples of external regulation.

Extrinsically motivated behavior can also be internally regulated. The process of internalization, which has been well studied in developmental psychology, is what allows people to take in an externally regulated behavior. Two operationalizations of internalization have dominated the field (Ryan & Connell, 1989). The first, called *introjection*, describes an external regulation that has been taken in and is now enforced by internal pressures (Meissner, 1981). The introjected person acts out of guilt, shame, anxiety, and pride. In other words, the person's sense of self-esteem has become contingent on living up to the internalized external standards. This type of regulation, even though it is internally driven, is not autonomous in nature, because there is no experience of volition attached to it. On the contrary, feelings of internal conflict and distress often accompany introjected regulation. An employee sticking to safety rules because he would feel guilty for not doing so displays introjected regulation.

Different from introjected regulation, *identification* describes a type of regulation in which the reason for doing the activity has been taken in (Kelman, 1958), such that the person acts out of personal conviction, and thereby feels volitional about it. It is therefore an autonomous type of extrinsic motivation. It still needs to be differentiated from intrinsic motivation as it is still done for an instrumental reason, and not out of pure enjoyment. Thus, if the same employee respects the safety rules because he understands that he may put other colleagues in danger by not doing so, he has identified with the importance of the socially requested behavior.

Ryan and Connell (1989) developed a way to measure these different types of motivations with elementary school children. By simply asking them why they did their homework, or why they would help someone in distress, and by providing them with reasons representing the different forms of motivation (which they could endorse on a Likert-type scale), the researchers found that these types of motivation were differentially related to important outcomes, such as coping strategies, effort, and enjoyment of school activities. This method has been widely applied in the fields of education, sport, exercise, parenting, leisure, and health behavior change, with similar results across these life domains (see Deci & Ryan, 2008; Vansteenkiste et al., 2010, for reviews). It has also recently been applied to the work domain, with a proliferation of scales to measure work motivation (Blais, Brière, Lachance, Riddle, & Vallerand, 1993; Gagné et al., 2010; Gagné, Forest, Vansteenkiste, Crevier-Braud, & Van den Broeck, 2012; Tremblay, Blanchard, Taylor, Pelletier, & Villeneuve, 2009). More importantly, these types of motivation do not yield the same outcomes. Autonomous forms of motivation (identified and intrinsic) in general lead to more positive outcomes, such as better performance, more positive affect, more energy, better physical and mental health, more persistence, and more cooperation, than controlled forms of motivation (external and introjected; Deci & Ryan, 2008).

Promoting Autonomous Motivation at Work

Postulating psychological needs allows us to predict what environmental factors, task characteristics, and social characteristics will foster the process of internalization and intrinsic motivation. By specifying these needs, one can predict that in a work environment where the selection of personnel is based on acquired knowledge, skills, and abilities, and where people are offered optimal challenges, where training and developmental opportunities are offered, and where constructive feedback is given, a person is more likely to feel competent. A work environment where strategic goals are explained to employees, participative management is used, where people can take initiative and make decisions, and where they have a voice is more likely to make workers feel autonomous. Finally, in a work environment where social interactions are encouraged through job design, let us say through team work, and where managers take the time to listen to their employees and empathize with them, a worker is more likely to feel high relatedness.

Not only has the theory been used to show how behaviors that support the three psychological needs influence performance and well-being (Baard et al., 2004), but it has also helped us understand why transformational leadership behavior influences performance, commitment to organizations, and job satisfaction (Bono & Judge, 2003). It has even recently been applied to show that occupational health and safety inspectors who support psychological needs when dealing with workplace conflicts are more effective in getting organizations to adhere to regulations (Burstyn, Jonasi, & Wild, 2010). In short, managers who provide a vision or goals with a good rationale for them, who consider their employees' needs and empathize with them, who provide them with choices and opportunities for initiative, and who believe in them, have employees who are more autonomously motivated.

The next question of interest is whether need-supportive managerial behaviors are trainable, and the answer is yes. Studies have indeed shown that training managers to be more supportive of the three needs enhances employee motivation, trust in management, commitment to the organization, and job satisfaction (Deci, Connell, & Ryan, 1989; see Su & Reeve, 2011 for a recent meta-analysis). But training is not enough. Managers also need to experience less pressure if they are to be autonomously motivated themselves and supportive of subordinate psychological needs (Pelletier, Lévesque, & Legault, 2002; Pelletier & Sharp, 2009), which means that organizational structure, culture, and practices are also important.

Job design also significantly influences autonomous work motivation. Jobs that provide variety, challenge, feedback, and decision latitude foster autonomous work motivation (Gagné, Senécal, & Koestner, 1997; Van den Broeck, Vansteenkiste, De Witte, & Lens, 2008). This can be achieved through job enrichment, team work, and participative management.

Moreover, employees whose values fit with those of their organization and group, and whose knowledge and abilities fit their job requirements, are more likely to experience high need satisfaction, which in turn is associated with their performance and commitment to the organization (Greguras & Diefendorff, 2009).

Individual Differences

As SDT puts human experience at the forefront, individual differences in how people appraise their environment become a crucial determinant of their motivation (Deci & Ryan, 1985b). Some people are more sensitive to environmental controls, and consequently feel controlled more often than others. These control-oriented people look for clues in the environment that will tell them what is expected of them, and feel pressured in initiating and regulating certain behaviors (Deci & Ryan, 1985a). They rely on environmental controls, such as deadlines, to regulate their behavior, and are hypothesized to be more likely to select jobs based on status and pay. In contrast, some people tend to experience more choice when initiating and regulating their behavior, and in a sense are more proactive than others. It is assumed that these autonomy-oriented people are more likely to select jobs that allow initiative, to interpret feedback as more informational, and to make choices based on their own interests and values. These causality orientations are assumed to emerge out of early need-supportive or need-thwarting experiences with significant others, such as parents, teachers, and peers. When the early environment satisfies the basic needs for autonomy, competence, and relatedness, people tend to develop a more autonomous orientation. Whereas people who are high on autonomy orientation tend to show behavior that is more consistent with their values and attitudes, and are consequently more likely to support the needs of others (Williams & Deci, 1996), people high on control orientation are more likely to show a Type-A behavior pattern, which is related to health problems (Deci & Ryan, 1985b). Autonomy orientation has indeed been positively related to work-related well-being, performance, and engagement (Baard et al., 2004; Deci et al., 2001; Gagné, 2003).

More recent research is looking beyond general causality orientations, by examining how values develop and affect our lives. People who hold more extrinsic values, such as financial success, image, and popularity, report lower well-being than people who hold more intrinsic values, such as affiliation, community, and self-acceptance (Grouzet et al., 2005;

Kasser & Ryan, 1993, 1996). People with intrinsic values tend to learn better and persist more, whereas those with extrinsic values cooperate less, hoard resources, act more prejudicially, and take more health risks (for an overview see Vansteenkiste, Soenens, & Duriez, 2008). Values seem to develop in a way that is similar to the causality orientations mentioned above: When needs are satisfied, people tend to adopt more intrinsic values relative to extrinsic values (Kasser, Koestner, & Lekes, 2002; Kasser, Ryan, Zax, & Sameroff, 1995). Education can also have an impact on the development of values, even at the adult age. It has been shown that law and business education students tend to adopt more extrinsic values, whereas undergraduate students in arts and science tend to adopt more intrinsic values during their education (Kasser & Ahuvia, 2002; Sheldon, 2005; Sheldon & Krieger, 2007). Intrinsic work values have also been related to interest for training, the ability of unemployed people to find a job, job satisfaction, engagement, and well-being (Van den Broeck et al., 2010; Vansteenkiste et al., 2007).

EXTENSIONS IN MANAGEMENT

SDT can be applied in numerous ways to positive organizational behavior. We cover a few of these applications, including work engagement, commitment, thriving, mindfulness, proactivity, prosocial work behavior, and psychological capital, though we believe that SDT has the potential to be applied in many other ways in management.

In organizational psychology, *work engagement* is a crucial organizational outcome, because it is linked to organizational effectiveness (Macey & Schneider, 2008). Conceptualizations of work engagement that are used by researchers and also by practitioners vary widely. Some conceptualize engagement as a trait, such as proactive personality and conscientiousness, others conceptualize it as a state, such as feelings of energy or organizational commitment, and yet others conceptualize it as a behavior, such as organizational citizenship behavior or personal initiative (Macey & Schneider, 2008). Meyer and Gagné (2008) argued that autonomous motivation is actually a good representation of the state of work engagement since it is defined as motivation through enjoyment and meaning. They also proposed need satisfaction as an essential ingredient for fostering work engagement, such that need satisfaction could actually serve as an explanatory mechanism for the effects of organizational interventions aimed at increasing work engagement.

Schaufeli and colleagues's conceptualization of work engagement is close to what would constitute an experiential outcome of autonomous motivation in SDT (Schaufeli, Salanova, González-Romá, & Bakker, 2002). The measure of engagement that emerged out of this conceptualization includes three components: vigor, which seems identical to the concept of vitality in SDT (Ryan & Frederick, 1997) and constitutes a core aspect of eudaimonic well-being; dedication, which likely emerges when people have fully internalized the importance of their assigned job tasks (Deci, Eghrari, Patrick, & Leone, 1994); and absorption, which has been used extensively as an indicator of intrinsic motivation and flow (Kowal & Fortier, 1999). The opposite of work engagement is burnout (González-Romá, Schaufeli, Bakker, & Lloret, 2006), and again, autonomous motivation has been shown to protect people against burnout (Fernet et al., 2010). Previous studies have also shown that the satisfaction of the needs for autonomy, competence, and relatedness is conducive to work engagement, while protecting against burnout (e.g., Van de Broeck et al., 2008). Indeed, when employees experience a sense of volition in carrying out their work tasks, feel effective in handling challenges, and feel a bond with their colleagues, they likely have more energy available to take up a greater work load or to persist in times of difficulty without burning out.

More recently, Spreitzer and her colleagues have developed a model of *thriving* at work partly based on SDT (Spreitzer, Sutcliffe, Dutton, Sonenshein, & Grant, 2005). Thriving is defined as a feeling of vitality combined with a sense of growing or developing in one's work, and its opposite is languishing or being stuck. Thriving could be considered as a good indicator of eudaimonic well-being and optimal functioning, and it has been related to innovative work behavior (Carmeli & Spreitzer, 2009). Thriving is said to occur when people are focused on the task, when they explore and when they meaningfully relate to others. Spreitzer et al. (2005) argued that such agentic behavior can only occur when one is autonomously motivated. Since autonomous motivation emerges out of the satisfaction of psychological needs, need satisfaction should be a good predictor of thriving. Indeed, thriving has been shown to be fostered by work environments that are high in trust and connectivity (Carmeli & Spreitzer, 2009), which is highly compatible with SDT's postulate regarding the role of psychological needs in fostering autonomous motivation.

Empowerment is another concept with clear links to SDT. Empowerment has been studied both in terms of organizational structural components aimed at decentralizing power in organizations, such as decision-making systems, organizational structures, and managerial styles, and as a psychological construct aimed at understanding the feeling of being empowered (Spreitzer & Doneson, 2005). Structural empowerment should in effect lead to psychological empowerment. Psychological empowerment has been defined as a Gestalt of four feelings, namely meaning, self-determination, competence, and impact (Thomas & Velthouse, 1990). Though the measure of psychological empowerment seems to reflect perceptions of the work environment more than feelings of empowerment per se, it is easy to link at least two of them, self-determination and competence, to two of the psychological needs proposed in SDT. One study in particular has shown that the five job characteristics from Hackman and Oldham's (1975) model (a way to provide structural empowerment) were related to psychological empowerment, which in turn was related to intrinsic work motivation (Gagné et al., 1997). Empowerment is thus another instance of a practice that can be better understood with the help of SDT.

Proactivity is also a desirable characteristic or behavior that has drawn much attention lately in organizational research. The concept emerged out of research on functional flexibility and role breadth (Cordery, Sevastos, Mueller, & Parker, 1993; Parker, Wall, & Jackson, 1997), which focused on how broadly workers define their role in an organization. These researchers have shown that autonomy is a strong predictor of such orientations. Proactive behavior is operationalized as being self-directed and innovative and as taking initiative in one's job (Parker, Williams, & Turner, 2006). Autonomy, trust, and support have been shown to be important antecedents of proactive work behavior (Parker et al., 2006), and overlap quite a bit with the psychological needs in SDT.

To reflect the importance of proactive work behavior for organizations, Griffin, Neal, and Parker (2007) have reconceptualized individual work performance in terms of three types, namely proficiency, adaptivity, and proactivity. While the first, proficiency, is as much associated with controlled and autonomous work motivation, the latter two are more strongly associated with autonomous work motivation (Gagné et al., 2012). These findings support Gagné and Deci's (2005) proposition that algorithmic tasks would be equally related to controlled and autonomous motivation, while heuristic tasks would require autonomous motivation. It also fits well with the idea that more complex and demanding activities require autonomous motivation to be well regulated (Green-Demers, Pelletier, & Ménard, 1997). With regards to adaptivity, research also shows how supporting the three psychological needs helps workers cope with and accept organizational change (Gagné, Koestner, & Zuckerman, 2000), and how autonomous motivation to use a new IT system is related to its adoption and usage

(Mitchell, Gagné, Beaudry, & Dyer, 2012). Parker, Bindl, and Strauss (2010) have recently proposed to study proactivity using the conceptualization of motivation offered by SDT, which they argue can help us better understand how to motivate this type of behavior in organizations. Grant, Nurmohamed, Ashford, and Dekas (2011) have recently shown that indeed, having a lot of personal initiative combined with having high autonomous work motivation and low controlled work motivation fosters proactive behaviors. Job applicants received more job offers and call center employees generated more revenue when they displayed such characteristics.

Commitment, defined as a "a force that binds an individual to a course of action of relevance to one or more targets" (Meyer & Herscovitch, 2001, p. 301), is yet another construct with strong links to the different types of motivation. Allen and Meyer (1990) proposed a tripartite conceptualization of *organizational commitment*, which includes affective commitment, defined as the emotional attachment and identification a person has to an organization, and that person's involvement in that organization; normative commitment, defined as a feeling of obligation or loyalty toward an organization; and continuance commitment, defined as the perceived economic cost of leaving an organization. Meyer, Becker, and Vandenberghe (2004) proposed that each form of commitment is likely to be related to a type of motivation, such that affective commitment would be linked to autonomous work motivation, normative commitment would be linked to introjected regulation, and continuance commitment would be linked to external regulation, which has been supported in research (Gagné et al., 2008) though the direction of causality is still a question of debate among researchers (Meyer, Parfyonova, & Gagné, 2010). Just like need satisfaction influences the development of autonomous work motivation, Meyer and Maltin (2010) speculated that need satisfaction may be more implicated in the development of affective commitment than in the development of normative and continuance commitment, though this remains to be tested.

Lastly, *mindfulness* has been a recent subject of inquiry in management, as the field seeks to exploit human strengths to the benefit of organizations and society (Dane, 2011; see also Barner & Barner, this volume). Mindfulness is considered as an important predictor of task performance (Dane, 2011), for sensing opportunities and threats, seizing opportunities, and optimally using assets (Gärtner, 2011). It has recently been applied to the management of information technology innovations (Mu & Butler, 2009), and to organizational learning (Levinthal, 2006). Though mindfulness is defined in various ways in management, SDT offers a potentially useful psychological definition that is rooted in its assumptions about human nature. Mindfulness is a state of consciousness and is defined as being aware of internal and external experience and reflecting upon this experience (Brown & Ryan, 2003). Mindfulness is positively related to effective self-regulation, interpersonal relationship quality, to holding intrinsic as opposed to extrinsic values, to reduced stress, and of course to eudaimonic well-being (Brown, Ryan, & Creswell, 2007; Weinstein, Brown, & Ryan, 2009). Mindfulness strengthens the association between intention and behavior (Chatzisarantis & Hagger, 2007), and has also been associated with more ecological and sustainable values, as well as with ethical decision-making, both of which have implications for organizational leadership (Brown & Kasser, 2005; Ruedy & Schweitzer, 2010). Mindfulness can also protect against the negative emotional effects of neuroticism (Feltman, Robinson, & Ode, 2009). It is likely to become a variable of interest in management and leadership training in the years to come.

Some enduring individual differences have also been a focus of interest to positive organizational psychology researchers. Such individual differences may influence people's work motivation through one of two processes. The first may operate through some form of resilience created by the traits. Individuals may be buffered from situational woes when they hold certain characteristics, such that their needs are not frustrated to the same extent. The second may be a function of how the environment is shaped by the individuals' traits, such that individuals may bring about need satisfaction just from "being" a certain way. We now discuss some of the traits that have been shown to influence organizational behavior.

Organizations care strongly about their *capital*, which not only includes financial capital, but also human capital (consisting of the knowledge held by individuals employed in organizations), social capital (consisting of the internal and external network of relationships of individuals employed in organizations), and psychological capital. The latter is defined as an individual's positive psychological state of development and consists of a Gestalt of four traits, namely self-efficacy, hope, optimism, and resilience (Luthans, Avey, Avolio, Norman, & Combs, 2006; see also Youssef & Luthans, this volume), all four of which are individual strengths that are theorized to affect motivation. They have also been related to job satisfaction, organizational commitment, and well-being (Avey, Reichard, Luthans, & Mhatre, 2011). It has also been shown that changes in individual psychological capital are related to changes in individual work performance (Peterson, Luthans, Avolio, Walumbwa, & Zhang, 2011). We argue that autonomous motivation may mediate these effects because each of the four traits that make up psychological capital are likely to affect the satisfaction of psychological needs, either through a buffering effect or through altering the context. This could be examined in future research.

Another Gestalt of four individual strengths that has been the recent focus of attention in management is that of core self-evaluations, consisting of self-efficacy, self-esteem, internal locus of control, and emotional stability (the inverse of neuroticism; Judge, Locke, & Durham, 1997). Core self-evaluations have been shown to predict job satisfaction and performance, and these effects have been shown to be mediated by autonomous motivation toward work goals (Judge, Bono, Erez, & Locke, 2005). Judge and colleagues explain that this is because "individuals with positive self-regard think of themselves as worthy, capable, and competent and therefore should be less influenced by external or introjected pressures" (p. 260). This may be due to the effects of core self-evaluations, once again, on the satisfaction of psychological needs.

Individual factors have not been extensively studied within the SDT framework, but the above review shows that there may be some potentially interesting individual differences worth examining. In short, it pays to not only look at contextual factors that are likely to influence work motivation and its outcomes, but to also consider individual differences that may affect how one appraises the work environment.

CONCLUSION

SDT is a theory of positive psychology because it focuses on how to promote optimal human functioning. Positive psychology could, however, not only be about looking at the world with rose-tainted glasses. It could also try to understand what can thwart human functioning (Gable & Haidt, 2005). SDT, by postulating basic psychological needs, offers a particularly good framework to equally understand the facilitation and thwarting of human functioning. As Seligman (2002) delineated, there are three pillars in positive psychology, namely subjective experience, individual characteristics, and positive institutions. Self-determination is able to address all three through specifying what constitutes optimal functioning, by determining individual characteristics such as motivational orientations and values, and by determining how institutions, including work organizations, can foster need satisfaction. This can be particularly useful in the study of organizational behavior in terms of helping us find the best practices to manage humans in organizations.

REFERENCES

Allen, N. J., & Meyer, J. P. (1990). The measurement and antecedents of affective, continuance, and normative commitment to the organization. *Journal of Occupational Psychology, 63,* 1–18.

Avey, J. B., Reichard, R. J., Luthans, F., & Mhatre, K. H. (2011). Meta-analysis of the impact of positive psychological capital on employee attitudes, behaviors and performance. *Human Resource Development Quarterly, 22,* 127–152.

Baard, P. P., Deci, E. L., & Ryan, R. M. (2004). Intrinsic need satisfaction: A motivational basis of performance and well-being in two work settings. *Journal of Applied Social Psychology, 34,* 2045–2068.

Blais, M. R., Brière, N. M., Lachance, L., Riddle, A. S., & Vallerand, R. J. (1993). L'inventaire des motivations au travail de Blais. [Blais's work motivation inventory]. *Revue Québécoise de Psychologie, 14,* 185–215.

Bono, J. E., & Judge, T. A. (2003). Self-concordance at work: Understanding the motivational effects of transformational leaders. *Academy of Management Journal, 46,* 554–571.

Brown, K. W., & Kasser, T. (2005). Are psychological and ecological well-being compatible? the role of values, mindfulness, and lifestyle. *Social Indicators Research, 74,* 349–368.

Brown, K. W., & Ryan, R. M. (2003). The benefits of being present: Mindfulness and its role in psychological well-being. *Journal of Personality and Social Psychology, 84,* 822–848.

Brown, K. W., Ryan, R. M., & Creswell, J. D. (2007). Mindfulness: Theoretical foundations and evidence for its salutary effects. *Psychological Inquiry, 18,* 211–237.

Burstyn, I., Jonasi, L., & Wild, T. C. (2010). Obtaining compliance with occupational health and safety regulations: A multilevel study using self-determination theory. *International Journal of Environmental Health Research, 20,* 271–287.

Carmeli, A., & Spreitzer, G. M. (2009). Trust, connectivity and thriving: Implications for innovative behaviors at work. *Journal of Creative Behavior, 43,* 169–191.

Chatzisarantis, N. L., & Hagger, M. S. (2007). Mindfulness and the intention-behavior relationship within the theory of planned behavior. *Personality and Social Psychology Bulletin, 33,* 663–676.

Cordery, J., Sevastos, P., Mueller, W., & Parker, S. K. (1993). Correlates of employee attitudes toward functional flexibility. *Human Relations, 46,* 705–723.

Dane, E. (2011). Paying attention to mindfulness and its effects on task performance in the workplace. *Journal of Management, 37,* 997–1018.

Deci, E. L., Connell, J. P., & Ryan, R. M. (1989). Self-determination in a work organization. *Journal of Applied Psychology, 74,* 580–590.

Deci, E. L., Eghrari, H., Patrick, B. C., & Leone, D. (1994). Facilitating internalization: The self-determination theory perspective. *Journal of Personality, 62,* 119–142.

Deci, E. L., Koestner, R., & Ryan, R. M. (1999). A meta-analytic review of experiments examining the effects of extrinsic rewards on intrinsic motivation. *Psychological Bulletin, 125,* 627–668.

Deci, E. L., & Ryan, R. M. (1985a). *Intrinsic motivation and self-determination in human behavior.* New York, NY: Plenum Publishing Co.

Deci, E. L., & Ryan, R. M. (1985b). The general causality orientations scale: Self-determination in personality. *Journal of Research in Personality, 19,* 109–134.

Deci, E. L., & Ryan, R. M. (2000). The "what" and "why" of goal pursuits: Human needs and the self-determination of behavior. *Psychological Inquiry, 11,* 227–268.

Deci, E. L., & Ryan, R. M. (2008). Facilitating optimal motivation and psychological well-being across life's domains. *Canadian Psychology*, *49*, 14–23.

Deci, E. L., Ryan, R. M., Gagné, M., Leone, D. R., Usunov, J., & Kornazheva, B. P. (2001). Need satisfaction, motivation, and well-being in the work organizations of a former eastern bloc country. *Personality and Social Psychology Bulletin*, *27*, 930–942.

Deci, E. L., & Vansteenkiste, M. (2004). Self-determination theory and basic need satisfaction: Understanding human development in positive psychology. *Ricerche di Psichologia*, *27*, 17–34.

Feltman, R., Robinson, M. D., & Ode, S. (2009). Mindfulness as a moderator of neuroticism–outcome relations: A self-regulation perspective. *Journal of Research in Personality*, *43*, 953–961.

Fernet, C., Gagné, M., & Austin, S. (2010). When does quality of relationships with coworkers predict burnout over time? The moderating role of work motivation. *Journal of Organizational Behavior*, *31*, 1163–1180.

Gable, S. L., & Haidt, J. (2005). What (and why) is Positive Psychology? *Review of General Psychology*, *9*, 103–110.

Gagné, M. (2003). The role of autonomy support and autonomy orientation in the engagement of prosocial behavior. *Motivation and Emotion*, *27*, 199–223.

Gagné, M., Chemolli, E., Forest, J., & Koestner, R. (2008). The temporal relations between work motivation and organizational commitment. *Psychologica Belgica*, *48*, 219–241.

Gagné, M., & Deci, E. L. (2005). Self-determination theory and work motivation. *Journal of Organizational Behavior*, *26*, 331–362.

Gagné, M., Forest, J., Gilbert, M. H., Aubé, C., Morin, E., & Malorni, A. (2010). The Motivation at Work Scale: Validation evidence in two languages. *Educational and Psychological Measurement*, *70*, 628–646.

Gagné, M., Forest, J., Vansteenkiste, M., Crevier-Braud, L., Van den Broeck, A. et al. (2012). Cross-cultural evidence for self-determination theory in the work domain. Unpublished manuscript, Concordia University.

Gagné, M., Koestner, R., & Zuckerman, M. (2000). Facilitating acceptance of organizational change: The importance of self-determination. *Journal of Applied Social Psychology*, *30*, 1843–1852.

Gagné, M., Senécal, C., & Koestner, R. (1997). Proximal job characteristics, feelings of empowerment, and intrinsic motivation: A multidimensional model. *Journal of Applied Social Psychology*, *27*, 1222–1240.

Gärtner, C. (2011). Putting new wines in old bottles: Mindfulness as a micro-foundation of dynamic capabilities. *Management Decision*, *49*, 253–269.

Goldstein, K. (1934/1995). *The organism: A holistic approach to biology derived from pathological data in man*. New York, NY: Zone Books.

González-Romá, V., Schaufeli, W. B., Bakker, A. B., & Lloret, S. (2006). Burnout and engagement: Independent factors or opposite poles? *Journal of Vocational Behavior*, *68*, 165–174.

Grant, A. M., Nurmohamed, S., Ashford, S. J., & Dekas, K. D. (2011). The performance implications of ambivalent initiative: The interplay of autonomous and controlled motivations. *Organizational Behavior and Human Decision Processes*, *116*, 241–251.

Green-Demers, I., Pelletier, L. G., & Ménard, S. (1997). The impact of behavioral difficult on the saliency of the association between self-determined motivation and environmental behaviors. *Canadian Journal of Behavioural Science*, *29*, 157–166.

Greguras, G. J., & Diefendorff, J. M. (2009). Different fits satisfy different needs: Linking person-environment fit to employee commitment and performance using self-determination theory. *Journal of Applied Psychology*, *94*, 465–477.

Griffin, M. A., Neal, A., & Parker, S. K. (2009). A new model of work role performance: Positive behavior in uncertain and interdependent contexts. *Academy of Management Journal*, *50*, 327–347.

Grolnick, W. S., & Ryan, R. M. (1987). Autonomy in children's learning: An experimental and individual difference investigation. *Journal of Personality and Social Psychology*, *52*, 890–898.

Grouzet, F. M., Kasser, T., Ahuvia, A., Dols, J. M. F., Kim, Y., Lau, S., ... Sheldon, K. M. (2005). The structure of goals across 15 cultures. *Journal of Personality and Social Psychology*, *89*, 800–816.

Hackman, J. R., & Oldham, G. R. (1975). Development of the Job Diagnostic Survey. *Journal of Applied Psychology*, *60*, 159–170.

Harter, S. (1981). A new self-report scale of intrinsic versus extrinsic orientation in the classroom: Motivational and informational components. *Developmental Psychology*, *17*, 300–312.

Judge, T. A., Bono, J. E., Erez, A., & Locke, E. A. (2005). Core self-evaluations and job and life satisfaction: The role of self-concordance and goal attainment. *Journal of Applied Psychology*, *90*, 257–268.

Judge, T. A., Locke, E. A., & Durham, C. C. (1997). The dispositional causes of job satisfaction: A core evaluations approach. *Research in Organizational Behavior*, *19*, 151–188.

Kahneman, D., Diener, E., & Schwartz, N. (1999). *Well-being: The foundations of hedonic psychology*. New York, NY: Russell Sage Foundation.

Kasser, T., & Ahuvia, A. C. (2002). Materialistic values and well-being in business students. *European Journal of Social Psychology*, *32*, 137–146.

Kasser, T., Koestner, R., & Lekes, N. (2002). Early family experiences and adult values: A 26-year, prospective longitudinal study. *Personality and Social Psychology Bulletin*, *28*, 826–835.

Kasser, T., & Ryan, R. M. (1993). A dark side of the American dream: Correlates of financial success as a central life aspiration. *Journal of Personality and Social Psychology*, *65*, 410–422.

Kasser, T., & Ryan, R. M. (1996). Further examining the American dream: Differential correlates of intrinsic and extrinsic goals. *Personality and Social Psychology Bulletin*, *22*, 280–287.

Kasser, T., Ryan, R. M., Zax, M., & Sameroff, A. J. (1995). The relations of maternal and social environments to late adolescents' materialistic and prosocial values. *Developmental Psychology*, *31*, 907–914.

Kelman, H. C. (1958). Compliance, identification and internalization, three processes of attitude change. *Journal of Conflict Resolution*, *2*, 51–60.

Kowal, J., & Fortier, M. S. (1999). Motivational determinants of flow: Contributions from self-determination theory. *Journal of Social Psychology*, *139*, 355–368.

Lepper, M. R., & Greene, D. (1975). Turning play into work: Effects of adult surveillance and extrinsic rewards on children's intrinsic motivation. *Journal of Personality and Social Psychology*, *31*, 479–486.

Levesque, C. S., & Pelletier, L. G. (2003). On the investigation of primed and chronic autonomous and heteronomous motivational orientations. *Personality and Social Psychology Bulletin*, *29*, 1570–1584.

Levinthal, D. (2006). Crossing an apparent chasm: Bridging mindful and less-mindful perspectives on organizational learning. *Organization Science, 17*, 502–513.

Luthans, F., Avey, J. B., Avolio, B. J., Norman, S. M., & Combs, G. M. (2006). Psychological capital development: Toward a micro-intervention. *Journal of Organizational Behavior, 27*, 387–393.

Macey, W. H., & Schneider, B. (2008). The meaning of employee engagement. *Industrial and organizational Psychology, 1*, 3–30.

Maslow, A. H. (1954). *Motivation and personality*. New York, NY: Harper.

Meissner, W. W. (1981). *Internalization in psychoanalysis*. New York, NY: International Universities Press.

Meyer, J. P., Becker, T. E., & Vandenberghe, C. (2004). Employee commitment and motivation: A conceptual analysis and integrative model. *Journal of Applied Psychology, 89*, 991–1007.

Meyer, J. P., & Gagné, M. (2008). Employee engagement from a self-determination theory perspective. *Industrial and Organizational Psychology, 1*, 60–62.

Meyer, J. P., & Herscovitch, L. (2001). Commitment in the workplace: Toward a general model. *Human Resource Management Review, 11*, 299–326.

Meyer, J. P., & Maltin, E. R. (2010). Employee commitment and well-being: A critical review, theoretical framework, and research agenda. *Journal of Vocational Behavior, 77*, 323–337.

Meyer, J. P., Parfyonova, N., & Gagné, M. (2010). Motivation and commitment. In S. Albrecht (Ed.), *Handbook of employee engagement*. UK: Edward Elgar.

Mitchell, J. I., Gagné, M., Beaudry, A., & Dyer, L. (2012). The moderating effect of motivation on the relationship between attitude and IT usage. *Computers in Human Behavior, 28*, 729–738.

Mu, E., & Butler, B. S. (2009). The assessment of organizational mindfulness processes for the effective assimilation of IT innovations. *Journal of Decision Systems, 18*, 27–51.

Murayama, K., Matsumoto, M., Izuma, K., & Matsumoto, K. (2010). Neural basis of the undermining effect of monetary reward on intrinsic motivation. PNAS Early Edition, 1–9. Retrieved from http://www.pnas.org/cgi/doi/10.1073/pnas.1013305107

Parker, S. K., Bindl, U. K., & Strauss, K. (2010). Making things happen: A model of proactive motivation. *Journal of Management, 36*, 827–856.

Parker, S. K., Wall, T. D., & Jackson, P. R. (1997). "That's not my job": Developing flexible employee work orientations. *Academy of Management Journal, 40*, 899–929.

Parker, S. K., Williams, H. M., & Turner, N. (2006). Modeling the antecedents of proactive behavior at work. *Journal of Applied Psychology, 91*, 636–652.

Pelletier, L. G., Lévesque, C. S., & Legault, L. (2002). Pressure from above and pressure from below as determinants of teachers' motivation and teaching behavior. *Journal of Educational Psychology, 94*, 186–196.

Pelletier, L. G., & Sharp, E. C. (2009). Administrative pressures and teachers' interpersonal behaviour in the classroom. *Theory and Research in Education, 7*, 174–183.

Peterson, S. J., Luthans, F., Avolio, B. J., Walumbwa, F. O., & Zhang, Z. (2011). Psychological capital and employee performance: A latent growth modeling approach. *Personnel Psychology, 64*, 427–450.

Reeve, J., & Tseng, C.-M. (2011). Cortisol reactivity to a teacher's motivating style: The biology of being controlled versus supporting autonomy. *Motivation and Emotion, 35*, 63–74.

Reis, H. T., Sheldon, K. M., Gable, S. L., Roscoe, J., & Ryan, R. M. (2000). Daily well-being: The role of autonomy, competence, and relatedness. *Personality and Social Psychology Bulletin, 26*, 419–435.

Rogers, C. (1951). *Client centered therapy.* Boston, MA: Houghton-Mifflin.

Ruedy, N. E., & Schweitzer, M. E. (2010). In the moment: The effect of mindfulness on ethical decision making. *Journal of Business Ethics, 95*, 73–87.

Ryan, R. M., Bernstein, J. H., & Brown, K. W. (2010). Weekends, work, and well-being: Psychological need satisfactions and day of the week effects on mood, vitality, and physical symptoms. *Journal of Social and Clinical Psychology, 29*, 95–122.

Ryan, R. M., & Connell, J. P. (1989). Perceived locus of causality and internalization: Examining reasons for acting in two domains. *Journal of Personality and Social Psychology, 57*, 749–761.

Ryan, R. M., & Deci, E. L. (2000). Self-determination theory and the facilitation of intrinsic motivation, social development, and well-being. *American Psychologist, 55*, 68–78.

Ryan, R. M., & Deci, E. L. (2003). On assimilating identities to the self: A self-determination theory perspective on internalization and integrity within cultures. In M. R. Leary & J. P. Tangney (Eds.), *Handbook on self & identity* (pp. 253–274). New York, NY: The Guilford Press.

Ryan, R. M., & Frederick, C. M. (1997). On energy, personality and health: Subjective vitality as a dynamic reflection of well-being. *Journal of Personality, 65*, 529–565.

Ryan, R. M., Huta, V., & Deci, E. L. (2008). Living well: A self-determination theory perspective on eudaimonia. *Journal of Happiness Studies, 9*, 139–170.

Schaufeli, W. B., Salanova, M., González-Romá, V., & Bakker, A. (2002). The measurement of engagement and burnout: A two sample confirmatory factor analytic approach. *Journal of Happiness Studies, 3*, 71–92.

Seligman, M. E. P. (2002). Positive psychology, positive prevention, and positive therapy. In C. R. Snyder & S. J. Lopez (Eds.), *Handbook of positive psychology* (pp. 3–9). New York, NY: Oxford University Press.

Sheldon, K., & Ryan, R. M. (2011). Positive psychology and self-determination theory: A natural interface. In V. I. Chirkov, R. M. Ryan & K. M. Sheldon (Eds.), *Human autonomy in cross-cultural context: Perspectives on the psychology of agency, freedom, and wellbeing* (pp. 33–44). New York, NY: Springer.

Sheldon, K. M. (2005). Positive value change during college: Normative trends and individual differences. *Journal of Research in Personality, 39*, 209–223.

Sheldon, K. M., Elliot, A. J., Kim, Y., & Kasser, T. (2001). What is satisfying about satisfying events? Testing 10 candidate psychological needs. *Journal of Personality and Social Psychology, 89*, 325–339.

Sheldon, K. M., Joiner, T. E., Pettit, J. W., & Williams, G. C. (2003). Reconciling humanistic ideals and scientific clinical practice. *Clinical Psychology: Science and Practice, 10*, 302–315.

Sheldon, K. M., & Krieger, L. K. (2007). Understanding the negative effects of legal education on law students: A longitudinal test and extension of self-determination theory. *Personality and Social Psychology Bulletin, 33*, 883–897.

Soenens, B., & Vansteenkiste, M. (2011). When is identity congruent with the self? A self-determination theory perspective. In S. J. Schwartz, K. Luyckx & V. L. Vignoles (Eds.), *Handbook of identity theory and research* (pp. 381–402). New York, NY: Springer.

Spreitzer, G. M., & Doneson, D. (2005). Musings on the past and future of employee empowerment. In T Cummings (Ed.), *Handbook of organizational development* (pp. 311–324). Thousand Oaks, CA: Sage.

Spreitzer, G. M., Sutcliffe, K., Dutton, J., Sonenshein, S., & Grant, A. M. (2005). A socially embedded model of thriving at work. *Organization Science, 16*, 537–549.

Su, Y., & Reeve, J. (2011). A meta-analysis of the effectiveness of intervention programs designed to support autonomy. *Educational Psychology Review, 23*, 159–188.

Thomas, K. W., & Velthouse, B. A. (1990). Cognitive elements of empowerment: An "interpretive" model of intrinsic task motivation. *Academy of Management Review, 15*, 666–681.

Tremblay, M. A., Blanchard, C. M., Taylor, S., Pelletier, L. G., & Villeneuve, M. (2009). Work extrinsic and intrinsic motivation scale: Its value for organizational psychology research. *Canadian Journal of Behavioural Science, 41*, 213–226.

Van den Broek, A., Vansteenkiste, M., De Witte, H., & Lens, W. (2008). Explaining the relationships between job characteristics, burnout and engagement: The role of basic psychological need satisfaction. *Work & Stress, 22*, 277–294.

Van den Broeck, A., Vansteenkiste, M., Lens, W., & De Witte, H. (2010). Unemployed individuals' work values and job flexibility: An explanation from expectancy-value theory and self-determination theory. *Applied Psychology: An International Review, 59*, 296–317.

Vansteenkiste, M., Lens, W., Soenens, B., & Luyckx, K. (2006). *Autonomy and relatedness among Chinese sojourners and applicants: Conflictual or independent predictors of well-being and adjustment? Motivation and Emotion, 30*, 273–282.

Vansteenkiste, M., Neyrinck, B., Niemiec, C. P., Soenens, B., De Witte, H., & Van Den Broeck, A. (2007). On the relations among work value orientations, psychological need satisfaction, and job outcomes: A self-determination theory approach. *Journal of Occupational and Organizational Psychology, 80*, 251–277.

Vansteenkiste, M., Niemiec, C. P., & Soenens, B. (2010). The development of the five mini-theories of self-determination theory: An historical overview, emerging trends, and future directions. In T. C. Urdan & S. A. Karabenick (Eds.), *Advances in motivation and achievement, v. 16A. The decade ahead: Theoretical perspectives on motivation and achievement* (pp. 105–165). London: Emerald.

Vansteenkiste, M., & Ryan, R. M. (in press). On psychological growth and vulnerability: Basic psychological need satisfaction and need frustration as an unifying principle. *Journal of Psychotherapy Integration*.

von Bertalanffy, L. (1968). *General systems theory*. New York, NY: G. Braziller.

Weinstein, N., Brown, K. W., & Ryan, R. M. (2009). A multi-method examination of the effects of mindfulness on stress attribution, coping, and emotional well-being. *Journal of Research in Personality, 43*, 374–385.

Williams, G. C., & Deci, E. L. (1996). Internalization of biopsychosocial values by medical students: A test of self-determination theory. *Journal of Personality and Social Psychology, 70*, 767–779.

THE JOB DEMANDS–RESOURCES MODEL: OVERVIEW AND SUGGESTIONS FOR FUTURE RESEARCH

Anja Van den Broeck, Joris Van Ruysseveldt, Els Vanbelle and Hans De Witte

Job design is considered among the most powerful contextual factors influencing worker well-being (Pinder, 2008). Accordingly, it has become a central topic in work and organizational psychology, leading to various models such as the Job Demand–Control model (JDC; Karasek, 1979) and the Effort–Reward Imbalance model (ERI; Siegrist, 1996). Recently, these were integrated and developed into the Job Demands–Resources model (JD–R model; Bakker & Demerouti, 2007; Demerouti, Bakker, Nachreiner, & Schaufeli, 2001; Schaufeli & Bakker, 2004). During the past decade, the JD–R model has given rise to a vast literature on how various job aspects might relate to individual and organizational outcomes.

The current chapter provides an overview of the JD–R literature and highlights some remaining issues feeding further theorizing and practice. We start off with describing the core assumptions of the JD–R model, as also pictured in Fig. 1. We detail the concepts of job demands and job resources and define burnout and work engagement as the most prominent outcomes of the energy-depleting and motivational process, respectively. Then we

Advances in Positive Organizational Psychology, Volume 1, 83–105

ISSN: 2046-410X/doi:10.1108/S2046-410X(2013)0000001007

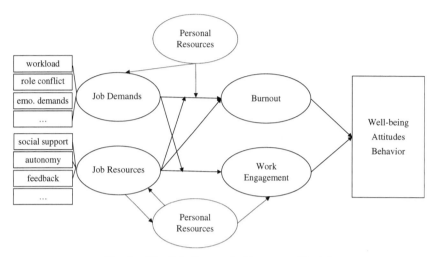

Fig. 1. The Job Demands–Resources Model.

detail the relationships between the job characteristics categories and employee well-being. We present the role of personal resources in the JD–R model and provide an overview of its empirical support. In the second part of this chapter, we highlight some remaining issues and indicate a couple of fruitful avenues for future research.

OVERVIEW OF THE JOB DEMANDS–
RESOURCES MODEL

The Theoretical Assumptions in a Nutshell

Job Demands and Job Resources
Several job characteristics have been suggested to influence workers' well-being. For example, Herzberg (1968) differentiated job characteristics that offset dissatisfaction such as social relations from job aspects that foster job satisfaction such as opportunities for advancement. While Hackman and Oldham (1976) focused on the motivational potential of job characteristics such as task identity and feedback, Karasek (1979) accentuated time pressure as a pivotal job demand. Together these models point out that various job characteristics may influence workers' functioning.

The JD–R model starts off with this assumption and maintains that these various job characteristics can be meaningfully categorized into job demands and job resources. *Job demands* are defined as "those physical, psychological, social, or organizational aspects of the job that require sustained physical and/or psychological (cognitive and emotional) effort or skills and are therefore associated with certain physiological and/or psychological costs" (Bakker & Demerouti, 2007, p. 312). *Job resources* are defined as "those physical, psychological, social, or organizational aspects of the job that are either/or (1) functional in achieving work goals, (2) reduce job demands and the associated physiological and psychological costs, (3) stimulate personal growth, learning, and development" (Bakker & Demerouti, 2007, p. 312).

According to the JD–R model, job demands and job resources can be located at the level of specific tasks (e.g., task interruptions, feedback from the task), work (e.g., workload, autonomy), social relations (e.g., social support from colleagues), and team (e.g., group work pressure). The JD–R model includes general job characteristics which were also part of previous models (e.g., Karasek, 1979), but remain highly relevant (Parker, Wall, & Cordery, 2001). It also encompasses general job characteristics typical for contemporary jobs (e.g., emotional demands), as well as job aspects that are specific for the occupation under study such as pupil misbehavior for teachers (Bakker, Hakanen, Demerouti, & Xanthopoulou, 2007), positive patient contacts for dentists (Hakanen, Bakker, & Demerouti, 2005), confrontation with pain and death for hospital nurses (Sundin, Hochwalder, & Lisspers, 2011), and unfriendly customer behavior for service employees (Walsh, 2011). Also home demands and resources (e.g., home overload, family support) have been investigated from a JD–R perspective (e.g., Hakanen, Schaufeli, & Ahola, 2008). The JD–R model thus taps into the broader context of one's job. It relates these demands and resources to several outcomes via burnout and work engagement.

Burnout and Work Engagement
While academics previously focused on the negative consequences of work (e.g., Siegrist, 1996), the JD–R model aligns with positive psychology, advocating the balanced study of the dark and bright side of employees' functioning (Seligman & Csikszentmihalyi, 2000). Accordingly, the model links job demands and job resources to both poor (i.e., burnout) and optimal well-being (i.e., work engagement).

Following Maslach and colleagues, *burnout* is defined as a syndrome mainly characterized by emotional exhaustion and cynicism.[1] Emotional exhaustion is a feeling of extreme physical and psychological fatigue, and overextension (Maslach et al., 2001). This energetic dimension of burnout is accompanied by an attitudinal component, cynicism, which reflects an excessive detachment from one's job and a lack of identification with one's tasks. Supplementing burnout, *work engagement* is defined as "a positive, fulfilling, work related state of mind" (Schaufeli, Salanova, Gonzaléz-Romá, & Bakker, 2002, p. 74). It is also mainly characterized by an energetic and an attitudinal component,[2] that is, vigor and dedication, respectively. Vigor pertains to feelings of energy and resilience while working. Dedication taps into one's identification with and enthusiasm for one's job.

The Energetic and Motivational Processes
The JD–R model considers the processes through which job characteristics may influence workers' functioning (see also Hackman & Oldham, 1976). Specifically, the JD–R model differentiates between an *energetic process* linking job demands to burnout, and a *motivational process* accounting for the job resources–work engagement relationship (Bakker & Demerouti, 2007). To detail these processes, the JD–R model builds upon various other theories (Schaufeli, Bakker, & Van Rhenen, 2009).

Drawing upon the stress adaptation model (Selye, 1956) and the state regulation model of compensatory control (Hockey, 1997), job demands are expected to arouse employees' nervous system and to activate their defense mechanisms. Employees will first try to withstand job demands and strive to keep up their performance level by activating additional energy. Continued exposure to high job demands increasingly wears out employees' energy reserves, resulting in exhaustion. Overextended employees may then try to escape from their job demands, for instance, by lowering their performance goals. As such, they gradually withdraw from their jobs making them prone to cynicism, and – hence – the burnout syndrome.

In contrast, job resources motivate employees. Job resources add to employees' total amount of resources (see conservation of resources theory (COR); Hobfoll, 2002). They also facilitate goal accomplishment (see goal-setting theory; Locke & Latham, 2002), foster the fulfillment of the psychological contract (Rousseau, 1995), enhance self-efficacy (see social-learning theory; Bandura, 1997), contribute to the psychological states of meaning, knowledge and responsibility (Hackman & Oldham, 1976), and/or satisfy the basic psychological needs for autonomy, competence, and relatedness (see self-determination theory; Gagné & Deci, 2005).

In addition, the lack of job resources is also – to some extent – considered to contribute to burnout, and cynicism in particular (Schaufeli & Bakker, 2004).

This is because, according to COR theory, individuals experience stress when they lack or lose highly valued resources.

Interactions between Job Demands and Job Resources
Besides their main effects, job demands and job resources are also considered to interact (Bakker & Demerouti, 2007). First, job resources may *buffer* the health-impairing impact of job demands. Employees encountering high job demands may thus feel less burned-out if they dispose of many job resources. This assumption builds on COR theory, stating that especially individuals lacking sufficient resources are prone to the impact of negative life events. The buffer hypothesis elaborates upon Karasek (1979), but expands his assumptions by suggesting that *several* different job resources can play a buffering role for *several* job demands.

Second, job demands are expected to *boost* the motivational effect of job resources (Bakker & Demerouti, 2007): job resources enhance work engagement particularly when job demands are high. This hypothesis is also grounded in COR theory, stating that individuals strive to protect, maintain, and increase their resources. These resources then become particularly salient under demanding conditions, boosting individuals' well-being, for example, in terms of work engagement. As such, the JD–R model picks up the active learning hypothesis (Karasek, 1979) holding that active (i.e., high demands/high control) jobs challenge employees most to develop new competencies or skills. Again, the JD–R model expands this assumption in considering various different job demands and job resources.

Personal Resources
Employees' functioning may not only be determined by situational (i.e., job) factors, but also by individual characteristics (see also Hackman & Oldham, 1976). Specifically, the JD–R model includes *personal resources*, which are defined as malleable lower-order, cognitive-affective personal aspects reflecting a positive belief in oneself or the world (Van den Heuvel, Demerouti, Bakker, & Schaufeli, 2010). Following COR theory, personal resources are considered as highly valued aspects, relating to resilience and contributing to individuals' potential to successfully control and influence the environment (Hobfoll, Johnson, Ennis, & Jackson, 2003). Personal resources may entail mental and emotional competence, self-efficacy, organizational based self-esteem, and optimism, among others (e.g., Xanthopoulou, Bakker, Demerouti, & Schaufeli, 2007).

Within the JD–R model, personal resources are ascribed three different roles (Xanthopoulou, Bakker, Demerouti et al., 2007). First, they are modeled as antecedents of job demands and job resources: They prevent the occurrence of job demands and foster the experience of job resources. Second, they are thought to moderate, that is, to attenuate, the health-impairing impact of job demands on well-being, much like job resources do. Third, personal resources are modeled as mediators through which job resources prevent burnout and enhance work engagement (Xanthopoulou, Bakker, Demerouti et al., 2007). Personal resources may thus explain the motivational process. By including personal resources, the JD–R model answers the call for more attention to the processes underpinning the relations between job characteristics and outcomes (Parker et al., 2001).

Empirical Assessment of the JD–R Model

Support for the Relations of Job Demands and Job Resources with Burnout and Engagement
The assumptions of the JD–R model have largely been supported in empirical research. First, numerous studies have supported the main effects of job demands and job resources, both cross-sectionally (e.g., Schaufeli & Bakker, 2004) and longitudinally (e.g., Hakanen, Bakker, & Jokisaari, 2011; Schaufeli et al., 2009), as well as on a weekly (Bakker & Bal, 2010) and day-to-day basis (e.g., Simbula, 2010; Xanthopoulou, Bakker, Demerouti, & Schaufeli, 2009). The results have been replicated within qualitative and quantitative designs alike (Freeney & Tiernan, 2009). Research also uncovered the motivational process by showing that job resources relate to burnout and work engagement through workers' perceptions of self-efficacy (Llorens, Schaufeli, Bakker, & Salanova, 2007) and the satisfaction of their basic psychological needs (Van den Broeck, Vansteenkiste, De Witte, & Lens, 2008).

Second, evidence has also been found for the buffer (Hakanen et al., 2005; King, De Chermont, West, Dawson, & Hebl, 2007) and the boost hypothesis (Bakker, Van Veldhoven, & Xanthopoulou, 2010; Hakanen et al., 2005). At the level of specific job demands and job resources, workload and emotional demands have, for example, been found to show a weaker health-impairing relationship with burnout when high job resources such as social support and autonomy are available (Bakker, Demerouti, & Euwema, 2005). The combination of high job demands and high job resources furthermore results in elevated levels of task enjoyment and commitment (Bakker, van Veldhoven, & Xanthopoulou, 2010). At the level of the job characteristics categories, Martin, Salanova, and Peiro (2007) evidenced that job demands boost the positive association between job resources and innovation.

Support for the Roles of Personal Resources
Several studies also supported the roles of personal resources. First, pertaining to their role as antecedents, personal resources such as organizational based self-esteem and optimism have also been shown to increase job resources over time (Xanthopoulou et al., 2009) while personal initiative assists in the accumulation of job resources through work engagement (Hakanen, Perhoniemi, & Toppinen-Tanner, 2008). Second, personal resources such as self-esteem and optimism have been found to buffer the association of time pressure with psychological distress (Mäkikangas & Kinnunen, 2003), while customer orientation buffers the association between job demands (e.g., role ambiguity and role overload) and burnout (Babakus, Yavas, & Ashill, 2009). Finally, Van den Broeck et al. (2008) indicated that satisfaction of the psychological needs mediated the health-enhancing relations of job resources with vigor, as a main component of work engagement; while self-efficacy, organization-based self-esteem and optimism have been shown to explain the positive consequences of job resources for engagement, both cross-sectionally (Llorens et al., 2007; Xanthopoulou, Bakker, Demerouti, et al., 2007) and on a day-to-day basis (Xanthopoulou et al., 2009).

Validation among Different Samples and Countries
The JD–R model has been validated across a broad range of professions, including high skilled (e.g., teachers, police officers, dentists, managers, nurses) and low skilled (e.g., call center agents, fast food employees, hotel personnel, temporary agency workers) service workers, production workers, students, and volunteers. Studies using heterogeneous samples and studies comparing blue and white collar workers further attest to the generalizability of the model (e.g., Van Ruysseveldt, Verboon, & Smulders, 2011).

The JD–R model was also found to be generally invariant across gender and age (Korunka, Kubicek, & Schaufeli, 2009). It has been validated in European countries such as Finland (Hakanen, Perhoniemi, et al., 2008), the Netherlands (Schaufeli et al., 2009), Belgium (Van den Broeck et al., 2008; Van Ruysseveldt, Proost, & Verboon, 2011), and Spain (e.g., Hakanen, Schaufeli, et al., 2008). Similar results have been reported in, for instance, China (Hu, Schaufeli, & Taris, 2011), Australia (Boyd et al., 2011), and Nigeria (e.g., Karatepe & Olugbade, 2009). The JD–R model has furthermore been shown to be *invariant* across the Netherlands and Spain

(Llorens, Bakker, Schaufeli, & Salanova, 2006), which provides further evidence for the cross-cultural stability of the relationships described in the JD–R model.

Examining Different Outcomes
Via burnout and work engagement, job demands and job resources have been shown to influence various other aspects of employees functioning. First, the JD–R model has successfully predicted well-being and health, in terms of psychosomatic complaints (Hakanen, Bakker, & Schaufeli, 2006), depression (Hakanen, Schaufeli, et al., 2008), the posttraumatic stress syndrome (Balducci, Fraccaroli, & Schaufeli, 2011), musculoskeletal disorders (Joling, Blatter, Ybema, & Bongers, 2008), and the fade-out of beneficial vacation effects (Kühnel & Sonnentag, 2011). Second, it has been related to work-related attitudes such as job satisfaction (Martinussen, Richardsen, & Burke 2007), organizational commitment (Hakanen, Schaufeli, et al., 2008), turnover intentions (Bakker, Demerouti, & Schaufeli, 2003), and the acceptance of organizational change (Van Emmerik, Bakker, & Euwema, 2009).

Third, job demands and job resources relate to workers' behavior in terms of presenteeism (Demerouti, Le Blanc, Bakker, Schaufeli, & Hox, 2009), absenteeism (Schaufeli et al., 2009), leaving one's profession (Jourdain & Chênevert, 2010), and early retirement (Schreurs, Van Emmerik, De Cuyper, Notelaers, & De Witte, 2011), as well as antisocial behavior (e.g., being a perpetrator of workplace bullying; Baillien, Rodriguez-Munoz, Van den Broeck, & De Witte, 2011). Job demands and resources also predict cooperative behavior, including in-role performance (Bakker, Van Emmerik, & Van Riet, 2008; Xanthopoulou et al., 2009), safety behavior (Hansez & Chmiel, 2010), and extra-role performance (e.g., helping behavior and innovativeness; Hakanen, Perhoniemi, et al., 2008). The JD–R model may therefore not only be instructive in explaining *workers'* functioning, but may also be able to understand the *organizations'* productivity.

Finally, workers' job demands and job resources and the related well-being outcomes may also affect others in one's environment. First, job demands and job resources predict work–home interference (WHI), both rated by the employee and his or her spouse (Hakanen, Peeters, & Perhoniemi, 2011; Mostert, Peeters, & Rost, 2011). They also influence employees' partner's and coworkers' functioning (Bakker, Demerouti, & Dollard, 2008; Westman, Bakker, Roziner, & Sonnentag, 2011).

Conclusion of This Overview

The JD–R model may be regarded as today's most comprehensive job characteristics model. It considers a broad range of job characteristics, categorized in terms of job demands and job resources and examines their relations with both negative (i.e., burnout) and positive (i.e., engagement) aspects of workers' well-being, which in turn relate to various individual outcomes, impacting organizations. The JD–R model also pays attention to the processes underlying these relationships as well as to how personal resources may affect job characteristics and their consequences. However, some issues remain. In the following section, we critically appraise these issues, which may hint at fruitful avenues for future research.

CRITICAL APPRAISAL OF THE JD–R MODEL AND SUGGESTIONS FOR FUTURE RESEARCH

Job Demands and Job Resources

As described above, the JD–R model parsimoniously categorizes job characteristics into job demands or job resources. This classification seems comprehensive, but also leaves some room for interpretation. Three observations can be made.

Classification of Particular Job Characteristics

On the one hand, some inconsistencies seem to exist in the classification of job characteristics into job demands or job resources. Job (in)security, for example, is often described as a job resource (Hu et al., 2011), but has also been included as a job demand (Mauno, Kinnunen, & Ruokolainen, 2007). The latter seems to align with the job insecurity literature, which defines job insecurity as a demanding aspect triggering particular coping styles, which seem to fit in the JD–R's energetic process. Future research might aim to advance JD–R theory by further examining its first basic premise about the categorization of various job characteristics.

On the other hand, particular job aspects are modeled both in terms of a job characteristic and as outcome. WHI, for example, has been classified not only as a job demand (Schaufeli et al., 2009), but also as an outcome (Mayo, Pastor, Cooper, & Sanz-Vergel, 2011), explaining the association between job demands and well-being (Van der Heijden, Demerouti, & Bakker, 2008;

Van Ruysseveldt, Proost, et al., 2011). Similarly, being bullied has been conceptualized as a job demand (Law, Dollard, Tuckey, & Dormann, 2011), but in line with the Three Way Model, it may also result from job demands and resources (Baillien et al., 2011; Balducci et al., 2011). Similarly, learning opportunities have often been integrated as a job resource (e.g., Schaufeli et al., 2009), but job-related learning can also be fueled by job resources such as job autonomy (Karasek, 1979), and hence, be modeled as an outcome of the motivational process (e.g., Van Ruysseveldt & Taverniers, 2010; Van Ruysseveldt, Verboon, et al., 2011). Theoretical and longitudinal empirical research disentangling job characteristics from their outcomes seems instructive and may add to the conceptual clarity of the JD–R model.

Differentiating Job Hindrances from Job Challenges
JD–R scholars have suggested that job demands only turn into job stressors when they reach a fairly high level (e.g., Mauno et al., 2007). Such curvilinear effects, however, received limited empirical support (for an overview, see Rydstedt, Ferrie, & Head, 2006), leading to the suggestion that not the *amount* of job demands, but the *type* of job demands causes these different results (e.g., Podsakoff, Lepine, & Lepine, 2007). As such, *job hindrances* (e.g., emotional demands, role problems, organizational politics, and hassles) are defined as obstacles that can be hardly overcome. They frustrate employees' needs and goal achievement, and therefore truly deplete workers' energy, leading to burnout. *Job challenges* (e.g., workload, time pressure, job complexity, and responsibility) equally tap into employees' energy, resulting in job strain. In contrast to job hindrances, however, job challenges may be overcome and may add to employees' development, goal achievement, and need satisfaction. As such, they may also elicit positive effects, such as work engagement.

    Empirical evidence supports this differentiation: The factor structure differentiating between job challenges and job hindrances is favored above a factor structure combining all job demands into one factor (Van den Broeck, De Cuyper, De Witte, & Vansteenkiste 2010; Van den Broeck, Vansteenkiste, & De Witte, 2009). Both a cross-sectional study (Van den Broeck et al., 2009, 2010) and a meta-analysis (Crawford, LePine, & Rich, 2010) furthermore indicated that – after controlling for the associations of job resources – job hindrances yield detrimental consequences in terms of burnout and work engagement, while job challenges relate positively to both burnout and work engagement. As such, the differentiation between job hindrances and job challenges may account for the previously unexplained positive relationship between particular job demands and work engagement in JD–R studies (e.g., Mauno et al., 2007; Van den Broeck et al., 2008). It might also spur future research opportunities clarifying the nature and relations of different job demands.

Broadened Demands and Resources

The JD–R model mainly addresses the job-level by framing the impact of job characteristics on well-being outcomes. However, interest seems to be growing to surpass the level of job design in the JD–R model and to incorporate also aspects at the level of the organization (e.g., organizational changes, innovation climate, safety climate, tele-work; Bakker, Demerouti, de Boer, & Schaufeli, 2003; Cifre, Salanova, & Rodriguez-Sanchez, 2011; Nielsen, Mearns, Matthiesen, & Eid, 2011) and aspects of human resources management (e.g., procedural fairness; strategic attention, strategic impact; staffing issues, communication; Boyd et al., 2011; De Cooman, Stynen, Sels, Van den Broeck, & De Witte, in press; Joling et al., 2008). This evolution extends the scope of the JD–R model and might spur interesting research.

One potential route for future research is to uncover the relations between the demands and resources at the different levels. Whereas most authors collapse all demands and resources into the broad categories of demands and resources, some authors differentiate these levels and put them in juxtaposition (Bakker, Van Emmerik et al., 2008; Lee & Akhtar, 2011; Weigl et al., 2010). Still others suggest that higher level aspects (i.e., HR-aspects) relate to worker well-being via lower level characteristics (i.e., task-related demands and resources; Castanheira & Chambel, 2010; Dollard & Bakker, 2010). As such, the JD–R model might help in opening the black box through which human resource policies relate to employee level outcomes (e.g., well-being and performance) and organizational success.

The Relations between Job Demands, Job Resources, Burnout, and Work Engagement

Thus far, the JD–R model has focused on the relations from job demands and job resources to burnout and work engagement. Although these relations seem to be well-established, two questions remain.

Longitudinal Relations and Stability

Several studies tapped into the longitudinal relations from the job characteristics to employee well-being, using prospective (e.g., Dikkers, Jansen, de Lange, Vinkenburg, & Kooij, 2010) and lagged designs (e.g., Boyd et al., 2011; Weigl et al., 2010; Xanthopoulou et al., 2009). The appropriate time lags within which job characteristics relate to employee well-being remain, however, unclear. Currently the time lags range from 4 months (Simbula, Gulielmi, & Schaufeli, 2011) to 35 years (Hakanen, Bakker, et al., 2011), with most studies using a one- to two-year time interval (e.g., Mauno et al., 2007; Sonnentag, Binneweis, & Mojza, 2010; Weigl et al., 2010). The selection of the time lag seems mostly based on practical issues, rather than on theoretical or methodological arguments. Future research could therefore advance the JD–R literature and the job design literature in general by uncovering the time it takes for job demands and job resources to impact on burnout and work engagement (see also De Lange, Taris, Kompier, Houtman, & Bongers, 2005).

The nature of the outcome might be one of the criteria to take into account in setting the appropriate time lag. Emotions might be studied using the shortest time lag, as they tend to be less stable over time (Ouweneel, Le Blanc, & Schaufeli, 2011). General health (Van der Heijden et al., 2008) and psychosomatic complaints (Boyd et al., 2011) may also be studied using a relatively short time lag, as they are perhaps also more subject to change than burnout and work engagement (Hakanen, Perhoniemi, et al., 2008; Sonnentag, Binnewies, & Mojza, 2010). More thorough observations are however needed to validate such conclusions and to set the appropriate time lag not in a relative, but in an absolute sense.

Interestingly, in general, burnout and work engagement in terms of general well-being aspects seem rather stable over time (i.e., stabilities ranging from .45 to .72; Hakanen, Perhoniemi, et al., 2008; Xantopoulou et al., 2009), irrespective of the time lag used. Similar stabilities have been reported for job demands and resources (Hakanen, Schaufeli, et al., 2008; Hakanen, Perhoniemi, et al., 2008). This seems to hint at a highly stable work environment for most workers, leaving little room for longitudinal lagged relations between job characteristics and well-being. Research confirms that prospective relations from job demands and job resources to burnout and work engagement are considerably reduced after controlling for initial levels of burnout and work engagement (e.g., Prieto, Salanova, Martinez, & Schaufeli, 2008).

Future research could therefore also adopt alternative designs to examine the impact of job demands and job resources on burnout and work engagement. First, transitions between jobs could be examined. Although job resources and work engagement seem most stable among workers staying in the same job, changes likely occur among workers making promotion or moving to other companies (De Lange, De Witte, & Notelaers, 2008).

Future research could expand this line of work to changes in job demands and burnout. Second, scholars could increasingly tap into intra-individual differences in job characteristics and well-being, for example, by using daily diary methods. Despite the stability at the inter-individual level, initial studies reveal that job resources and work engagement vary within employees, with employees experiencing higher engagement on days they report higher job resources (Simbula, 2010; Xanthopoulou et al., 2009). Within-person designs may be further used to examine whether fluctuations in both job demands and job resources influence employees' burnout and engagement.

Gain and Loss Cycles

Some studies also tapped into the reversed causation and reciprocity in the relations between job characteristics and employees' well-being, leading to the study of gain or loss cycles. Within positive gain cycles, job resources stimulate work engagement which, in turn, increase job resources, fostering engagement (e.g., Llorens et al., 2007). Loss cycles refer to processes in which burnout induces losses of resources and an accumulation of job demands, which subsequently results in burnout (Ten Brummelhuis, Ter Hoeven, Bakker, & Peper, 2011). Both gain and loss cycles can be grounded in COR theory. In short, the availability of resources allows individuals to accumulate more resources, and in the long run the resulting "resource caravans" reinforce positive outcomes. Conversely, loss cycles reflect the idea that a lack of resources results in even greater resource loss. To date, evidence for the existence of gain spirals in the JD–R model is mixed: While some studies could establish positive relations from work engagement to job resources (e.g., Simbula, Guglielmi, & Schaufeli, 2011; Weigl et al., 2010; Xanthopoulou et al., 2009), others could not replicate these results (Boyd, Winefield, & Bakker, 2008; Hakanen, Bakker, et al., 2011). Similarly, some scholars provided evidence for loss cycles regarding job demands (Ten Brummelhuis, ter Hoeven, Bakker, & Peper, 2011; Van der Heijden et al., 2008) and job resources (Houkes, Winants, & Twellaar, 2008), while others did not (Prieto et al., 2008). Perhaps some moderators such as workers' motivation may come into play (Ten Brummelhuis et al., 2011) or particular transitions are needed for changes in particular job characteristics to occur (De Lange et al., 2008). In general, these reciprocal relations hint at job crafting, that is, the process in which workers physically or cognitively change their tasks and social relations at work (e.g., Tims, Bakker, & Derks, 2012).

Buffer and Boost Hypotheses

As a particular strength, the JD–R model considers *various* job demands to yield health-impairing consequences, and *various* job resources to enhance employees' well-being, allowing for the grouping of the job characteristics in their respective categories. From this assumption, it might be suggested that a diverse set of job demands may interact with a diverse set of job resources. However, few studies provided evidence for the interaction between the *categories* of job demands and job resources, even though different methods are used, such as the ratio approach, balancing job demands and job resources (Hu et al., 2011, see also Siegrist, 1996) or the quadrant approach using a median split procedure (Hu et al., 2011, see also Karasek, 1979) or cluster analysis (Van den Broeck, De Cuyper, Luyckx, & De Witte, 2012).

Recently, the job resources category was found to buffer the impact of job demands on workplace bullying via structural equation modeling (Van den Broeck, Baillien, & De Witte, 2011), which might stimulate the use of this methodology to further examine the interactions between the job characteristics categories, also in terms of the boosting hypothesis. Future research may also focus on potential moderators. Job resources might, for example, particularly buffer the negative impact of the most detrimental job demands in a particular job (e.g., emotional demands for home care workers; Xanthopoulou, Bakker, Dollard, et al., 2007). Additionally, following COR theory, various resources might be necessary to overcome the burden of job demands. In line with this view, the presence of organizational resources (e.g., innovative climate; King et al., 2007) has been shown to alleviate the negative association of work demands, perhaps because organizational resources give rise to various job resources. Alternatively, the combination of personal and job resources might be most powerful in buffering job demands. In support of this view, internal locus of control and self-efficacy have been indicated as necessary personal attributions for job control to attenuate the health-impairing impact of job demands on affective strain and muscoskeletal pain (Meier, Semmer, Elfering, & Jacobshagen, 2008). Similarly, particularly the combination of motivation and job resources was indicated to buffer the associations of job demands with burnout (Fernet, Guay, & Senécal, 2004).

Personal Resources

Scholars might further advance the role of personal characteristics in the JD–R model, for instance, in terms of the roles of personal resources and the introduction of personal demands.

Roles of Personal Resources

Initial research indicates that the roles of personal resources can be extended. First, several studies stressed the main effects of personal resources such as organizational based self-esteem and optimism (Xanthopoulou et al., 2009), perfectionism, avoidance and active coping (Houkes et al., 2008), mental and emotional competences (Prieto et al., 2008), humor (Van den Broeck, Van der Elst, Dikkers, De Lange, & De Witte, 2012) on burnout and engagement, after controlling for job demands and resources. Although the latter remained the most important predictors, these findings highlight the additional importance of employees' positive beliefs in themselves and their potential to control the environment for their work-related well-being. Future research might further examine this and thereby focus on personal resources which can easily be trained in the context of work (e.g., organizational based self-esteem).

Second, the mediating role of personal resources can be extended to the relationship between job demands and burnout. In line with this view and building upon COR theory, coping has been shown to explain the association of job demands with burnout and work engagement (Alarcon, Edwards, & Menke, 2011). Also motivation in terms of intrinsic motivation (Rubino, Luksyte, Perry, & Volpone, 2009) and the satisfaction of the psychological needs (Van den Broeck et al., 2008) fulfills this role, which seems to indicate that motivation might also assist in understanding the impact of the energetic process.

Third, the moderating role of personal resources could also be extended. In addition to buffering job demands, personal resources might strengthen the positive effects of job resources. In line with this idea and the person-environment-fit literature, the pursuit of intrinsic values was shown to increase the relations between autonomy and learning opportunities in the prediction of work engagement and exhaustion (Van den Broeck, Van Ruysseveldt, Smulders, & De Witte, 2011). Similarly, proactiveness could enhance the positive impact of social support on work engagement over time (Dikkers et al., 2010).

Personal Demands

Previous job design models and empirical evidence indicate that personal aspects such as overcommitment might make workers vulnerable for the negative impact of job demands or impede them to benefit from positive aspects (Van Vegchel, De Jonge, Bosma, & Schaufeli, 2005). Recent research seems to hint at such detrimental factors in the realm of the JD–R model too. For example, workers holding deficits in their cognitive control system seemed to develop heightened levels of burnout when confronted

with emotional dissonance (Diestel & Schmidt, 2011). Personal characteristics putting an additional burden on employees' might be labeled as
personal demands, and the JD–R model can constitute a valuable framework to further examine their impact on job design, burnout, and work
engagement. The focus on personal demands might also have practical
relevance, as individuals holding personal demands might be particularly
vulnerable to develop burnout and a lack of work engagement.

CONCLUSION

In general, abundant research validated the JD–R model, and attested to its
integrative character. As such, the JD–R model has become well-established
and inspired a great amount of research on employee well-being. However,
some lacunas and discrepancies emerged, which might open interesting new
research possibilities. Future studies might, for example, focus upon the
basic premises of the JD–R model and provide a solid frame for the categorization of job demands and job resources. We also call for meticulous
future research tapping into the direct and reciprocal relations between job
demands, job resources, burnout, and work engagement. Finally, the JD–R
theory can further develop the role of personal characteristics, thereby
integrating suggestions of previous studies. We hope these ideas challenge
researchers to take the JD–R model into the next decennium for the benefit
of workers and organizations alike.

NOTES

1. Sometimes also (reduced) personal accomplishment is included as a component
of burnout. However, there are several reasons to consider it as a less important
aspect (e.g., Maslach, Schaufeli, & Leiter, 2001). For example, reduced personal
accomplishment was only added to the burnout syndrome because it emerged out of
the initial factor analysis examining burnout. It associates less strongly with
emotional exhaustion and cynicism (which correlate among each other) and it yields
different antecedents and consequences.

2. Initially, also absorption was included as a component of work engagement, as
it emerged as a characterizing feature of engaged employees in qualitative research
(Schaufeli & Bakker, 2001). Based on further studies indicating vigor and dedication
as the main components of work engagement, acceptance seems to be growing that
these components constitute the "core" of work engagement (Bakker, Schaufeli,
Leiter, & Taris, 2008).

REFERENCES

Alarcon, G. M., Edwards, J. M., & Menke, L. E. (2011). Student burnout and engagement: A test of the conservation of resources theory. *Journal of Psychology*, *145*, 211–227.

Babakus, E., Yavas, U., & Ashill, N. J. (2009). The role of customer orientation as a moderator of the job demand-burnout-performance relationship: A surface-level trait perspective. *Journal of Retailing*, *85*, 480–492.

Baillien, E., Rodríguez-Muñoz, A., Van den Broeck, A., & De Witte, H. (2011). Do demands and resources affect target's and perpetrators' reports of workplace bullying? A two-wave cross-lagged study. *Work & Stress*, *25*, 128–146.

Bakker, A. B., & Bal, P. M. (2010). Weekly work engagement and performance: A study among starting teachers. *Journal of Occupational and Organizational Psychology*, *83*, 189–206.

Bakker, A. B., & Demerouti, E. (2007). The job demands-resources model: State of the art. *Journal of Managerial Psychology*, *22*, 309–328.

Bakker, A. B., Demerouti, E., & Dollard, M. (2008). How job demands influence partners' experience of exhaustion: Integrating work-family conflict and crossover theory. *Journal of Applied Psychology*, *93*, 901–911.

Bakker, A. B., Demerouti, E., de Boer, E., & Schaufeli, W. B. (2003). Job demands and job resources as predictors of absence duration and frequency. *Journal of Vocational Behaviour*, *62*, 341–356.

Bakker, A. B., Demerouti, E., & Euwema, M. (2005). Job resources buffer the impact of job demands on burnout. *Journal of Occupational Health Psychology*, *10*, 170–180.

Bakker, A. B., Demerouti, E., & Schaufeli, W. B. (2003). Dual processes at work in a call centre: An application of the job demands-resources model. *European Journal of Work and Organizational Psychology*, *12*, 393–417.

Bakker, A. B., Hakanen, J. J., Demerouti, E., & Xanthopoulou, D. (2007). Job resources boost work engagement, particularly when job demands are high. *Journal of Educational Psychology*, *99*, 274–284.

Bakker, A. B., Schaufeli, W. B., Leiter, M. P., & Taris, T. W. (2008). Work engagement: An emerging concept in occupational health psychology. *Work & Stress*, *22*, 187–200.

Bakker, A. B., Van Emmerik, IJ. H., & Van Riet, P. (2008). How job demands, resources, and burnout predict objective performance: A constructive replication. *Anxiety, Stress, and Coping*, *21*, 309–324.

Bakker, A. B., van Veldhoven, M., & Xanthopoulou, D. (2010). Beyond the demand-control model: Thriving on high job demands and resources. *Journal of Personnel Psychology*, *9*, 3–16.

Balducci, C., Fraccaroli, F., & Schaufeli, W. B. (2011). Workplace bullying and its relation with work characteristics, personality, and post-traumatic stress symptoms: an integrated model. *Anxiety, Stress and Coping*, *24*, 499–513.

Bandura, A. (1997). *Self-efficacy: The exercise of control.* New York, NY: W.H. Freeman.

Boyd, C. M., Bakker, A. B., Pignata, S., Winefield, A. H., Gillespie, N., & Stough, C. (2011). A longitudinal test of the job demands-resources model among Australian university academics. *Applied Psychology: An International Review*, *60*, 112–140.

Boyd, D., Winefield, A., & Bakker, A. B. (2008). A longitudinal test of the job demands-resources model in Australian university staff. *International Journal of Psychology*, *43*, 225.

Castanheira, F., & Chambel, M. J. (2010). Reducing burnout in call centers through HR practices. *Human Resource Management, 49,* 1047–1065.

Cifre, E., Salanova, M., & Rodriguez-Sanchez, A. M. (2011). Dancing between theory and practice: Enhancing work engagement through work stress intervention. *Human Factors and Ergonomics in Manufacturing & Service Industries, 21,* 269–286.

Crawford, E. R., LePine, J. A., & Rich, B. L. (2010). Linking job demands and resources to employee engagement and burnout: A theoretical extension and meta-analytic test. *Journal of Applied Psychology, 95,* 834–848.

De Cooman, R., Stynen, D., Sels, L., Van den Broeck, A., & De Witte, H. (in press). How job characteristics relate to need satisfaction and autonomous motivation: Implications for work effort. *Journal of Applied Social Psychology.*

De Lange, A. H., De Witte, H., & Notelaers, G. (2008). Should I stay or should I go? Examining the longitudinal relation between job resources and work engagement for stayers versus movers. *Work & Stress, 22,* 201–223.

De Lange, A. H., Taris, T. W., Kompier, M. A. J., Houtman, I. L. D., & Bongers, P. M. (2005). Different mechanisms to explain the reversed effects of mental health on work characteristics. *Scandinavian Journal of Work, Environment and Health, 31,* 3–14.

Demerouti, E., Bakker, A. B., Nachreiner, F., & Schaufeli, W. B. (2001). The job demands-resources model of burnout. *Journal of Applied Psychology, 86,* 499–512.

Demerouti, E., Le Blanc, P., Bakker, A. B., Schaufeli, W. B., & Hox, J. (2009). Present but sick: A three-wave study on job demands, presenteeism and burnout. *Career Development International, 14,* 50–68.

Diestel, S., & Schmidt, K. H. (2011). The moderating role of cognitive control deficits in the link from emotional dissonance to burnout symptoms and absenteeism. *Journal of Occupational Health Psychology, 16,* 313–330.

Dikkers, J. S., Jansen, P. G., de Lange, A. H., Vinkenburg, C. J., & Kooij, D. (2010). Proactivity, job characteristics, and engagement: A longitudinal study. *Career Development International, 15,* 59–77.

Dollard, M. F., & Bakker, A. B. (2010). Prosocial safety climate as a precursor to conducive work environments, psychological health problems and employee engagement. *Journal of Occupational and Organizational Psychology, 83,* 579–599.

Escobari, D. (2012). Imperfect detection of tax evasion in a corrupt tax administration. *Public Organization Review, 12*(4), 317–330.

European Commission. (2007). Undeclared work in the European Union. Special Euro-barometer No. 284, 135 pp.

European Commission. (2012) Taxation trends in the European Union: 2012 edition. Eurostat, 269 pp.

Fernet, C., Guay, F., & Senécal, C. (2004). Adjusting to job demands: The role of work, self-determination and job control in predicting burnout. *Journal of Vocational Behavior, 65,* 39–56.

Freeney, Y. M., & Tiernan, J. (2009). Exploration of the facilitators of and barriers to work engagement in nursing. *International Journal of Nursing Studies, 46,* 1557–1565.

Gagné, M., & Deci, E. L. (2005). Self-determination theory and work motivation. *Journal of Organizational Behavior, 26,* 331–362.

Hackman, J., & Oldham, G. (1976). Motivation through design of work – Test of a theory. *Organizational Behavior and Human Performance, 16,* 250–279.

Hakanen, J. J., Bakker, A. B., & Demerouti, E. (2005). How dentists cope with their job demands and stay engaged: The moderating role of job resources. *European journal of Oral Sciences, 113*, 479–487.

Hakanen, J. J., Bakker, A. B., & Jokisaari, M. (2011). A 35-year follow-up study on burnout among Finnish employees. *Journal of Occupational Health Psychology, 16*, 345–360.

Hakanen, J. J., Bakker, A. B., & Schaufeli, W. B. (2006). Burnout and work engagement among teachers. *Journal of School Psychology, 43*, 495–513.

Hakanen, J. J., Peeters, M. C. W., & Perhoniemi, R. (2011). Enrichment processes and gain spirals at work and at home: A 3-year cross-lagged panel study. *Journal of Occupational and Organizational Psychology, 84*, 8–30.

Hakanen, J. J., Perhoniemi, R., & Toppinen-Tanner, S. (2008). Positive gain spirals at work: From job resources to work engagement, personal initiative and work-unit innovativeness. *Journal of Vocational Behaviour, 73*, 78–91.

Hakanen, J. J., Schaufeli, W. B., & Ahola, K. (2008). The job demands–resources model: A three-year cross-lagged study of burnout, depression, commitment, and work engagement. *Work & Stress, 22*, 224–241.

Hansez, I., & Chmiel, N. (2010). Safety behavior: Job demands, job resources, and perceived management commitment to safety. *Journal of Occupational Health Psychology, 15*, 267–278.

Herzberg, F. (1968). *Work and the nature of man*. London: Crosby.

Hobfoll, S. E. (2002). Social and psychological resources and adaptation. *Review of General Psychology, 6*, 307–324.

Hobfoll, S. E., Johnson, R. J., Ennis, N. E., & Jackson, A. P. (2003). Resource loss, resource gain, and emotional outcomes among inner-city women. *Journal of Personality and Social Psychology, 84*, 632–643.

Hockey, G. F. (1997). Compensatory control in the regulation of human performance under stress and high workload: A cognitive-energetical framework. *Biological Psychology, 45*, 73–93.

Houkes, I., Winants, Y. H., & Twellaar, M. (2008). Specific determinants of burnout among male and female general practitioners: A cross-lagged panel analysis. *Journal of Occupational and Organizational Psychology, 81*, 249–276.

Hu, Q., Schaufeli, W. B., & Taris, T. W. (2011). The job demands-resources model: An analysis of additive and joint effects of demands and resources. *Journal of Vocational Behavior, 79*, 181–190.

Joling, C. I., Blatter, B. M., Ybema, J. F., & Bongers, P. M. (2008). Can favorable psychosocial work conditions and high work dedication protect against the occurrence of work-related musculoskeletal disorders? *Scandinavian Journal of Work Environment & Health, 34*, 345–355.

Jourdain, G., & Chênevert, D. (2010). Job demands-resources, burnout and intention to leave the nursing profession: A questionnaire survey. *International Journal of Nursing Studies, 47*, 709–722.

Karasek, R. (1979). Job demands, job decision latitude, and mental strain – Implications for job redesign. *Administrative Science Quarterly, 24*, 285–308.

Karatepe, O. M., & Olugbade, O. A. (2009). The effects of job and personal resources on hotel employees' work engagement. *International Journal of Hospitality Management, 28*, 504–512.

King, E. B., De Chermont, K., West, M., Dawson, J. F., & Hebl, M. R. (2007). How innovation can alleviate negative consequences of demanding work contexts: The influence of climate for innovation on organizational outcomes. *Journal of Occupational and Organizational Psychology, 80*, 631–645.

Korunka, C., Kubicek, B., & Schaufeli, W. B. (2009). Work engagement and burnout: Testing the robustness of the job demands-resources model. *The Journal of Positive Psychology, 4*, 243–255.

Kühnel, J., & Sonnentag, S. (2011). How long do you benefit from vacation? A closer look at the fade-out of vacation effects. *Journal of Organizational Behavior, 32*, 125–143.

Law, R., Dollard, M. F., Tuckey, M. R., & Dormann, C. (2011). Psychosocial safety climate as a lead indicator of workplace bullying and harassment, job resources, psychological health and employee engagement. *Accident Analysis and Prevention, 43*, 1782–1793.

Lee, J. S., & Akhtar, S. (2011). Effects of the workplace social context and job content on nurse burnout. *Human Resource Management, 50*, 227–245.

Llorens, S., Bakker, A. B., Schaufeli, W. B., & Salanova, M. (2006). Testing the robustness of job demands-resources model. *International Journal of Stress Management, 13*, 378–391.

Llorens, S., Schaufeli, W. B., Bakker, A. B, & Salanova, M. (2007). Does a positive gain spiral of resources, efficacy beliefs and engagement exist? *Computers in Human Behaviour, 23*, 825–841.

Locke, E., & Latham, G. (2002). Building a practically useful theory of goal setting and task motivation – A 35-year odyssey. *American Psychologist, 57*, 705–717.

Mäkikangas, A., & Kinnunen, U. (2003). Psychosocial work stressors and well-being: Self-esteem and optimism as moderators in a one-year longitudinal sample. *Personality and Individual Difference, 35*, 537–557.

Martin, P., Salanova, M., & Peiro, J. M. (2007). Job demands, job resources and individual innovation at work: Going beyond Karasek's model? *Psicothema, 19*, 621–626.

Martinussen, M., Richardsen, A. M., & Burke, R. J. (2007). Job demands, job resources and burnout among police officers. *Journal of Criminal Justice, 35*, 239–249.

Maslach, C., Schaufeli, W. B., & Leiter, M. P. (2001). Job burnout. *Annual Review of Psychology, 52*, 397–422.

Mauno, S., Kinnunen, U. M., & Ruokolainen, M. (2007). Job demands and resources as antecedents of work engagement: A longitudinal study. *Journal of Vocational Behaviour, 70*, 149–171.

Mayo, M., Pastor, J. C., Cooper, C., & Sanz-Vergel, A. I. (2011). Achieving work-family balance among Spanish managers and their spouses: A demands-control perspective. *International Journal of Human Resource Management, 22*, 331–350.

Meier, L. L., Semmer, N. K., Elfering, A., & Jacobshagen, N. (2008). The double meaning of control: Three-way interactions between internal resources, job control, and stressors at work. *Journal of Occupational Health Psychology, 13*, 244–258.

Mostert, K., Peeters, M., & Rost, I. (2011). Work-home interference and the relationship with job characteristics and well-being: a South African study among employees in the construction industry. *Stress and Health, 27*, E238–E251.

Nielsen, M. B., Mearns, K., Matthiesen, S. B., & Eid, J. (2011). Using the Job demands-resources model to investigate risk perception, safety climate and job satisfaction in safety critical organizations. *Scandinavian Journal of Psychology, 52*, 465–475.

Ouweneel, E., Le Blanc, P. M., & Schaufeli, W. B. (2011). Flourishing students: A longitudinal study on positive emotions, personal resources, and study engagement. *Journal of Positive Psychology, 6*, 142–153.

Parker, S. K., Wall, T. D., & Cordery, J. L. (2001). Future work design research and practice: Towards an elaborated model of work design. *Journal of Occupational and Organisational Psychology, 74*, 413–440.

Pinder, C. (2008). *Work motivation in organisational behaviour* (2nd ed.). New York, NY: Psychology Press.

Podsakoff, N. P., Lepine, J. A., & Lepine, M. A. (2007). Differential challenge stressor-hindrance stressor relationships with job attitudes, turnover intentions, turnover and withdrawal behaviour: A meta-analysis. *Journal of Applied Psychology, 92*, 438–454.

Prieto, L. L., Salanova, M., Martinez, I., & Schaufeli, W. B. (2008). Extension of the Job-demands resources model in the prediction of burnout and engagement among teachers over time. *Psicothema, 20*, 354–360.

Rousseau, D. M. (1995). *Psychological contracts in organisations: Understanding written and unwritten agreements.* Thousand Oaks, CA: Sage.

Rubino, C., Luksyte, A., Perry, S. J., & Volpone, S. D. (2009). How do stressors lead to burnout? The mediating role of motivation. *Journal of Occupational Health Psychology, 14*, 289–304.

Rydstedt, L. W., Ferrie, J., & Head, J. (2006). Is there support for curvilinear, relationships between psychosocial work characteristics and mental well-being? Cross-sectional and long-term data from the Whitehall II study. *Work & Stress, 20*, 6–20.

Schaufeli, W. B., & Bakker, A. B. (2001). Werk en welbevinding. Naar een positieve benadering in de Arbeids- en Gezondheidspsychologie [Work and well-being. Toward a positive approach of occupational health psychology]. *Gedrag & Organisatie, 5*, 229–253.

Schaufeli, W. B., & Bakker, A. B. (2004). Job demands, job resources, and their relationship with burnout and engagement: A multi-sample study. *Journal of Organizational Behavior, 25*, 293–315.

Schaufeli, W. B., Bakker, A. B., & Van Rhenen, W. (2009). How changes in job demands and resources predict burnout, work engagement, and sickness absenteeism. *Journal of Organizational Behavior, 30*, 893–917.

Schaufeli, W. B., Salanova, M., Gonzaléz-Romá., V., & Bakker, A. B. (2002). The measurement of engagement and burnout: A confirmatory factor analytic approach. *Journal of Happiness Studies, 3*, 71–92.

Schreurs, B., Van Emmerik, H., De Cuyper, N., Notelaers, G., & De Witte, H. (2011). job demands-resources and early retirement intention: Differences between blue- and white-collar workers. *Economic and Industrial Democracy, 32*, 47–68.

Seligman, M., & Csikszentmihalyi, M. (2000). Positive psychology – An introduction. *American Psychologist, 55*, 5–14.

Selye, H. (1956). *The stress of life.* New York, NY: McGraw-Hill.

Siegrist, J. (1996). Adverse health effects of high effort-low reward conditions. *Journal of Occupational Health Psychology, 1*, 27–41.

Simbula, S. (2010). Daily fluctuations in teachers' well-being: A diary study using the job demands-resources model. *Anxiety, Stress and Coping, 23*, 563–584.

Simbula, S., Guglielmi, D., & Schaufeli, W. B. (2011). A three-wave study of job resources, self-efficacy, and work engagement among Italian schoolteachers. *European Journal of Work and Organizational Psychology, 20*, 285–304.

Sonnentag, S., Binnewies, C., & Mojza, E. J. (2010). Staying well and engaged when demands are high: The role of psychological detachment. *Journal of Applied Psychology, 95*, 965–976.

Sundin, L., Hochwalder, J., & Lisspers, J. (2011). A longitudinal examination of generic and occupational specific job demands, and work-related social support associated with burnout among nurses in Sweden. *Work: A Journal of Prevention, Assessment & Rehabilitation, 38,* 389–400.

Ten Brummelhuis, L. L., ter Hoeven, C. L., Bakker, A. B., & Peper, B. (2011). Breaking through the loss cycle of burnout: The role of motivation. *Journal of Occupational and Organizational Psychology, 84,* 268–287.

Tims, M., Bakker, A. B., & Derks, D. (2012). Development and validation of the job crafting scale. *Journal of Vocational Behavior, 80,* 173–186.

Van den Broeck, A., Baillien, E., & De Witte, H. (2011). Workplace bullying: A perspective from the job demands-resources model. *South African Journal of Industrial Psychology, 37,* 879–891.

Van den Broeck, A., De Cuyper, N., De Witte, H., & Vansteenkiste, M. (2010). Not all job demands are equal: Differentiating job hindrances and job challenges in the job demands-resources model. *European Journal of Work and Organizational Psychology, 19,* 735–759.

Van den Broeck, A., De Cuyper, N., Luyckx, K., & De Witte, H. (2012). Employees' job demands-resources profiles, burnout and work engagement: A person-centred examination. *Economic and Industrial Democracy, 33,* 691–706.

Van den Broeck, A., Van der Elst, T., Dikkers, J., De Lange, A., & De Witte, H. (2012). This is funny: On the beneficial role of self-enhancing and affiliative humour in job design. *Psicothema, 24,* 87–93.

Van den Broeck, A., Van Ruysseveldt, J., Smulders, P., & De Witte, H. (2011). Does an intrinsic work value orientation strengthen the impact of job resources? A perspective from the job demands-resources model. *European Journal of Work and Organizational Psychology, 20,* 581–609.

Van den Broeck, A., Vansteenkiste, M., & De Witte, H. (2009). Are some job demands positively related to job well-being? Further evidence for the differentiation between job hindrances and job challenges/demands. In M. Salanova & A. M. Rodríguez-Sánchez (Eds.), *Looking for the positive side of occupational health at work. Colección e-psique* (pp. 88–105). Castellón: Publicacions Universitat Jaume I.

Van den Broeck, A., Vansteenkiste, M., De Witte, H., & Lens, W. (2008). Explaining the relationships between job characteristics, burnout, and engagement: The role of basic psychological need satisfaction. *Work and Stress, 22,* 277–294.

Van den Heuvel, M., Demerouti, E., Bakker, A. B., & Schaufeli, W. B. (2010). Personal resources and work engagement in the face of change. In J. Houdmont & S. Leka (Eds.), *Contemporary occupational health psychology: Global perspectives on research and practice* (pp. 124–150). Chichester, UK: Wiley.

Van der Heijden, B. I., Demerouti, E., & Bakker, A. B. (2008). Work-home interference among nurses: Reciprocal relationships with job demands and health. *Journal of Advanced Nursing, 62,* 572–584.

Van Emmerik, IJ. H., Bakker, A. B., & Euwema, M. C. (2009). Explaining employees' evaluations of organisational change with the job demands-resources model. *Career Development International, 14,* 594–613.

Van Ruysseveldt, J., Proost, K., & Verboon, P. (2011). The role of work-home interference and workplace learning in the energy-depletion process. *Management Revue, 22,* 151–168.

Van Ruysseveldt, J., & Taverniers, J. (2010). Al werkend leren. De actief leren-hypothese van Karasek revisited [Learning while working. Karasek's active learning hypothesis revisited]. *Gedrag & Organisatie, 23,* 1–18.

Van Ruysseveldt, J., Verboon, P., & Smulders, P. (2011). Job resources and emotional exhaustion: The mediating role of learning opportunities. *Work & Stress, 25,* 205–223.

Van Vegchel., N., De Jonge, J., Bosma, H., & Schaufeli, W. B. (2005). Reviewing the Effort-Reward Imbalance model: Drawing up the balance of 45 empirical studies. *Social Science & Medicine, 60,* 1117–1131.

Walsh, G. (2011). Unfriendly customers as a social stressor – An indirect antecedent of service employees' quitting intention. *European Management Journal, 29,* 67–78.

Weigl, M., Hornung, S., Parker, S. K., Petru, R., Glaser, J., & Angerer, P. (2010). Work engagement accumulation of task, social, personal resources: A three-wave structural equation model. *Journal of Vocational Behavior, 77,* 140–153.

Westman, M., Bakker, A. B., Roziner, I., & Sonnentag, S. (2011). Crossover of job demands and emotional exhaustion within teams: A longitudinal multilevel study. *Anxiety, Stress and Coping, 24,* 561–577.

Xanthopoulou, D., Bakker, A. B., Demerouti, E., & Schaufeli, W. B. (2007). The role of personal resources in the job demands-resources model. *International Journal of Stress Management, 14,* 121–141.

Xanthopoulou, D., Bakker, A. B., Demerouti, E., & Schaufeli, W. B. (2009). Reciprocal relationships between job resources, personal resources and work engagement. *Journal of Vocational Behavior, 74,* 235–244.

Xanthopoulou, D., Bakker, A. B., Dollard, M. F., Demerouti, E., Schaufeli, W. B., Taris, T. W., & Schreurs, P. J. G. (2007). When do job demands particularly predict burnout? The moderating role of job resources. *Journal of Managerial Psychology, 22,* 766–786.

DOES PERSONALITY MATTER? A REVIEW OF INDIVIDUAL DIFFERENCES IN OCCUPATIONAL WELL-BEING

Anne Mäkikangas, Taru Feldt, Ulla Kinnunen and Saija Mauno

Despite working in the same workplace and sharing the same working conditions, employees' occupational well-being may vary considerably as a result of differences in their personalities, motivation, and personal goals. This is an issue that has attracted the attention of many scholars over the years. However, the role of personality in employee well-being is not yet fully understood for several reasons. First, the diversity of personality constructs used in occupational well-being research is striking, and it seems that no consensus exists as to what are the core constructs of personality that really matter in promoting or impairing employee well-being at work. Second, the occupational well-being literature has thus far focused largely on single personality characteristics, ignoring the employee as a complete person simultaneously possessing many personality traits (or dispositions), characteristic adaptations, and life narratives, all of which together may play a role in an employee's occupational well-being. Third, the rise of positive psychology and related constructs has presented research on personality and occupational well-being with an additional challenge.

Advances in Positive Organizational Psychology, Volume 1, 107–143
ISSN: 2046-410X/doi:10.1108/S2046-410X(2013)0000001008

The key question from this viewpoint is: What kind of personality promotes employees' positive occupational well-being, including work engagement (WE)?

To shed further light on these fundamental issues in the current occupational well-being literature, we aim in this chapter, first, to introduce a holistic framework for personality research that will lay a foundation for a better understanding of the role of different personality constructs and their mutual relationships in employees' emotions and behavior at work. Second, we briefly trace the history of personality research in the context of occupational well-being, and look at the mechanisms via which personality plays a role in occupational well-being. Finally, we present the results of our qualitative review of the literature on the relationships between personality and WE, and on the basis of reflections on our review, conclude by suggesting avenues for future personality research in the work context. The holistic framework for personality research and mechanisms of personality in occupational well-being processes are used as tools to discuss the results of the literature review.

WE, defined as a positive, fulfilling, work-related state of mind, characterized by vigor, dedication, and absorption (Schaufeli, Salanova, González-Romá, & Bakker, 2002), was selected as the key target of the review, as it is one of the central constructs in the realm of positive occupational health psychology (Bakker & Demerouti, 2008). In addition, owing to the fact that the history of WE research is still relatively young and the majority of previous research has focused on its work-related antecedents, the purpose of the chapter is to draw together the empirical knowledge gained thus far on its association with personality characteristics. The ultimate aim is to identify future research targets and promote the use of positive psychology in the occupational context.

HOLISTIC APPROACH TO HUMAN PERSONALITY

In the context of occupational health psychology, personality has usually been depicted from the perspective of single traits, dispositions, or their combinations. However, there is a clear need to better understand personality as a whole. For this reason, an integrative framework of personality is presented in order to give a more comprehensive and cohesive picture of how the different personality constructs relate to each other. In recent years, several holistic models of human personality have been presented. For example, such models have been formulated by Dan McAdams (1995), Brian

Little (2007), Robert McCrae and Paul Costa Jr. (1999), and Brent Roberts and Dustin Wood (2006). In this chapter, we briefly introduce one of these models, that is, the *three-tiered conceptual framework of personality* by McAdams and his colleagues (McAdams, 1995; McAdams & Adler, 2006; McAdams & Olson, 2010; McAdams & Pals, 2006). This comprehensive and multifaceted model conceptualizes human personality via a developing pattern of (1) dispositional traits, (2) characteristic adaptations, and (3) constructive life narratives (see Fig. 1). Each of these three levels possesses its own characteristics for describing and understanding personality.

The first level of personality describes the basic individual tendencies formed in gene–environment interaction throughout the individual's development. This level contains temperament (e.g., irritability, activity, frequency of smiling, and an approach or avoidant posture to unfamiliar events; Rothbart, Ahadi, & Evans, 2000), personality traits (e.g., the Big Five; McCrae & Costa, 2003), and personality dispositions (e.g., optimism; Scheier & Carver, 1985) that describe the fundamental and broad differences between individuals. In many respects, these differences show consistency

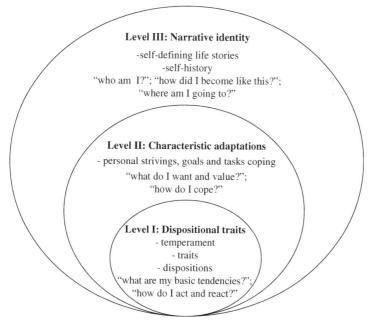

Fig. 1. Conceptual Framework of Personality (Adapted from McAdams, 1995).

across different situations and over time (McAdams & Adler, 2006). Thus, the first level captures the basic tendencies characterizing an individual's inclinations to act and react in accordance with her or his life circumstances across the life course.

The second level includes characteristic adaptations. These are descriptions of personal strivings, life tasks, and coping strategies that are connected to specific times, situations, and social roles (McAdams, 1995). Thus, level 2 characteristics are motivational, social-cognitive, and developmental adaptations that have a close connection with the individual's life context (McAdams & Pals, 2006). Whereas dispositional traits describe what a person is generally like, characteristic adaptations portray more situation-related psychological processes, such as how a person copes with particular kinds of stressors.

The third, and the broadest, level of personality represents integrative and evolving self-defining life stories. This so-called "narrative identity" reconstructs the individual's past life and creates the future; together these give a person's life meaning (McAdams & Adler, 2006). Narrative identity is a psychological construction of self in the modern world that is strongly shaped by the surrounding culture, contextual factors, and social relations. Culture guides what kinds of life stories are available and how to express them. Life stories are made and reconstructed every day and they give a unique meaning to individual lives and a feeling of continuity (McAdams & Pals, 2006). By constructing life stories, a person combines dispositional traits, life tasks, and goals, and creates a coherent life story.

PERSONALITY IN THE OCCUPATIONAL WELL-BEING CONTEXT

Researchers have long known that individual differences exist in the extent to which people effectively respond to and cope with stressful situations. According to Semmer and Meier (2009, p. 99), there is a tendency in current stress research to emphasize individual differences to the point where stress is reduced to nothing but idiosyncratic appraisals and coping styles, invalidating such concepts as "environmentally induced stress." In fact, as long ago as 1966, Lazarus stated that no objective criterion is sufficient to describe a situation as stressful and that only the person experiencing the event can do so. However, it is worth bearing in mind that, originally, in stress theory, environmental and external stressors were emphasized. Thus, in emphasizing individual differences, the importance of the nature and scope of environmental factors that have the potential to create strain for individuals in workplaces should not be neglected.

Earliest Research Focused on Single Dispositions

It can reasonably be concluded that the associations between stressors and strain do not hold for everyone in the same way (Spector, 2003). One explanation for these individual differences can be sought in personality. From the viewpoint of stress and strain, personality traits and dispositions can be divided into two broad categories. On the one hand, there are dispositions that make persons vulnerable to stress and strain. On the other hand, there are dispositions that make them resilient – stress-resistant – in this regard. Although several personality variables may function as vulnerability or resiliency factors, the earliest research in the area tended to be dominated by those which may be viewed solely as vulnerability factors.

One of the first personality constructs to receive considerable attention in stress research is *Type A behavior*. This pattern was first identified as a potential contributor to strain-related outcomes by cardiologists Friedman and Rosenman in the 1950s. Type A individuals display high levels of concentration and alertness, achievement striving, competiveness, time urgency, and aggressiveness. Of these components, anger/hostility is often regarded as the major toxic component of the Type A behavior pattern. The evidence to date suggests that hostility is predictive of coronary heart disease (CHD) and all-cause mortality (see Miller, Smith, Turner, Guijarro, & Hallet, 1996, for a meta-analysis).

Negative affectivity, a construct that overlaps to some extent with neuroticism, has also received much research attention over the past few decades in stress research. Negative affectivity (NA) refers to a relatively stable predisposition to experience negative emotional states (Watson & Clark, 1984). Persons who are high in NA are more inclined to experience psychological strain and other negative outcomes in their work setting. NA is seen as a factor that may influence the experience and perception of, as well as reactions to, stress factors, but at the same time it may be influenced by these factors (Spector, Zapf, Chen, & Frese, 2000).

Furthermore, people differ in their beliefs about the world and their relationship with it. Several personality variables account for this difference. Among these are locus of control, sense of coherence, self-efficacy, self-esteem, and optimism. All have been under study for a long time, and they can be considered as representing resilience factors.

Locus of control represents the extent to which people believe that the rewards they receive in life can be controlled by their own personal actions (Rotter, 1966). Research in this area distinguishes between individuals who have an internal locus of control (i.e., those who believe that they can control their own lives) and individuals who have an external locus of control (i.e., those who believe that their lives are controlled by outside influences, such as other people or fate). It has been shown that work locus of control – the extent to which people attribute reward at work to their own behavior – in particular is substantially related to employee well-being and more weakly to perceived work stressors (see Wang, Bowling, & Eschleman, 2010, for a meta-analysis). Accordingly, persons with an internal locus of control have higher job satisfaction and lower levels of burnout and job-induced tension, and report less role ambiguity, conflict, and overload compared to those with an external locus of control.

Sense of coherence describes a personality disposition via three components: comprehensibility, a belief that the world makes sense, that information about the environment is ordered, consistent, and explicable; manageability, a belief that sufficient resources are available for meeting internal and external stimuli and demands; and meaningfulness, a feeling that demands are challenges worthy of investment and engagement (Antonovsky, 1987). A high sense of coherence is assumed to promote an individual's health and well-being through its central role in generating a more resilient choice of strategies for coping with environmental stressors. In occupational health research it has been found that employees with a high sense of coherence perceive less stressors in their work and score higher in occupational well-being than others (for a review, see Feldt, 2000).

As with locus of control and sense of coherence, *self-efficacy* has also consistently been shown to be positively related to well-being. These three concepts are, of course, not identical, but they overlap (Semmer & Meier, 2009, p. 105). Self-efficacy refers to a belief in one's general capacity to handle tasks (Bandura, 1989), and it has similarity not only with locus of control, but also with *self-esteem*. Overall, self-esteem describes the degree to which one experiences feelings of self-worth (Rosenberg, 1965, 1979). Both self-efficacy and self-esteem seem especially important in dealing with negative feedback and failure in terms of distress (Bandura, 1989; Brockner, 1988). *Optimism* is distinct from control-related concepts as it does not require that the course of events is influenced by one's own actions. Rather, it includes the belief that things are likely to turn out reasonably well anyway (Scheier & Carver, 1985). Optimism has been shown to influence stress appraisals, well-being, and coping strategies; that is, optimistic persons have fewer feelings of stress, report higher well-being, and cope more actively with problems (Carver & Scheier, 1999). Optimism has also shown a strong positive association with other personality dispositions, such as sense of coherence (Feldt, Mäkikangas, & Aunola, 2006).

Combinations of Dispositions, Coping, and Goals

In recent years, in the realm of occupational well-being, personality research has focused on different combinations of personality dispositions that relate to an individual's positive evaluation of the self, control beliefs, and having a favorable orientation to the future. For example, according to Judge and his colleagues (Judge, Locke, Durham, & Kluger, 1998), self-esteem, self-efficacy, emotional stability (i.e., reversed neuroticism), and locus of control compose a single broad construct of *core self-evaluations*. The theoretical model is based on an assumption that core self-evaluation constructs are relatively stable and affect all our appraisals concerning ourselves and the world around us. The propagators of this theoretical model suggest that this broad personality construct predicts action over time and over situations, and offers more information about behavior than single constructs. The core self-evaluation construct (measured by the core self-evaluations scale that produces a positive estimate of these personality dispositions; see Judge, Erez, Bono, & Thoresen, 2003) in particular has been associated with high levels of job satisfaction (Srivastava, Locke, Judge, & Adams, 2010) and better health (Kammeyer-Mueller, Judge, & Scott, 2009).

Similarly, the concept of *psychological capital* (PsyCap) combines four personality characteristics, namely self-efficacy, optimism, hope, and resiliency (Luthans, 2002a,b). A meta-analysis of 51 studies shows that PsyCap is associated with desirable employee attitudes (i.e., job satisfaction, organizational commitment, psychological well-being) and with organizational citizenship behavior and job performance (Avey, Reichard, Luthans, & Mhatre, 2011). In addition, a second-order personality concept, named "personal resources," unifying typically positive beliefs about one's self (e.g., self-esteem, self-efficacy) and the world (e.g., optimism), has been used in the context of occupational health psychology (Mäkikangas, 2007; Xanthopoulou, Bakker, Demerouti, & Schaufeli, 2007, 2009a). These kinds of personal resources are assumed to promote well-being by, for example, successful coping (e.g., active and flexible coping) and favorable health behaviors (see Feldt et al., 2006).

In addition to the personality dispositional traits described above, characteristic adaptations (McAdams, 1995) are also widely studied in occupational well-being research. One of these characteristic adaptations is coping, which emerged in work stress research already in the late 1970s. Perhaps the most often used definition of coping comes from Lazarus and Folkman (1984), who define coping as behavioral and cognitive attempts to manage, tolerate, or reduce the stressful demands of a situation. On the one hand, dispositional traits might trigger certain coping responses (Carver & Connor-Smith, 2010; Connor-Smith & Flachsbart, 2007). On the other hand, it has been argued that coping responses are also disposition-like, implying that people tend to use similar coping strategies across situations (Carver & Connor-Smith, 2010).

We also know that some coping behaviors are likely to result in more positive individual outcomes and adjustment, whereas other behaviors are less effective or even maladjustive (for reviews, see, e.g., Aldwin & Revenson, 1987; Carver & Connor-Smith, 2010; Zeidner & Saklofske, 1996). Overall, these previous studies, including those in the field of occupational health psychology (for reviews, see Dewe, Cox, & Ferguson, 1993; Dewe, O'Driscoll, & Cooper, 2010), have shown that problem-focused strategies, referring to active problem-solving behavior with high cognitive effort, often result in positive well-being and health outcomes. In contrast, emotion-focused coping, including behaviors that seek to reduce or eliminate negative emotions arising in a stressful situation, is not an effective way to manage adverse life events in the long run. This is particularly true of avoidant coping (i.e., wishful thinking, escapism, using stimulants).

In recent years, personal goal pursuit has also received increasing attention in occupational well-being research (for a review, see Hyvönen, 2011). Like coping, personal goals are located on level 2 in McAdam's (1996) holistic personality model. Personal goals are considered as "interpersonal represen-tations of desired states," and can be outcomes, events, or processes (Austin & Vancouver, 1996). Such goals can range from short-term goals (e.g., completing a work project) to goals that are present throughout the life course (e.g., taking care of one's health and well-being). Personal goals can, for example, guide the regulation of behavior, form criteria for self-evaluation, and instigate various plans and strategies to cope with environmental demands (Karoly, 1993). Personal goals are crucial in channeling people's behavior, which in turn has an impact on their health and well-being (for a review, see Feldt, Hyvönen, Oja-Lipasti, Kinnunen, & Salmela-Aro, 2012).

When investigating the content of personal goals, the focus is on what a person is oriented toward achieving in the future, uncovering wants, wishes, concerns, and intentions. The contents of goals have typically been investigated in relation to general life goals or to specific areas of life – such as work and career. Work-related personal goals include, for example, competence (e.g., job performance and professional development), progression (advancing to a higher position or promotion), well-being (e.g., job satisfaction, work-life balance), job change (e.g., change in career by changing one's organization, position, or professional field), job security (e.g., receiving a permanent contract), and organizational (e.g., to promote the success of an organization) and financial (e.g., better pay) goals (see, e.g., Hyvönen, Feldt, Salmela-Aro, Kinnunen, & Mäkikangas, 2009).

MECHANISMS THROUGH WHICH PERSONALITY AFFECTS OCCUPATIONAL WELL-BEING

Personality may play various roles in the stress process, as shown by Bolger and Zuckerman (1995). They divide the stress process into two fundamental stages: stressor exposure and stressor reactivity. As we are not focusing solely on environmental stressors (or demands) in the present chapter, we use the term "work characteristics" to cover both negative (demands) and positive (resources) characteristics of work. Thus, slightly modifying Bolger and Zuckerman's (1995) framework, we consider exposure as the extent to which a person is likely to experience a given work characteristic either negatively (such as job demands) or positively (such as job resources). Reactivity is the extent to which a person is likely to show emotional or physical reactions to work characteristics (whether experienced as demands or as resources). Stated simply, exposure refers to how situations are appraised, and reactivity to different reactions to these situations.

Following these fundamental mechanisms of exposure and reactivity, several links between personality, work characteristics, and occupational well-being are possible (see Fig. 2). The first possibility – labeled the *null model* – is that personality does not affect either exposure or reactivity to work characteristics; consequently, personality does not play any role in relation to work characteristics or occupational well-being (i.e., work characteristics have only a main effect on occupational well-being) (Fig. 2a). The second possibility is the *differential exposure model* which assumes that personality affects exposure but not reactivity to work characteristics; once

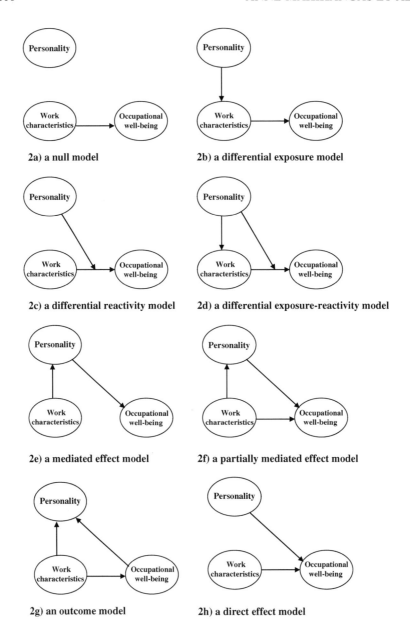

Fig. 2. Theoretical Links Between Personality, Work Characteristics, and Occupational Well-Being.

these characteristics (or events) in the workplace occur, they affect everyone in the same way (Fig. 2b). In this model, the ways in which employees react to work characteristics are seen as a mediating pathway between personality and occupational well-being. The third possibility is that there are personality differences in reactivity to work characteristics but not in exposure to work characteristics. According to this *differential reactivity model*, personality affects outcomes by moderating the effects of work characteristics on well-being outcomes (Fig. 2c); that is, personality operates as a moderator variable (see Baron & Kenny, 1986). The fourth possibility is the *differential exposure-reactivity model* (Fig. 2d), which combines the two previous models under the same process. This model assumes that personality affects both exposure and reactivity in the associations between work characteristics and occupational well-being.

In addition to these hypothetical links discussed by Bolger and Zuckerman (1995), personality may also play a role of a mediator between work characteristics and occupational well-being, resulting in a *mediated effect model* (Fig. 2e). In line with this model, it is possible that work characteristics may modify an employee's personality, which, in turn, leads to changes in that person's occupational well-being. What is more, a direct association between work characteristics and occupational well-being is also possible along with an indirect link via personality, resulting in a *partially mediated effect model* (Fig. 2f).

Personality may also operate as an outcome in relation to work characteristics and occupational well-being, as hypothesized by the *outcome model* (Fig. 2g); that is, work characteristics may lead to changes in personality both directly and indirectly, when work characteristics lead to changes in occupational well-being, which, in turn, cause changes in employees' personality. For example, excessive workload might decrease an employee's well-being; this may then induce a negative change in personality, for example, in terms of lowered self-esteem or efficacy. The final possibility – labeled the *direct effect model* (Fig. 2h) – assumes that personality and work characteristics each lead independently to changes in occupational well-being. According to this model, employees' personality is linked to their occupational well-being irrespective of the work characteristics they perceive in their working environment.

Next we shall discuss how personality – in line with the mechanisms presented above – has been examined in the context of positive work psychology. Our discussion is based on a literature review of the research on personality and WE.

A QUALITATIVE REVIEW OF PERSONALITY AND WORK ENGAGEMENT

The personality characteristics reviewed in this chapter have typically been examined in relation to occupational ill-being (e.g., burnout, symptoms) or job attitudes such as job satisfaction. Recently, in the tail wind of positive psychology, we have witnessed a renewed interest in work motivation processes, and the WE construct, in particular, has been intensively examined (Albrecht, 2010; Bakker & Demerouti, 2008; Bakker & Leiter, 2010). While the correlates of some dispositional traits (i.e., self-efficacy, optimism) have already been included in WE reviews (see Halbesleben, 2010), the aim of this chapter is to provide a more comprehensive view of this issue by reviewing, first, what kinds of personality characteristics have been investigated together with WE, and second, what mechanism(s) have gained most research support.

Criteria for Searching Studies

The PsycINFO database (from 1967 to present) was used to find studies for the review. The literature search was conducted in August 2011. In addition to the key concept of "work engagement" (or "job engagement"), the following terms were used as keywords or were mentioned in the study abstract: "personality," "individual differences," "personality differences." Besides these, umbrella terms ("core self-evaluations," "psychological capital," and "personal resources"), and the single personality characteristics included in these second-order constructs were used. These were "self-efficacy," "self-esteem," "locus of control," "neuroticism/emotional stability," "optimism," "hope," and "resiliency." Furthermore, "sense of coherence," "personal goals," and "coping" were used as keywords. In addition, to be eligible, studies had to (a) present original empirical results, (b) be reported in English, (c) be conducted among working populations, and (d) have a main focus on the association between WE and personality. Studies that merely reported such an association in the correlation matrix of the study variables were excluded from the review.

We found 28 studies that met our criteria. These studies are summarized in Table 1. In many cases, the studies also included other constructs (such as burnout, job performance), but this review focuses only on results regarding the association between personality and WE.

Inspection of the studies in Table 1 showed that the majority of the samples used were drawn from European countries (Scandinavia 10 samples, central Europe 9, and southern Europe 3), but there were also three samples from Africa, and one sample each from Asia, Russia, and the United States. Over half of the studies were cross-sectional ($n = 15$), nine studies used longitudinal designs with wide variation in time lags (from 3 months to 18 years), and four studies used diary data collected typically during one working week. Statistical analyses were typically performed via Structural Equation Modeling (SEM) ($n = 9$), or regression analysis ($n = 9$). Multilevel modeling was used in five studies. Latent Growth Curve (LGC) analysis was used in three studies that also had the longest follow-ups (from 10 to 18 years) (Salmela-Aro & Nurmi, 2007; Salmela-Aro et al. 2009, Salmela-Aro et al., 2011).

Results of the Review

The first target of the review was to find out what personality characteristics had been found to be associated with WE. As shown in Table 1, the great majority of the articles investigated dispositional traits (75%), and thus, in terms of McAdams' (1995) model, focused on level 1 personality constructs. The most popular single dispositional trait in the realm of WE research was self-efficacy, which was the main construct in six studies. Neuroticism was investigated in five studies, together with either extraversion or all the Big Five traits. There were also some sporadic findings relating to optimism, self-esteem, sense of coherence, and temperament characteristics. Personal resources was the most often investigated umbrella construct in relation to WE ($n = 4$). Only one study linking core self-evaluations and WE was found, and none linking psychological capital and WE. In addition, such concepts as locus of control, hope, and resiliency did not yield any matches with WE.

The second target of the review was to explore the mechanisms between personality, work characteristics, and WE that gained most support from the results. Of the results presented in Table 1, 64% supported the direct effect model; that is, personality characteristics were associated either positively or negatively with WE. In addition, 15% of the findings supported the mediated effect model, 9% the differential reactivity model (i.e., personality functioned as a moderator), and 7.5% the outcome model. However, it should be noted that these mechanisms do not rule each other out. For example, if the outcome model was supported in a longitudinal setting, the results typically also supported the direct effect model,

Table 1. Summary Table of Work Engagement Studies in Relation to Personality.

Author(s)	Participants, Design and Analysis	Personality Characteristic(s)	Job Characteristic(s)	Main Results in Relation to Personality and WE
Bledow, Schmitt, Frese, and Kühnel (2011)	German software developers ($n = 49$), web-based survey twice a day over a period of nine consecutive days, HLM	Positive and negative affectivity	Positive work events (praise from the supervisor, being asked for help, and being involved in planning and decision-making processes), negative work events (making errors, working under time pressure, and conflicts with colleagues and/or supervisor)	(1) Positive affectivity related to high WE (*direct effect model*) (2) Negative affectivity related to high WE (when positive affectivity was controlled for) (*direct effect model*) (3) Positive affectivity moderated the relationship between positive work events and WE (*differential reactivity model*) *Note:* Positive and negative work events related to WE, but when mood and affectivity were added into the model, the relation of work events become nonsignificant
Fourie, Rothmann, and van de Vijver (2008)	South African nonprofessional counselors ($n = 165$), cross-sectional, SEM	Sense of coherence	Job characteristics (job demands, job resources)	(1) Sense of coherence related to high work wellness (latent factor formed by WE and burnout) (*direct effect model*)

Gudbergsson, Fosså, & Dahl (2008)	Norwegian cancer survivors (*n* = 513) and control group (*n* = 700), cross-sectional, regression analysis	Neuroticism, extraversion	Work demands, control, support	(2) Positive job characteristics related to high work wellness (*direct effect model*) (3) Job characteristics mediated the sense of coherence – work wellness relation (*differential exposure model*) (1) Extraversion related to high WE (*direct effect model*) (2) Work demands, control and support related to low WE (*direct effect model*)
Hakanen & Lindbohm (2008)	Finnish breast cancer survivors (*n* = 389), referents (*n* = 560), cross-sectional, SEM	Optimism, pessimism	Organizational climate, social support at work, avoidance behavior of supervisor/colleagues	(1) Optimism related to high WE in whole data (*direct effect model*) (2) Organizational climate and social support related to high WE, whereas avoidance behavior of supervisor and colleagues related to low WE in whole data (*direct effect model*) (3) Optimism moderated the relationship between avoidance behavior by supervisor and

Table 1. (*Continued*)

Author(s)	Participants, Design and Analysis	Personality Characteristic(s)	Job Characteristic(s)	Main Results in Relation to Personality and WE
				organizational climate on WE among cancer survivors (*differential reactivity model*)
Heuven, Bakker, Schaufeli, and Huisman (2006)	Cabin attendants from a European airline company (*n* = 154), cross-sectional, regression analysis	Self-efficacy	Job demands (emotionally charged interactions with passengers, feeling rules), emotional dissonance	(1) Self-efficacy related to high WE (*direct effect model*) (2) Emotional dissonance related to low WE (*direct effect model*) (3) Self-efficacy moderated the relationship between emotional dissonance and WE (*differential reactivity model*)
Hyvönen et al. (2009)	Young Finnish managers (*n* = 747), cross-sectional, goal content analysis, ANCOVA	Personal work goals	—	(1) Personal job changes goals related to low WE, vigor, and dedication (*direct effect model*) (2) Personal well-being goals related to low vigor and dedication (*direct effect model*)

Hyvönen, Feldt, Tolvanen, and Kinnunen (2010)	Young Finnish managers (*n* = 747), cross-sectional, GLM	Personal work goals	Effort, reward, effort–reward imbalance	(1) High reward and low effort – reward imbalance related to high WE (*direct effect model*) (2) Personal work goals partially mediated reward – WE and effort–reward imbalance – WE relations (*partially mediated effect model*) (3) Personal work goals fully mediated effort – WE relation (*mediated effect model*) (4) Personal work goals moderated reward – WE relation (*differential reactivity model*)
Karatepe & Olugbade (2009)	Nigerian hotel employees (*n* = 130), cross-sectional, SEM	Self-efficacy, trait competitiveness	Supervisor support	(1) Self-efficacy related to high absorption (*direct effect model*) (2) Trait competitiveness related to high WE and its dimensions (*direct effect model*) (3) Supervisory support and trait competitiveness related to high self-efficacy (*outcome model*)

Table 1. (*Continued*)

Author(s)	Participants, Design and Analysis	Personality Characteristic(s)	Job Characteristic(s)	Main Results in Relation to Personality and WE
Kim, Shin, & Swanger (2009)	Employees working for quick-service restaurants in United States (*n* = 187), cross-sectional, regression analysis	Extraversion, agreeableness, conscientiousness, neuroticism, openness to experience	Skill variety, customer verbal aggression	(1) Conscientiousness related to high WE, vigor, and absorption (*direct effect model*) (2) Neuroticism related to low WE and vigor (*direct effect model*) (3) Conscientiousness and agreeableness related to high professional efficacy (positively worded burnout dimension) (*direct effect model*) (4) Skill variety related to high WE and its dimensions (*direct effect model*)
Langelaan, Bakker, van Doornen, and Schaufeli (2006)	Heterogeneous sample of Dutch employees (*n* = 572), cross-sectional, discriminant analysis, logistic regression analysis	Temperament (strength of excitation, strength of inhibition, and mobility), extraversion, neuroticism	—	(1) Employees with high WE were characterized by high extraversion, low neuroticism, and high mobility[c] (2) Extraversion, low neuroticism, and mobility related to high WE (*direct effect model*)

Leung, Wu, Chen, and Young (2011)	Supervisory-subordinate dyads (n = 304) working in Chinese hotels, a three-wave longitudinal study with three-month time lags, HLM	Neuroticism (T1)	Workplace ostracism (T1)	(1) Workplace ostracism related to low WE (*direct effect model*) (2) Neuroticism at T1 moderated the relationship between workplace ostracism at T1 and WE at T2 (*differential reactivity model*)
Mauno, Kinnunen, and Ruokolainen (2007)	Finnish health care employees (n = 409), a two-wave longitudinal study, two-year time lag, regression analysis	Organization-based self-esteem (OBSE)	Management quality job control job insecurity time pressures at work; work-family conflict	(1) OBSE predicted high vigor, dedication, and absorption (*direct effect model*) *Note:* When the baseline of each WE dimension was controlled for, OBSE did not predict WE (2) Job insecurity predicted low dedication and job control high dedication, when the baseline of dedication was controlled for (*direct effect model*)
Mostert & Rothmann (2006)	South African police members (n = 1794), cross-sectional, regression analysis	Extraversion, emotional stability, agreeableness, conscientiousness	Job demands, lack of resources	(1) Extraversion, emotional stability and conscientiousness related to high WE (*direct effect model*)

Table 1. (*Continued*)

Author(s)	Participants, Design and Analysis	Personality Characteristic(s)	Job Characteristic(s)	Main Results in Relation to Personality and WE
				(2) Job demands and lack of resources related to low WE (*direct effect model*)
Rantanen, Mauno, Kinnunen, and Rantanen (2011)	Heterogeneous sample of Finnish employees (*n* = 527), cross-sectional, regression analysis	Coping strategies: avoidance-focused, emotion-focused, problem-focused	Work-to-family conflict, family-to-work conflict	(1) Problem-focused coping related to high WE and emotion-focused coping to low WE (*direct effect model*) (2) Family-to-work conflict related to low WE (*direct effect model*)
Rich, Lepine, and Crawford (2010)	Caucasian firefighters and their supervisors (*n* = 245), cross-sectional, SEM	Core self-evaluations	Value congruence, perceived organizational support	(1) Core self-evaluations related to high job engagement (*direct effect model*) (2) Value congruence and perceived organizational support related to high job engagement (*direct effect model*)
Richardsen, Burke, and Martinussen (2006)	Norwegian police officers (*n* = 150), cross-sectional study, regression analysis	Type A: Achievement Striving (AS) and Impatience-Irritation (II)	Job demands (overtime work, leadership responsibilities, work conflicts, work-family conflict), job resources	(1) AS related to high WE (*direct effect model*)

			(autonomy, social support from co-workers, social support from supervisor)	
Salanova, Llorens, and Schaufeli (2011)	Spanish secondary-school teachers (n = 274), a two-way longitudinal study with eight-month time lag, SEM	Self-efficacy	—	(1) Job-related positive affect-mediated self-efficacy at T1 – WE at T2 relation[a] (2) Job-related positive affect mediated WE at T1 – self-efficacy at T2 relation[a]
Salmela-Aro and Nurmi (2007)	Finnish academically educated employees (baseline n = 297), a five-wave longitudinal study with time lags of two or four years, LGC	Self-esteem	—	(1) Self-esteem and its increase during university studies predicted high WE 10 years later (*direct effect model*)
Salmela-Aro, Tolvanen, and Nurmi (2009)	Finnish academically educated employees (baseline n = 292), a six-wave longitudinal study with time lags of two, four, or six years, LGC	Achievement strategies: optimistic strategy, task avoidance strategy	—	(1) Optimistic achievement strategy and its increase during studies predicted high WE 10, 14, and 17 years later (*direct effect model*) (2) Task avoidance strategy during studies predicted low WE 10, 14, and 17 years later (*direct effect model*)

Table 1. (*Continued*)

Author(s)	Participants, Design and Analysis	Personality Characteristic(s)	Job Characteristic(s)	Main Results in Relation to Personality and WE
Salmela-Aro, Tolvanen, and Nurmi (2011)	Finnish academically educated employees (baseline $n = 292$), a six-wave longitudinal study with time lags of two, four, or six years, LGC	Social strategies: optimistic strategy, self-handicapping strategy, social withdrawal	—	(1) Social optimistic strategy and its increase during university studies predicted high WE 18 years later (*direct effect model*) (2) Self-handicapping and social withdrawal strategy predicted low WE 18 years later (*direct effect model*)
Simbula, Guglielmi, & Schaufeli (2011)	Italian schoolteachers ($n = 104$), a three-wave longitudinal study, four-month time lags, SEM	Self-efficacy	Job resources (opportunities to learn and develop, co-workers' support, supervisor support)	(1) Self-efficacy at T1 predicted high WE at T2 and T3 (*direct effect model*) (2) WE at T1 predicted high self-efficacy at T2 and T3 (*outcome model*) (3) Job resources at T1 predicted high WE at T2 (*direct effect model*) (4) WE at T1 predicted high job resources at T2[b]
Tims, Bakker, and Xanthopoulou (2011)	Employees working for temporary work agency or an industrial	Self-efficacy, optimism	Transformational leadership style	(1) Daily self-efficacy related to high daily WE (*direct effect model*)

Study	Sample/Method	Personal resource	Findings
	consultancy firm in the Netherlands (*n* = 42), general questionnaire and daily survey of five consecutive days, multilevel analysis		(2) Daily transformational leadership related to high daily WE (*direct effect model*) (3) Daily optimism fully mediated transformational leadership – WE relation (*mediated effect model*)
van den Heuvel, Demerouti, Schreurs, Bakker, and Schaufeli (2009)	Employees from a variety of public and private organizations (*n* = 238), cross-sectional, regression analysis	Personal resources (self-efficacy, optimism, mastery, meaning in life), coping (acceptance, positive reinterpretation), meaning-making	(1) Self-efficacy, optimism, and meaning in life related to high WE (*direct effect model*) (2) Meaning-making related to high WE, when meaning in life-variable was not controlled for (*direct effect model*)
Weigl et al. (2010)	German hospital physicians (*n* = 416), a three-wave longitudinal study, 14- and 19-month time lags, SEM	Active coping behavior	Job control, work relationships (1) Job control, work relationships, and active coping at T1 predicted high WE at T2 (*direct effect model*) (2) Job control and active coping at T2 predicted high WE at T3 (*direct effect model*) (3) WE at T1 predicted active coping at T2 (*outcome model*)

Table 1. (*Continued*)

Author(s)	Participants, Design and Analysis	Personality Characteristic(s)	Job Characteristic(s)	Main Results in Relation to Personality and WE
				(4) WE at T2 predicted high job control and good work relationships at T3[b]
				(5) WE at T2 predicted active coping at T3 (*outcome model*)
				(6) WE at T2 mediated the relations between job control at T1 and at T3, work relationships at T1 and at T3, and active coping at T1 and at T3[d]
Xanthopoulou et al. (2007)	Employees working for engineering and electronics company in the Netherlands ($n = 714$), cross-sectional, SEM	Personal resources (self-efficacy, organizational-based self-esteem, optimism)	Job resources (autonomy, social support, supervisory coaching, professional development)	(1) Personal and job resources related to high WE (*direct effect model*)
				(2) Personal resources mediated job resources – WE relation (*mediated effect model*)
				(3) Job resources mediated personal resources – WE relation (*differential exposure model*)

Xanthopoulou et al. (2009a)	Employees working for engineering and electronics company in the Netherlands (n = 163), two-wave full panel design with 18-month time lags, SEM	Personal resources (self-efficacy, organizational-based self-esteem, optimism)	Job resources (autonomy, social support, supervisory coaching, professional development, performance feedback)	(1) Personal and job resources at T1 predicted high WE at T2 (*direct effect model*) (2) WE at T1 predicted high personal resources at T2 (*outcome model*) (3) WE at T1 predicted high job resources at T2[b]
Xanthopoulou, Bakker, Demerouti, and Schaufeli (2009b)	Employees from a Greek fast-food company, participating in both general questionnaire and diary survey (n = 42), multilevel analysis	Personal resources (self-efficacy, OBSE, optimism)	Job resources (autonomy, supervisory coaching, team climate)	(1) Day-level personal resources fully mediated day-level autonomy – day-level WE relation (*mediated effect model*) (2) Day-level self-efficacy fully mediated day-level coaching – WE relation (*mediated effect model*) (3) Day-level optimism partially mediated day-level coaching – WE (*partially mediated effect model*) (4) Previous days' coaching had a positive lagged effect on next days' WE, through the full mediation of next days' optimism (*mediated effect model*)

Table 1. (*Continued*)

Author(s)	Participants, Design and Analysis	Personality Characteristic(s)	Job Characteristic(s)	Main Results in Relation to Personality and WE
Xanthopoulou, Bakker, Heuven, Demerouti, and Schaufeli (2008)	Flight attendants from a European airline company participating in both general questionnaire and diary survey ($n = 44$), multilevel analysis	Self-efficacy	Colleague support	(1) Self-efficacy related to high WE (*direct effect model*) (2) Colleague support associated with high self-efficacy (*outcome model*) (3) Colleague support associated with high WE (*direct effect model*)

[a] Job-related affects as mediators between personality and WE.
[b] Reversed causality relation between work characteristic(s) and work engagement.
[c] Discriminant analysis, predictive relations were not modeled for.
[d] WE at T2 as mediator between work characteristic(s) at T1 and T3 and between personality at T1 and T3.

producing a reciprocal cycle. It is also important to acknowledge that the large majority of studies focused only on investigating the direct and moderating effects of personality. In other words, many of the possible mechanisms were not investigated.

More detailed inspection of the review results shows that self-efficacy was positively related to WE in five out of six studies. The cross-sectional self-efficacy studies mainly found in favor of a direct association with WE, whereas in the longitudinal studies (Salanova et al., 2011; Simbula et al., 2011) both the direct effect and outcome models gained support. Thus, it seems that self-efficacy and WE are reciprocally related over time. In the case of the personal resources construct, which combined self-efficacy, self-esteem, and optimism, the reciprocal pattern between personality and WE over time was typically found (Xanthopoulou et al., 2007; Xanthopoulou et al., 2009a).

Of the Big Five traits, extraversion and conscientiousness were consistently positively associated with high WE levels, whereas a negative association between neuroticism and WE was found in only half of the studies. Interestingly, in one study (Kim et al., 2009), agreeableness was positively associated with professional efficacy, which is the only positively worded burnout dimension. However, no far-reaching conclusions can be drawn from the associations reported between the Big Five traits and WE, because all the reviewed studies utilized cross-sectional designs and the majority of them tested only the direct effects model. There was nevertheless one fresh exception. In the study by Langelaan et al. (2006), a person-centered approach was used; that is, engaged and burned-out employees were identified and their characteristics were sought by simultaneously examining several personality traits and temperament characteristics. The main results of this study were that neuroticism was negatively and extraversion was positively related to WE.

In addition to the dispositional trait studies discussed above, the review included seven studies with a focus on level 2 personality constructs (McAdams, 1995). Work-related goals were investigated in two studies (Hyvönen et al., 2009; Hyvönen et al., 2010). The content categories of the goals were determined in relation to whether the goals enhanced or diminished WE. For example, personal goals relating to well-being or job change were associated with lower WE, whereas organizational goals (i.e., relating to the success or performance of the organization) were related to higher levels of WE.

Two of the studies showed that an increase in optimistic achievement or social strategies (i.e., a succession of psychological processes characterized by optimism, mastery beliefs, and high level of effort) predicted high levels of WE, while task avoidance, self-handicapping, or social withdrawal associated with low levels of subsequent WE (Salmela-Aro et al., 2009; Salmela-Aro et al., 2011). With respect to coping, two out of three studies showed a significant association between a specific coping strategy and WE. Weigl et al. (2010) showed that active, problem-focused coping (e.g., being persistent and creative in problem-solving) was related to higher WE, which, in turn, promoted more active coping over time. On the basis of their longitudinal findings, the authors suggest that there is a positive reciprocal association between active coping strategies and WE. Subsequently, Rantanen et al. (2011) found that problem-focused coping was associated with higher and emotion-focused coping with lower WE, although these relationships were not very strong.

In sum, the different studies appear to have many common elements, which allow us to build a picture of the personality traits that associate with occupational well-being. It seems that people with high self-efficacy, optimism, and high emotional stability have a particular way of dealing with reality (Semmer & Meier, 2009, p. 108). Such people tend to interpret their environment basically as benign. For example, they expect things to go well, they accept setbacks and failures as normal, and not as indicative of their own lack of worthiness, and they tend to see life as something that can be influenced and acted upon. Thus, in many cases, it is not the objective situation per se, but the way people deal with it that determines the outcome. However, it should be remembered that chronically stressful working conditions overtax people's resources, impairing not only their health but also their coping resources. Therefore, people in this situation seem to be unable to deal with problems that other people manage to deal with effectively. Clearly, we need more knowledge about the cross-lagged effects between these phenomena.

SUGGESTION FOR FUTURE RESEARCH IN POSITIVE OCCUPATIONAL HEALTH PSYCHOLOGY

Our review shows that although personality has been a relatively popular topic in recent WE research, there is also room for new research perspectives. The majority of the reviewed studies focused on level 1 personality constructs, that is, dispositional traits. More specifically, most of these studies focused on single dispositional traits, while there is an evident lack of studies relating WE to the new second-order personality constructs, such as core self-evaluations and psychological capital. Thus, in the future, these relatively new second-order personality constructs would merit examination in relation to WE.

Typically, the reviewed studies included only little or no discussion at all about the grounds on which particular dispositional traits were selected for study and what personality components they represented. In future research, more effort needs to be dedicated to understanding the connection between different dispositional traits and their place in understanding personality as a whole. To address this deficiency, more research on the construct validity of personality constructs is needed. As this chapter shows, a large number of different constructs purport to describe dispositional traits. In many cases, however, the line between these constructs (e.g., self-efficacy, optimism, hope, locus of control) is thin, while there is also considerable overlap between them (i.e., they correlate highly). This might in part be a problem of measurement; that is, questionnaires cannot capture the theoretical differences between these constructs. However, this might also be a problem specific to psychological research: there are more constructs than there are phenomena to measure. In either case, the strong association that exists between the different personality constructs should be better acknowledged, as has been done in the core self-evaluation theory or psychological capital concept. Thus, it remains unclear how many different constructs are needed and how they are hierarchically ordered. Construct validity studies are needed for this purpose. The research evidence relating to higher-order personality constructs is promising. For example, it has been shown that the core self-evaluation construct associates more strongly with job satisfaction than its components separately (Judge, Erez, Bono, & Thoresen, 2002). The core self-evaluations also predicted job satisfaction over and above the Big Five and positive/negative affectivity typologies (Judge, Heller & Klinger, 2008).

The second option to enrich understanding of dispositional traits is offered by personality types consisting of clusters of traits. By adopting a person-centered approach (Laursen & Hoff, 2006; Magnusson, 1999), it is possible to investigate the different combinations of dispositional traits within individuals. For example, in the area of personality psychology, the Big Five characteristics are often clustered, producing different personality types (e.g., resilient, overcontrolled, and undercontrolled) (Herzberg & Roth, 2006; Robins, John, Caspi, Moffitt, & Stouthamer-Loeber, 1996).

The results of the longitudinal studies reviewed here showed that personality and WE are reciprocally related. This result is consistent with

Conservation of Resources theory, according to which different kinds of resources are likely to accumulate (Hobfoll, 1989). Overall, the review results support the plasticity principle, which posits that personality preserves its plasticity over the life span (Caspi, Roberts, & Shiner, 2005; Roberts & Wood, 2006). According to this principle, personality or dispositional traits are open systems that can change at any age due to interaction with the environment. Consequently, personality and work experiences are in a relation of correspondence with each other throughout the life course; that is, personality influences and are influenced by work experiences. However, it should be noted that the majority of the reviewed studies were cross-sectional. Hence, more longitudinal studies are required. In the case of level 2 personality constructs (e.g., personal goals, coping) in particular, it is vital to understand and acknowledge the context and life course viewpoint.

The mechanisms typically used and developed to depict the stress process were also useful in modeling the work motivation process. Studying mediating links in the work motivation process is especially fruitful, as it helps to understand what kinds of processes are involved in high versus low work motivation. An example of this kind of enlargement is the study by Salanova et al. (2011). They found that job-related positive affect mediated the reciprocal relations between self-efficacy and WE. As stated in Broaden-and-Build theory, positive emotions and psychological resiliency (characterized by positive emotionality, optimism, openness to new experiences, and an energetic approach to life; Tugade & Fredrickson, 2004) affect each other reciprocally. Positive emotions build psychological resilience over the life course, which in turn helps the resilient individual to cope with, and also recover from, demanding and negative emotional experiences (Fredrickson, 1998, 2001; Tugade et al., 2004).

Furthermore, the relation between different personality levels is an important research target, that is, how a person's basic tendencies manifest themselves on the behavioral level. The literature review showed that in particular the linkages between dispositional traits, coping strategies, and WE are replete with interesting research questions. First, it could be examined in which on-the-job situations coping plays a mediating or moderating role between dispositional traits and WE. It could be expected, on the basis of stress and coping theories (Dewe et al., 1993; Dewe et al., 2010; Lazarus & Folkman, 1984; Zeidner & Saklofske, 1996), that coping matters, particularly when stressors are present. For example, coping may serve as a buffering resource in much the same manner as job resources (control, support) buffer against job stressors in relation to WE.

Dispositional traits, in turn, might predispose individuals to use specific coping styles in the work context. Hence, coping forms the mediating mechanism between personality and WE. Another interesting question is whether there is a positive spiral between certain dispositional traits, coping behaviors, and WE. To answer this question would naturally require a study with a longitudinal design.

Despite the interpersonal nature of the present-day work, all of the reviewed studies focused on the association between personality and WE within an individual employee. However, it is also essential to consider team/group processes, since personality characteristics may have different consequences in team work. For example, self-esteem is consistently associated with high self-rated well-being and happiness, yet at the same time studies have also addressed its possible dark side in group processes. For example, there is evidence that people with high self-esteem have self-enhancement tendencies (Bosson, Brown, Zeigler-Hill, & Swann, 2003) and demonstrate stronger in-group favoritism, both of which may increase prejudice and discrimination (Baumeister, Campbell, Krueger, & Vohs, 2003). Hence, the interpersonal processes and group dynamics of different personalities as well as their possible impact on collective well-being should be also explored along with the perspective of the individual employee.

As the last-mentioned issue indicates, context also needs to be taken into account in personality research. According to McAdams (1995), culture and its norms always determine how personality traits manifest themselves. For example, in the work context, social norms guide employees' behavior (Schein, 1999). Organizational social norms often render some behaviors, moods, or attitudinal reactions more appropriate than others, thereby creating a culture, climate, or morale in which the organization's members start behaving, thinking, or feeling in accordance with those social norms (Schein, 1999). Thus, it is reasonable to argue that in the work context, the organizational culture, social norms, and the individual person's roles are all important, since they delimit how an individual's personality characteristics are acted out. Hence, it should be noted that in the work context an individual's basic tendencies never appear as such, but are embellished by the immediate social environment.

Finally, in order to develop effective interventions to facilitate employees' WE, we need to gather more information about which personality constructs or their combinations are most powerful in this respect. In this chapter, we have shown that while many personality characteristics have been studied as antecedents of high WE, we do not as yet know enough about how to strengthen certain personal characteristics. One promising relatively new area in the realm of occupational health psychology is the study of level 2 personality constructs, that is, personal goals and strategies that offer more concrete intervention possibilities than dispositional traits. All in all, the findings of this review show that personality is strongly associated with WE. The mechanisms that produce this association are, however, far from clear. In the future, this relationship needs to be examined in more detail. In this regard utilizing longitudinal data and more comprehensive models of personality would be helpful. We expect research of this kind to bring personality and occupational health psychology more closely together, and thus diversify our knowledge.

REFERENCES

Albrecht, S. L. (Ed.). (2010). *Handbook of employee engagement: Perspectives, issues, research and practice*. Glos, UK: Edward Elgar.

Aldwin, C. M., & Revenson, T. A. (1987). Does coping help? A re-examination of the relation between coping and mental health. *Journal of Personality and Social Psychology, 53*, 337–348.

Antonovsky, A. (1987). *Unraveling the mystery of health: How people manage stress and stay well*. San Francisco, CA: Jossey-Bass.

Avey, J. B., Reichard, R. J., Luthans, F., & Mhatre, K. H. (2011). Meta-analysis of the impact of positive psychological capital on employee attitudes, behaviors, and performance. *Human Resource Development Quarterly, 22*, 127–152.

Austin, J. T., & Vancouver, J. B. (1996). Goal constructs in psychology: Structure, process, and content. *Psychological Bulletin, 120*, 338–375.

Bakker, A. B., & Demerouti, E. (2008). Towards a model of work engagement. *Career Development International, 13*, 209–223.

Bakker, A. B., & Leiter, M. P. (Eds.). (2010). *Work engagement: A handbook of essential theory and research*. New York, NY: Psychology Press.

Bandura, A. (1989). Human agency in social cognitive theory. *American Psychologist, 44*, 1175–1184.

Baron, R. M., & Kenny, D. A. (1986). The moderator-mediator variable distinction in social psychology research. Conceptual, strategic, and statistical considerations. *Journal of Personality and Social Psychology, 51*, 1173–1182.

Baumeister, R. F., Campbell, J. D., Krueger, J. I., & Vohs, K. D. (2003). Does high self-esteem cause better performance, interpersonal success, happiness, or healthier lifestyles? *Psychological Science in the Public Interest, 4*, 1–44.

Bledow, R., Schmitt, A., Frese, M., & Kühnel, J. (2011). The affective shift model of work engagement. *Journal of Applied Psychology, 96*, 1246–1257.

Bolger, N., & Zuckerman, A. (1995). A framework for studying personality in the stress process. *Journal of Personality and Social Psychology, 69*, 890–902.

Bosson, J. K., Brown, R. P., Zeigler-Hill, V., & Swann, W. B., Jr. (2003). Self-enhancement tendencies among people with high explicit self-esteem: The moderating role of implicit self-esteem. *Self and Identity, 2*, 169–187.

Brockner, J. (1988). *Self-esteem at work: Research, theory and practice.* Lexington, MA: Lexington Books.

Carver, C. S., & Connor-Smith, J. (2010). Personality and coping. *Annual review of psychology, 61,* 679–704.

Carver, C. S., & Scheier, M. (1999). Optimism. In C. R. Snyder (Ed.), *Coping: The psychology of what works* (pp. 182–204). New York, NY: Oxford University Press.

Caspi, A., Roberts, B., & Shiner, R. (2005). Personality development: Stability and change. *Annual Review of Psychology, 56,* 453–484.

Connor-Smith, J. K., & Flachsbart, C. (2007). Relations between personality and coping: Meta-analysis. *Journal of Personality and Social Psychology, 93,* 1080–1107.

Dewe, P., Cox, T., & Ferguson, E. (1993). Individual strategies for coping with stress and work: A review. *Work & Stress, 7,* 5–15.

Dewe, P. J., O'Driscoll, M., & Cooper, C. L. (2010). *Coping with job stress. A review and critique.* Singapore: Wiley-Blackwell.

Feldt, T. (2000). *Sense of coherence. Structure, stability and health promoting role in working life.* Jyväskylä Studies in Education, Psychology, and Social Research, 158. Jyväskylä University Printing House, Jyväskylä.

Feldt, T., Hyvönen, K., Oja-Lipasti, T., Kinnunen, U., & Salmela-Aro, K. (2012). Do work ability and job involvement channel later personal goals in retirement? An 11-year follow-up study. *International Archives of Occupational and Environmental Health, 85,* 547–558.

Feldt, T., Mäkikangas, A., & Aunola, K. (2006). Sense of coherence and optimism: A more positive approach to health. In L. Pulkkinen, J. Kaprio & R. J. Rose (Eds.), *Socioemotional development and health from adolescence to adulthood* (pp. 286–305). New York, NY: Cambridge University Press.

Fourie, L., Rothmann, S., & van de Vijver, R. J. R. (2008). A model of work wellness for non-professional counsellors in South Africa. *Stress and Health, 24,* 35–47.

Fredrickson, B. L. (1998). What good are positive emotions? *Review of General Psychology, 2,* 300–319.

Fredrickson, B. L. (2001). The role of positive emotions in positive psychology. The Broaden-and-Build theory of positive emotions. *American Psychologist, 56,* 218–226.

Gudbergsson, S., Fosså, S., & Dahl, A. (2008). Is cancer survivorship associated with reduced work engagement? A NOCWO study. *Journal of Cancer Survivorship, 2,* 159–168.

Hakanen, J., & Lindbohm, M.-L. (2008). Work engagement among breast cancer survivors and the referents: The importance of optimism and social resources at work. *Journal of Cancer Survivorship, 2,* 283–295.

Halbesleben, J. (2010). A meta-analysis of work engagement: Relationships with burnout, demands, resources, and consequences. In A. B. Bakker & M. P. Leiter (Eds.), *Work engagement. A handbook of essential theory and research* (pp. 102–118). Sussex, UK: Psychology Press.

Herzberg, P. Y., & Roth, M. (2006). Beyond resilients, undercontrollers, and overcontrollers? An extension of personality prototype research. *European Journal of Personality, 20,* 5–28.

Heuven, E., Bakker, A. B., Schaufeli, W. B., & Huisman, N. (2006). The role of self-efficacy in performing emotion work. *Journal of Vocational Behavior, 69,* 222–235.

Hobfoll, S. E. (1989). Conservation of resources. A new attempt at conceptualizing stress. *American Psychologist, 44,* 513–524.

Hyvönen, K. (2011). *Personal work goals put into context. Associations with work environment and occupational well-being*. Jyväskylä Studies in Education, Psychology and Social Research, 409. Jyväskylä University Printing House, Jyväskylä.

Hyvönen, K., Feldt, T., Salmela-Aro, K., Kinnunen, U., & Mäkikangas, A. (2009). Young managers' drive to thrive: A personal work goal approach to work engagement and burnout. *Journal of Vocational Behavior, 75*, 183–196.

Hyvönen, K., Feldt, T., Tolvanen, A., & Kinnunen, U. (2010). The role of goal pursuit in the interaction between psychosocial work environment and occupational well-being. *Journal of Vocational Behavior, 76*, 406–418.

Judge, T. A., Erez, A., Bono, J. E., & Thoresen, C. J. (2002). Are measures of self-esteem, neuroticism, locus of control, and generalized self-efficacy indicators of a common core construct? *Journal of Personality and Social Psychology, 83*, 693–710.

Judge, T. A., Erez, A., Bono, J. E., & Thoresen, C. J. (2003). The core self-evaluation scale: Development of a measure. *Personnel Psychology, 56*, 303–331.

Judge, T. A., Heller, D., & Klinger, R. (2008). The dispositional sources of job satisfaction: A comparative test. *Applied Psychology: An International Review, 57*, 361–372.

Judge, T. A., Locke, E. A., Durham, C. C., & Kluger, A. N. (1998). Dispositional effects on job and life satisfaction: The role of core evaluations. *Journal of Applied Psychology, 83*, 17–34.

Kammeyer-Mueller, J. D., Judge, T. A., & Scott, B. A. (2009). The role of core self-evaluations in the coping process: Testing an integrative model. *Journal of Applied Psychology, 94*, 177–195.

Karatape, O., & Olugbade, O. (2009). The effects of job and personal resources on hotel employees' work engagement. *International Journal of Hospitality Management, 28*, 504–512.

Karoly, P. (1993). Mechanism of self-regulation: A system view. *Annual Review of Psychology, 44*, 23–52.

Kim, H. J., Shin, K. H., & Swanger, N. (2009). Burnout and engagement: A comparative analysis using the Big Five personality dimensions. *International Journal of Hospitality Management, 28*, 96–104.

Langelaan, S., Bakker, A. B., van Doornen, L., & Schaufeli, W. B. (2006). Burnout and work engagement: Do individual differences make a difference? *Personality and Individual Differences, 40*, 521–532.

Laursen, B., & Hoff, E. (2006). Person-centered and variable-centered approaches to longitudinal data. *Merrill-Palmer Quarterly, 52*, 377–389.

Lazarus, R. S., & Folkman, S. (1984). *Stress, appraisal, and coping*. New York, NY: Springer.

Leung, A. S. M., Wu, L. Z., Chen, Y. Y., & Young, M. N. (2011). The impact of workplace ostracism in service organizations. *International Journal of Hospitality Management, 30*, 836–844.

Little, B. R. (2007). Prompt and circumstance: The generative context of personal projects analysis. In B. R. Little, K. Salmela-Aro & S. D. Phillips (Eds.), *Personal project pursuit: Goals, action, and human flourishing* (pp. 51–93). Mahwah, NJ: Lawrence Erlbaum Associates.

Luthans, F. (2002a). Positive organizational behaviour: Developing and managing psychological strengths. *Academy of Management Executive, 16*, 57–75.

Luthans, F. (2002b). The need for and meaning of positive organizational behavior. *Journal of Organizational Behavior, 23*, 695–706.

Magnusson, D. (1999). On the individual: A person-oriented approach to developmental research. *European Psychologist, 4*, 205–218.

Mäkikangas, A. (2007). *Personality, well-being and job resources. From negative paradigm towards positive psychology.* Jyväskylä Studies in Education, Psychology and Social Research, 320. Jyväskylä University Printing House, Jyväskylä.

Mauno, S., Kinnunen, U., & Ruokolainen, M. (2007). Job demands and resources as antecedents of work engagement: A longitudinal study. *Journal of Vocational Behavior, 70*, 149–171.

McAdams, D. (1995). What do we know when we know a person? *Journal of Personality, 63*, 365–396.

McAdams, D., & Adler, J. (2006). How does personality develop? In D. K. Mroczek & T. D. Little (Eds.), *Handbook of personality development* (pp. 469–492). Mahwah, NJ: Lawrence Erlbaum Associates.

McAdams, D., & Olson, B. D. (2010). Personality development: Continuity and change over the life course. *Annual Review of Psychology, 61*, 517–542.

McAdams, D., & Pals, J. L. (2006). A new big five: Fundamental principles for an integrative science of personality. *American Psychologist, 61*, 204–217.

McCrae, R. R., & Costa, P. T., Jr. (1999). A five-factor theory of personality. In L. A. Pervin & O. P. John (Eds.), *Handbook of personality: theory and research* (2nd ed., pp. 139–153). New York, NY: Guilford.

McCrae, R. R., & Costa, P. T., Jr. (2003). *Personality in adulthood: A Five-Factor Theory perspective* (2nd ed.). New York, NY: Guilford.

Miller, T. Q., Smith, T. W., Turner, C. W., Guijarro, M. L., & Hallet, A. J. (1996). A meta-analytic review of research on hostility and physical health. *Psychological Bulletin, 119*, 322–348.

Mostert, K., & Rothmann, S. (2006). Work-related well-being in the South African police service. *Journal of Criminal Justice, 34*, 479–491.

Rantanen, M., Mauno, S., Kinnunen, U., & Rantanen, J. (2011). Do individual coping strategies help or harm in the work-family conflict situation? *International Journal of Stress Management, 18*, 24–48.

Rich, B. L., Lepine, J. A., & Crawford, E. R. (2010). Job engagement: Antecedents and effect on job performance. *Academy of Management Journal, 53*, 617–635.

Richardsen, A. M., Burke, R. J., & Martinussen, M. (2006). Work and health outcomes among police officers: The mediating role of police cynicism and engagement. *International Journal of Stress Management, 13*, 555–574.

Roberts, B., & Wood, D. (2006). Personality development in the context of the neo-socioanalytic model of personality. In D. K. Mroczek & T. D. Little (Eds.), *Handbook of personality development* (pp. 11–39). Mahwah, NJ: Lawrence Erlbaum.

Robins, R. W., John, O. P., Caspi, A., Moffitt, T. E., & Stouthamer-Loeber, M. (1996). Resilient, overcontrolled, and undercontrolled boys: Three replicable personality types. *Journal of Personality and Social Psychology, 70*, 157–171.

Rothbart, M. K., Ahadi, S. A., & Evans, D. E. (2000). Temperament and personality: Origins and outcomes. *Journal of Personality and Social Psychology, 78*, 122–135.

Rotter, J. B. (1966). Generalized expectancies for internal versus external control of reinforcement. *Psychological Monographs, 80*, 1–28.

Rosenberg, M. (1965). *Society and the adolescent self-image.* Princeton, NJ: Princeton University Press.

Rosenberg, M. (1979). *Conceiving the self.* New York, NY: Basic Books.

Salanova, M., Llorens, S., & Schaufeli, W. (2011). "Yes, I can, I feel good, and I just do it!" On gain cycles and spirals of efficacy beliefs, affect, and engagement. *Applied Psychology: An International Review, 60,* 255–285.

Salmela-Aro, K., & Nurmi, J.-E. (2007). Self-esteem during university studies predicts career characteristics 10 years later. *Journal of Vocational Behavior, 70,* 463–477.

Salmela-Aro, K., Tolvanen, A., & Nurmi, J.-E. (2009). Achievement strategies during university studies predict early career burnout and engagement. *Journal of Vocational Behavior, 75,* 162–172.

Salmela-Aro, K., Tolvanen, A., & Nurmi, J.-E. (2011). Social strategies during university studies predict early career work burnout and engagement: 18-year longitudinal study. *Journal of Vocational Behavior, 79,* 145–157.

Schaufeli, W., Salanova, M., González-Romá, V., & Bakker, A. (2002). The measurement of engagement and burnout: A two sample confirmatory factor analytic approach. *Journal of Happiness Studies, 3,* 71–92.

Schein, E. (1999). *The corporate culture survival guide – sense and nonsense about culture change.* San Francisco, CA: Jossey-Bass.

Scheier, M., & Carver, C. S. (1985). Optimism, coping, and health: Assessment and implication of generalized outcome expectancies. *Health Psychology, 4,* 219–247.

Semmer, N., & Meier, L. (2009). Individual differences, work stress and health. In C. Cooper, J. Quick & M. Scharbracq (Eds.), *International handbook of work and health psychology* (3rd ed., pp. 99–122). New York, NY: Wiley.

Simbula, S., Guglielmi, D., & Schaufeli, W. (2011). A three-wave study of job resources, self-efficacy, and work engagement among Italian schoolteachers. *European Journal of Work and Organizational Psychology, 20,* 285–304.

Spector, P. (2003). Individual differences in health and well-being in organizations. In D. Hoffman & L. Tetric (Eds.), *Health and safety in organizations. A multilevel perspective* (pp. 29–55). San Francisco, CA: Jossey-Bass.

Spector, P., Zapf, D., Chen, P., & Frese, M. (2000). Why negative affectivity should not be controlled in job stress research: Don't throw out the baby with the bath water. *Journal of Organizational Behavior, 21,* 69–85.

Srivastava, A., Locke, E. A., Judge, T. A., & Adams, J. W. (2010). Core self-evaluations as causes of satisfaction: The mediating role of seeking task complexity. *Journal of Vocational Behavior, 77,* 255–265.

Tims, M., Bakker, A. B., & Xanthopoulou, D. (2011). Do transformational leaders enhance their followers' daily work engagement? *The Leadership Quarterly, 22,* 121–131.

Tugade, M. M., & Fredrickson, B. L. (2004). Resilient individuals use positive emotions to bounce back from negative emotional experiences. *Journal of Personality and Social Psychology, 86,* 320–333.

Van den Heuvel, M., Demerouti, E., Schreurs, B., Bakker, A. B., & Schaufeli, W. B. (2009). Does meaning-making help during organizational change? Development and validation of a new scale. *Career Developmental International, 14,* 508–533.

Wang, Q., Bowling, N., & Eschleman, K. (2010). A meta-analytic examination of work and general locus of control. *Journal of Applied Psychology, 95,* 761–768.

Watson, D., & Clark, L. A. (1984). Negative affectivity: The disposition to experience aversive emotional sates. *Psychological Bulletin, 96,* 465–490.

Weigl, M., Hornung, S., Parker, S. K., Petru, R., Glaser, J., & Angerer, P. (2010). Work engagement accumulation of task, social, personal resources: A three-wave structural equation model. *Journal of Vocational Behavior, 77,* 140–153.

Zeidner, M., & Saklofske, D. (1996). Adaptive and maladaptive coping. In M. Zeidner & N. S. Endler (Eds.), *Handbook of coping. Theory, research and applications* (pp. 505–532). New York, NY: Wiley.

Xanthopoulou, D., Bakker, A. B., Demerouti, E., & Schaufeli, W. B. (2007). The role of personal resources in the job demands-resources model. *International Journal of Stress Management, 14,* 121–141.

Xanthopoulou, D., Bakker, A. B., Demerouti, E., & Schaufeli, W. B. (2009a). Reciprocal relationships between job resources, personal resources, and work engagement. *Journal of Vocational Behavior, 74,* 235–244.

Xanthopoulou, D., Bakker, A. B., Demerouti, E., & Schaufeli, W. B. (2009b). Work engagement and financial returns: A diary study on the role of job and personal resources. *Journal of Occupational and Organizational Psychology, 82,* 183–200.

Xanthopoulou, D., Bakker, A. B., Heuven, E., Demerouti, E., & Schaufeli, W. B. (2008). Working in the sky: A diary study on work engagement among flight attendants. *Journal of Occupational Health Psychology, 13,* 345–356.

PSYCHOLOGICAL CAPITAL THEORY: TOWARD A POSITIVE HOLISTIC MODEL

Carolyn M. Youssef-Morgan and Fred Luthans

Although the importance of employee satisfaction and well-being has been given considerable attention by organizational psychology scholars and practicing managers for decades, recently there has been a sharper focus on the role that positivity in general may play in the workplace. The positive psychology movement made a call about a dozen years ago to redirect more research and practice toward a better understanding of optimal human functioning as opposed to the almost sole preoccupation with the negative and dysfunctional (Peterson & Seligman, 2004; Seligman & Csikszentmihalyi, 2000). Since the workplace is one of the most significant contexts for the best (and the worst) of human functioning, this call has been answered in organizational psychology with a number of positively oriented conceptualizations and growing research. Specifically, we coined the term psychological capital (PsyCap) to address positivity in the workplace at the individual level, defining it as:

> an individual's positive psychological state of development that is characterized by:
> (1) having confidence (self-efficacy) to take on and put in the necessary effort to succeed at challenging tasks; (2) making a positive attribution (optimism) about succeeding now and in the future; (3) persevering toward goals and, when necessary, redirecting paths to goals (hope) in order to succeed; and (4) when beset by problems and adversity, sustaining and bouncing back and even beyond (resiliency) to attain success. (Luthans, Youssef, & Avolio, 2007, p. 3)

Advances in Positive Organizational Psychology, Volume 1, 145–166
Copyright © 2013 by Emerald Group Publishing Limited
ISSN: 2046-410X/doi:10.1108/S2046-410X(2013)0000001009

Conceptually, PsyCap goes beyond the four identified psychological resources of hope, efficacy, optimism, and resiliency along several dimensions that are discussed in detail throughout this chapter. Empirically, PsyCap has been found to be a valid and measurably reliable higher-order, latent multidimensional construct (Luthans, Avolio, Avey, & Norman, 2007) and to explain significant variance in desired attitudinal and behavioral outcomes beyond study participants' demographics and established positively oriented OB constructs such as core self-evaluations, personality traits, and person-organization and person–job fit (Avey, Luthans, & Youssef, 2010).

The empirical research has taken off and demonstrates significant support for the contributions of PsyCap in the workplace in terms of employee attitudes, behaviors, and performance (e.g., see the recent meta-analysis by Avey, Reichard, Luthans, & Mhatre, 2011). Yet, to date, an overarching conceptual framework that can organize and guide the positive agenda in terms of theory development, empirical research, and integration within the existing and future organizational psychology literature has been generally lacking. With the growing body of empirical evidence serving as the point of departure, the time has come for a more holistic model of positivity from which PsyCap theory can be developed. Our proposed model goes beyond just the boundaries of the workplace by integrating relationships and health. This whole-person perspective makes the model particularly relevant for the interdisciplinary study and practice of positivity in general and helps in effectively positioning the contributions of PsyCap within the broader spectrum of existing organizational psychology theories and findings as found in the other chapters of this book.

MEANING AND RELEVANCE OF POSITIVITY IN THE WORKPLACE

Positive organizational scholars define positivity as "elevating processes and outcomes" (Cameron & Caza, 2004, p. 731). Thus, a better understanding of positive processes requires the investigation of the explanatory mechanisms that can account for the manifestation of "intentional behaviors that depart from the norm of a reference group in honorable ways" (Spreitzer & Sonenshein, 2003, p. 209). Positivity also focuses on outcomes that "dramatically exceed common or expected performance ... spectacular results, surprising outcomes, extraordinary achievements ... exceptional performance" (Cameron, 2008, p. 8). This "positive deviance" clearly goes beyond ordinary success or effectiveness.

This outcome-oriented perspective on positivity is also consistent with Luthans' (2002, p. 59) definition of positive organizational behavior (POB) as "the study and application of positively oriented human resource strengths and psychological capacities that can be measured, developed, and effectively managed for performance improvement in today's workplace." A critical component of POB is its demonstrable impact on work perform- ance. This perspective emphasizes the strategic business value of positivity, which has been widely supported by empirical research (Avey et al., 2011; Luthans, Avolio et al., 2007; Lyubomirsky, King, & Diener, 2005; Peterson, Luthans, Avolio, Walumbwa, & Zhang, 2011).

UNIQUE CHARACTERISTICS OF POSITIVITY AND NEGATIVITY

A close examination of the unique characteristics of positivity and negativity can shed light on the need for distinct positively oriented theoretical frameworks in the workplace. At least three characteristics can be identified. First, positivity and negativity trigger different thought–action repertoires. For example, according to Fredrickson's (2003) broaden-and-build model, positivity has a broadening effect on thought–action repertoires, and a building effect on physical, social, and psychological resources. On the other hand, negativity yields narrower, more specific action tendencies, such as fight-or-flight responses to threatening situations. As a result of these differences, the outcomes of negativity tend to be viewed as more direct, immediate, and readily observable, while the outcomes of positivity tend to be viewed as distal, vague, uncertain, and under-specified (Wright & Quick, 2009). This may be one of the reasons for the heavy emphasis of scientific research in general on negativity. On the other hand, in order for the contributions of positivity to be adequately conceptualized and measured, broader theoretical frameworks are needed, both in terms of the impact of positivity and the stretch of time over which that impact unfolds.

Second, positivity can be evasive. Negativity tends to present intense, urgent signals for our attention, energy, and action. These signals are learned at an early age, which can push our natural heliotropic tendencies (inclination toward positivity) to the sidelines. Negativity usually signals maladaptation and promotes immediate action to avoid undesirable consequences. On the other hand, there are rarely clear immediate conse-quences for ignoring (or at least delaying) positivity. Thus, natural positive tendencies may be suppressed (e.g., in the name of professionalism, desire for continuous improvement, or simply time pressures). They may need to be stimulated by the intentional mobilization of cognitive, affective, and social resources to overcome the externally induced pressures reinforcing negativity. While both positivity and negativity are necessary for the reali-zation of positive outcomes, negativity alone can lead to rigidity. Positivity needs to be promoted as a balancing mechanism for facilitating the benefits of both positivity and negativity (Baumeister, Bratslavsky, Finkenauer, & Vohs, 2001; Cameron, 2008).

Third, negativity tends to exhibit a narrow singularity, but positivity requires a more global perspective. One negative characteristic can result in system failure, but one positive characteristic does not necessarily result in success (Cameron, 2008). For example, it is easier for a person's positive reputation to be marred by one incident of misconduct, but one honorable act does not "cleanse" a person's negative reputation. A person's failure in one area of life can have far-reaching effects on other areas (e.g., spillover effects in the work–life balance literature; see also Crain & Hammer, this volume), but a person's exceptional success in one area does not guarantee success in others. While extreme positivity in every aspect of life is not required for optimal functioning, research supports the existence of thresholds. For example, flourishing has been distinguished not only from mental illness, but also from languishing, a neutral state where mental illness may be absent, but where hollowness or emptiness are experienced (Keyes, 2002). The tipping point between flourishing and languishing seems to occur at a positivity-to-negativity ratio of about 3:1 in work emotions and interactions, about 5:1 in more complex settings such as top management team communications, and as high as 6:1 or more in marital relationships (Fredrickson & Losada, 2005; Gottman, 1994; Losada & Heaphy, 2004).

This imbalance of the positive over the negative stems from evidence that negative events tend to have a stronger and longer lasting impact than good events on the human self-concept, memory, information processing, and relationships, as well as a wide variety of psychological and behavioral outcomes (Baumeister et al., 2001). Fredrickson uses the metaphor of a sailing ship where the mast is about three times or longer than the keel. The keel can represent negativity. It is needed to prevent the ship from flounder-ing around or even falling flat, but the more dominant mast supporting the sails (representing positivity) is needed for moving full speed ahead in the desired direction. This critical distinction between positivity and negativity further indicates the need for unique models for understanding positivity, and specifically highlights the need for such models to be holistic in nature, capturing a broader context for the mechanisms and outcomes of positivity.

DEFINITION OF POSITIVITY

Based on these unique characteristics, we define positivity as "*an integrated system of antecedents, processes, practices, and outcomes that can be readily identified and agreed upon by diverse observers and stakeholders as uniquely surpassing standards of adequate functioning and adding sustainable value to both the individual and the context.*" This broader "integrated system" perspective is consistent with the notion that positivity tends to be multifaceted, created by a broader set of antecedents, and resulting in more distal outcomes than does negativity. Moreover, this definition emphasizes that one positive dimension of a system (at individual, group, or organization levels) does not constitute positivity until it has been considered in conjunction with the other components of that system.

Furthermore, a common critique of positivity is its subjectivity in that what is positive in one context may be negative in another (Fineman, 2006). Spreitzer and Sonenshein (2003) refer to the norms of a reference group as the standard toward which exceptional behavior can be compared. We expand on this notion in two ways. First, our integrated system perspective addresses not only outward behavior but also the antecedents, processes, and outcomes surrounding the desirable behavior. This systems perspective may yield a deeper understanding of "authentic" positivity, rather than just positive manifestations that may be derived from compensatory mechanisms (Wright & Quick 2009), social desirability, or impression management. In addition, we incorporate the identification and consensus of diverse observers and stakeholders in our definition in order to emphasize their active role as judges in the process of positivity, as well as their potentially divergent interests and stakes in the process. While some dimensions of positivity may be socially constructed, we concur with Peterson and Seligman (2004) that there is significant convergence in what constitutes positivity even in the presence of these differences. We believe that this convergence can be meaningfully conceptualized through the development of holistic models that actively engage a diverse group of observers and stakeholders from different life domains.

Following the argument that positivity and negativity are not necessarily polar opposites (see Peterson & Chang, 2002), we would argue that the definition of positivity should account for performance that uniquely surpasses standards. If positivity can be achieved by quantitatively exceeding standards, then existing models and findings can be extrapolated to the positive end of the continuum. While exceeding standards is important for success in many life domains, we would argue that positivity should not only be defined as "more" but also "different." Interestingly, although it is mathematically impossible to add more "above average" units without inflating what's considered average, well-intentioned scholars and practitioners continue to pursue just that. For example, the term work engagement is often associated with many studies that are at their core simply studying higher levels of commitment (Bakker & Schaufeli, 2008), a Bachelor's degree has become the new high school diploma in the job market but with no significant improvement in actual performance (Oloffson, 2009), and spouses seem to increasingly have exceedingly unrealistic expectations of each other (Seligman, 1998).

On the other hand, the uniqueness aspect in our definition of positivity means that it may need to be fundamentally distinct, not just more of the same (and even potentially "too much of a good thing," Diener, Ng, & Tov, 2009). Combined with the integrated system perspective described above, this uniqueness will likely be manifested as a process of optimizing various dimensions of the system, rather than maximizing each dimension. Maximization is usually best observed in ceteris paribus conditions. On the other hand, optimization requires a holistic perspective in order to balance various dimensions in conjunction, rather than in isolation of each other.

In the context of positivity, optimization recognizes that more is not always better. For example, optimal functioning has been demonstrated when satisfaction is maximized with some life domains (e.g., relationships) while being at moderate levels in others (e.g., income, education; Oishi, Diener, & Lucas, 2007). In other words, optimal functioning is a dynamic balancing process, rather than a sought after destination where all dimensions of life are somehow "topped off." It may necessitate more of some dimensions but less of others, and the right "mix" may change over time. Empirically, optimization is more readily testable when positivity is conceptualized from a whole-person or integrated system perspective. If only maximization or minimization is conceptualized, it becomes a hedonic ideology, or a science of rarities and outliers that may be interesting and thought-provoking, but inaccessible for everyday application and thus of limited generalizability.

Finally, our definition of positivity emphasizes adding value. While this value does not have to be financial in nature, positive outcomes are imperative for most conceptualizations of positivity. They are consistent with the notion of identification and consensus by observers and stakeholders. Our definition does not negate that the value added may be terminal or intrinsic, or that even the simplest pleasures in life "count" without necessarily leading to bigger and better accomplishments. However, the definition adds an element of responsibility in that value added to the individual should be complementary to, rather than at the expense of, the context.

PROPOSED HOLISTIC FRAMEWORK OF POSITIVITY AND PSYCAP

As indicated, the purpose of this chapter is to build out from the emerging positivity and PsyCap research literature, as well as from various more established relevant domains of study, a proposed positive holistic conceptual framework or model that permeates the boundaries of the workplace. Fig. 1 summarizes our proposed model.

The unique contribution of this model is its emphasis on the underlying mechanisms for positivity and PsyCap that invoke reciprocal causal relationships across life domains. We think these fundamental mechanisms can help in the theoretical explanations and understanding of positivity at work and beyond and are now explored. Health (physical and mental), relationships (personal, social, and work), and work have been selected as a starting point toward a holistic model of positivity and PsyCap. Future researchers can expand the boundaries of this model by adding more areas, but we anticipate that the underlying mechanisms proposed in this chapter would promote comparable linkages across other life domains as well. As shown in Fig. 1, three underlying mechanisms for positivity and PsyCap, namely agency, malleability and sociability, are identified.

Unique about the proposed model are the reciprocal relationships across life domains. Distinct from simply related variables, or even cause–effect relationships, reciprocity indicates that each variable causally influences and is causally influenced by the others. Reciprocity may occur simultaneously or over time, directly or indirectly (i.e., through mediating variables and processes), and in isolation or under the influence of other factors

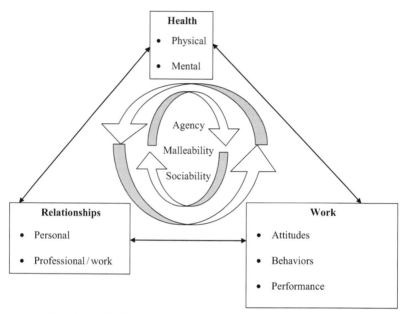

Fig. 1. A Holistic Model of Positivity at Work and Beyond.

(i.e., interactions, moderators). Dynamic, reciprocal relationships that can unfold into positive, self-reinforcing spirals (Fredrickson, 2003) have been supported in positivity research (Demerouti, 2012; Salanova, Bakker, & Llorens, 2006; Walter & Bruch, 2008). Furthermore, these positively oriented relationships have been demonstrated to operate through unique mechanisms that can be conceptually and empirically distinguished from the recognized negative spillover effects, as well as the more neutral aspects of work–life balance (Greenhaus & Powell, 2006).

Incorporating reciprocal causal relationships in our model recognizes the holistic nature of positivity and helps conceptualize its complex relationships and underlying mechanisms. Since the emphasis of this chapter is on conceptualizing the underlying mechanisms that can reciprocally and causally trigger positivity and PsyCap across life domains, a detailed discussion of the literature supporting the relationships between specific dimensions of health, relationships, and work is beyond the scope of this chapter. However, comprehensive reviews are available in the positive psychology literature (e.g., see Lyubomirsky, King, et al., 2005; Lyubomirsky, Sheldon, & Schkade, 2005).

MECHANISM #1: HUMAN AGENCY

Foundational to many organizational psychology theories is conation (Hilgard, 1980), or the assumption that humans are capable of and motivated to influence their environments and alter the course of events through their intentional actions. Historically, conation has been recognized as an integral pillar of psychology, along with cognition and affect. More recently, Bandura's (1997) social cognitive theory (SCT) popularized conation under the more commonly used term "agency" (Bandura, 2008).

DRAWING FROM SOCIAL COGNITION AND EFFICACY

One of the critical underlying theoretical mechanisms shared among PsyCap's four constituent psychological resources is a cognitive, agentic, developmental capacity representing "one's positive appraisal of circumstances and probability for success based on motivated effort and perseverance" (Luthans, Avolio et al., 2007, p. 550). PsyCap draws from Bandura's SCT, which posits triangular reciprocal causal relationships between the individual, the environment, and behavior itself and focuses on at least five vital components for agentic processing: symbolizing, forethought, observation, self-regulation, and self-reflection. It is through the interaction between the person (cognitions, emotions), behavior (self and others), and other social and contextual environmental factors that learning and growth occur. This triangular interaction leads to confidence in the ability to intentionally (agentically) take control over one's future and destiny (i.e., people are both products and producers of their behavior and life course). This form of agency in turn motivates the following: (a) positive cognitions, such as proactive self-regulation and positive expectancies, about the future; (b) positive emotions such as subjective well-being and moods; (c) positive self-directed behaviors, such as investing time, effort, and other resources, in attempting challenging goals; and (d) positive influences on others and the environment through effective leadership of innovation and social reform. Over time, these positive outcomes and others accrue from the exercise of a combination of personal, proxy (socially mediated through others' abilities), and collective (pooled resources and collaborative efforts) efficacy (Bandura, 2008).

Efficacy as an integral constituent of PsyCap can be defined as "one's belief about his or her ability to mobilize the motivation, cognitive resources, and courses of action necessary to execute a specific action within a given context" (Stajkovic & Luthans, 1998b, p. 66). Based on SCT, there are four recognized approaches to efficacy development: successful mastery, vicarious learning or modeling, social persuasion, and physiological and psychological arousal (Bandura, 1997). Efficacy has been supported as one of the strongest predictors of performance at work (Stajkovic & Luthans, 1998a), and in numerous other life domains (Bandura, 1997), making it particularly relevant for our proposed positive holistic model. However, efficacy is also widely recognized to be domain-specific, which arguably may have prohibited conceptual and empirical efforts exploring its cross-context transfer.

We argue that the contributions of human agency to positivity and PsyCap go far beyond the recognized impact of domain-specific efficacy, which has received the most attention in research and practice. The development of self-efficacy has been successfully accomplished in numerous domains with significant performance outcomes (see Chapter 2 of Luthans, Youssef, et al., 2007, for a comprehensive review). However, this domain-specific approach to understanding and developing efficacy may not have captured the full impact of the agentic mechanisms developed and utilized in the process of repeatedly and simultaneously building efficacy across different life domains. This is an example of approaching a very positive construct (efficacy) from a "deficit" perspective. While an efficacious person is likely to be motivated to pursue more challenging goals within the same context, the mechanisms through which efficacy translates into agency to pursue new and unfamiliar goals in different contexts remain unclear. This leaves the otherwise efficacious person in the odd condition of lacking in efficacy whenever exposed to a new context. Without efficacy, the agentic pursuit of new challenges comes to a halt. This, of course, hinders subsequent successful mastery experiences, one of the primary ways to build efficacy. This disconnect in the literature is rather surprising, considering that earlier theory building on efficacy conceptualized it in terms of three dimensions: magnitude, strength, and generality. Thus, this leaves open the possibility that efficacy may be transferrable across life domains.

We propose that a broader perspective on agency as an underlying mechanism for positivity and PsyCap can help resolve this seeming dilemma. We argue that as the efficacy development process is simulta-neously activated in multiple domains, and as efficacy incrementally increases with the successful pursuit of more challenging goals in these domains, a higher-order sense of overall agentic control also builds up toward a threshold that can trigger increase in efficacy and interactions across domains. In other words, increasing levels of efficacy in multiple domains may reach a tipping point. Before that tipping point, building domain-specific efficacy will be primarily related to positive outcomes in that particular domain, but may be unrelated to, or even lead to negative outcomes in other domains. For example, drawing from established neurological research (e.g., Miller & Cohen, 2001), it is understandable that when an unfamiliar task is pursued, building efficacy may consume a significant amount of attention, energy, and resources, until a reasonable level of mastery is achieved. This may even come at the expense of other life domains, which may be viewed as distractions.

However, we argue that human agency can help determine and control the standards of what is perceived as "reasonable" (e.g., through symbolizing and observation), allocate adequate resources to the pursuit of those standards (e.g., through self-regulation), and consciously anticipate and monitor performance in other life domains (e.g., through forethought and self-reflection). These social cognitive processes can act as checks and balances that help prevent efficacy building in one life domain from becoming an uncontrollable obsession. As the threshold or tipping point is determined to have been achieved, emphasis is likely to agentically shift back to a more holistic perspective of optimizing across domains for higher overall positivity and PsyCap. Various life domains can then be agentically allied toward enriching, rather than competing with each other (Greenhaus & Powell, 2006).

At this point, we want to emphasize that our purpose is not to critique SCT and efficacy theories. On the contrary, we uphold them as foundational to our framework. Our goal is to simply reemphasize the basic tenets of these theories, which seem to have been too often obscured by narrow applications in empirical research.

AGENCY ACROSS LIFE DOMAINS

Once again, the model proposes reciprocal causal relationships across life domains. Several specific agentic mechanisms can trigger the direction and intensity of these linkages. First, we argue that a higher-order sense of overall agency and control is built based on the number of simultaneous domains being efficaciously pursued and the progress being made in these domains. The emphasis here is on optimization and the synergies realized as a tipping point is achieved in relation to efficacy in each domain. Each domain is influenced by the others, not just additively but in conjunction.

For example, individuals are more likely to perceive themselves to be "in control" of their life and destiny when faced with a challenge in one life domain if the majority of the other life domains seem to be "in order" or progressing at a desirable rate than if extremely successful in one domain to the detriment of others.

Second, the life domains with the highest efficacy levels will likely act as the drivers and catalysts for other domains, rather than obsessions that may compromise development in these domains. Third, the domains with high efficacy do not become the center of attention and focus, but rather the safety net or safe haven that can provide much-needed recharging of energy and resources, and the cushion or buffer that can absorb stress and strain. Drawing again from Fredrickson's (2003) broaden-and-build model, the positive emotions associated with agentic processing in high-efficacy domains can become a source of psychological resources to draw from in order to develop agency to pursue efficacy development in other domains. Thus, the direction of causality triggered by agency as an underlying mechanism within a holistic framework of positivity is likely to flow from the domains with the highest efficacy levels to those with lower efficacy, through additive, compensatory (buffering), and interactive mechanisms.

Similar propositions can be made for the other three constituents of PsyCap, namely hope, resiliency, and optimism, as well as PsyCap in general as a multidimensional construct. For example, hope's agentic component of willpower can help mobilize the determination and motivation for complex, balanced, multi-domain goal pursuit, while its pathway or waypower component can facilitate the development and optimization of new or unexplored paths toward blocked goals. Resiliency's bouncing back capacity can facilitate growth and learning in the face of adversity and crossing the thresholds that can lead to cross-domain positivity. Optimism can help create more positive appraisals of circumstances, which can facilitate agentic thinking. These connections are emerging areas of research that can yield a better understanding of human agency toward a more holistic model of positivity and PsyCap.

MECHANISM #2: HUMAN MALLEABILITY

While the first mechanism highlights the integral role that human agency and intentions play in motivating and executing the behavioral, cognitive, and volitional processes necessary for increased positivity and PsyCap across life domains, it is important to note that human agency alone is largely limited by an individual's existing capabilities and resources. However, fortunately, human capabilities and psychological resources are not necessarily static. Specifically, research supports that about half of the variance in happiness and life satisfaction (i.e., positivity, broadly defined) is relatively set for adults. Importantly, and counter to conventional wisdom, only about 10 percent is determined by situational circumstances, but 40 percent is still open to change through intentional activity (for empirical support of these percentages see Lyubomirsky, Sheldon, et al., 2005). Thus, in this second mechanism we build out from the existing literature that distinguishes between fixed and developable capacities in adults and make the case for the role that human malleability plays in positivity and PsyCap.

TRAIT–STATE CONTINUUM

In the positive organizational behavior literature, stable traits and changing states have been presented on a conceptual continuum (Luthans & Youssef, 2007). One of the continuum extremes includes genetically determined or so-called hard-wired "pure" traits (e.g., intelligence, inherited characteristics). The opposite extreme includes continuously changing, or sometimes even unpredictable "pure" states (e.g., moods or fleeting emotions). Between those two extremes, "trait-like" characteristics tend to be relatively stable over time but may show some small incremental changes over one's lifespan. Thus, these are located closer to the "pure" traits end of the continuum. "State-like" characteristics, on the other hand, such as the now widely recognized positive core construct of PsyCap and its constituent psychological resources of efficacy, hope, optimism, and resilience (see Luthans, Avolio et al., 2007; Luthans, Youssef et al., 2007), have been empirically demonstrated to be open to agentic development and management through relatively short experimental training interventions (e.g., see Luthans, Avey, Avolio, & Peterson, 2010; Luthans, Avey, & Patera, 2008). In addition, "state-like" PsyCap has been empirically shown to fall between emotional states on the "pure state" and core self-evaluations and personality traits on the "trait-like" portion of the continuum (Luthans, Avolio, et al., 2007). Within-individual PsyCap change over time has also been demonstrated in a recent longitudinal study (Peterson et al., 2011).

Further support for these trait–state continuum distinctions can also be found in the extant organizational behavior literature. For example, Chaplin, John, and Goldberg (1988) found that people do not view traits and states as abstract social concepts, but as prototype-based categories that have a graded internal structure and fuzzy boundaries, defined by ideal (or extreme) attribute values. On one extreme, prototypical traits are stable, long-lasting, and internally caused, and on the opposite extreme, prototypical states are temporary, brief, and caused by external circumstances.

Empirically, traits and trait-like characteristics have also been shown to correlate differently than states and state-like capacities to other variables, and less directly to various outcomes (e.g., Chen, Whiteman, Gully, & Kilcullen, 2000). Zuckerman (1983) offered three helpful criteria in making the distinction when measuring traits and states: (a) both show high internal consistency, but states show lower (but still significant) retest reliability, (b) state measures correlate more highly with other state measures than with trait measures and vice versa (showing convergent and divergent validity between traits and states), and (c) trait test scores before and after relevant changes in arousal levels show no change, but state test scores do change. Also, as a guideline for the distinction between traits and states, Wright (1997) proposed that stability over six months can be considered supportive of the trait-like nature of a construct.

MALLEABILITY ACROSS LIFE DOMAINS

We propose that human malleability triggers reciprocal causal relationships across life domains toward overall positivity through several specific mechanisms. First, human malleability is about change. Although change can be positive, it poses a paradox in that change tends to be more strongly stimulated by negativity. While as described earlier positive heliotropic tendencies continuously promote positivity, negativity tends to send more intense signals of maladaptation and urgency for change. If negativity is allowed to prevail, the resultant change can be characterized by narrowness and rigidity. This excessive negativity can result in either passive responses such as cynicism and apathy, or active but destructive reactions such as aggression and rebellion. On the other hand, if only positive stimuli are considered, valuable negative information may be ignored or discounted, and meaningful, productive change may give way to Pollyannaish hedonism. Positive growth requires balancing the positive and the negative (Baumeister et al., 2001; Cameron, 2008). For example, resilience requires both the exposure to threats or risk factors and a positive reaction to these factors (Norman, Luthans, & Luthans, 2005).

We argue that this dynamic balance between the positive and negative is more likely to result from optimizing across a broader range of life domains than from focusing on one highly positive or one highly negative domain. As discussed earlier in the context of agency, the sole focus on one highly positive domain can become obsessive and detrimental to success in other domains and overall optimal functioning. Research also supports a within-domain tendency to invest more time, affect, and cognitive energy in the negative than the positive aspects of a domain. For example, threatening personal relationships tend to receive more thought time than supportive ones, and blocked personal goals get more thought time than open and available options (Klinger, Barta, & Maxeiner, 1980). Since negativity tends to be characterized by singularity (one negative characteristic renders a whole system dysfunctional; Cameron, 2008), it follows that when intense negative stimuli exist in a domain of life, they are likely to prevail, causing that whole domain to be perceived in a negative light.

On the other hand, a holistic perspective that incorporates various life domains allows positive aspects of a domain to support weaknesses and vulnerabilities in another through providing valuable resources. For example, resources such as social support may help overcome the challenges of a demanding job (Schaufeli & Bakker, 2004). This social support is a critical resource that can be drawn from strong relationships, which can be professional, social, or personal. Not only can physical, social, and psychological resources buffer the stress and strain of a highly demanding job, but they can also be conducive to higher engagement and commitment through mechanisms that are clearly distinct from those leading to burnout and negativity (Bakker & Schaufeli, 2008). Importantly, the integrative process of dynamically (malleably) allocating resources from predominantly positive life domains to meet the demands of more negative ones can yield the positivity ratios or tipping points discussed earlier (Fredrickson & Losada, 2005; Gottman, 1994; Losada & Heaphy, 2004). This in turn leads to higher overall positivity that may not be achievable through compartmentalization and single-domain emphasis.

Successful development and growth (malleability) in one domain can also provide informative feedback on the extent of stability and malleability of one's various abilities and resources, which can then be adapted toward more targeted change in other domains. Thus, the direction of causality triggered by malleability as an underlying mechanism within a holistic framework of positivity will likely flow from the domains and contexts with more informative content and feedback about one's flexibility, adaptability, and growth potential, to those that are relatively novel or yet to be explored. However, unlike agentic mechanisms where we have proposed the direction of causality to flow from domains with the highest efficacy levels, in malleability mechanisms the informative content and feedback need not be highly positive, but rather balanced. As explained earlier, highly positive or highly negative content may hinder change or limit its effectiveness. A balance of positive and negative information allows for the strategic allocation of energy and resources toward developing state-like characteristics that offer a reasonable level of malleability to facilitate positive change.

MECHANISM #3: HUMAN SOCIABILITY

Social psychology was originally defined as "the psychic planes and currents that come into association" (Ross, 1909, p. 409). This individual in association can take multiple forms such as socialization, social comparisons, and other forms of inter-individual cognitive uniformities. While human agency and malleability go hand in hand in integrating the willingness and ability to grow and develop, self-reliance may not be the answer to every one of life's opportunities and challenges. As social beings, humans have the desire and the ability to mobilize resources from their social context toward the pursuit of personal and social goals. This may occur in the absence of some critical personal resources, or when these resources are not malleable to development and management. Interaction with others can also yield significant synergies as personal resources are pooled toward the pursuit of symbiotic goals. Furthermore, human agency can also be triggered through social interactions, such as through vicarious learning, persuasion, and social support (Bandura, 1997).

SOCIAL CHARACTERISTICS

Several social characteristics are particularly relevant for positivity. The first, and most basic, is that people are universally and innately driven by a strong need for belongingness (Maslow, 1962), or what we refer to as "sociability for its own sake." Basic needs, such as belongingness, derive their motivational power from being irreducible to other needs, motives, or drives. They encompass cognitive as well as affective components, and are instrumental in eliciting goal-directed behavior toward their satisfaction. They are also consequential in terms of long-term behavioral, psychological, and health outcomes (Baumeister & Leary, 1995). Thus, the direction of causality will likely consistently flow from the domain of relationships to other life domains, with positive relationships with others triggering overall higher positivity (Diener & Seligman, 2002) that can in turn influence productivity at work and better health.

Second, human sociability is critical for the creation, reinforcement, and adaptation of identity, or what we refer to as "sociability as a vehicle of self-discovery" (i.e., the procedural value of sociability). Feedback from others, both directly or through perceived approval and affirmation (or even occasional rejection or exclusion), can increase self-awareness and create a context for self-discovery. Internalizing feedback can also shape and enrich who we are through the following: (a) enhancing self-efficacy; (b) promoting stronger agency and self-regulation in order to meet others' high expectations; and (c) providing a secure base for human malleability to facilitate identity change and growth (Roberts, 2007). Thus, linkages with the mechanisms of human agency and human malleability cannot be overlooked. While human sociability is directly tied to relationships, within this particular characteristic, sociability becomes most significant in the life domains where identity is being most actively constructed and developed. For example, an unfamiliar context such as a new job may mobilize sociability mechanisms toward the construction of a new work identity.

Third, human sociability is vital for the creation of social capital. Social capital refers to the resources built, expanded, or utilized through networks of relationships, including financial, human, and PsyCap (Adler & Kwon, 2002; Luthans & Youssef, 2004). We refer to this social capital as "sociability as means-to-an-end" (i.e., the instrumental value of sociability). Social capital can expand one's resource-producing capacities, facilitate goal achievement in various life domains, and promote overall positivity (Baker & Dutton, 2007). For example, there is an extensive body of literature associating social support with a wide range of positive health (Cohen, 2004) and work performance outcomes (Glaser, Tatum, Nebeker, Sorenson, & Aiello 1999), through the process of providing the necessary resources to buffer stress. On the other hand, negative interactions or loneliness have been shown to induce stressors that can drain one's available physical and psychological resources (Cacioppo et al., 2002).

While social capital is conceptually linked to relationships, it is the potency of these networks of relationships that contribute to resource creation, rather than just the number and depth of the relationships. This resource creation is what makes human sociability particularly relevant for positivity. For example, weak ties (Granovetter, 1973) have been found to positively relate to employment, career advancement, and new knowledge transfer (Inkpen & Tsang, 2005). It follows that within this particular mechanism, the direction of causality will flow from life domains with the highest potential for social capital creation to those with lower potential. A classic example would be when a casual acquaintance with the right contacts is approached to facilitate getting a good job or a promotion.

Finally, positivity is socially grounded. That is, it is a dynamically, incrementally, and collaboratively defined phenomenon. Positivity is not an individualistic, static, absolute concept (Duck, 2007). It is what could be referred to as "sociability as environmental dynamism" (i.e., the contextual value of sociability). What is considered positive in some cultures may be considered negative in others (Fineman, 2006), and that in turn may depend on the time, place, or other situational characteristics of such consideration. In other words, human sociability, and consequently positivity as a socially embedded concept, should be viewed as an open-ended enterprise, a work-in-progress, or "unfinished business," rather than as a final state.

SOCIABILITY ACROSS LIFE DOMAINS

Human sociability can trigger the proposed reciprocal causal relationships in positivity across life domains through mechanisms that can be analogous to diffusion and osmosis in the physical sciences. Underlying human sociability is the assumption that people are willing to be in positions of vulnerability and dependence on others, especially where their agency and malleability may be in question. This openness or vulnerability can be compared to a permeable surface that allows for two-way exchanges. In the physical sciences, it is recognized that the higher the gradient differential across mediums, the more exchanges are likely to take place. This causes more pronounced changes in both mediums, until they exhibit similar characteristics or concentrations.

Similarly, life domains with the highest "gradient differentials" in positivity may trigger a positivity cycle where PsyCap can be developed and nurtured across domains. For example, starting a new job in a highly positive work environment may facilitate positive changes in health and relationships for an individual who has suffered from working in an excessively negative workplace in the past. Similarly, starting a relationship with a positive individual can change the outlook of a negative person about life in general, including work and health. On the other hand, even if the "gradient" is small or nonexistent, passive diffusion (back and forth motion of molecules) will still take place. However, the transfer would be comparable to the recognized spillover (Judge & Ilies, 2004) or emotional contagion effects (Barsade, 2002), which to date have not conceptualized or empirically tested the potential effects of those "gradient differentials." This is another example of the need to recognize thresholds and tipping points within a framework of dynamic equilibrium in our holistic model of positivity.

Highly positive encounters, relative to oneself, are proposed to make the strongest impact in terms of triggering the positivity cycle across life domains. Therefore, it follows that highly negative encounters in one domain can also trigger a negative spiral across life domains. We argue that this potential negative impact is also necessary to restore balance and allow positivity to remain grounded in reality (i.e., Fredrickson's mast and keel metaphors). The dynamic exchange across "gradient differentials" protects both "mediums" from extreme, Pollyannaish positivity or excessive, dysfunctional negativity. It can result in a dynamic equilibrium where exchanges continue to take place while keeping extreme positivity and negativity in check. This is another example of the importance of balance and optimization, rather than maximization, in conceptualizing overall positivity.

However, positivity is not only facilitated by passive exchanges across "gradient differentials." Human agency and malleability mechanisms are also in place to allow for "selective permeability" (also recognized in the physical sciences). This is where individual volition, choices, and ability to adapt and change can selectively manage and control exchanges so that they are not detrimental for performance or well-being in one or more domains or for overall positivity and PsyCap. This capacity for change may explain occasions where experiencing setbacks or catastrophic events in one life domain, or observing others' misfortunes, may simultaneously trigger spontaneous negative reactions such as anger or sadness, as well as more intentional positive reactions, such as gratitude, compassion, empathy, and helping behavior.

A FINAL WORD

In conclusion, in order to contribute to a needed conceptual foundation and better understanding of positivity in general and PsyCap in particular, we have proposed and supported a positive holistic model. The underlying mechanisms of human agency, malleability, and sociability are identified as helping to explain the role that positivity and PsyCap plays in the dynamic, reciprocal interaction between work, relationships, and health toward optimal life functioning. With this chapter we hope to make a contribution toward a comprehensive theory of positivity and PsyCap in and beyond the workplace.

REFERENCES

Adler, P. S., & Kwon, S. (2002). Social capital: Prospects for a new concept. *Academy of Management Review, 27*, 17–40.

Avey, J. B., Luthans, F., & Youssef, C. M. (2010). The additive value of positive psychological capital in predicting attitudes and behaviors. *Journal of Management, 36*, 430–452.

Avey, J. B., Reichard, R., Luthans, F., & Mhatre, K. (2011). Meta-analysis of the impact of positive psychological capital on employee attitudes, behaviors and performance. *Human Resource Development Quarterly, 22*, 127–152.

Baker, W., & Dutton, J. E. (2007). Enabling positive social capital in organizations. In J. Dutton & B. R. Ragins (Eds.), *Exploring positive relationships at work* (pp. 325–345). New York, NY: Lawrence Erlbaum.

Bakker, A. B., & Schaufeli, W. B. (2008). Contexts of positive organizational behavior. *Journal of Organizational Behavior, 29*, 147–261.

Bandura, A. (1997). *Self-efficacy: The exercise of control.* New York, NY: Freeman.

Bandura, A. (2008). An agentic perspective on positive psychology. In S. J. Lopez (Ed.), *Positive psychology: Exploring the best in people* (pp. 167–196). Westport, CT: Greenwood.

Barsade, S. G. (2002). The ripple effect: Emotional contagion and its influence on group behavior. *Administrative Science Quarterly, 47*, 644–675.

Baumeister, R. F., Bratslavsky, E., Finkenauer, C., & Vohs, K. D. (2001). Bad is stronger than good. *Review of General Psychology, 5*, 323–370.

Baumeister, R. F., & Leary, M. R. (1995). The need to belong: Desire for interpersonal attachments as a fundamental human motivation. *Psychological Bulletin, 117*, 497–529.

Cacioppo, J. T., Hawkley, L. C., Crawford, E., Ernst, J. M., Burleson, M. H., Kowalewski, R. B., et al. (2002). Loneliness and health: Potential mechanisms. *Psychosomatic Medicine, 64*, 407–417.

Cameron, K. S. (2008). Paradox in positive positive organizational change. *Journal of Applied Behavioral Science, 44*, 7–24.

Cameron, K. S., & Caza, A. (2004). Contributions to the discipline of positive organizational scholarship. *American Behavioral Scientist, 47*, 731–739.

Chaplin, W. F., John, O. P., & Goldberg, L. R. (1988). Conceptions of states and traits: Dimensional attributes with ideals as prototypes. *Journal of Personality and Social Psychology, 54*, 541–557.

Chen, G., Whiteman, J. A., Gully, S. M., & Kilcullen, R. N. (2000). Examination of relationships among trait-like individual differences, state-like individual differences, and learning performance. *Journal of Applied Psychology, 85*, 835–847.

Cohen, S. (2004). Social relationships and health. *American Psychologist, 59*, 676–684.

Demerouti, E. (2012). The spillover and crossover of resources among partners: The role of work–self and family–self facilitation. *Journal of Occupational Health Psychology, 17*, 184–195.

Diener, E., Ng, W., & Tov, W. (2009). Balance in life and declining marginal utility of diverse resources. *Applied Research in Quality of Life, 3*, 277–291.

Diener, E., & Seligman, M. E. (2002). Very happy people. *Psychological Science, 13*, 81–84.

Duck, S. W. (2007). Finding connections at the individual/dyadic level. In J. Dutton & B. R. Ragins (Eds.), *Exploring positive relationships at work* (pp. 179–186). New York, NY: Lawrence Erlbaum.

Fineman, S. (2006). On being positive: Concerns and counterpoints. *Academy of Management Review, 31*, 270–291.

Fredrickson, B. L. (2003). Positive emotions and upward spirals in organizations. In K. S. Cameron, J. E. Dutton & R. E. Quinn (Eds.), *Positive organizational scholarship* (pp. 63–175). San Francisco, CA: Berrett-Koehler.

Fredrickson, B. L., & Losada, M. F. (2005). Positive affect and the complex dynamics of human flourishing. *American Psychologist, 60*, 678–686.

Glaser, D. N., Tatum, B. C., Nebeker, D. M., Sorenson, R. C., & Aiello, J. R. (1999). Workload and social support: Effects on performance and stress. *Human Performance, 12*, 155–176.

Gottman, J. M. (1994). *What predicts divorce?* Hillsdale, NJ: Erlbaum.

Granovetter, M. S. (1973). The strength of weak ties. *American Journal of Sociology, 78*, 1360–1380.

Greenhaus, J. H., & Powell, G. N. (2006). When work and families are allies: A theory of work-family enrichment. *Academy of Management Review, 31*, 72–92.

Hilgard, E. R. (1980). The trilogy of mind: Cognition, affection, and conation. *Journal of the History of the Behavioral Sciences, 16*, 107–117.

Inkpen, A. C., & Tsang, E. W. K. (2005). Social capital, networks, and knowledge transfer. *Academy of Management Review, 30*, 146–165.

Judge, T. A., & Ilies, R. (2004). Affect and job satisfaction: A study of their relationship at work and at home. *Journal of Applied Psychology, 89*, 661–673.

Keyes, C. (2002). The mental health continuum: From languishing to flourishing in life. *Journal of Health and Social Behavior, 43*, 207–222.

Klinger, E., Barta, S. G., & Maxeiner, M. E. (1980). Motivational correlated through content frequency and commitment. *Journal of Personality and Social Psychology, 39*, 1222–1237.

Losada, M. F., & Heaphy, E. (2004). The role of positivity and connectivity in the performance of business teams. *American Behavioral Scientist, 47*, 740–765.

Luthans, F. (2002). The need for and meaning of positive organizational behavior. *Journal of Organizational Behavior, 23*, 695–706.

Luthans, F., Avey, J. B., Avolio, B. J., & Peterson, S. J. (2010). The development and resulting performance impact of positive psychological capital. *Human Resource Development Quarterly, 21*, 41–67.

Luthans, F., Avey, J. B., & Patera, J. L. (2008). Experimental analysis of a web-based training intervention to develop positive psychological capital. *Academy of Management Learning and Education, 7*, 209–221.

Luthans, F., Avolio, B. J., Avey, J. B, & Norman, S. M. (2007). Psychological capital: Measurement and relationship with performance and satisfaction. *Personnel Psychology, 60*, 541–572.

Luthans, F., & Youssef, C. M. (2004). Human, social, and now positive psychological capital management. *Organizational Dynamics, 33*, 143–160.

Luthans, F., & Youssef, C. M. (2007). Emerging positive organizational behavior. *Journal of Management, 33*, 321–349.

Luthans, F., Youssef, C. M., & Avolio, B. J. (2007). *Psychological capital: Developing the human competitive edge.* Oxford, UK: Oxford University Press.

Lyubomirsky, S., King, L., & Diener, E. (2005). The benefits of frequent positive affect: Does happiness lead to success? *Psychological Bulletin, 131*, 803–855.

Lyubomirsky, S., Sheldon, K. M., & Schkade, D. (2005). Pursuing happiness: The architecture of sustainable change. *Review of General Psychology, 9*, 111–131.

Maslow, A. (1962). *Toward a psychology of being*. Princeton, NJ: Van Nostrand.

Miller, E. K., & Cohen, J. D. (2001). An integrative theory of prefrontal cortex function. *Annual Review of Neuroscience, 24,* 167–202.

Norman, S., Luthans, B., & Luthans, K. (2005). The proposed contagion effect of hopeful leaders on the resiliency of employees and organizations. *Journal of Leadership and Organizational Studies, 12,* 55–64.

Oishi, S., Diener, E., & Lucas, R. (2007). The optimum level of well-being: Can people be too happy? *Perspectives on Psychological Science, 2,* 346–360.

Oloffson, K. (2009, December 8). The job market: Is a college degree worth less? *Time*. Retrieved from http://www.time.com/time/business/article/0,8599,1946088,00.html#ixz z1E37BMJDk

Peterson, C., & Chang, E. (2002). Optimism and flourishing. In C. Keyes & J. Haidt (Eds.), *Flourishing: Positive psychology and the life well-lived* (pp. 55–79). Washington, DC: American Psychological Association.

Peterson, C., & Seligman, M. (2004). *Character strengths and virtues: A handbook and classification*. New York, NY: Oxford University Press.

Peterson, S. J., Luthans, F., Avolio, B. J., Walumbwa, F. O., & Zhang, Z. (2011). Psychological capital and employee performance: A latent growth modeling approach. *Personnel Psychology, 64,* 427–450.

Roberts, L. M. (2007). From proving to becoming: How positive relationships create a context for self-discovery and self-actualization. In J. Dutton & B. R. Ragins (Eds.), *Exploring positive relationships at work* (pp. 29–45). New York, NY: Lawrence Erlbaum.

Ross, E. A. (1909). Discussion: What is social psychology? *Psychological Bulletin, 6,* 409–411.

Salanova, M., Bakker, A. B., & Llorens, S. (2006). Flow at work: Evidence for an upward spiral of personal and organizational resources. *Journal of Happiness Studies, 7,* 1–22.

Schaufeli, W. B., & Bakker, A. B. (2004). Job demands, job resources, and their relationship with burnout and engagement: A multi-sample study. *Journal of Organizational Behavior, 25,* 293–315.

Seligman, M. E. P. (1998). *Learned optimism*. New York, NY: Pocket Books.

Seligman, M. E. P., & Csikszentmihalyi, M. (2000). Positive psychology. *American Psychologist, 55,* 5–14.

Spreitzer, G., & Sonenshein, S. (2003). Positive deviance and extraordinary organization. In K. Cameron, J. K. Dutton & R. Quinn (Eds.), *Positive organizational scholarship* (pp. 207–224). San Francisco, CA: Berrett Koehler.

Stajkovic, A. D., & Luthans, F. (1998a). Self-efficacy and work-related performance: A meta-analysis. *Psychological Bulletin, 124,* 240–261.

Stajkovic, A. D., & Luthans, F. (1998b). Social cognitive theory and self-efficacy. *Organizational Dynamics, 26,* 62–74.

Walter, F., & Bruch, H. (2008). The positive group affect spiral: A dynamic model of the emergence of positive affective similarity in work groups. *Journal of Organizational Behavior, 29,* 239–261.

Wright, T. A. (1997). Time revisited in organizational behavior. *Journal of Organizational Behavior, 18,* 201–204.

Wright, T. A., & Quick, J. C. (2009). Special issue: The emerging positive agenda. *Journal of Organizational Behavior, 30,* 147–336.

Zuckerman, M. (1983). The distinction between trait and state scales is not arbitrary: Comment on Allen and Potkay's "On the arbitrary distinction between traits and states." *Journal of Personality and Social Psychology, 44,* 1083–1086.

TOWARD A MORE CONTEXTUAL, PSYCHOLOGICAL, AND DYNAMIC MODEL OF EMOTIONAL INTELLIGENCE

Oscar Ybarra, Ethan Kross, David Seungjae Lee, Yufang Zhao, Adrienne Dougherty and Jeffrey Sanchez-Burks

Our world is a quantifiable one, and so are people. Assigning numbers to behavioral and cognitive phenomena allows for relationships to be tested, categorizations to be made, and predictions about what people are likely to do. However, scores about people can be misapplied. Imagine an organization that is interested in revamping its culture by emphasizing communication and cooperation across boundaries and in general making the tenor of the interactions among personnel more positive. One key to helping with this may be to focus on employee emotional intelligence (EI), provide assessments of these capacities, and educate where gaps seem apparent. Maybe some employees are having difficulty recognizing their emotions or those of others, which can create problems in social interaction, while others' difficulties stem from challenges to controlling frustrations at work. Depending on the size of the organization, this could be a very involved and

Advances in Positive Organizational Psychology, Volume 1, 167–187
ISSN: 2046-410X/doi:10.1108/S2046-410X(2013)0000001010

costly undertaking. The hope is that the culture will be improved, along with the organizations' efficiency and performance.

But what if the predictive validity of EI tests was minimal? This is a valid concern, especially with recent meta-analyses indicating that when cognitive ability and personality measures are controlled for, the relationship between EI measures and a variety of consequential outcomes, such as work outcomes, academic outcomes, and life outcomes, is remarkably small (O'Boyle, Humphrey, Pollack, Hawver, & Story, 2011; Van Rooy & Viswesvaran, 2004).[1] Such evidence contradicts popular notions surrounding the promise and "big idea" behind EI, in which it was claimed that EI can matter more than IQ in life success (Goleman, 1995). The evidence also does not align with more recent claims from researchers. For example, Cherniss (2010, p. 184) noted that, "This big idea is that success in work and life depends on more than just the basic cognitive abilities typically measured by IQ tests and related measures; it also depends on a number of personal qualities that involve the perception, understanding, and regulation of emotion."

With such concerns regarding the predictive validity of EI, organizational decision makers might not bother following through with the assessments they had planned to help overhaul their organization's culture. However, as researchers, our concern is a different one, and that is to consider ways to increase the predictive value of EI. In this chapter, we offer a set of suggestions for how to refine the way EI is conceptualized to enhance its predictive utility. We aim to do this by creating a synthesis based on two principles:

- *Principle 1*: A useful model of EI needs to delineate the nature and influence of the social context in order to understand *when* and *why* people apply their EI skills.
- *Principle 2*: A useful model of EI needs to integrate fundamental conceptions of *how* the mind works – namely, by defining the interaction between intuitive (automatic) and deliberative (controlled) mental processes – to fully capture the psychology of EI and the flexibility with which people make sense of their social worlds and are influenced by it.

We begin by reviewing briefly the diverse approaches to conceptualizing EI. We then elaborate the two principles of our EI model and discuss their implications for theory, research, and practice.

CONCEPTUALIZING AND ASSESSING EMOTIONAL INTELLIGENCE

Researchers have undertaken many approaches to conceptualizing and assessing EI. Some approaches combine self-reported EI with broader personality constructs. Other approaches are based on so-called ability measures of EI, whether as tendencies people can self-report (Tett, Fox, & Wang, 2005) or as assessments developed to measure specific components of EI (e.g., Nowicki & Duke, 1994). We briefly survey the literature to arrive at a working understanding of what EI is currently thought to be (for more extensive reviews, see Mayer, Roberts, & Barsade, 2008; Zeidner, Matthews, Roberts, 2009).

Mixed Models

So-called mixed models, in addition to assessing qualities that appear related to EI abilities, also consider factors participants self-report on, such as their motives, self-assessments, and coping tendencies. Examples include the Emotional Quotient Inventory (EQ-i; Bar-On, 1997), the Self-Report Emotional Intelligence Test (SREIT; Schutte et al., 1998), and the Multidimensional Emotional Intelligence Assessment (MEIA; Tett et al., 2005). Because mixed approaches overlap with other personality traits and assess self-judgments rather than "abilities," it has been suggested that they do not provide real assessments of EI (Mayer et al., 2008). For example, studies have reported correlations above .70 between the EQ-i and the Big Five personality scales (e.g., Brackett & Mayer, 2003). However, more recent work appears to embrace such overlap and suggests this is consistent with the view that the General Factor of Personality is equal to trait EI (e.g., Linden et al., 2012).

Ability Models

In contrast to mixed models, ability models focus on single abilities, such as how people reason about emotions (e.g., Roseman, 1984) or how emotions influence thought (e.g., Frijda, 1988; Isen, Johnson, Mertz, & Robinson, 1985). Other potential abilities include facial recognition, emotion perception and recognition (Banziger, Grandjean, & Scherer, 2009; Ekman & Friesen, 1975;

Matsumoto et al., 2000; Nowicki & Duke, 1994; O'Sullivan, 1982; Sanchez-Burks & Huy, 2009), and emotion management (e.g., Freudenthaler & Neubauer, 2007; Gross, 1998; Kross, Ayduk, & Mischel, 2005). The interest in distinct abilities seems to be based in part on their separate historical and intellectual traditions. For example, research on emotion management is closely tied to impulse control and coping (e.g., Lazarus, 1994) and is rooted in part in the clinical tradition (e.g., Ellis, 2001).

Integrative Models

Finally, some models bring together separate abilities thought to be related to EI. The main integrative model is the four-branch model, which deals with people's ability to recognize emotions in self and others, use emotion to influence thought, understand emotions, and manage emotions (Mayer & Salovey, 1997; Mayer et al., 1997). Some researchers, though, consider the abilities contained within this model to be a little arbitrary, as it is unclear what criteria beyond the researchers' judgment is used to include some abilities over others (Roberts, Matthews, & Zeidner, 2010).

RECONCEPTUALIZING EMOTIONAL INTELLIGENCE

Given the many approaches to studying EI, it is challenging to understand what EI actually is. Such a lack of conceptual coherence promotes confusion among researchers and potential misunderstandings by the public. This does not, however, imply that EI is of no use. Current research and conceptions provide important early steps in the study of EI. Our aim is to elaborate these steps and provide a framework to help guide theoretical development and research on EI. One aspect of our approach is to consider the social context in which EI-related tools are applied (Principle 1). An explicit focus on social context can ground the concept and study of EI. The second element of our approach is to take seriously the notion that EI involves a set of mental processes, not just a score a person is given on an EI test. By delving deeper into the psychology of EI and relating it to widely accepted dual-process models (Principle 2), we delineate a conception of EI that is more dynamic and flexible. The model thus embraces the reality that people's behaviors and decisions are bound to context as much as the person's characteristics. The present conception also may help explain why individuals thought to be high on EI can enact ineffective behavior in some situations – which no current model of EI can do. We turn to the two principles of our framework next.

Principle 1: Social Context Matters

Implied in many discussions of EI is the idea that how people manage aspects of the social environment is important for success. For example, some of the subscales of the EQ-i (Bar-On, 1997) converge onto an inter-personal factor, and many of the ability models deal with emotion recognition in others (e.g., Matsumoto et al., 2000; Nowicki & Duke, 1994) and the ability to manage emotions in others (e.g., Mayer, Salovey, & Caruso, 2002). Popular treatments have also moved beyond the term *emotional intelligence* and refer to *social intelligence* (Goleman, 2006) to make explicit the connection between EI and social and interpersonal processes. Despite these suggestions, current EI conceptions do little to fully explicate the importance of the social context in which people apply their EI toolkit and at times have attempted to distance themselves from earlier formulations that focused on the social realm, such as work on social intelligence (e.g., Mayer, Caruso, & Salovey, 1999; for reviews of some of the early work on social intelligence, see Kihlstrom & Cantor, 1989).

But earnestly focusing on social context broadens the promise of EI, helping it address puzzling questions such as why it is that otherwise emotionally intelligent individuals crumble when faced with temptation, such as President Clinton with Monica Lewinsky. President Clinton won two elections – achievements based in part on the careful navigation of the social and perilous world of US politics. But the Lewinsky debacle resulted from a failure to read the social landscape and control his emotions. Usually, the explanation for such occurrences is based on the so-called "big idea behind EI," that successful people with high IQ's can falter, which leaves room for other abilities such as EI to help explain such shortfalls – meaning they must have been low on EI or some aspect of it (Cherniss, 2010). However, Clinton clearly demonstrated the capacity to be "emotionally intelligent" in other situations. For example, he was adept at negotiating difficult treaties between opposing factions and when interacting with opposing parties in Congress.

Dealing with such discrepancies necessitates greater elaboration of the role of context in EI, and that is why we make the context an explicit element of this analysis. This consideration will make clear that the social world people navigate can shape and constrain a person's EI (for similar arguments in the domain of personality, see Mischel & Shoda, 1995).

Contexts Activate Goals in People that can Impair Emotional Intelligence
People pursue varied goals throughout the day, some chronic and some more short term in nature. A classic study in social psychology highlights how chronic versus short-term goals can conflict in ways that consequentially influence behavior. Darley and Batson (1973) were interested in studying the power of context to influence helping behavior. The participants of their study involved seminary students. In the study, the seminary students had the goal to deliver a talk on either the parable of the Good Samaritan or a non-helping topic. In addition, participants were randomly assigned to a condition in which they either thought they had enough time to get to the hall where they would deliver their talk or a different condition in which they were told they were late. On their way to deliver the talk the students were presented with a powerful contextual event that was directly relevant to their task but also conflicted with the task goal – as they were making their way to give the talk they encountered a man slumped in an alleyway in need of help. So, what did the results show?

The findings were striking and indicated that the seminary students, whether or not they were to give a speech on the Good Samaritan or the non-helping topic, were more likely to help when they were not in a hurry to give their talk. Some hurried students even literally stepped over the person in the alleyway. Here you have a group of people who is undertaking what might be considered intensive EI training, in the sense that they are honing their skills in reading others and being more sympathetic. Half of them were even off to give a talk on helping. But when presented with the opportunity to read a potentially problematic social situation in which a person needs help, many of them faltered because of a pressing goal activated by the context. It is unclear how any available conception of EI would explain such a finding (see Fig. 1 for a standard view of EI and how it is thought to affect outcomes).

Other ironic effects abound when the social context is considered more closely. It is understood by a growing number of researchers that people greatly value and strive for positive social connections. In an extensive review, Trivers' (1971) concluded that people are driven to establish relationships with others, at times even at great cost to the self (also see Baumeister & Leary, 1995). This drive to create social and emotional bonds emerges and asserts itself even in work- and task-related contexts. Research has shown, for example, that when formal groups were put in place to

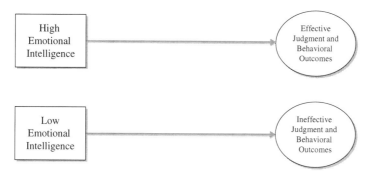

Fig. 1. Standard Model of EI Effects on Outcomes.

perform tasks relevant to organizational goals, informal groups – such as employees from different units gathering to eat lunch – were spontaneously created as a response to people's need for social contact (e.g., Sayles, 1957). More recently, researchers have shown that the social conditions at work predict people's mortality levels (Shirom, Toker, Alkaly, Jacobson, & Balicer, 2011).

However, the power of social goals can also bleed into other judgments and behaviors to create biases. People, for example, are faster to notice information with social versus nonsocial implications (Ybarra, Chan, & Park, 2001), and when getting to know someone, people are biased to ask for information that tells them about the person's social versus work-related qualities (Wojciszke, Bazinska, & Jawoski, 1998). Even while sleeping we tend to think about other people (McNamara, McLaren, Smith, Brown, & Stickgold, 2005), and at times even see social cues where there are none, such as in clouds (Humphrey, 1976). These biases may become elevated when people's need to be socially accepted and connected to others is thwarted, regardless of what their EI capacities might be. In such cases, people tend to focus on information related to fulfilling the need to connect (Gardner, Pickett, & Brewer, 2000), which can limit their ability to take in information relevant to the task at hand and blind them to other aspects of the social environment. Such unfulfilled social needs can also induce negative emotional reactions that impair people's ability to reason (e.g., Baumeister, Twenge, & Nuss, 2002). So, core goals for people – to connect with others and to have positive social relationships – vary by context and the current situation and can put mental blinders on people that can actually result in compromised EI.

The above discussion suggests that a more complete model of EI needs to incorporate information about context, social goals, and potential conflict in activated goals. Such considerations would suggest that the EI process is fluid and at times open to inefficiencies. It suggests that situational factors that pit task versus social goals can create conflict in people and even override outcomes at the core of EI (cf. Sanchez-Burks, 2005). For instance, rather than shelving an emotional reaction in response to a colleague's feedback, a person might carry that experience into the next meeting, which could influence team dynamics and their ability to complete the task at hand. At other times situational forces can make people feel lacking in positive social connections and may lead them to misread social information or, as we will discuss in Principle 2 of our analysis, short-circuit higher-level reasoning processes when such processes are most needed.

Context Influences Target Emotional Displays in Addition to Personal Mental Biases
In addition to not explicitly considering issues of dynamic motivation or the perpetual goal conflicts that comprise social life, current EI models assume that assessments of the social world – given a person has scored high on some measure of EI – are static and valid. It is comforting to assume so, but just as smart people can be foolish for a host of reasons (also see Sternberg, 2002), people who score high on EI may also exhibit socially ineffective behavior for a host of reasons. In addition to being overtaken by situationally triggered goals, another way this can happen is by assuming that the emotions of others can actually be recognized as most EI models assume. Although many models of social and person perception share this bias with EI conceptions – focusing on the perceiver (i.e., the person and their EI level) – social understanding is ultimately the product of perceiver hypotheses but also the actual stimulus that is being perceived.

For example, in complex and mixed-motive environments in which people deal with strangers or competitors, those being perceived many times enact unpredictable behaviors or limit the degree to which they are "readable" (Ybarra et al., 2010). At best, a person high on EI would be expected not to render a judgment of another person in such cases, but no conception or assessment of EI has been created to capture this "skeptical" approach to information presented by others. At worst, the person will inaccurately infer the target's emotions, triggering a cascade of additional assumptions that could potentially lead to a suboptimal way of interacting. Just like people can see faces in clouds, they may see emotional expressions in others that are not there in mixed-motive environments. Ecologically valid models of EI need to incorporate such knowledge of others and the social conditions that are more or less likely to trigger attempts not to be figured out and predicted (e.g., Ybarra et al., 2010).

Certain social environments can also shape the construals people make and inferences they draw. Although various psychological and behavioral processes are in place that prompt people to form social connections with others, people are also attuned to potential interpersonal costs, such as being betrayed by a coworker, overlooked by a boss, or treated with disrespect in front of other employees. This sensitivity to potential costs can create barriers to positive social connections as people have lower thresholds for noticing the bad and drawing negative inferences about others, and higher thresholds for accepting at face value others' positive acts (Ybarra, 2001, 2002; Ybarra, Schaberg, & Keiper, 1999). One implication of this is that contexts that emphasize values related to competitiveness, distrust, and behavioral practices harmful to the "social glue" could trigger less-than-generous and erroneous inferences and thus ineffective EI, due in part to supporting some beliefs over others (e.g., "My colleagues only care about themselves"), but also due to social stress and diminished cognitive resources, as we discuss under Principle 2.

Summary: Principle 1 of our analysis suggests that an explicit exposition of the social context and the situations in which people apply their EI skills is needed to enhance current conceptions of EI. Such considerations help inform the *when* and *why* of EI. We could all be interested in or even immersed in EI training, but if other goals are activated by the context, conflict may occur and our best intentions to understand and problem-solve in social situations can be compromised. Further, even though all people have a need to connect, when such a need is unfulfilled, they may actually exhibit low EI despite having scored high on an EI assessment. A better understanding of the context thus can also help explain *why* people considered emotionally intelligent can be socially ineffective as a function of context – a scenario no current model of EI addresses.

Next, we turn to Principle 2, which highlights the importance of incorporating knowledge concerning the intuitive and deliberate processes that govern how the mind operates to develop a more comprehensive model of EI.

Principle 2: The Mental Processes Involved in Emotional Intelligence

Many times in EI studies participants are asked to judge scenarios or facial stimuli and then describe what they have seen or complete self-report personality-type inventories. At other times participants are presented with hypothetical descriptions of social situations and asked to report how they and the other person in the situation would feel. Communicating and reporting such opinions and feelings are very conscious activities (e.g., Smith & DeCoster, 2000) and they can be cognitively demanding. We refer to this aspect of EI as *deliberate* – individuals consciously use their EI to judge and analyze social and emotional situations or internal reactions. On the other hand, research from other areas has begun to show that processes related to EI can actually be carried out automatically, with little awareness. We refer to this as the *intuitive* aspect of EI, and discuss the deliberate–intuitive distinction presently. As we elaborate in the next section, taking seriously the distinction between deliberate and intuitive processes adds dynamism and context sensitivity to our framework, but it also suggests novel hypotheses and implications.

Two General Abilities and Two Types of Processing for Emotional Intelligence

Although EI instruments assess a variety of so-called abilities, here we focus on two meta-capabilities that are common to many EI models – *emotion recognition* and *emotion control*. We realize that no exhaustive test of EI-related assessments has been conducted. However, the two meta-capabilities of emotion recognition and control can be considered the workhorses of social navigation. Beyond this, our framework also incorporates the two types of information processing discussed above – *intuitive* and *deliberate* processing. What this does is help place our framework in the context of similarly distinctive dual-process models used in various disciplines, including social cognition, cognitive science, reasoning and rationality, personality, behavioral economics, and emotion regulation, for example (e.g., Chaiken & Trope, 1999; Smith & DeCoster, 2000; Stanovich & West, 2000).

Emotion recognition traditionally deals with people's ability to determine in the self and others which emotions are being felt or expressed verbally and nonverbally and is rooted in earlier work on nonverbal sensitivity (e.g., Buck, 1984; Rosenthal, Hall, DiMatteo, Rogers, & Archer, 1979). Emotion control refers to a person's ability to manage moods and emotions in self and others, usually in the service of maintaining or creating positive affective states and eliminating or minimizing negative ones (e.g., Clark & Isen, 1982).

Both emotion recognition and control can operate through a deliberate process. An employee, for example, can consciously focus on what his boss is saying and attend to the boss' facial expressions and gestures to infer what the boss wants done. In terms of emotion control, a unit leader could guide their attention to think differently about the impending downsizing of the unit. This conscious frame switching could help quell personal distress but could also suggest different ways of helping the affected employees.

In the majority of EI models, emotion recognition and control are considered to operate through a deliberate process (Mayer & Salovey, 1997; for an exception, see Fiori, 2009), and research indicates that there are deliberate components to the operation of both of these skills. For example, individuals who suffer from autism spectrum disorder, in order to recognize faces effectively, rely on the deliberate application of rules and knowledge to make inferences about what another person is feeling (e.g., Winkielman, McIntosh, & Oberman, 2009). In terms of emotion control, psychotherapeutic techniques are based on a conscious, controlled approach in which therapists raise awareness in clients about distressing emotions and events and provide them with conscious activities to practice controlling such reactions (Ellis, 2001). In fact, researchers have been able to manipulate the particular deliberate manner in which people approach a negative emotional experience – for instance, whether they immerse themselves or take a step back from it, with findings indicating that the ability to take a step back and consider more information about the social situation helps to buffer against reexperiencing intense negative emotions (Kross & Ayduk, 2011). Deliberate steps taken by a unit leader to distance herself from the distress of impending layoffs, for example, may be effective for managing emotions (for related discussion see Mischel, DeSmet, & Kross, 2006).

Deliberately implemented skills are critical to helping people interact effectively in social contexts, but their use is restricted in part by a person's level of cognitive resources. Fortunately, these skills can also operate *intuitively* through a process that is more immune to one's cognitive resource level (e.g., Smith & DeCoster, 2000). A service provider, for example, might readily notice among a group of jockeying customers one who is smiling and seems friendly, even if they are not aware of why that person captured their attention. With regard to emotion control, a team leader, almost impulsively, could speak up and rally his or her team when the team has suffered a setback and the members are overcome with disappointment.

Recent research has delved deeper into the intuitive operation of EI-related abilities. For example, in terms of emotion recognition, research indicates that people can recognize the valence of faces (positive, negative) even when the faces are presented too fast to engage higher-level cognitive skills (e.g., Clark, Winkielman, & McIntosh, 2008). Recent findings also suggest that some elements of emotion control can occur quite efficiently with little deliberation (for reviews see Bargh & Williams, 2007; Mauss, Bunge, & Gross, 2007). In one study, researchers primed participants with words related to controlling or expressing their emotions, and this was done to activate these emotion-related goals. Participants then filled out a mood questionnaire and were led to experience anger. They then completed a posttest mood questionnaire. The findings indicated participants with the "control" goal expressed less anger at Time 2 than participants for whom the goal of "express" had been activated (Mauss, Cook, and Gross, 2007, Experiment 1). This was the case even though participants were unaware that the goal concepts had been activated. Such findings provide evidence of an efficient, intuitive type of process.

Other work that has documented the operation of efficient, automatic processes comes from research on theory of mind and the understanding of psychological states related to behavior. Understanding emotions in others is intertwined with the perception of others' psychological states. Comparative and developmental approaches to theory of mind have shown that perceivers can immediately grasp the meaning of others' acts or aspects of their mental states without thinking extensively about the available information (e.g., Iacaboni et al., 2005; Qureshi, Apperly, & Samson, 2010).

Although we argue that the operation of EI can occur quite efficiently through intuitive processing, it does not mean this type of processing will always be effective. Its effectiveness depends to a large extent on the veracity of the social and contextual information on which it is based. If the available intuitive process is based on well-crafted habits of mind and prior emotion recognition and control that was adaptive given the prevailing context, then the process can be useful. But if the intuitive processes are not well tuned to past social experience and social reality, they may actually get the person in a lot of trouble. For example, having been part of an overly competitive organizational environment could lead a person to see interpersonal threats at a new job even when there are no threats. Basing final judgments on such initial inferences could then create a host of interpersonal problems. In cases such as these, conscious and deliberate processes are useful in order to unlearn potentially ineffective ways of relating to others, and for controlling and modulating initial assessments of others to correct for inaccurate inferences.

However, because deliberate processing tends to be more controlled and linked to limited cognitive resources, such processing should influence emotion recognition only to the extent that people are not cognitively overloaded or fatigued. Similarly, if people are under time pressure, or if they are not motivated to undertake such deliberate processing (cf. Smith & DeCoster, 2000), emotion recognition (or control) could be compromised – instead of reserving judgment about the emotion being perceived, for instance, an individual might jump to conclusions and judge inaccurately. In another example, the employee lacking sleep and overwhelmed by the tasks piling up on his desk may not have the cognitive resources to discern the boss' intent (assuming he or she has little experience with the boss), which could compromise subsequent performance on the job.

The above discussion suggests that people can be flexible in how they integrate their EI abilities, playing them off each other to arrive at effective assessments of their social surroundings, but this use of deliberate processing to restrain or inform intuitive processes is restricted by the availability of limited cognitive resources. However, EI-related abilities can become efficient and automatized through practice, much like other skills. This bodes well for employees who want to develop their EI. It suggests that, although work or life can be stressful and fatiguing, well practiced skills and abilities can be executed with little need for cognitive resources (Bargh & Chartrand, 1999; Smith & DeCoster, 2000). In order for this to happen, however, people need to put themselves in situations in which they can practice, develop, and apply these abilities.[2]

In sum, Principle 2 contends that two factors influence a person's EI: (a) the availability of cognitive resources and (b) the determination of appropriate individual reactions. Recall that, even though a skill can be executed efficiently does not imply appropriateness, as skills at times may be based on a history of imperfect social understanding and they can be misapplied. In some cases it may thus make sense to more carefully consider or "shelve" these inferences before acting on them. Many times the outcomes of intuitive processes are proposed solutions that need to be monitored for appropriateness given the current context, which requires cognitive resources. The level of individual cognitive resources thus allows for various idiosyncrasies in how people manifest their EI, but so does the degree to which people practice and make more intuitive some EI reactions over others.

MOTIVATION AND THE TWO PRINCIPLES MOVING FORWARD

At different points in discussing Principles 1 and 2 we have highlighted the power of people's goals and motivations to shape EI. Here we consider people's motivation more broadly. In fact, in our conception, it is difficult to separate motivation from the two principles, as the three elements many times interact to produce a wide range of EI-related outcomes. The examples and research we reviewed can be used to highlight these inter-actions, and also, moving forward, suggest ways in which these and other ideas can be tested.

One example has to do with automatic and deliberate processes (Principle 2) related to how people understand psychological states such as theory of mind, which matters when assessing emotions in others. Some of this research has shown that when people perform theory of mind tasks under cognitive load, they can still carry out simple calculations to arrive at some understanding of others (e.g., Qureshi et al., 2010). In day-to-day life, different contexts (Principle 1) could give rise to time pressure or to different motivations, such as not wanting to be in the company of a certain individual or feeling bored at a meeting. The time pressure in the former case and the lack of motivation in the latter could actually reduce cognitive resources and the extent to which people attend to those around them, thus limiting deliberate processing related to EI. This does not mean perceivers in these situations would fail to achieve any understanding, but that emotional understanding is likely to be of a more simple and generic quality, even though a person might have received a high score on some traditional EI assessment.

However, if we assume people who are higher on EI compared to those lower on EI should extract richer understandings of others' mental states and more complex reasons for others' emotions, studies could be done comparing high and low EI participants under conditions of cognitive load or no load. One expectation would be that under no load conditions both high and low EI participants would extract rich emotion understandings, but that under load only those higher on EI would continue to do so. According to our framework, this would assume the EI abilities of those high in EI are well practiced and intuitive. If the EI abilities are not intuitive – which is difficult to measure with current assessments of EI – then what might be expected is that under cognitive load even participants considered high on EI would be ineffective (see Fig. 2 for a depiction of this possibility). As this example makes clear, without knowing anything about a person's EI abilities in terms of whether they can be applied automatically, or the degree to which the testing context depletes cognitive resources, it is difficult to ascertain what high or low EI is. For example, the second outcome, if obtained, would suggest that part of what makes for effective EI

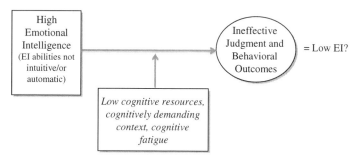

Fig. 2. Reconceptualized Model of High EI Effects on Outcomes: Dual Process Considerations.

is the availability of cognitive resources and/or EI abilities that are well practiced and intuitive and not open to disruption from stressful contexts.

The study on the Good Samaritan situation (Darley & Batson, 1973) provides an example of how the three elements – context, dual processes, and motivation – might interact in other ways. The seminary students who were in a hurry were under a different motivational state than those not in a hurry, and this motivational state was determined by context (Principle 1: different information received from instructors). Many people due to their current context have experienced deadlines, which changes what they value and their priorities – that is, their motivation. For the seminary students who thought they were late, their goal caused many of them to disregard the person in need of help, which could have stemmed from various processes involving automatic and deliberate EI (Principle 2). For example, one possibility is that they just did not notice the person. Another is that they noticed the person but they categorized the situation incorrectly. A third possibility is that the students accurately categorized the situation but overrode the assessment through a deliberate process and decided they could not help due to the pressing goal.

To disentangle these possibilities, researchers could have participants perform a similar task, but at the end assess memory for the critical incident (person in need of help). If participants in the time pressure condition, regardless of EI level, could not remember the person in need, this would suggest that the induced motivational state directed cognitive processing away from the person and the social situation. Alternatively, it is possible that participants lower on EI would show poor memory but those high in EI good memory and accurate categorization of the critical incident.

This would suggest that even when an assessment of the critical situation was made correctly, the pressing goal overrode EI inferences and intentions to help. Viewed without consideration for context and the conflicting goals they can elicit, such an outcome might in actuality suggest low EI, as depicted in the top panel of Fig. 3. But it could just as well be that on a different day, free of conflicting goals, the seminary students might have been quite willing to help (like those in the control group; see bottom panel of Fig. 3), which might lead some observers in this case to attribute high EI to them for being able to read the situation and for being generous. But the inference of low EI in the former case and high EI in the latter is less than clear without consideration of the principles we have outlined here.

The current discussion should help demonstrate that three elements we are proposing to help reconceptualize EI are pieces in an interactive mental system. The elements can interact and align in different ways, providing more nuanced explanations of how effective EI emerges but also helping to suggest a variety of hypotheses that could be tested in future research and ultimately help explain why individuals thought to be high on EI can enact ineffective behavior in other situations.

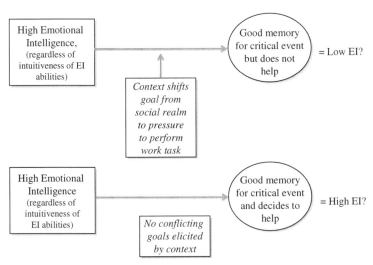

Fig. 3. Reconceptualized Model of High EI Effects on Outcomes: Context × Motivation Considerations.

CONCLUSION

Many questions remain regarding EI, so we concur with many of our colleagues' previous calls for further study of EI to help address these issues. But we would add that what is also needed is more conceptual work that takes social context seriously and provides a model of mental processes (at different levels) given what is known in the psychological literature. In this vein, we have proposed one approach for doing this. It is our hope that by delving deeper into both the social context and psychology of EI researchers and practitioners will have more guidance and knowledge at their disposal to pursue questions and projects that can help unlock the promise of EI.

NOTES

1. These analyses focus on measures specifically labeled as EI. Other approaches to the study of EI-relevant abilities exist, as we discuss under the section dealing with ability measures. Most of the research assessing predictive validity (in meta-analyses controlling for other important factors) has focused on specific measures of EI, whether as integrated EI abilities or self-report trait or "mixed" models.

2. Most skills follow the path of explicit practice to automaticity, from being deliberate to becoming more automatic and intuitive. This is not to say that skill acquisition cannot occur implicitly and with little awareness (Bargh & Chartrand, 1999; Lewicki et al., 1992).

REFERENCES

Bargh, J. A., & Chartrand, T. L. (1999). The unbearable automaticity of being. *American Psychologist, 54*, 462–479.

Bargh, J. A., & Williams, L. E. (2007). The nonconscious regulation of emotion. In J. Gross (Ed.), *Handbook of emotion regulation* (pp. 429–445). New York, NY: Guilford.

Bar-On, R. (1997). *Bar-On emotional quotient inventory: Technical manual.* Toronto, ON: Multi-Health Systems.

Banziger, T., Grandjean, D., & Scherer, K. R. (2009). Emotion recognition from expressions in face, voice, and body: The Multimodal Emotion Recognition Test (MERT). *Emotion, 9*, 691–704.

Baumeister, R., & Leary, M. (1995). The need to belong: Desire for interpersonal attachments as a fundamental human motivation. *Psychological Bulletin, 117*, 497–529.

Baumeister, R. F., Twenge, J. M., & Nuss, C. (2002). Effects of social exclusion on cognitive processes: Anticipated aloneness reduces intelligent thought. *Journal of Personality and Social Psychology, 83*, 817–827.

Brackett, M., & Mayer, J. (2003). Convergent, discriminant, and incremental validity of competing measures of emotional intelligence. *Personality and Social Psychology Bulletin, 29*, 1147–1158.

Buck, R. (1984). *The communication of emotion.* New York, NY: Guilford Press.

Chaiken, S., & Trope, Y. (Eds.). (1999). *Dual process theories in social psychology.* New York, NY: Guilford Press.

Cherniss, C. (2010). Emotional intelligence: New insights and further clarifications. *Industrial and Organizational Psychology, 3*, 183–191.

Clark, M. S., & Isen, A. M. (1982). Toward understanding the relationship between feeling states and social behavior. In A. Hastorf & A. M. Isen (Eds.), *Cognitive social psychology.* New York, NY: Elsevier.

Clark, T. F., Winkielman, P., & McIntosh, D. N. (2008). Autism and the extraction of emotion from briefly presented facial expressions: Stumbling at the first step of empathy. *Emotion, 8*, 803–809.

Darley, J. M., & Batson, C. D. (1973). From Jerusalem to Jericho: A study of situational and dispositional variables in helping behavior. *Journal of Personality and Social Psychology, 27*, 100–108.

Ekman, P., & Friesen, W. V. (1975). *Unmasking the face: A guide to recognizing emotions from facial clues.* Englewood Cliffs, NJ: Prentice-Hall.

Ellis, A. (2001). *Overcoming destructive beliefs, feelings and behaviors.* New York, NY: Prometheus Books.

Fiori, M. (2009). A new look at emotional intelligence: A dual process framework. *Personality and Social Psychology Review, 13*, 21–44.

Freudenthaler, H. H., & Neubauer, A. C. (2007). Measuring emotional management abilities: Further evidence of the importance to distinguish between typical and maximum performance. *Personality and Individual Differences, 42*, 1561–1572.

Frijda, N. H. (1988). *The laws of emotions.* Mahwah, NJ: Erlbaum.

Gardner, W. L., Pickett, C. L., & Brewer, M. B. (2000). Social exclusion and selective memory: How the need to belong influences memory for social events. *Personality and Social Psychology Bulletin, 26*, 286–296.

Goleman, D. (1995). *Emotional intelligence: Why it can matter more than IQ.* New York, NY: Bantam.

Goleman, D. (2006). *Social intelligence: The new science of human relationships.* New York, NY: Bantam.

Gross, J. J. (1998). The emerging field of emotion regulation: An integrative review. *Review of General Psychology, 2*, 271–299.

Humphrey, N. K. (1976). The social function of intellect. In P. P. G. Bateson & R. A. Hinde (Eds.), *Growing points in ethology* (pp. 303–317). Cambridge: Cambridge University Press.

Iacaboni, M., Molnar-Szakacs, I., Gallese, V., Buccino, G., Mazziotta, J. C., & Rizzolatti, G. (2005). Grasping the intentions of others with one's own mirror neuron system. *PLoS Biology, 3*, 529–535.

Isen, A. M., Johnson, M. M. S., Mertz, E., & Robinson, G. F. (1985). The influence of positive affect on the unusualness of word associations. *Journal of Personality and Social Psychology, 48*, 1413–1426.

Kihlstrom, J. F., & Cantor, N. (1989). Social intelligence and personality: There's room for growth. In R. S. Wyer & T. K. Srull (Eds.), *Advances in social cognition* (Vol. 2, pp. 197–214). Hillsdale, NJ: Erlbaum.

Kross, E., & Ayduk, O. (2011). Making meaning out of negative experiences by self-distancing. *Current Directions in Psychological Science, 20,* 187–191.

Kross, E., Ayduk, O., & Mischel, W. (2005). When asking "'why'" does not hurt: Distinguishing rumination from reflective processing of negative emotions. *Psychological Science, 16,* 709–715.

Lazarus, R. S. (1994). *Emotion and adaptation.* Oxford, UK: Oxford University Press.

Lewicki, P., Hill, T., & Czyzewska, M. (1992). Nonconscious acquisition of information. *American Psychologist, 47,* 796–801.

Linden, D., van der, Tsaousis, Y., & Petrides, K. V. (2012). Overlap between general factors of personality in the Big Five, giant three, and trait emotional intelligence. *Personality and Individual Differences, 53,* 175–179.

Matsumoto, D., LeRoux, J., Wilson-Cohn, C., Raroque, J., Kooken, K., Ekman, P., ... Goh, A. (2001). A new test to measure emotion recognition ability: Matsumoto and Ekman's Japanese and Caucasian brief affect recognition test (JACBART). *Journal of Nonverbal Behavior, 24,* 179–209.

Mauss, I. B., Bunge, S. A., & Gross, J. J. (2007). Automatic emotion regulation. *Social and Personality Psychology Compass, 1,* 146–167.

Mauss, I. B., Cook, C., & Gross, J. J. (2007). Automatic emotion regulation during anger provocation. *Journal of Experimental Social Psychology, 43,* 698–711.

Mayer, J. D., Caruso, D., & Salovey, P. (1999). Emotional intelligence meets traditional standards for an intelligence. *Intelligence, 27,* 267–298.

Mayer, J. D., Roberts, R. D., & Barsade, S. G. (2008). Human abilities: Emotional intelligence. *Annual Review of Psychology, 59,* 507–536.

Mayer, J. D., & Salovey, P. (1997). What is emotional intelligence? In P. Salovey & D. Sluyter (Eds.), *Emotional development and emotional intelligence: Educational implications* (pp. 3–31). New York, NY: Basic.

Mayer, J. D., Salovey, P., & Caruso, D. (1997). *Emotional IQ test.* Needham, MA: Virtual Knowledge.

Mayer, J. D., Salovey, P., & Caruso, D. R. (2002). *Mayer-Salovey-Caruso emotional intelligence test (MSCEIT) user's manual.* Toronto, ON: MHS Publ.

McNamara, P., McLaren, D., Smith, D., Brown, A., & Stickgold, R. (2005). A "Jekyll and Hyde" within: Aggressive versus friendly interactions in REM and non-REM dreams. *Psychological Science, 16,* 130–136.

Mischel, W., DeSmet, A., & Kross, E. (2006). Self-regulation in the service of conflict resolution. In M. Deutsch, P. T. Coleman & E. C. Marcus (Eds.), *Handbook of conflict resolution* (pp. 294–313). San Francisco, CA: Jossey-Bass.

Mischel, W., & Shoda, Y. (1995). A cognitive-affective system theory of personality: Reconceptualizing situations, dispositions, dynamics and invariance in personality structure. *Psychological Review, 102,* 246–268.

Nowicki, S., Jr., & Duke, M. (1994). Individual differences in the nonverbal communication of affect: The diagnostic analysis of nonverbal accuracy scale. *Journal of Nonverbal Behavior, 18,* 9–35.

O'Boyle, E. H., Humphrey, R. H., Pollack, J. M., Hawver, T. H., & Story, P. A. (2011). The relation between emotional intelligence and job performance: A meta-analysis. *Journal of Organizational Behavior, 32,* 788–818.

O'Sullivan, M. (1982). Measuring the ability to recognize facial expressions of emotion. In P. Ekman (Ed.), *Emotion in the human face* (pp. 281–317). Cambridge, UK: Cambridge University Press.

Qureshi, A., Apperly, I. A., & Samson, D. (2010). Executive function is necessary for perspective-selection, not Level-1 visual perspective-calculation: Evidence from a dual-task study of adults. *Cognition, 117*, 230–236.

Roberts, R. D., Matthews, G., & Zeidner, M. (2010). Emotional intelligence: Muddling through theory and measurement. *Industrial and Organizational Psychology, 3*, 140–144.

Roseman, I. J. (1984). Cognitive determinants of emotion. *Review of Personality and Social Psychology, 5*, 11–36.

Rosenthal, R., Hall, J. A., DiMatteo, M. R., Rogers, P. L., & Archer, D. (1979). *Sensitivity to nonverbal communication*. Baltimore, MD: Johns Hopkins University Press.

Sanchez-Burks, J. (2005). Protestant relational ideology: The cognitive underpinnings and organizational implications of an American anomaly. *Research in Organizational Behavior, 26*, 263–305.

Sanchez-Burks, J., & Huy, Q. (2009). Emotional aperture: The accurate recognition of collective emotions. *Organization Science, 20*, 22–34.

Sayles, L. R. (1957). Work group behavior and the larger organization. In C. M. Arensburg, (Ed.), *Research in industrial human relations* (pp. 131–145). New York, NY: Harper & Row.

Schutte, N., Malouff, J., Hall, L., Haggerty, D., Cooper, J., Golden, C., & Dornheim, L. (1998). Development and validation of a measure of emotional intelligence. *Personality and Individual Differences, 25*, 167–177.

Shirom, A., Toker, S., Alkaly, Y., Jacobson, O., & Balicer, R. (2011). Work-based predictors of mortality: A 20-year follow-up of healthy employees. *Health Psychology, 30*, 268–275.

Smith, E. R., & DeCoster, J. (2000). Dual process models in social and cognitive psychology: Conceptual integration and links to underlying memory systems. *Personality and Social Psychology Review, 4*, 108–131.

Stanovich, K. E., & West, R. F. (2000). Individual differences in reasoning. Implications for the rationality debate. *Behavioral and Brain Sciences, 23*, 645–726.

Sternberg, R. J. (2002). Smart people are not stupid, but they sure can be foolish: The imbalance theory of foolishness. In R. J. Sternberg (Ed.), *Why smart people can be so stupid* (pp. 232–242). New Haven, CT: Yale University Press.

Tett, R. P., Fox, K. E., & Wang, A. (2005). Development and validation of a self-report measure of emotional intelligence as a multidimensional trait domain. *Personality and Social Psychology Bulletin, 31*, 859–888.

Trivers, R. L. (1971). The evolution of reciprocal altruism. *The Quarterly Review of Biology, 46*, 35–57.

Van Rooy, D., & Viswesvaran, C. (2004). Emotional intelligence: A meta-analytic investigation of predictive validity and nomological net. *Journal of Vocational Behavior, 65*, 71–95.

Winkielman, P., McIntosh, D. N., & Oberman, L. (2009). Embodied and disembodied emotion processing: Learning from and about typical and autistic individuals. *Emotion Review, 1*, 178–190.

Wojciszke, B., Bazinska, R., & Jaworski, M. (1998). On the dominance of moral categories in impression formation. *Personality and Social Psychology Bulletin, 24*, 1251–1263.

Ybarra, O. (2001). When first impressions don't last: The role of isolation and adaptation processes in impression revision. *Social Cognition, 19*, 491–520.

Ybarra, O. (2002). Naive causal understanding of valenced behaviors and its implications for social information processing. *Psychological Bulletin, 128*, 421–441.

Ybarra, O., Chan, E., & Park, D. C. (2001). Young and old adults' concerns with morality and competence. *Motivation and Emotion*, *25*, 85–100.

Ybarra, O., Keller, M., Chan, E., Garcia, S., Sanchez-Burks, J., Rios Morrison, K., & Baron, A. (2010). Being unpredictable: Friend or foe matters. *Social Psychological and Personality Science*, *1*, 259–267.

Ybarra, O., Schaberg, L. A., & Keiper, S. N. (1999). Favorable and unfavorable target expectancies and social information processing. *Journal of Personality and Social Psychology*, *77*, 698–709.

Zeidner, M., Matthews, G., & Roberts, R. (2009). *What we know about emotional intelligence: How it affects learning, work, relationships and our mental health.* Cambridge, MA: MIT Press.

THE ROLE OF MINDFULNESS IN FOSTERING TRANSFORMATIONAL LEARNING IN WORK SETTINGS

Robert W. Barner and Charlotte P. Barner

This chapter explores how the practice of mindfulness offers an important and seldom reviewed pathway to transformational learning in work settings. We also delineate the ways in which this transformational process enables individuals, and the organizations in which they work, to meet challenging work conditions while supporting personal growth. In doing so, we align our focus with the tenets of positive organizational psychology by positioning mindfulness as a positive experiential state that supports both employee well-being and improved organizational performance (Bakker & Schaufeli, 2008; Ko & Donaldson, 2011). The construct of individual mindfulness has been defined as "the awareness that arises out of intentionally attending in an open and discerning way to whatever is arising in the present moment" (Shapiro, 2009, p. 555), with a mindfulness state described as "being in-the-moment aware of internal and external stimuli in a nonjudgmental and nonreactive way" (Barner, 2011, p. 19). We discuss five mechanisms by which mindfulness may serve as a key for transformational learning and present four applications of mindfulness in work settings.

Advances in Positive Organizational Psychology, Volume 1, 189–210
ISSN: 2046-410X/doi:10.1108/S2046-410X(2013)0000001011

INTRODUCTION TO CONCEPTS

The concepts of "mindfulness" and "transformational learning" arise from several domains (i.e., traditional and positive psychology, organizational and social sciences, human and organizational learning and development) and are researched within numerous contexts. Given the need to be sensitive to the complexities of multiple levels for analyses (Hitt, Beamish, Jackson, & Mathieu, 2007), our discussion of individual mindfulness in organizations is centered on the micro level of analysis. This construct of individual mindfulness differs from two constructs at the macro, or organizational, level of analysis: "collective mindfulness" – the practices and processes high-reliability organizations employ to increase organizational reliability – and "mindful organizing" (Langer, 2000; Weick & Putman, 2006; Weick & Roberts, 1993; Weick & Sutcliffe, 2007; Weick, Sutcliffe, & Obstfeld, 2002).

Perspectives of Individual Mindfulness

Eastern and Western perspective on mindfulness are continuing to overlap (Fulton & Siegel, 2005), and an increasing number of empirical studies use mindfulness constructs that acknowledge both Eastern and Western views (Barner, 2011; Shapiro & Carlson, 2009; Wallace & Hodel, 2008; Wallace & Shapiro, 2006). These two views share a common purpose of mindfulness – a healthy, balanced mind for a life of well-being (Carmody & Baer, 2008; Kabat-Zinn, 1990, 2003; Walach et al., 2007). The Eastern view sees mindfulness from a holistic perspective, while the Western view tends to examine the impact of mindfulness on a single dimension such as decision making, improving memory, managing stress, or cognitive flexibility. Both views hold the important practices of intentionality and awareness; with the opposite condition – "mindlessness" – viewed as a state in which an individual is inattentive and on "autopilot"; a state characterized by an imbalanced, rigid mindset (Barner, 2011; Langer, 2000; Yeganeh, 2006). An important distinction between these two views is the attention given to addressing emotions and thoughts. Eastern mindful practice (Kabat-Zinn, 1990) regards emotions and thoughts as impermanent and so strives to help individuals "let go" of these experiences. Western approaches to mindfulness (Langer, 1997, 2000) tend to emphasize the control and management of thoughts, with relative little attention given to the role that emotions play in experience.

Mindfulness has been treated as both a process and a trait, with the prevailing view being that mindfulness has qualities that reflect both states and traits (Baer, Smith, Hopkins, Krietemeyer, & Toney, 2006; Bishop et al., 2004; Brown & Ryan, 2004), depending on how the construct of mindfulness is operationalized. That is, whether the researcher's attention is directed to the changes in thoughts, emotions, and physiological reactions that occur within a given mindful practice session, or to those cumulative long-term, positive changes in personal well-being that have been found to be associated with sustained practice of mindfulness over several weeks or months (Davidson, 2010).

Researchers agree that individual mindfulness can be learned (Walsh & Shapiro, 2006; Walach et al., 2007). The methods of learning and practicing mindfulness vary across domains and extend from mental focusing activities to a combination of mind-and-body activities (i.e., breathing techniques, mindfulness meditation, prayerful focus, mindfulness-based stress reduction, and walking). Research indicates that a mindfulness practitioner obtains significant benefits for the mind, body, and spirit; and changes in all three areas enable the individual to create a life of holistic well-being.

Mindfulness' Role in Transformational Learning

Mezirow (2000) describes "transformational learning" as "the process by which we transform our taken-for-granted frames of reference (meaning perspectives, habits of mind, and mind-sets) to make them more inclusive, discriminating, open, emotionally capable of change, and reflective" (pp. 7–8). Implied in this definition is that transformational learning is reflected in the development of a new and broader perspective of oneself and one's world – a perspective that encourages one to question deeply held assumptions and to remain receptive to exploring new possibilities for personal change. Mezirow (1991) suggests that transformational learning is typically triggered by a critical life event that is personally disorienting and traumatic, such as facing a critical career change, a serious illness, or the death of a loved one.

There is much to suggest that mindfulness offers a different avenue to transformation, one that *does not* require the sudden onset of traumatic and painful life experiences. The alternative view is that mindfulness allows personal transformation to take the form as an intentional process (Elias, 2000; Healy, 2001) that represents the gradual "unfolding" of a person's potential. This perspective – that personal transformation can occur gradually over time – is consistent with the positions held by many theorists (Daloz, 2000; Taylor, 2000). We contend (Barner & Barner, 2011) that mindfulness practice supports transformational learning not through a direct attack on our personal assumptions, but by helping individuals understand the manner in which their assumptions are personally and culturally constructed.

Mindfulness' transformational properties reside in the evidence that when individuals are mindful they more fully attend to, and are more nonjudgmentally receptive of, their life experiences. By adopting this receptive state, they discover how to be open to what those experiences reveal. This relationship between mindfulness and openness is closely aligned with the Eastern view and definition (Shapiro, 2009) of mindfulness as a state of mind that is nonjudgmentally open and receptive to present experience. Thus, we have proposed (Barner & Barner, 2011) five mechanisms through which mindfulness fosters transformational learning (Table 1).

Attending to the Present Moment

Mindful individuals are more likely to be more open to experiences, as reflected in the ability to engage fully in the present moment by limiting intruding thoughts (Leary & Tate, 2007), by reducing cognitive filtering

Table 1.   Five Mechanisms of Mindfulness for Transformational Learning in Work Settings.

Five Mechanisms of Mindfulness for Transformation Learning
1. *Attending to the present moment* To be present in the moment in order to be open to unfolding experiences
2. *Assuming a nonjudgmental attitude* To attend to fields of awareness without internal censoring or filtering in order to be nonjudgmental of self and others
3. *Being fully aware of embedded experiences* To be aware of one's external life events and internal landscape in order to understand one's construction of experiences
4. *Staying engaged with perceived challenging life experiences* To remain highly aware of one's responses within challenging experiences in order to lessen emotional reactivity under conditions of stress
5. *Viewing thoughts and feelings as transitory experiences* To disidentify from and change one's relationship to thoughts and feelings in order to view experiences as transitory phenomena, separate from sense of self

(Brown, Ryan, & Creswell, 2007), and by increasing attentional skills (Chambers, Lo, & Allen, 2008; Jha, Krompinger, & Baime, 2007). The result is that a mindful individual is less likely to respond in reactive and habitual ways. Instead, when mindful, one is more inclined to pause and "introduce a 'space' between one's perception and response" (Bishop et al., 2004, p. 232). This moment of full attention, in which the individual pauses without acting in an automatic, habitual fashion, represents an experiential state that supports deep personal learning (Jarvis, 2006).

Assuming a Nonjudgmental Attitude
Being mindful helps individuals develop the ability to attend to whatever enters their fields of awareness without internal censoring or filtering, and to dispassionately observe their thoughts, emotions, and bodily sensations. This state of mind has been shown to be related to increased learning (Lillis & Hayes, 2007) and to reduce verbal defensiveness when confronted with self-threatening experiences (Feldman-Barrett, Williams, & Fong, 2002). The ability to assume a nonjudgmental stance is viewed as a critical component of practicing mindfulness (Germer, Siegel, & Fulton, 2005; Shapiro, Carlson, Astin, & Freedman, 2006) and is a necessary condition for reducing reactivity to challenging life experiences (Bishop et al., 2004; Hodgins, 2008).

Being Fully Aware of Embedded Experiences
Mindfulness involves assuming a stance of nonjudgmental awareness of external life events *and* that internal landscape comprised of individuals' thoughts, feelings, and bodily reactions (Kabat-Zinn, 2003). This full awareness of the external and internal allows individuals to better under-stand their responses to life events and, in so doing, increases the degree of latitude and choice they have in constructing those experiences (Bishop et al., 2004).

Staying Engaged with Perceived Challenging Life Experiences
Individuals often have difficulty staying fully engaged with life experi-ences when those experiences call into question critical self-assumptions (Aronson, 1998; Brown, Ryan, Creswell, & Niemiec, 2008). In this regard, Mezirow (2000) cautions that "transformative learning, especially when it involves subjective reframing, is often an intensely threatening emotional experience" (p. 6). In such situations, one's typical reaction is to disengage from learning or minimize or deny information that may challenge one's

cherished view of self; which, over time, eliminates opportunities for personal transformation.

Several studies suggest that mindfulness practice increases the ability to stay fully engaged within threatening experiences (Bishop et al., 2004; Brown et al., 2007) by achieving higher states of emotional self-regulation and lessening emotional reactivity under conditions of stress (Arch & Craske, 2006; Baer, Smith, & Allen, 2004; Ortner, Kilner, & Zelazo, 2007). Such findings extend beyond self-reports to include measures in brain activation patterns that reflect less emotional reactivity to stressful stimuli (Davidson et al., 2003). These adaptive response patterns appear to be closely related to what Maddi and Hightower (1999) termed a "transformational coping pattern" of engagement and adaptation to difficult life experiences. In contrast, the less adaptive "regressive coping pattern" is characterized by the tendency to deny or minimize the negative life experiences.

Viewing Thoughts and Feelings as Transitory Experiences
A consistently noted feature of mindfulness practice is that over time practitioners come to view the flow of emotions and thoughts they experience as transitory phenomena that are separate from their underlying sense of self (Brown et al., 2008). This means disidentifying from *and* changing one's relationship to thoughts and feelings – "I observe that I have this thought/feeling" rather than "I am this thought/feeling." For example, an employee who receives critical feedback from her manager might engage in negative rumination regarding this experience – "I can't do anything right." Without being mindful, she would attempt to control these thoughts – "I shouldn't be upset, stop being upset." Through practicing mindfulness, she observes these thoughts as transitional experiences separate from who she is, and learns to let go.

Support for this position comes from Thompson and Waltz's (2008) study involving 167 college students. They found strong correlations between two measures of mindfulness and measures of self-acceptance and self-esteem. The researchers concluded that mindfulness might cause individuals to view their experiences as transitory phenomena and to attend to personal experiences in a more open and nonjudgmental fashion. Therefore, they suggest that mindfulness may play a pivotal role in fostering a view of self that is more unconditional and less self-evaluative.

Additional evidence comes from Farb et al. (2007) who exposed 20 adults who completed an eight-week course in meditation, and 16 adults in a non-training control group, to negative or positive self-trait words. Comparisons of these two groups' MRI images showed different brain wave activation patterns. Compared with the control group's brain patterns, trained participants were found to produce a "distinct experiential mode in which thoughts, feelings, and bodily sensations are viewed less as being good or bad integral to the 'self' and treated more as transient mental events that can be simply observed" (p. 320).

These studies and others' research (Shapiro & Carlson, 2009; Wallace & Shapiro, 2006) contend that extended mindfulness meditation practice can bring about a view of self that is more fluid and less constrained by contingent assessments of self-worth. When one considers the difficulty many individuals face in remaining open to information that can challenge views of self (Aronson, 1998; Thibodeau & Aronson, 1992), we believe that the ability to make this shift in perspective is particularly important to personal transformation.

APPLICATIONS OF MINDFULNESS IN WORK SETTINGS

Studies documenting mindfulness' applications to work settings have encompassed such areas as reductions in cognitive failures (Herndon, 2008), improved working memory (Jha, Stanley, Kiyonaga, Wong, & Gelfand, 2010), and sustained attention (Jha et al., 2007). We suggest four additional areas of applications where mindfulness can foster transformational learning in work settings.

Supporting Personal Transformation in High-Stress Work Environments

A substantial body of research has demonstrated the positive role that mindfulness can play in reducing stress and increasing well-being (Carmody & Baer, 2008; Chang et al., 2004; Kabat-Zinn, 1990, 2003). What gives mindfulness-based stress reduction a transformational quality is its emphasis on having individuals alter their *relationships* to stress-related thoughts and emotions, rather than the *content* of those thoughts and emotions.

This transformational change through mindfulness is reflected in Kabat-Zinn's (1990) position that "[i]f we can change the way we see, we can change the way we respond" (p. 241). Through this altered relationship, individuals develop the ability to stay fully engaged with threatening experiences (Bishop et al., 2004; Brown et al., 2007), to disidentify from stressful thoughts and emotions (Brown et al., 2008; Thompson & Waltz, 2008), and to become less emotionally reactive to stressful work events (Baer et al., 2004; Arch & Craske, 2006; Ortner et al., 2007), including layoffs and employment uncertainties (Barner, 2011; Jacobs & Blustein, 2008). The outcome of these collective changes is that mindfulness practitioners come to experience potentially stressful events with greater equanimity and emotional balance.

Transformational changes were revealed in a study (Healy, 2001) on the long-term effects of meditation practice involving nine health care professionals who were experienced (>3 years) practitioners. During their interviews, several participants discussed how learning to calmly and dispassionately observe their thoughts and feelings helped them become less reactive within stressful work situations. Based on results of participant themes, Healy (2001) concluded that mindfulness meditation fostered transformational changes in participants.

A high-stress work environment that requires composure and stress management is a call center service operation since service representatives' customers are frequently angry or frustrated. Walach et al.'s (2007) study of 12 service workers who completed an eight-week mindfulness program reported lower work-related stress after completing the program, when compared to the 11 control group participants. Once again, mindfulness participants reported changes that extended beyond better stress management, to include changes such as being able to pause before responding to customers and being less reactive when encountering stressful situations with customers and coworkers.

Military combat units who are awaiting deployment (Adler, McGurk, Stetz, & Bliese, 2003; Bolton, Lit, Britt, Adler, & Roemer, 2001) experience a particularly stressful work environment. Such military groups serve as a unique research population given that stress levels for military personnel have been found to increase over the length of pre-deployment periods (Stanley, Schaldach, Kiyonaga, & Jha, 2011). Jha et al. (2010) conducted an eight-week program in mindfulness meditation training for 31 military personnel awaiting deployment (control $n = 17$). Participants who received training demonstrated improved working memory capacity, as well as increased positive affect and decreased negative affect (measured by the Positive and Negative Affect Schedule), with no such improvements found for controls. In addition, improvements in both areas were directly related to the time spent in mindfulness meditation practice.

A similar study by Stanley et al. (2011) involved 34 Marine reservists who received training (control $n = 21$) prior to deployment to Iraq, 21 of the 34 participants had previous deployment experience. While awaiting deployment, 13 participants in the experimental group faced additional work stressors from being employed in such high-stress occupations as emergency medical care, firefighting, and law enforcement. Participants' self-reported levels of mindfulness scores (Five Facet Mindfulness Questionnaire, FFMQ) from pre- and post-training were compared. Their pre- and post-training self-reported stress level scores (Perceived Stress Scale) were also assessed. This study's findings showed that the eight-week mindfulness meditation program was directly related to self-reported reductions in participants' stress levels. A significant outcome of training noted by several participants was reductions in the traumatic stress symptoms that they had been experiencing as the result of previous deployments.

Enhancing the Abilities of Professionals in Helping Roles

Mindfulness further appears to support transformational learning for professionals in helping roles (i.e., counselors, social workers, nurses,) through effective stress management within helping relationships, enhancement of empathy and understanding, and development of compassion. Maintaining composure during emotionally laden, high-stress encounters is a challenge many helping professionals face. Over time, the stress of addressing these challenges can cause increased anxiety, emotional exhaustion, and impaired performance (Blegen, 1993; Radeke & Mahoney, 2000; Rosenberg & Pace, 2006; Stamm, 1995).

Mindfulness training has proven beneficial in enabling helping professionals to more effectively manage work-related stressors. Beddoe and Murphy (2004) found that a relatively brief (8–12 weeks) mindfulness meditation course helped nurses reduce job-related stress and increase their levels of empathy when working with patients. Similarly, in a qualitative study involving social work students, Birnbaum (2008) found that mindfulness training strengthened the emotional self-regulation of participants and encouraged them to explore issues regarding their relationships with their field supervisors and their practice. Birnbaum (2008) concluded that these mindfulness sessions create "an 'accompanying place' for the students where thoughts, feelings and dilemmas can be observed in a supportive and non-evaluative way" (p. 838). Mindfulness training has also been shown to reduce stress symptoms in first-year medical students (Hassed, de Lisle, Sullivan, & Pier, 2008), nurses and nurse aides (Cohen-Katz, Wiley, Capuano, Baker, & Shapiro, 2004; Mackenzie, Poulin, & Seidman-Carlson, 2006), and health care professionals (Healy, 2001; Shapiro, Astin, Bishop, & Cordova, 2005).

McGarrigle and Walsh (2011) conducted an eight-week mindfulness-based stress management program for 12 social work professionals (11 women). Pre- and post-test comparisons of the Mindfulness Attention and Awareness Scale (MAAS) showed significant increases in mindfulness and associated reductions in stress measured by the Perceived Stress Scale. In addition, at the start of each training session participants made personal journal entries reflecting on their experiences of self-care and compassion. These journals were then made anonymous, collected, transcribed verbatim, and independently coded by two researchers for themes related to mindfulness, compassion, and self-care. Findings showed that participants noted significant changes in the way in which they regarded their work and interacted with their clients, as well as increased ability to manage daily stress. One participant observed that, "The information has changed the way I do my job, work with clients and in my personal life" (p. 223).

Helping professionals must also be able to establish rapport with and fully attend to the needs of their clients. Mindful practice can increase feelings of empathy (Healy, 2001; Schure, Christopher, & Christopher, 2008; Shapiro, Brown, & Biegel, 2007) and intersubjectivity (Surrey, 2005). Glomb, Duffy, Bono, and Yang (2011) suggest that mindfulness fosters the development of empathy by creating a state of "meta-cognitive awareness" (p. 132) in which individuals become more aware of their own emotions and the emotions of others. These changes, in turn, can lead to substantial positive effects in how those in helping roles are able to form deep connections with those they are assisting.

Physicians' ability to listen deeply without judgment, and to stay in the moment without distraction, has been identified as an important quality in making more accurate and complete medical diagnoses and more effective interventions (Connelly, 2005; Epstein, 1999). Shapiro, Schwartz, and Bonner's (1998) study using mindfulness training (seven-week MBSR program) with medical and premedical students found that empathy increased after the training (pre/post self-reports using Empathy Construct Rating Scale).

Closely related to empathy is the development of compassion – defined as "noticing another person's suffering, empathically feeling that person's pain, and acting in a manner intended to ease the suffering" (Lilius et al., 2008, pp. 194–195). Compassionate actions might involve providing emotional support or work flexibility that helps others cope and lessens their distress. A variety of research indicates that mindfulness can increase an individual's sense of compassion toward others. First, when experiencing compassion from others in their workplace, individuals have reported experiencing higher levels of positive emotions, increased perceptions of positive regard from their coworkers, and greater connections to their organizations (Frost, Dutton, Worline, & Wilson, 2000; Lilius et al., 2008). Shapiro et al. (2005) found that along with improved management of stress, mindfulness training fostered the development of greater empathy and self-compassion in participants. Beitel, Ferrer, and Cecero's (2005) study with 103 undergraduate students found correlations between mindfulness scores and increased compassionate concern for others (assessed using the Inter-personal Reactivity Index). Mindfulness meditation practice has also been correlated with self-reports of increased compassion in counselors (Lesh, 1970) and graduate counseling students (Schure et al., 2008).

The increased sense of compassion that helping professionals gain through mindful practice is reflected in the comments of a school psychologist, one of the helping professionals in Healy's (2001) study, who explained that a benefit he derived from mindfulness meditation practice was that "you can put your life in perspective ... And you also realize how much in common you have with everyone who walks by you. So there's a sense, there's really much more of a universal sense of affection" (p. 187).

Strengthening Work Relationships

Given the substantial mindfulness research results supporting personal transformation in high-stress work settings and enhancing helping professional's abilities, a reasonable expectation is that mindfulness may have implications for positively strengthening work relationships. Burgoon, Berger, and Waldron (2000) contend that mindfulness can strengthen individuals' workplace interpersonal communications by increasing receptivity to performance feedback, reducing stereotyping, and supporting collaboration for constructive conflict management.

The premise that mindfulness fosters positive workplace interpersonal communications is supported by Moore and Malinowski's (2009) study. They found that mindfulness meditation practitioners scored higher than non-meditators on measures of cognitive flexibility – the ability to shift behaviors in response to different situational contexts – and attentional functions, with results directly related to levels of meditation practice. This increased cognitive flexibility, they concluded, "provides the mental space to detect incorrect and unwholesome cognitive evaluations, which would usually go unnoticed and would lead to mistaken attitudes and emotions, which in turn would affect our well-being" (p. 183).

Pruitt and McCollum (2010) conducted qualitative interviews with seven advanced mindfulness meditation practitioners (> 10 years' experience). The results provide interesting insights into the potential relationships between mindfulness and work relationships, even though the study was limited to a small, homogenous group (Caucasians ages 52–70, with 5 being female). Participants revealed several themes suggesting that extended practice in mindfulness meditation resulted in enhanced personal relationships, as demonstrated through greater acceptance of themselves and others; reduced reactivity when confronted with difficult situations; a greater feeling of compassion toward self and others; and a stronger sense of connectivity with others. Greater feelings of acceptance were also found to relate to experiencing less anger, fear, or blame toward others. In interpreting the relationships found between participants' meditation practice and reductions in reactivity, the researchers noted that participants "believed that their meditation practice helped them to be more aware of their emotional vulnerabilities," which, in turn, resulted in reduced reactivity and helped participants "be more patient and calm with others who activated those triggers" (p. 143).

Reduced reactivity through mindfulness appears to be closely related to the concept of increased response flexibility (Siegel, 2007), the ability to pause during situations to consider alternative options for action, rather than responding in a habitual and autonomic manner. Glomb et al. (2011) propose that mindfulness may strengthen work relationships, in part, by increasing an individual's response flexibility within work settings. Based on interviews with 20 work professionals who were experienced (> 1 year) mindfulness practitioners, the researchers concluded that mindfulness allows "a more thoughtful consideration of how (and whether) to react to work events rather than 'jump' impulsively and reactively" (p. 129).

Brown and Ryan (2004) contend that the mindfulness construct is closely associated with that of emotional intelligence (EI), given the emphasis that mindfulness places on being aware of one's current emotional state, and that awareness of ones' emotional state is viewed as an important aspect of EI. Support for this position comes from two related studies performed by Chu (2010). In surveying 351 full-time employees within private and public sectors in Taiwan, Chu (2010) found that when compared with their less experienced counterparts, participants who possessed greater mindfulness meditation experiences exhibited higher levels of EI and reported less perceived stress and high levels of mental health. The second study evaluated the impact of meditation training on EI scores for 10 graduate students who had no prior meditation experience, compared with an equal number of control group participants. Findings showed that the training improved scores on EI, perceived stress, and mental health. Two important implications of this study are that differences in EI appear to be associated with trait and state measures of mindfulness, and that EI can be accentuated through mindfulness-based meditation practice.

Performing Effectively within Diverse Populations

As mindfulness appears to play a role in strengthening work relationships, the next question that arises is whether mindfulness can enhance individuals' abilities to work effectively within a diverse workforce. Research findings supporting this idea show that mindfulness can help reduce prejudice, stereotyping, and worldview defense.

In a study involving 32 undergraduate students, Lillis and Hayes (2007) compared the effectiveness of two training options in reducing prejudice. Option one involved the mindfulness training approach known as acceptance and commitment therapy (ACT), and option two was an educational lecture on racial differences. Prejudice was assessed by having participants evaluate their positions using a 1 to100 scale on four behavioral areas: "[1] plans to join diversity organizations or [2] seek out diverse experiences, [3] willingness to be the lone individual of their ethnic group at social gatherings, and [4] the belief that their actions can overcome racial boundaries" (p. 393). All participants received mindfulness training and education, with the difference being the order in which the interventions occurred. Results showed that ACT training reduced prejudicial attitudes when assessed through a one-week follow-up, with no similar reductions in prejudice found for the lecture condition.

Mindfulness may also help reduce worldview defense. Brown et al. (2008) defined "worldviews" as "reflecting values, ideals, or beliefs about the world and the place of the individual or group in it, [that] provides a sense of shared meaning and order that acts to affirm personal and group identify" (p. 81). Individuals who display a high degree of worldview defense are more likely to experience conflict or anger when they feel that an outside group represents potential threats to their cultural worldviews (Greenberg et al., 1990).

Niemiec et al. (2010) conducted a series of seven studies with 64 undergraduates that examined the relationship between trait mindfulness, worldview defense, and mortality salience (MS, fears related to thoughts about death). The study's guiding hypothesis was that given that an individual's worldview helps reduce the anxiety associated with MS, "then under conditions of MS people should defend their belief systems by derogating those who question, oppose, or threaten the cultural worldview" (p. 345). One of these studies involved inducing an MS condition by having participants imagine their emotions in envisioning their own death. Control group participants were asked to imagine their emotions in watching television. Both groups were later asked to rate their reactions to an author who was described as being a foreigner and who had supposedly written either a pro-US or an anti-US essay. Results showed that although MS increased pro-US bias in both groups, this bias was significantly lower for those participants who scored higher in trait mindfulness.

Another of Niemiec et al.'s (2010) seven studies involved 109 Caucasian undergraduate participants (71% male; 29% female, ages 18–38 years). Participants were asked to read a criminal case wherein the defendant was accused of racial discrimination in the workplace by an employee. In one condition the defendant was described as being a black racist, and in the other a white racist. Some participants were exposed to the MS condition, with the results showing that under the MS condition participants rated the Caucasian defendant more favorably than they did the black defendant. Once again, however, these results were modified by mindfulness, with participants who scored higher in trait mindfulness revealing less bias in favor of Caucasian defendants.

Niemiec et al.'s (2010) studies suggest that trait mindfulness helped moderate participants' worldview defense when MS fears were generated. Additional support for this conclusion comes from other research (Brown et al., 2008; Eisenberger, Lieberman, & Williams, 2003) showing that mindfulness can reduce the degree of defensiveness that individuals experience when exposed to the threat of social exclusion by peers or strangers.

When viewed together, the findings from these studies on prejudice, stereotyping, and worldview defense suggest that mindfulness may help individuals perform more effectively within diverse populations.

LONG-TERM TRANSFORMATIONAL OUTCOMES OF MINDFULNESS

As suggested earlier, over time mindfulness can support personal transformation through the gradual "unfolding" of a person's potential (Daloz, 2000; Elias, 2000; Healy, 2001; Taylor, 2000). Given this position, one would expect that transformational outcomes would become increasingly enhanced with extended mindfulness training and long-term practice. Indeed, available research supports this position.

Shapiro (1992) compared the outcome goals set by 27 participants who volunteered in either a two-week or a three-month mindfulness meditation retreat. Findings revealed that over time participants shifted from adopting more pragmatic goals aimed at emotional and cognitive regulation ("want to control my stress better"), to goals related to self-exploration ("want to learn more about myself"), and finally spiritual goals ("want to go beyond my narrow ego") (pp. 27–28). Similar shifts in meditation goals – from the instrumental to the spiritual – were noted in cancer patients within the Mackenzie, Carlson, Munoz, and Speca (2007) study. The five transformational themes for these cancer patient participants were increased spirituality, greater self-control, increased personal growth, awareness of their medical condition as shared emotional experience, and greater openness to change. Mackenzie et al.'s (2007) study concluded that meditation training resulted in participants' significant transformation:

> Underlying this process is a theme of personal growth. With this comes the further development of positive qualities, beyond the symptom reduction documented over the course of the initial program. A growing spirituality of feeling increasingly interconnected with others is part of this personal growth. Qualities of gratitude, compassion and equanimity may be the ultimate culmination of practice. (p. 66)

The relative durability of transformational changes resulting from extended mindful practice is also revealed in changes in behavioral patterns. Salmon, Santorelli, and Kabat-Zinn (1998) found that participants who had completed mindfulness training continued to show positive outcomes in productive coping patterns to life events when evaluated in a three-year, post-training completion follow up. Finally, these studies are supported by research that evaluated the neurological impact of long-term meditation, as revealed by the ability to maintain increased attention (Carter et al., 2005; Jha et al., 2007; Lazar et al., 2005), and increased positive affect and reduced reactivity to stressful emotional responses (Davidson et al., 2003).

CAVEATS AND FUTURE RESEARCH

Certain methodological caveats must be considered before drawing definitive conclusions regarding mindfulness' applications to transformational learning in work contexts. First, as noted, Eastern and Western definitions of mindfulness arise from different views regarding factors such as the importance placed on assuming a stance of nonjudgmental receptivity toward experience and the degree to which mindfulness includes attention to external *and* subjective experiences. These differences lend themselves to varying research methodologies, yet one will encounter research that mistakenly uses the Eastern and Western perspectives interchangeably.

How researchers operationalize mindfulness is a factor that introduces an element of variation into research. Research conclusions may be constrained by the different self-report instruments for assessing mindfulness (i.e., FFMQ, MAAS) or by mindfulness interventions and practices (i.e., MBSR). Little is known about the comparative efficacy of different mindfulness training approaches.

Further, much of what is known about transformational learning comes from studies performed within academic settings. There is a dearth of available research focused on mindfulness' application to transformational learning within work contexts. Additional research within this area, with attention given to discrete population groups (i.e., entry-level professionals, leaders, human services providers) would be valuable.

Finally, important recommendations for future research involve the effects of mindfulness on team performance. While there are studies at the macro-level (i.e., mindful organizing), the majority of mindfulness research has focused on the individual (micro) level of analysis. The opportunity exists for new empirical research directed at the group or team (meso) level. A few studies covered in this chapter point to the potential benefits of these unexplored research areas; for example, the application of mindfulness training in learning cohorts to increase cooperation (Birnbaum, 2008) and facilitate learning (Stanley et al., 2011). Undoubtedly, further research is needed within these areas. In summary, unexplored areas include how changes and increases in mindfulness at the team level may play a role in employee satisfaction, team dynamics, and broader organizational performance.

CONCLUSION

In this chapter we suggested that individual's mindfulness can support transformation learning in work settings. We discussed how this transformation is revealed in such outcomes as decreasing reactivity and disassociation from thoughts and emotions within stressful experiences, increasing empathy and compassion, enhancing interpersonal communications and relationships, and reducing prejudices and worldview defense. Collectively, these studies suggest that mindfulness supports long-term changes in one's openness to experiences; and this, in turn, acts to sustain positive, significant transformational changes in individuals. These changes – revealed in positive emotional, behavioral, physical, and neurological outcomes – have critical implications for employee well-being and improved performance in work settings.

REFERENCES

Adler, A. B., McGurk, D., Stetz, M. C., & Bliese, P. D. (2003, March). Military occupational stressors in garrison, training, and deployed environments. Paper presented at the NIOSH/APA Symposia, Toronto, Canada.

Arch, J. J., & Craske, M. G. (2006). Mechanism of mindfulness: Emotion regulation following a focused breathing induction. *Behavior Research and Therapy*, *44*, 1849–1858.

Aronson, E. (1998). Dissonance, hypocrisy, and the self-concept. In E. Haron-Jones & J. S. Mills (Eds.), *Cognitive dissonance theory: Revival with revisions and controversies*. Washington, DC: American Psychological Association.

Baer, R., Smith, G. T., & Allen, K. B. (2004). Assessment of mindfulness by self-report. *Assessment*, *11*, 191–206.

Baer, R. A., Smith, G. T., Hopkins, J., Krietemeyer, J., & Toney, L. (2006). Using self-report assessment methods to explore facets of mindfulness. *Assessment*, *13*, 27–45.

Bakker, A. B., & Schaufeli, W. B. (2008). Positive organizational behavior: Engaged employees in flourishing organizations. *Journal of Organizational Behavior*, *29*, 147–154.

Barner, C. P. (2011). *Understanding the role of mindfulness in the professional's experience of recently being laid off: An interpretive study*. Publication No. 3465639. Retrieved from http://udini.proquest.com/view/understanding-the-role-of-pqid:2428776301/

Barner, R. W., & Barner, C. P. (2011). The relationship between mindfulness, openness to experience, and transformational learning. In C. Hoare (Ed.), *Handbook of reciprocal adult development & learning* (pp. 347–362). New York, NY: Oxford University Press.

Beddoe, A. E., & Murphy, S. O. (2004). Does mindfulness decrease stress and foster empathy among nursing students? *Journal of Nursing Educations*, *43*, 305–312.

Beitel, M., Ferrer, E., & Cecero, J. J. (2005). Psychological mindedness and awareness of self and others. *Journal of Clinical Psychology*, *61*, 739–750.

Birnbaum, L. (2008). The use of mindfulness training to create an "accompanying place" for social work students. *Social Work Education*, *27*, 837–852.

Bishop, S., Lau, M., Shapiro, S. L., Carlson, L., Anderson, N. D., Carmody, J., … Devins, G. (2004). Mindfulness: A proposed operational definition. *Clinical Psychology: Science and Practice*, *11*, 230–241.

Blegen, M. A. (1993). Nurses' job satisfaction: A meta-analysis of related variables. *Nursing Research*, *42*, 36–41.

Bolton, E., Lit, B., Britt, T., Adler, A., & Roemer, L. (2001). Reports of prior exposure to potentially traumatic events and PTSD in troops poised for deployment. *Journal of Traumatic Stress*, *14*, 249–256.

Brown, K. W., & Ryan, R. M. (2004). Perils and promise in defining and measuring mindfulness: Observations from experience. *Clinical Psychology: Science and Practice*, *11*, 242–248.

Brown, K. W., Ryan, R. M., & Creswell, J. D. (2007). Mindfulness: Theoretical foundations and evidence for its salutary effects. *Psychological Inquiry*, *18*, 211–237.

Brown, K. W., Ryan, R. M., Creswell, J. D., & Niemiec, C. (2008). Beyond me: Mindful responses to social threat. In H. A. Wayment & J. J. Bauer (Eds.), *Transcending self-interest: Psychological explorations of the quiet ego* (pp. 75–84). Washington, DC: American Psychological Association.

Burgoon, J. K., Berger, C. R., & Waldron, V. R. (2000). Mindfulness and interpersonal communication. *Journal of Social Issues*, *56*, 105–127.

Carmody, J., & Baer, R. A. (2008). Relationships between mindful practice and levels of mindfulness, medical and psychological symptoms and well-being in a mindfulness-based stress reduction program. *Journal of Behavioral Medicine*, *31*, 23–33.

Carter, O. L., Presti, D. E., Callistemon, C., Ungerer, Y., Liu, G. B., & Pettigrew, J. D. (2005). Meditation alters perceptual rivalry in Tibetan Buddhist monks. *Current Biology*, *15*, R412–R413.

Chambers, R., Lo, B. C. Y., & Allen, N. B. (2008). The impact of intensive mindfulness training on attentional control, cognitive style, and affect. *Cognitive Therapy and Research*, *32*, 303–322.

Chang, V. Y., Palesh, O., Caldwell, R., Glasgow, N., Abramson, M., Luskin, F., ... Koopmann, C. (2004). The effects of a mindfulness-based stress reduction program on stress, mindfulness self-efficacy, and positive states of mind. *Stress and Health*, *20*, 141–147.

Chu, L. (2010). The benefits of meditation vis-à-vis emotional intelligence, perceived stress and negative mental health. *Stress and Health*, *26*, 169–180.

Cohen-Katz, J., Wiley, S., Capuano, T., Baker, D., & Shapiro, S. (2004). The effects of mindfulness-based stress reduction on nurse stress and burnout: A quantitative and qualitative study. *Holistic Nursing Practice*, *18*, 302–308.

Connelly, J. (2005). Narrative possibilities: Using mindfulness in clinical practice. *Perspectives in Biology and Medicine*, *48*, 84–94.

Daloz, L. A. P. (2000). Transformative learning for the common good. In J. Mezirow (Ed.), *Learning as transformation: Critical perspectives on a theory in progress* (pp. 103–123). San Francisco, CA: Jossey-Bass.

Davidson, R. J. (2010). Empirical explorations of mindfulness: Conceptual and methodological conundrums. *Emotion*, *10*, 8–11.

Davidson, R. J., Kabat-Zinn, J., Schumacher, J., Rosenkranz, M., Muller, D., Santorelli, S. F., ... Sheridan, J. F. (2003). Alterations in brain and immune function produced by mindfulness meditation. *Psychosomatic Medicine*, *65*, 564–570.

Eisenberger, N., Lieberman, M., & Williams, K. D. (2003). Does rejection hurt? An fMRI study of social exclusion. *Science*, *302*, 290–292.

Elias, D. (2000). One strategy for facilitating transformative learning: Synergic inquiry. In A. Wiessner, S. R. Meyer & D. A. Fuller (Eds.), *Challenges of practice: Transformative learning in action*. Proceedings of the 3rd international transformative learning conference (pp. 135–138). New York, NY: Teachers College Columbia University.

Epstein, R. E. (1999). Mindful practice. *Journal of the American Medical Association*, *282*, 833–839.

Farb, N. A. S., Segal, Z. V., Mayberg, M, Bean, J., McKeon, D., Fatima, Z., & Anderson, A. K. (2007). Attending to the present: Mindfulness meditation reveals distinct neural modes of self-reference. *Social Cognitive and Affective Neuroscience, 2,* 313–322.

Feldman-Barrett, L., Williams, N., & Fong, G. T. (2002). Defensive verbal behavior assessment. *Personality and Social Psychology Bulletin, 28,* 776–788.

Frost, P. J., Dutton, J. E, Worline, M. C., & Wilson, A. (2000). Narratives of compassion in organizations. In S. Fineman (Ed.), *Emotion in organizations* (pp. 25–45). London: Sage.

Fulton, P. R., & Siegel, R. D. (2005). Buddhist and Western psychology: Seeking common ground. In C. K. Germer, R. D. Siegel & P. R. Fulton (Eds.), *Mindfulness and psychotherapy* (pp. 28–51). New York, NY: Guilford Press.

Germer, C. K., Siegel, R. D., & Fulton, P. R. (Eds.). (2005). *Mindfulness and psychotherapy.* New York, NY: Guilford Press.

Glomb, T. M., Duffy, M. K., Bono, J. E., & Yang, T. (2011). Mindfulness at work. *Research in Personnel and Human Resources Management, 30,* 115–157.

Greenberg, J., Pyszczynski, T., Solomon, S., Rosenblatt, A., Veeder, M., Kirkland, S., & Lyon, D. (1990). Evidence for terror management II: The effects of mortality salience on reactions to those who threaten or bolster the cultural worldview. *Journal of Personality and Social Psychology, 58,* 308–318.

Hassed, C., de Lisle, S., Sullivan, G., & Pier, C. (2008). Enhancing the health of medical students: Outcomes of an integrated mindfulness and lifestyle program. *Advances in Health Science Education: Theory and Practice, 144,* 387–398.

Healy, M. F. (2001). *The insight (Vipassana) meditation transformational learning process: A phenomenological study.* Publication No. 0493371931. Retrieved from URL: http://proxy.libraries.smu.edu/login?url = http://search.proquest.com.proxy.libraries.smu.edu/docview/276263753?accountid = 6667

Herndon, F. (2008). Testing mindfulness with perceptual and cognitive failures: External vs. internal encoding, and the cognitive failures questionnaire. *Personality and Individual Differences, 44,* 32–41.

Hitt, M. A., Beamish, P. A., Jackson, S. E., & Matheiu, J. E. (2007). Building theoretical and empirical bridges across levels: Multilevel research in management. *Academy of Management Journal, 50,* 1385–1399.

Hodgins, H. (2008). Motivation, threshold for threat, and quieting the ego. In H. A. Wayment & J. Bauer (Eds.), *Transcending self-interest: Psychological explorations of the quiet ego* (pp. 117–124). Washington, DC: American Psychological Association.

Jacobs, S., & Blustein, D. L. (2008). Mindfulness as a coping mechanism for employment uncertainty. *Career Development Quarterly, 52,* 172–180.

Jarvis, R. (2006). *Toward a comprehensive theory of human learning.* New York, NY: Routledge/Falmer Press.

Jha, A. P., Krompinger, J. K., & Baime, M. J. (2007). Mindfulness training modifies subsystems of attention. *Cognitive, Affective & Behavioral Neuroscience, 7,* 102–119.

Jha, A. P., Stanley, E. A., Kiyonaga, A., Wong, L., & Gelfand, L. (2010). Examining the protective effects of mindfulness training on working memory and affective experience. *Emotion, 10,* 54–64.

Kabat-Zinn, J. (1990). *Full catastrophic living: Using the wisdom of your body and mind to face stress, pain, and illness.* New York, NY: Dell.

Kabat-Zinn, J. (2003). Mindfulness-based interventions in context: Past, present, and future. *Clinical Psychology: Science and Practice, 10,* 144–156.

Ko, I., & Donaldson, S. I. (2011). Applied positive organizational psychology: The state of the science and practice. In S. I. Donaldson, M. Csikszentmihalyi & J. Nakamura (Eds.), *Applied positive psychology: Improving everyday life, health, schools, work, and society* (pp. 137–154). New York, NY: Psychology Press.

Langer, E. J. (1997). *The power of mindful learning.* Cambridge: Da Capo Press.

Langer, E. J. (2000). Mindful learning. *Current Directions in Psychological Science, 9,* 220–223.

Lazar, S. W., Kerr, C., Wasserman, R. H., Gray, J. R., Greve, D., Treadway, M. T., & Fischl, B. (2005). Meditation experience is associated with increased cortical thickness. *NeuroReport, 16,* 1893–1897.

Leary, M. R., & Tate, E. B. (2007). The multi-faceted nature of mindfulness. *Psychological Inquiry, 18,* 251–255.

Lesh, T. V. (1970). Zen meditation and the development of empathy in counselors. *Journal of Humanistic Psychology, 10,* 39–74.

Lillis, J., & Hayes, S. C. (2007). Applying acceptance, mindfulness, and values to the reduction of prejudice: A pilot study. *Behavioral Modification, 31,* 389–411.

Lilius, J. M., Worline, M. C., Maitlis, S., Kanov, J., Dutton, J. E., & Frost, P. (2008). The contours and consequences of compassion at work. *Journal of Organizational Behavior, 29,* 193–218.

Mackenzie, C. S., Poulin, P. A., & Seidman-Carlson, R. (2006). A brief mindfulness-based stress reduction intervention for nurses and nurse aides. *Applied Nursing Research, 19,* 105–109.

Mackenzie, M., Carlson, L. E., Munoz, M., & Speca, M. (2007). A qualitative study of self-perceived effects of mindfulness-based stress reduction (MBSR) in a psychosocial oncology setting. *Stress and Health, 23,* 59–69.

McGarrigle, T., & Walsh, C. (2011). Mindfulness, self-care, and wellness in social work: Effects of contemplative training. *Journal of Religion & Spirituality in Social Work: Social Thought, 30,* 212–233.

Maddi, S. R., & Hightower, M. (1999). Hardiness and optimism expressed as coping patterns. *Consulting Psychology Journal: Practice and Research, 51,* 95–105.

Mezirow, J. (1991). *Transformative dimensions of adult learning.* San Francisco, CA: Jossey-Bass.

Mezirow, J. (Ed.). (2000). *Learning as transformation: Critical perspectives on a theory in progress.* San Francisco, CA: Jossey-Bass.

Moore, A., & Malinowski, P. (2009). Meditation, mindfulness cognitive flexibility. *Consciousness and Cognition, 18,* 176–186.

Niemiec, C. P., Brown, K. W., Kashdan, T. B., Cozzolino, P. J., Breen, W. E., Levesque-Bristol, C., & Rayan, R. M. (2010). Being present in the face of existential threat: The role of trait mindfulness in reducing defensive responses to mortality salience. *Journal of Personality and Social Psychology, 2,* 344–356.

Ortner, C. N. M., Kilner, J. S., & Zelazo, P. D. (2007). Mindfulness meditation and reduced emotional interference on a cognitive task. *Motivation and Emotion, 31,* 271–283.

Pruitt, I. T., & McCollum, E. E. (2010). Voices of experienced meditators: The impact of meditation practice on intimate relationships. *Contemporary Family Therapy, 32,* 135–154.

Radeke, J. T., & Mahoney, M. J. (2000). Comparing the personal lives of psychotherapists and research psychologists. *Professional Psychology: Research and Practice, 31,* 82–84.

Rosenberg, T., & Pace, M. (2006). Burnout among mental health professionals: Special considerations for the marriage and family therapist. *Journal of Marital and Family Therapy, 32,* 87–99.

Salmon, P. G., Santorelli, S. F., & Kabat-Zinn, J. (1998). Intervention elements promoting adherence to mindfulness-based stress reduction programs in the clinical behavioral medicine setting. In S. A. Shumaker, E. Schron, J. Ockene & W. McBee (Eds.), *Handbook of health behavior change* (2nd ed., pp. 239–266). New York, NY: Springer.

Schure, M. B., Christopher, J., & Christopher, S. (2008). Mind-body medicine and the art of self-care: Teaching mindfulness to counseling students through yoga, meditation, and qigong. *Journal of Counseling & Development, 86,* 47–56.

Shapiro, D. H. (1992). A preliminary study of long term meditators: Goals, effects, religious orientation, cognitions. *Journal of Transpersonal Psychology, 24,* 23–39.

Shapiro, S. (2009). The integration of mindfulness and psychology. *Journal of Clinical Psychology, 65,* 555–560.

Shapiro, S., & Carlson, L. E. (2009). *The art and science of mindfulness: Integrating mindfulness into psychology and the helping professions.* Washington, DC: American Psychological Association.

Shapiro., S., Carlson, L. E., Astin, J., & Freedman, B. (2006). Mechanisms of mindfulness. *Journal of Clinical Psychology, 62,* 373–386.

Shapiro, S. L., Astin, J. A., Bishop, S. R., & Cordova, M. (2005). Mindfulness-based stress reduction for health care professionals: Results from a randomized trial. *International Journal of Stress Management, 12,* 164–176.

Shapiro, S. L., Brown, K. W., & Biegel, G. M. (2007). Teaching self-care to caregivers: Effects of mindfulness-based stress reduction on the mental health of therapists in training. *Training and Education in Professional Psychology, 1,* 105–115.

Shapiro, S. L., Schwartz, G. E., & Bonner, G. (1998). Effects of mindfulness-based stress reduction on medical and premedical students. *Journal of Behavioral Medicine, 21,* 581–599.

Siegel, D. J. (2007). *The mindful brain: Reflection and attainment in the cultivation of well-being.* New York, NY: Norton.

Stamm, B. H. (Ed.). (1995). *Secondary traumatic stress: Self-care issues for clinicians, researchers, and educators.* Lutherville, MD: Sidran Press.

Stanley, E. A., Schaldach, J. M., Kiyonaga, A., & Jha, A. P. (2011). Mindfulness-based mind fitness training: A case study of a high-stress predeployment military cohort. *Cognitive and Behavioral Practice, 18,* 566–576.

Surrey, J. L. (2005). Relationship psychotherapy, relational mindfulness. In C. K. Germer, R. D. Siegal & P. R. Fulton (Eds.), *Mindfulness and psychotherapy* (pp. 91–110). New York, NY: Guilford Press.

Taylor, E. W. (2000). Analyzing research on transformative learning theory. In J. Mezirow (Ed.), *Learning as transformation: Critical perspectives on a theory in transition* (pp. 285–328). San Francisco, CA: Jossey-Bass.

Thibodeau, R., & Aronson, E. (1992). Taking a closer look: Reasserting the role of the self-concept in dissonance theory. *Personality and Social Psychology Bulletin, 18,* 591–602.

Thompson, B. L., & Waltz, J. A. (2008). Mindfulness, self-esteem, and unconditional self-acceptance. *Journal of Rational-Emotive & Cognitive-Behavior Therapy, 26,* 119–126.

Walach, H., Nord, E., Zier, C., Dietz-Waschkowski, B., Kersig, S., & Schupback, H. (2007). Mindfulness-based stress reduction as a method for personnel development: A pilot evaluation. *International Journal of Stress Management, 14,* 188–198.

Wallace, B. A., & Hodel, B. (2008). *Embracing mind: The common ground of science and spirituality.* Boston, MA: Shambhala.

Wallace, B. A., & Shapiro, S. L. (2006). Mental balance and well-being: Building bridges between Buddhism and Western psychology. *American Psychologist, 67,* 690–701.

Walsh, R., & Shapiro, S. L. (2006). The meeting of meditative disciplines and Western psychology. *American Psychologist, 6,* 227–239.

Weick, K. E., & Putnam, R. (2006). Organizing as mindfulness: Eastern wisdom and Western knowledge. *Journal of Management Inquiry, 15,* 275–287.

Weick, K. E., & Roberts, K. H. (1993). Collective mind in organizations: Heedful interrelating on flight decks. *Administrative Science Quarterly, 38,* 357–381.

Weick, K. E., Sutcliffe, K., & Obstfeld, D. (2002). High reliability: The power of mindfulness. In F. Hesselbein & R. Johnson (Eds.), *On high performance organizations: A leader to leader guide* (pp. 7–18). San Francisco, CA: Jossey-Bass.

Weick, K. E., & Sutcliffe, K. M. (2007). *Managing the unexpected: Resilient performance in an age of uncertainty* (2nd ed.). San Francisco, CA: Jossey-Bass.

Yeganeh, B. (2006). *Mindful experiential learning.* Case Western Reserve University. Retrieved from http://etd.ohiolink.edu/view.cgi/Yeganeh%20Bauback.pdf?acc_num = case11630 23095

ORGANIZATIONAL SOCIALIZATION AND NEWCOMERS' PSYCHOLOGICAL CAPITAL AND WELL-BEING

Jamie A. Gruman and Alan M. Saks

Organizational socialization is the process through which new hires adjust to their new roles and become effective members of an organization. Katz (1980) defines the socialization period as the "introductory events and activities by which individuals come to know and make sense out of their newfound work experiences" (p. 88). Other definitions of organizational socialization also describe it as a learning process that involves learning new attitudes, behaviors, and ways of thinking (Klein & Weaver, 2000).

In this chapter, we aim to expand this approach to organizational socialization by including more than just knowledge acquisition and learning. We argue that the emphasis in the socialization literature on information and learning is too narrow given the current challenges facing employees and organizations. New hires need to be able to function in organizations that face increasing uncertainty, challenges, and competitive pressures. This means that socialization programs must do more than simply provide newcomers with exhaustive amounts of information (Rollag, Parise, & Cross, 2005). Clearly, becoming an effective organizational member today requires more than just information.

Advances in Positive Organizational Psychology, Volume 1, 211–236
ISSN: 2046-410X/doi:10.1108/S2046-410X(2013)0000001012

The chapter is organized in five sections. First, we discuss how organizational socialization has traditionally been viewed as an information and learning process. Second, we show that the dominant approach for socializing newcomers (i.e., organizational socialization tactics) is grounded in the information perspective. Third, we discuss how organizational socialization should go beyond learning and focus on the development of newcomers' psychological capital (i.e., hope, optimism, self-efficacy, and resiliency) and well-being. Fourth, we present a new approach to organizational socialization that we call Socialization Resources Theory (SRT) that aims to develop newcomers' psychological capital and enhance their well-being. In the final section of the chapter, we discuss the implications of this new approach to organizational socialization for research and practice.

ORGANIZATIONAL SOCIALIZATION AND LEARNING

From the start, organizational socialization has been all about learning. In fact, most definitions of organizational socialization are very explicit about this and the general notion that socialization involves learning "the ropes" of a particular organizational role (Fisher, 1986). Socialization has been described as a sense-making and learning process in which newcomers acquire a variety of types of information and knowledge to become effective members of the organization (Klein & Weaver, 2000).

In her review of the organizational socialization literature, Fisher (1986) described socialization as primarily a learning and change process. She suggested four primary categories or types of learning content: (1) organizational values, goals, culture, and so on; (2) work group values, norms, and friendships; (3) how to do the job and the required skills and knowledge; and (4) personal change and development in terms of identity, self-image, and motive structure. She suggests that "the first task of the socializing organization or agent may be to convince the newcomer that learning or adaptation on his or her part is necessary" or what she refers to as preliminary learning. Newcomers must learn "*what* to learn" and "whom to learn from" (pp. 105–106).

The two most recent reviews of organizational socialization also describe socialization as a learning process. Ashforth, Sluss, and Harrison (2007) state that learning is the heart of socialization:

> For socialization to effectively bring the newcomer into the fold, the newcomer should
> come to know and understand (i.e., learn) the norms, values, tasks, and roles that typify

group and organizational membership. As such, newcomer learning lies "at the heart of any organizational socialization model." (p. 16)

In a similar vein, Klein and Heuser (2008) view socialization "fundamentally as a process of learning about a new or changed role and the environment surrounding that role" (p. 321). As such, they focused on what newcomers need to learn during socialization. As described by Klein and Heuser (2008),

> The socialization content approach views socialization as primarily a learning process in which newcomers acquire a variety of information, attitudes, and behaviors in order to become more effective organizational members. (p. 296)

Saks and Ashforth (1997a) developed a multilevel process model of organizational socialization in which cognitive sense-making, uncertainty reduction, and learning intervenes between socialization factors and socialization outcomes. As described by Saks and Ashforth, "the focus of the model is information and learning which is consistent with recent research showing that organizational socialization is primarily a learning process" (p. 238).

Along these lines, several models of organizational socialization have treated learning as a direct outcome of socialization practices and as a mediating variable for the relationship between socialization practices and outcomes. For example, Ashforth, Sluss, and Harrison's (2007) integrative model places learning as a mediating variable between socialization processes and newcomer adjustment. According to the authors, "content appears to offer tremendous potential as the major linchpin between socialization processes and short- and long-term newcomer adjustment" (p. 31).

Klein and Heuser's (2008) framework of the socialization literature links three socialization practices (organizational tactics and practices, socialization agents, and newcomer proactivity) to learning outcomes, which then lead to proximal outcomes (e.g., role clarity), which lead to distal outcomes (e.g., job satisfaction). Along these lines, a number of studies have found that learning mediates the relationship between socialization practices such as orientation training, socialization tactics, mentoring, socialization agent helpfulness, and proactive behaviors and socialization outcomes (Allen, McManus, & Russell, 1999; Ashforth, Sluss, & Saks, 2007; Cooper-Thomas & Anderson, 2002; Klein, Fan, & Preacher, 2006; Klein & Weaver, 2000).

Following the learning approach, there has been increasing research attention on the so-called content of socialization (Klein & Heuser, 2008). This research focuses on identifying and measuring knowledge in various domains and considers indicators of learning as the most appropriate criteria for socialization (Klein & Heuser, 2008). Several measures of socialization learning content have been developed (Chao, O'Leary-Kelly, Wolf, Klein, & Gardner, 1994; Cooper-Thomas & Anderson, 2002; Haueter, Macan, & Winter, 2003; Ostroff & Kozlowski, 1992). These measures generally consist of various content dimensions of learning and knowledge with respect to newcomers' tasks, role, work group, and the organization (e.g., history, goals).

Klein and Heuser (2008) recently developed an expanded socialization content typology (i.e., the information and behaviors individuals need to acquire in order to be effective organizational members) that consists of 12 content dimensions that newcomers need to learn for effective socialization. They used an instructional systems approach to connect the socialization content dimensions to learning outcomes and the socialization practices (what they refer to as orienting activities) that will be most effective for newcomers to learn the socialization-content dimensions.

In summary, the prevailing perspective of organizational socialization has not changed much over the last 25 years. Socialization models and research have considered learning to be the most direct and important outcome of organizational socialization. It has even been suggested that "greater attention needs to be given to learning outcomes as learning is the most direct socialization outcome" (Klein & Heuser, 2008, p. 296). In addition, most organizations use an informational approach to orienting new hires, and managers view the on-boarding process primarily as a means of providing newcomers with information (Rollag et al., 2005). As described in the next section, the emphasis on learning has been accompanied by an approach to socialization that involves the use of socialization tactics that provide information to reduce newcomer uncertainty.

SOCIALIZATION TACTICS AND NEWCOMER ADJUSTMENT

Just as learning has been regarded as the primary outcome of organizational socialization, the socialization literature has emphasized one approach for the socialization literature has emphasized one approach for the socialization of newcomers – socialization tactics (Klein & Heuser, 2008).

Van Maanen and Schein (1979) define socialization tactics as "the ways in which the experiences of individuals in transition from one role to another are structured for them by others in the organization" (p. 230). Socialization tactics can be used by managers when socializing newcomers into the organization or at various boundary passages.

Van Maanen and Schein (1979) identified six tactical dimensions and described how they influence newcomers' custodial, content-innovative, or role-innovative responses. Jones (1986) suggested that Van Maanen and Schein's six tactics represent two opposing dimensions that he called *institutionalized* and *individualized socialization*.

According to Jones (1986), the collective, formal, sequential, fixed, serial, and investiture tactics encourage newcomers to passively accept preset roles, thus reproducing the organizational status quo. These institutionalized tactics provide newcomers with information that reduces the uncertainty inherent in early work experiences and reflect a more structured and formalized socialization process. At the opposite end of the socialization continuum, the individual, informal, random, variable, disjunctive, and divestiture tactics encourage newcomers to question the status quo and to develop their own unique approach to their roles. Thus, individualized socialization reflects an absence of structure such that newcomers are socialized more by default than design (Ashforth, Saks, & Lee, 1998). As a result, individualized tactics might increase the uncertainty and anxiety of early work experiences (Jones, 1986).

The results of two meta-analyses found that institutionalized socialization tactics are negatively related to role ambiguity, role conflict, and intentions to quit, and positively related to fit perceptions, self-efficacy, social acceptance, job satisfaction, organizational commitment, job performance, and a custodial role orientation (Bauer, Bodner, Erdogan, Truxillo, & Tucker, 2007; Saks, Uggerslev, & Fassina, 2007). In addition, a number of studies have found that institutionalized socialization tactics are associated with a greater amount of information acquisition and learning which mediates the relationship between socialization tactics and outcomes (Ashforth, Sluss, & Saks, 2007; Cooper-Thomas & Anderson, 2002; Saks & Ashforth, 1997b). In effect, what socialization tactics do is shape the information that newcomers receive (Jones, 1986). The theoretical and conceptual underpinning for socialization tactics is uncertainty reduction theory which is also the basis for the learning or content approach to socialization.

In summary, the socialization literature has been dominated by research on socialization tactics and learning outcomes. Fig. 1 shows the linkages between socialization tactics, learning, and proximal and distal socialization outcomes. The model shows that socialization tactics have a direct effect on learning, and learning is an antecedent of proximal adjustment outcomes and distal socialization outcomes (Klein & Heuser, 2008; Saks & Ashforth, 1997a). This model reflects the current state of the socialization literature.

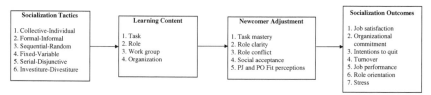

Fig. 1.   Traditional Model of Organizational Socialization.

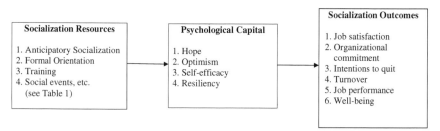

Fig. 2.   Model of Organizational Socialization and Psychological Capital.

We believe, however, that there is much more to organizational socialization than socialization tactics and learning. In the next section, we argue that organizational socialization needs to consider other direct outcomes in addition to learning that represent a more positive approach to organizational socialization.

NEWCOMER PSYCHOLOGICAL CAPITAL AND WELL-BEING

In this section, we argue for a new perspective on organizational socialization that goes beyond learning as the primary outcome of organizational socialization. Instead, we suggest a more positive approach that focuses on developing the psychological capital (PsyCap) and well-being of newcomers (see Fig. 2).

As noted by Klein and Heuser (2008), starting in a new position can be a difficult and turbulent transition that leads to confusion, anxiety, doubt, and disorientation. These difficulties call for more than information to make a newcomer an effective member of an organization today. Such challenges can be effectively managed through the development of psychological capital. Psychological capital is a positive psychological state-like characteristic involving confidence to succeed at challenging tasks (self-efficacy), making personal attributions for positive outcomes (optimism), persisting toward goals and changing paths when necessary (hope), and bouncing back from adversity (resiliency) (Luthans, Youssef, & Avolio, 2007).

Research on PsyCap has found that it is related to supervisor performance ratings and objective performance (Avey, Nimnicht, & Graber Pigeon, 2010; Luthans, Avey, Clapp-Smith, & Li, 2008). Follower PsyCap has been shown to fully mediate the relationship between leader PsyCap and performance ratings (Walumbwa, Peterson, Avolio, & Hartnell, 2010), in addition to the relationship between supportive organizational climate and performance (Luthans, Norman, Avoilo, & Avey, 2008).

A recent meta-analysis (Avey, Reichard, Luthans, & Mhatre, 2011) found that PsyCap has significant correlations with many traditional socialization outcomes such as job satisfaction (corrected $r = .54$, $p < .05$), organizational commitment (corrected $r = .48$, $p < .05$), turnover intentions (corrected $r = -.32$, $p < .05$), and stress and anxiety (corrected $r = -.29$, $p < .05$). PsyCap also correlates significantly with behaviors such as organizational citizenship behaviors (corrected $r = .45$, $p < .05$) and employee performance (corrected $r = .26$, $p < .05$). Additionally, the value of PsyCap as a higher-order construct has been suggested by the observation that PsyCap has a more consistent relationship with performance and job satisfaction than the individual variables that comprise it (Luthans, Avolio, Avey, & Norman, 2007). Indeed, this is the purported value of PsyCap as a higher order construct.

We argue that PsyCap represents a new and important way to think about the socialization and adjustment of newcomers with important implications for newcomers' well-being. PsyCap and the four constructs that comprise it represent important proximal outcomes of organizational socialization and are antecedents of traditional socialization outcomes. In addition to being positively associated with such outcomes, PsyCap may also promote another outcome of increasing interest to organizational scholars – workplace well-being. In fact, each of the constructs comprising PsyCap is crucial for one's psychological and work-related well-being (e.g., Xanthopoulou, Bakker, Demerouti, & Schaufeli, 2009).

Thus, as suggested in Fig. 2, an important focus of organizational socialization should be to socialize newcomers so that they have high levels of self-efficacy, optimism, hope, and resiliency. This will, in turn, lead to traditional socialization outcomes such as job satisfaction and result in a higher level of newcomers' well-being. Following is a brief description of the four main constructs of PsyCap and well-being.

Self-Efficacy

Of the four constructs comprising the higher-order PsyCap construct, self-efficacy has the strongest conceptual and empirical foundation (Luthans & Youssef, 2007). Based on original work by Bandura (1997), Luthans and his colleagues define self-efficacy as "an individual's conviction (or confidence) about his or her abilities to mobilize the motivation, cognitive resources, and courses of action needed to successfully execute a specific task within a given context" (Stajkovic & Luthans, 1998, p. 66).

Self-efficacy is the only PsyCap construct that has been studied in the socialization literature. In one of the earliest studies, Saks (1995) found that newly hired entry-level accountants who received more entry training had higher post-training task-relevant self-efficacy. In addition, initial self-efficacy moderated the relationship between training and socialization outcomes, and post-training self-efficacy mediated the relationship between training and socialization outcomes. Saks (1995) concluded that "the success of socialization programs may be improved if they are designed to increase newcomers' self-efficacy" (p. 224).

Hope

Snyder, Rand, and Sigmon (2005) define hope as the belief that people can discover pathways to their goals (pathways thinking) and find the motivation to use the pathways (agentic thinking). Hope is distinguished from self-efficacy by the equal importance placed on two forms of thinking (Luthans, 2002a) and the fact that self-efficacy concerns situation-specific goals whereas hope includes cross-situational goals (Snyder et al., 2005). Because newcomers enter organizations with their own goals and are expected to achieve work-related goals, an important objective of socialization should be to develop newcomers' hope with respect to their capacity to set and achieve their work and career goals.

Optimism

Optimism refers to having positive outcome expectancies and/or making positive attributions for events (Luthans, 2002a). Optimists expect good things to happen to them (Carver & Scheier, 2005), and when they experience bad events, they make external, specific, unstable attributions

(Seligman, 2006). Optimism differs from hope in that optimism does not address pathways thinking, and includes expectancies about outcomes achieved via forces outside of oneself (Luthans & Youssef, 2007). Newcomers are often apprehensive about their ability to succeed in their new job and role, so developing their optimism about their ability to succeed in their new role and the organization is important.

Resiliency

Unlike the other three PsyCap elements, resiliency is a reactive construct (Luthans, Vogelgesang, & Lester, 2006). Resiliency involves maintaining positive adjustment, coping successfully, and bouncing back when facing challenging conditions, including those involving positive change (Luthans, 2002b). The PsyCap conceptualization of resiliency focuses on the adaptive use of assets to address risks, and the interplay between the risks one faces and one's repertoire of assets (Luthans & Youssef, 2007). Early failures and setbacks can be especially unsettling for new hires who need to be able to bounce back from the inevitable challenges they will face during the socialization process. Therefore, the development of resiliency is important for newcomers during their socialization.

Workplace Well-Being

As indicated earlier, in addition to predicting traditional socialization outcomes, another outcome that PsyCap might promote among newcomers is well-being which has for the most part been absent in the socialization literature (see Fig. 2). Building on the definition of well-being provided by Ryan and Deci (2001), workplace well-being can be conceptualized as optimal psychological functioning and experience at work.

Organizational research has shown that well-being is negatively associated with turnover (Wright & Bonett, 2007), and positively associated with job performance (Wright & Cropanzano, 1999). In fact, Wright (2010) notes that differences in well-being can account for up to 25% of the variance in job performance. Well-being at work may also reduce organizations' healthcare costs by improving employees' cardiovascular health (Wright, 2010).

We propose that PsyCap may be a significant precursor to workplace well-being among newcomers partly because the constructs that comprise PsyCap involve, in varying ways, adaptive perceptions that promote happiness. For example, as noted above, self-efficacy involves a "conviction" that one can achieve a certain level of performance, and hope is a "belief" that one can find and use pathways to goals. These sorts of adaptive perceptions help to foster well-being by orienting people toward positive construal of their experiences (Lyubomirsky, 2001). Specifically, PsyCap may help newcomers perceive, evaluate, and conceptualize challenges in more positive ways (Lyubomirsky, 2001). As Fisher (2010) notes "It is important to remember that happiness and positive attitudes are not directly created by environments or events ..., but rather by individuals' perceptions, interpretations, and appraisals of those environments and events" (p. 396).

Research within and outside organizations has demonstrated that the individual constructs of hope (Park, Peterson, & Seligman, 2004), optimism (Mäkikangas & Kinnunen, 2003), self-efficacy (Liu, Siu, & Shi, 2010), and resiliency (Tugade & Fredrickson, 2004) are, indeed, positively associated with well-being. Additionally, recent empirical studies have demonstrated a positive association between PsyCap and well-being (Avey, Luthans, Smith, & Palmer, 2010; Culbertson, Fullagar, & Mills, 2010).

In summary, we believe that the time has come for socialization research and practice to go beyond learning outcomes and focus on the development of newcomers' PsyCap and well-being. However, the traditional approach to socializing newcomers through socialization tactics is largely focused on providing information and reducing uncertainty. Is this also an effective approach for developing newcomers' PsyCap and well-being? In the next section, we consider the potential for socialization tactics to develop newcomers' PsyCap and well-being and we introduce a new approach to organizational socialization called Socialization Resources Theory (SRT).

SOCIALIZATION RESOURCES THEORY AND PSYCHOLOGICAL CAPITAL

How can the socialization process be designed to develop the PsyCap of newcomers? Although socialization tactics have been linked to learning and other socialization outcomes, it is questionable how effective they will be in developing newcomers' PsyCap. Bauer et al. (2007) did find a significant relationship between socialization tactics and self-efficacy in their meta-analysis but the correlations were relatively small and the two highest ones were for the social tactics (i.e., serial and investiture), which indicates the importance of social capital.

Ashforth, Myers, and Sluss (2012) have suggested that the social tactics are most likely to facilitate the development of PsyCap because social support and social validation reinforce PsyCap. However, what this means in terms of socialization practices is unclear because socialization tactics are a "black box" when it comes to the specific activities that they involve (Ashforth, Sluss, & Harrison, 2007). This is because socialization tactics measure the structure of the socialization process or what Van Maanen and Schein (1979) refer to as the "structural side" of organizational socialization not the actual activities, events, or content of socialization.

Of greater importance for the development of newcomers' PsyCap is the actual information they receive and the experiences they have rather than *how* the information is received. Thus, we argue that socialization tactics are not sufficient to develop positive organizational psychology outcomes such as PsyCap. In fact, a recent study found that none of the socialization tactics were correlated with employee engagement, which is considered to be a positive psychology outcome (Saks & Gruman, 2011).

The question then is how do you socialize newcomers to develop each of the psychological capital constructs? We argue that this involves providing newcomers with resources that are necessary for the development of each of the PsyCap constructs. We refer to this approach as *Socialization Resources Theory* (SRT; Saks & Gruman, 2012).

Conceptually based on the Job Demands-Resources Model (Bakker & Demerouti, 2007), SRT is a new approach to organizational socialization that focuses on the resources newcomers require for successful adjustment to their jobs, roles, and the organization. It consists of a comprehensive set of resources that newcomers can draw on to manage the transition to work or changes in work roles. The basic premise of SRT is that the transition to a new job or role is inherently challenging and stressful, and that presenting newcomers with the resources they need to cope with these challenges is the most effective and efficient way to foster PsyCap and well-being.

SRT is built on both the academic and practitioner literatures and consists of 17 dimensions which address specific socialization resources that can be used to develop newcomers' PsyCap and well-being (see Tables 1 and 2) and facilitate newcomer adjustment and socialization. The 17 dimensions correspond to four time periods: (1) prior to entry; (2) immediately after entry; (3) following orientation (social capital resources and work-related resources); and (4) following the formal socialization/on-boarding period.

Table 1.   Socialization Resources Theory Dimensions.

SRT Dimension by Socialization Period	Definition	Sample Questions
Period: Prior to Entry		
1. Anticipatory Socialization	Contacting new hires before their first day on the job	Are newcomers contacted after they are hired by members of the organization?
Period: Immediately After Entry		
2. Formal Orientation	The extent and nature of the orientation	Do newcomers participate in an orientation program after they are hired?
3. Proactive Encouragement	Encouraging newcomers to be proactive (e.g., asking for help) during socialization	Are newcomers encouraged to meet and interact with members of the organization?
4. Formal Assistance	Assignment of a buddy or mentor	Are newcomers assigned a "buddy" after they are hired?
Period: Following Orientation – Social Capital Resources		
5. Social Events	Holding formal events (e.g., lunches) for new hires to become acquainted with others	Are there company-sponsored social events organized for new hires?
6. Socialization Agents	Insiders going out of their way to help the new hire	Do organizational members offer help and assistance to new hires?
7. Supervisor Support	Care, concern, and assistance displayed by immediate supervisor.	Do supervisors provide help and assistance to new hires?
8. Relationship Development	Informal time made for the new hire to meet and get to know others	Is time made for new hires to meet members of their department and the organization?
Period: Following Orientation – Work-related Resources		
9. Job Resources	Material and physical resources are ready and available for new hires	Are newcomers provided with all of the resources they need to perform their job?
10. Personal Planning	Expectations, plans, and work goals have been established for new hires	Are newcomers given specific work objectives that they are expected to achieve?
11. Training	Formal programs providing newcomers with the knowledge and skills required to effectively perform their jobs	Are newcomer provided with training related to their job and role after they are hired?

Table 1. (*Continued*)

SRT Dimension by Socialization Period	Definition	Sample Questions
12. Assignments	Nature of newcomers' early assignments in terms of job characteristics (e.g., task variety) and other characteristics of work (e.g., working with others)	Are newcomers given considerable control in how they perform their job?
13. Information	Providing new hires with information about their jobs, role, and the organization	Do co-workers go out of their way to provide new hires with information about how things are done in the organization?
14. Feedback	Providing newcomers with accurate and timely feedback on their job performance and work-related behavior	Do new hires receive ongoing feedback about their job performance?
15. Recognition and Appreciation	Newcomers receive acknowledgement and praise for their effort and performance	Do new hires receive praise and compliments when they do a good job?
Period: Following Formal Socialization/On-boarding Period		
16. Follow-up	Organization follows-up with new hires after the formal orientation period has ended to check adjustment	Are there follow-up events to see how well new hires are adjusting?
17. Program Evaluation	Organization evaluates its orientation and socialization practices	Are newcomers asked to provide feedback about the helpfulness of the new hire orientation program?

Each dimension pertains to specific socialization events (as opposed to general experiences or learning content), and involves concrete socialization behaviors (as opposed to a subjective accounts).

Below, we describe how each of the PsyCap constructs have been developed by Luthans and associates through a process they refer to as PsyCap intervention (PCI: Luthans, Avey, Avolio, Norman, & Combs, 2006; Luthans, Avey, Avoilo, & Peterson, 2010; Luthans, Avey, & Patera, 2008) and explain how the associated SRT dimensions (italicized) can be leveraged to foster the personal resources that represent PsyCap.

Table 2.   Socialization Resources Theory Dimensions for Promoting the
                Components of Psychological Capital.

Psychological Capital Component	Socialization Resources Theory Dimensions
Self-efficacy	
Enactive mastery	Training, assignments, job resources
Vicarious learning	Supervisor support, training, formal assistance, relationship development
Verbal persuasion	Supervisor support, feedback, recognition and appreciation
Hope	
Hope finding	Formal orientation
Hope bonding	Social capital resources, personal planning
Hope enhancing	Personal planning, information, training, social capital resources
Hope reminding	Social capital resources, Follow-up
Optimism	Personal planning, feedback, recognition and appreciation, social capital resources
Resiliency	
Risk-focused strategies	Anticipatory socialization, formal orientation
Asset-focused strategies	Formal assistance, assignments, training
Process-focused strategies	Assignments, formal assistance, feedback, supervisor support

Self-Efficacy

Self-efficacy can be developed through enactive mastery, vicarious learning, and verbal persuasion (Bandura, 1997). In the PCI, mastery experiences are fostered by having participants establish goals and subgoals, and explain how they will be accomplished. Vicarious learning occurs as participants observe peers approach their own goals and discuss how their goals were achieved. This is enhanced by verbal persuasion from the facilitator and group members regarding the achievability of each individual's goals. These and other techniques are addressed by SRT, which provides a framework for incorporating self-efficacy building experiences into the socialization process. These experiences can be grouped according to the three primary sources of self-efficacy information.

Enactive Mastery
Experiencing success in mastering specific challenges is likely to have the greatest impact on self-efficacy because the most powerful source of

self-efficacy-related information is derived from one's own attempts to exert control over the environment (Bandura, 1997; Maddux, 2005). *Training* that helps newcomers learn and practice job-related tasks allows them to experience success first-hand and is likely to have a strong impact on the development of their self-efficacy. As indicated earlier, training has been found to be positively related to newcomers' self-efficacy (Saks, 1995). In a similar vein, early *assignments* that challenge, but don't overwhelm, newcomers will produce comparable results, but only to the extent that newcomers have the *job resources* they need to perform their duties properly. Providing newcomers with early work experiences in situations where the probability of success is high is an effective strategy for fostering self-efficacy (Luthans et al., 2007).

Vicarious Learning

Self-efficacy beliefs are influenced by observing the behavior of others. Therefore, having *supervisor support* who model high self-efficacy and demonstrate success in their endeavors will foster the self-efficacy of new-comers. However, the degree to which observation impacts self-efficacy depends largely on the degree to which observed others are similar to the observer (Maddux, 2005). Therefore, early entry *training* that includes models similar to the newcomers (in terms of age, gender, etc.) successfully engaging in work-related tasks will have a greater impact on newcomer self-efficacy than observing dissimilar others or a supervisor. Similarly, providing *formal assistance* in the form of a buddy may allow newcomers to observe similar others successfully perform comparable duties, thus boosting the newcomers' confidence. Less structured processes, such as *relationship development*, may also provide effective role models more indirectly, and produce equivalent gains in self-efficacy.

Verbal Persuasion

Throughout the training discussed above, positive reinforcement in the form of expressions of confidence by trainers can further boost self-efficacy. Once training is complete, continued reinforcement in the form of *supervisor support* can promote the transfer of self-efficacy training to the job itself. This support can include encouraging newcomers to take small risks that can lead to small successes (Maddux, 2005), and highlighting to the newcomers that their successes are due to their own effort. *Feedback* that lets newcomers know when they are succeeding and how to modify their efforts to achieve greater success will also promote self-efficacy, as will *recognition and appreciation* for good work.

Hope

Lopez et al. (2004) describe four strategies for enhancing hope: hope finding, bonding, enhancing, and reminding. Although Lopez et al. (2004) discuss these strategies in a psychotherapeutic context, they are equally applicable in an organizational context. Each of these strategies is elaborated below along with the SRT dimensions that can incorporate each strategy.

Hope Finding

Hope finding involves boosting people's expectations for success and can involve telling stories that emphasize agentic and pathways thinking. These forms of thinking can easily be incorporated into the stories of an organization's history that are often included in *formal orientation* programs. Highlighting the early and prior goals of the organization, actions taken to achieve these goals, and strategies implemented to address challenges can help to instill hope among new employees as soon as they begin working.

Hope Bonding

Hope bonding refers to the formation of a sound alliance between two individuals in pursuit of goals. Lopez et al. (2004) note that the goals negotiated in therapy, for example, "depend largely on the bonding component, defined as the positive personal attachment between [two people] that results from working together on a shared activity. Bonding ... usually is expressed in terms of liking, trusting, and respect for one another, in addition to a feeling of mutual commitment and understanding in the activity (Bordin, 1994)" (p. 393).

   In the context of organizational socialization, hope bonding largely involves the alliance that forms between newcomers, their supervisors, and new colleagues. *Supervisor support* creates the trusting, respectful relationship that supports the *personal planning* that includes the formation of goals, help conceiving of pathways to the attainment of goals, and encouragement to pursue goals. Additionally, developing new relationships (*relationship development*) that further support these processes can foster hope (Lopez et al., 2004). Thus, during socialization, all of the SRT social capital resources (items 5–8 in Table 1) should be positively associated with hope among newcomers.

Hope Enhancing

As noted above, in PsyCap, hope is conceptualized as a goal-directed process that involves pathways thinking and agentic thinking. Hope enhancing cultivates these forms of thinking and entails having individuals conceive goals more clearly, produce various pathways to goals, marshal the energy to pursue goals, and view difficulties to the achievement of goals as challenges. Hope-enhancing practices include establishing clear, specific goals, breaking large goals into subgoals, thinking of different routes to the achievement of goals and choosing the best one, mentally rehearsing what to do if an impediment to a goal is encountered, recalling previous successful goal pursuits, and redirecting energy when a goal becomes unattainable (Lopez et al., 2004; Luthans, Avey, et al., 2010).

As suggested above, *personal planning* is the primary vehicle through which goal selection and clarification will occur in the socialization process. Other resources such as *information* and *training* may help newcomers learn about relevant goals and pathways, and develop the motivation to pursue them; however, more social resources may also be necessary to help newcomers realize their goals. Pathways to goals and the agency to pursue them can then be effectively developed through *supervisor support* and the other social capital resources which can provide ideas and feedback regarding the viability of pathways, and regular encouragement for goal attainment.

Hope Reminding

Hope reminding involves encouraging the regular use of hopeful cognitions. Newcomers should be encouraged to identify goal-related thoughts and self-defeating thoughts on a regular basis. This can be achieved via the SRT social capital resources, such as *supervisor support* and *socialization agents*, and also by regular *follow-up* with newcomers.

Optimism

In their PCI, Luthans, Avey, et al. (2006, 2008, 2010) build optimism indirectly by fostering hope. They note that generating pathways to the achievement of goals and planning to overcome obstacles to these goals provides a foundation for the positive expectations that characterize optimism. Luthans and his colleagues also suggest that this process is enhanced by group feedback, observing others plan for goal attainment, and challenging negative thoughts.

Socialization resources that might be especially important for developing optimism include personal planning, feedback, and recognition and appreciation. With *personal planning*, newcomers will know what the expectations are for their performance and they will have specific and challenging goals that are under their own control and which they will be motivated to achieve. This sets the stage for them to attribute goal accomplishment and positive outcomes to themselves. Also important is *feedback* from coworkers and supervisors that is accurate and timely. Feedback should help newcomers understand that goal achievement and positive work outcomes are the result of their own motivation and hard work. Finally, *recognition and appreciation* should help to reinforce newcomers' belief that they are responsible for their performance and positive outcomes. A lack of recognition and appreciation could cause newcomers to question their performance and might lead to external attributions for positive outcomes.

The social capital socialization resources will also be important for the development of optimism. As noted by Luthans, Youssef, and Avolio (2007), simple workplace friendships and informal social events can stimulate the development of optimism. Thus, the four social capital resources should help newcomers develop optimism.

In summary, when personal planning, feedback, and recognition and appreciation are used in combination and accompanied by social support, newcomers should begin to develop optimism that will result in personal attributions for positive outcomes that, over time, will become permanent and pervasive. At the same time, newcomers will learn to attribute negative outcomes to external, temporary, and situation specific factors (Luthans, Youssef, & Avolio, 2007).

Resiliency

All of the methods discussed for promoting the preceding PsyCap constructs should also impact the development of resiliency. As noted by Luthans, Vogelgesang, et al. (2006), "In terms of convergence, we propose that these other PsyCap factors may act as pathways to resiliency (i.e., those who are hopeful, optimistic, and confident are more likely to bounce back from adversity than those who are not)" (p. 29). In their PCI, Luthans and associates capitalize on positive construals to foster resiliency by helping participants become aware of the thoughts and feelings they have when facing hardships. They also foster resiliency by building awareness of personal assets such as skills and social networks that are available to individuals and by encouraging them to think about, and leverage, these resources in the face of adversity.

During the socialization process, a key resource for newcomers will involve the acquisition of knowledge and skills necessary to perform one's tasks and assume a new role. Thus, *training* is an important resource for the development of newcomers' resiliency. In addition, the SRT social capital resources of *supervisor support* and *socialization agents* in addition to *formal assistance* should help to foster newcomer resiliency by providing opportunities for newcomers to receive *feedback* and become aware of, and change maladaptive thoughts and feelings they may be having as they adjust to their new roles. These social resources can also bring to the attention of newcomers resources that are available to them about which they may be unaware. Along these lines, providing newcomers with all of the specific *job resources* they need to accomplish their work will also foster resiliency.

Masten and Reed (2005) suggest that there are three basic strategies for promoting resiliency: Risk-focused, asset-focused, and process-focused strategies. Risk-focused strategies involve reducing people's exposure to hazardous experiences. As an example of a risk-focused strategy, Masten and Reed (2005) note school reforms that attempt to reduce the stressfulness of school transitions for adolescents. We suggest that organizational practices that reduce the stressfulness of work transitions will be equally effective at fostering resiliency among newcomers. For example, getting in touch with newcomers before they start work and advising them of what to expect (*anticipatory socialization*) should promote resiliency and positive adjustment. Also, a well-structured *formal orientation* that teaches newcomers about important rules, policies, and procedures will help them avoid difficulties and adjust more quickly.

An especially relevant type of orientation program is realistic orientation programs for new employee stress or ROPES. ROPES are designed to teach coping skills for the most important stressors that newcomers will encounter (Wanous & Reichers, 2000). ROPES provide newcomers with emotion-focused and problem-focused coping skills that will enable them to recover from difficulties and setbacks that can occur during the socialization process and buffer the effects of job demands and stressors. Thus, orientation programs designed according to ROPES would seem to be especially effective for developing newcomers' resiliency.

Asset-focused strategies involve increasing the amount of, quality of, or access to resources available to people. Assigning a buddy or mentor (*formal assistance*) can foster resiliency by providing social support and helping newcomers cope with the stress and confusion associated with assuming a new role. Providing newcomers with early work *assignments* that allow them to gain pertinent experience and build relevant skills will help them cope effectively with hurdles and challenges they may face. *Training* is also an example of an asset-focused strategy given its importance for the development of newcomers' human capital (Luthans, Youssef, & Avoilo, 2007).

Process-focused strategies attempt to influence processes that activate the mastery motivation system. Mastery motivation involves approaching tasks with enthusiasm, confidence, and persistence (Shiner, Masten, & Roberts, 2003). Sutcliffe and Vogus (2003) note that mastery motivation is activated when individuals have experiences that contribute to their growth, competence, and confidence, and that this is likely to occur when individuals exercise judgment, recover from mistakes, and observe role models who demonstrate these behaviors. As might be expected, one variable that can activate this system is self-efficacy (Masten & Reed, 2005). However, the experiences that activate the mastery motivation system are likely to foster hope and optimism also, which underscores why resiliency can be increased, partly, through the development of the other three PsyCap constructs (Luthans, Vogelgesang, et al., 2006).

For organizational newcomers, early job *assignments* that provide graduated mastery experiences, buddies, or mentors (*formal assistance*) who model how to recover from mistakes, *feedback,* and *supervisor support* are all socialization resources that can activate the mastery motivation system and cultivate resiliency.

IMPLICATIONS FOR RESEARCH AND PRACTICE

In this chapter, we have offered a new perspective and approach to organizational socialization based on positive organizational psychology. In particular, we have argued that socialization should focus on the development of newcomers' PsyCap and well-being and that this can be achieved by providing newcomers with socialization resources. In effect, we have suggested a new slate of independent and dependent variables for organizational socialization. This has implications for socialization research and practice.

For starters, research is needed to investigate the relationships between the socialization resources and each of the PsyCap constructs. For example, to what extent do the socialization resources predict each of the PsyCap states and what resources are most important? We have begun to try answering this question in a study that involved 152 undergraduate management co-op students on a four-month work-term. We found that the socialization resources were significantly related to the four PsyCap states to varying degrees with correlations ranging from .17 to .56.

The strongest relationships were for hope and optimism followed by self-efficacy and resiliency. Among the socialization resources, relationship development and job resources were related to all four PsyCap states, and information, feedback, and socialization agents were related to at least three of the PsyCap states. Although these results are preliminary, they do suggest that socialization resources are related to PsyCap to varying degrees. Additional research is needed on full-time newcomers to learn more about the extent to which each of the socialization resources predicts the four PsyCap constructs.

Another area worth pursuing is research that investigates the relationship between newcomers' PsyCap and their well-being. In our own work we have found that the constructs that comprise PsyCap, and PsyCap itself, are associated with the well-being of newcomers. In a sample of 90 organizational newcomers, we found that self-efficacy, optimism, hope, and overall PsyCap are all positively associated with job satisfaction, affective organizational commitment, and employee engagement with correlations ranging from .24 to .59. Resiliency had a significant positive correlation with job satisfaction ($r = .31$).

A final area worthy of research would involve experimental interventions that are designed to develop each of the PsyCap constructs in newcomers. As indicated earlier, Luthans and colleagues have shown that the PsyCap of employees can be developed through PCI. Similar interventions (Socialization PsyCap interventions or SocPCI) might be tested for their effects on the PsyCap and well-being of newcomers. At least one study has already shown that a self-efficacy intervention can increase the self-efficacy of newcomers (McNatt & Judge, 2008). One area that would seem especially worth pursuing is ROPES. A study by Fan and Wanous (2008) found that a ROPES intervention that involved graduate students from Asia attending a large university in the United States resulted in lower pre-entry expectations and stress at the end of the orientation program, and higher academic and interaction adjustment six and nine months after the program. Future research might test the effects of a ROPES intervention on newcomers' PsyCap. As indicated earlier, ROPES seems especially relevant for the development of newcomers' resiliency.

In terms of practice, organizations should begin to think about the on-boarding and orientation of new hires as something that should involve more than information and learning. Rather, they should think about providing newcomers with the resources they need to develop each of the PsyCap states. This might involve a socialization resource audit to determine newcomers' level of PsyCap and the extent to which an organization provides the socialization resources listed in Table 1.

Recently hired employees can be asked to complete a survey to measure their PsyCap to identify areas of weakness and the extent to which any of the PsyCap states require more attention. A socialization resource audit can involve a review of the dimensions in Table 1 which can be rated in terms of the extent to which they are being provided to newcomers. The results of this audit can indicate what resources are not being provided to newcomers and should be included in existing socialization programs. In combination, these two audits can indicate what PsyCap states need more attention during the socialization process and what socialization resources need to be included in existing socialization programs. Table 2 can then be used to identify what socialization resources should be emphasized for the purpose of developing a particular PsyCap state.

Finally, organizations can implement SocPCI based on the PCI developed by Luthans and colleagues. As indicated earlier, PCI involves a two-hour training session with exercises aimed at enhancing and integrating the development of the PsyCap dimensions such as breaking personally relevant goals into sub goals, considering alternate pathways to these goals if obstacles surface, and receiving feedback from others about more obstacles and pathways. These kinds of exercises can be added onto existing orientation and training programs.

CONCLUSION

For the last several decades, socialization research has focused on socialization tactics and learning-related outcomes. In this chapter, we have argued that a new approach to organizational socialization is required for today's constantly changing, uncertain, and competitive work environment. Along these lines, we believe that socialization research and practice will benefit from an approach that has its basis in positive organizational psychology and focuses on newcomers' PsyCap and well-being.

SRT offers organizations and researchers a new way to think about, study, and design socialization programs that, we believe, will better help newcomers build personal resources associated with success, well-being, and positive outcomes. This will make them effective members of their organization and also provide their organization with the ability to compete and survive in an increasingly uncertain, competitive, and challenging world.

REFERENCES

Allen, T. D., McManus, S. E., & Russell, J. E. A. (1999). Newcomer socialization and stress: Formal peer relationships as a source of support. *Journal of Vocational Behavior, 54,* 453–470.

Ashforth, B. E., Myers, K. K., & Sluss, D. M. (2012). Socialization perspectives and positive organizational scholarship. In K. S. Cameron & G. M. Spreitzer (Eds.), *The Oxford handbook of positive organizational scholarship* (pp. 537–551). New York, NY: Oxford University Press.

Ashforth, B. E., Saks, A. M., & Lee, R. T. (1998). Socialization and newcomer adjustment: The role of organizational context. *Human Relations, 51,* 897–926.

Ashforth, B. E., Sluss, D. M., & Harrison, S. H. (2007). Socialization in organizational contexts. In G. P. Hodgkinson & J. K. Ford (Eds.), *International review of industrial and organizational psychology.* Chichester, UK: Wiley.

Ashforth, B. E., Sluss, D. M., & Saks, A. M. (2007). Socialization tactics, proactive behavior, and newcomer learning: Integrating socialization models. *Journal of Vocational Behavior, 70,* 447–462.

Avey, J. B., Luthans, F., Smith, R. M., & Palmer, N. F. (2010). Impact of positive psychological capital on employee well-being over time. *Journal of Occupational Health Psychology, 15,* 17–28.

Avey, J. B., Nimnicht, J. L., & Graber Pigeon, N. (2010). Two field studies examining the association between positive psychological capital and employee performance. *Leadership and Organization Development Journal, 31,* 384–401.

Avey, J. B., Reichard, R. J., Luthans, F., & Mhatre, K. H. (2011). Meta-analysis of the impact of positive psychological capital on employee attitudes, behaviors, and performance. *Human Resource Development Quarterly, 22,* 127–152.

Bakker, A. B., & Demerouti, E. (2007). The job demands-resources model: State of the art. *Journal of Managerial Psychology, 22,* 309–328.

Bandura, A. (1997). *Self-efficacy: The exercise of control.* New York, NY: Freeman.

Bauer, T. N., Bodner, T., Erdogan, B., Truxillo, D. M., & Tucker, J. S. (2007). Newcomer adjustment during organizational socialization: A meta-analytic review of antecedents, outcomes, and methods. *Journal of Applied Psychology, 92,* 707–721.

Carver, C. S., & Scheier, M. F. (2005). Optimism. In C. R. Snyder & S. J. Lopez. (Eds.), *Handbook of positive psychology.* New York, NY: Oxford University Press.

Chao, G. T., O'Leary-Kelly, A. M., Wolf, S., Klein, H. J., & Gardner, P. D. (1994). Organizational socialization: Its content and consequences. *Journal of Applied Psychology, 79,* 730–743.

Cooper-Thomas, H., & Anderson, N. (2002). Newcomer adjustment: The relationship between organizational socialization tactics, information acquisition and attitudes. *Journal of Occupational and Organizational Psychology, 75,* 423–437.

Culbertson, S. S., Fullagar, C. J., & Mills, M. J. (2010). Feeling good and doing great: The relationship between psychological capital and well-being. *Journal of Occupational Health Psychology, 15,* 421–433.

Fan, J., & Wanous, J. P. (2008). Organizational and cultural entry: A new type of orientation program for multiple boundary crossings. *Journal of Applied Psychology, 93,* 1390–1400.

Fisher, C. D. (1986). Organizational socialization: An integrative review. In K. M. Rowland & G. R. Ferris (Eds.), *Research in personnel and human resources management* (Vol. 4, pp. 101–145). Greenwich, CT: JAI Press.

Fisher, C. D. (2010). Happiness at work. *International Journal of Management Reviews, 12,* 384–412.

Haueter, J. A., Macan, T. H., & Winter, J. (2003). Measurement of newcomer socialization: Construct validation of a multidimensional scale. *Journal of Vocational Behavior, 63,* 20–39.

Jones, G. R. (1986). Socialization tactics, self-efficacy, and newcomers' adjustments to organizations. *Academy of Management Journal, 29,* 262–279.

Katz, R. (1980). Time and work: Toward an integrative perspective. In B. Staw & L. L. Cummings (Eds.), *Research in organizational behavior* (Vol. 2, pp. 81–127). Greenwich, CT: JAI Press.

Klein, H. J., Fan, J., & Preacher, K. J. (2006). The effects of early socialization experiences on content mastery and outcomes: A meditational approach. *Journal of Vocational Behavior, 68,* 96–115.

Klein, H. J., & Heuser, A. E. (2008). The learning of socialization content: A framework for researching orientating practices. *Research in Personnel and Human Resources Management, 27,* 279–336.

Klein, H. J., & Weaver, N. A. (2000). The effectiveness of an organizational-level orientation training program in the socialization of new hires. *Personnel Psychology, 53,* 47–66.

Liu, J., Siu, O.-L., & Shi, K. (2010). Transformational leadership and employee well-being: The mediating role of trust in the leader and self-efficacy. *Applied Psychology: An International Review, 59,* 454–479.

Lopez, S. J., Snyder, C. R., Magyar-Moe, J. L., Edwards, L. M, Teramoto Pedrotti, J., Janowski, K., ... Pressgrove, C. (2004). Strategies for accentuating hope. In P. A. Linley & S. Joseph (Eds.), *Positive psychology in practice* (pp. 388–404). Hoboken, NJ: Wiley.

Luthans, F. (2002a). Positive organizational behavior: Developing and managing psychological strengths. *Academy of Management Executive, 16,* 57–72.

Luthans, F. (2002b). The need for and meaning of positive organizational behavior. *Journal of Organizational Behavior, 23,* 695–706.

Luthans, F., Avey, J. B., Avolio, B. J., Norman, S. M., & Combs, G. J. (2006). Psychological capital development: Toward a micro-intervention. *Journal of Organizational Behavior, 27,* 387–393.

Luthans, F., Avey, J. B., Avolio, B. J., & Peterson, S. J. (2010). The development and resulting impact of positive psychological capital. *Human Resource Development Quarterly, 21,* 41–67.

Luthans, F., Avey, J. B., Clapp-Smith, R., & Li, W. (2008). More evidence on the value of Chinese workers' psychological capital: A potentially unlimited competitive resource? *The International Journal of Human Resource Management, 19,* 818–827.

Luthans, F., Avey, J. B., & Patera, J. L. (2008). Experimental analysis of a web-based training intervention to develop positive psychological capital. *Academy of Management Learning and Education, 7,* 209–221.

Luthans, F., Avolio, B. J., Avey, J. B., & Norman, S. M. (2007). Positive psychological capital: Measurement and relationship with performance and satisfaction. *Personnel Psychology, 60,* 541–572.

Luthans, F., Norman, S. M., Avoilo, B. J., & Avey, J. B. (2008). The mediating role of psychological capital in the supportive organizational climate–employee performance relationship. *Journal of Organizational Behavior, 29,* 219–238.

Luthans, F., Vogelgesang, G. R., & Lester, P. B. (2006). Developing the psychological capital of resiliency. *Human Resource Development Review, 5,* 25–44.

Luthans, F., & Youssef, C. M. (2007). Emerging positive organizational behavior. *Journal of Management, 33*, 321–349.

Luthans, F., Youssef, C. M., & Avolio, B. J. (2007). *Psychological capital: Developing the human competitive edge.* Oxford, UK: Oxford University Press.

Lyubomirsky, S. (2001). Why are some people happier than others? The role of cognitive and motivational processes in well-being. *American Psychologist, 56*, 239–249.

Maddux, J. E. (2005). Self-efficacy: The power of believing you can. In C. R. Snyder & S. Lopez (Eds.), *Handbook of positive psychology* (pp. 277–287). New York, NY: Oxford University Press.

Mäkikangas, A., & Kinnunen, U. (2003). Psychosocial work stressors and well-being: self-esteem and optimism as moderators in a one-year longitudinal sample. *Personality and Individual Differences, 35*, 537–557.

Masten, A. S., & Reed, M.-G. J. (2005). Resiliency in development. In C. R. Snyder & S. J. Lopez. (Eds.), *Handbook of positive psychology* (pp. 74–88). New York, NY: Oxford University Press.

McNatt, D. B., & Judge, T. A. (2008). Self-efficacy intervention, job attitudes, and turnover: A field experiment with employees in role transition. *Human Relations, 61*, 783–810.

Ostroff, C., & Kozlowski, S. W. J. (1992). Organizational socialization as a learning process: The role of information acquisition. *Personnel Psychology, 45*, 849–874.

Park, N., Peterson, C., & Seligman, M. E. P. (2004). Strengths of character and well-being. *Journal of Social and Clinical Psychology, 23*, 603–619.

Rollag, K., Parise, S., & Cross, R. (2005). Getting new hires up to speed quickly. *MIT Sloan Management Review, 46*, 35–41.

Ryan, R. M., & Deci, E. L. (2001). On happiness and human potentials: A review of research on hedonic and eudemonic well-being. *Annual Review of Psychology, 52*, 141–166.

Saks, A. M. (1995). Longitudinal field investigation of the moderating and mediating effects of self-efficacy on the relationship between training and newcomer adjustment. *Journal of Applied Psychology, 80*, 211–225.

Saks, A. M., & Ashforth, B. E. (1997a). Organizational socialization: Making sense of the past and present as a prologue for the future. *Journal of Vocational Behavior, 51*, 234–279.

Saks, A. M., & Ashforth, B. E. (1997b). Socialization tactics and newcomer information acquisition. *International Journal of Selection and Assessment, 5*, 48–61.

Saks, A. M., & Gruman, J. A. (2011). Getting newcomers engaged: The role of socialization tactics. *Journal of Managerial Psychology, 26*, 383–402.

Saks, A. M., & Gruman, J. A. (2012). Getting newcomers on-board: A review of socialization practices and introduction to socialization resources theory. In C. Wanberg (Ed.), *The Oxford handbook of organizational socialization* (pp. 27–55). New York, NY: Oxford University Press.

Saks, A. M., Uggerslev, K. L., & Fassina, N. E. (2007). Socialization tactics and newcomer adjustment: A meta-analytic review and test of a model. *Journal of Vocational Behavior, 70*, 413–446.

Seligman, M. E. P. (2006). *Learned optimism: How to change your mind and your life.* New York, NY: Vintage Books.

Shiner, R. L., Masten, A. S., & Roberts, J. M. (2003). Childhood personality foreshadows adult personality and life outcomes two decades later. *Journal of Personality, 71*, 1145–1170.

Snyder, C. R., Rand, K. L., & Sigmon, D. R. (2005). Hope theory: A member of the positive psychology family. In C. R. Snyder & S. J. Lopez. (Eds.), *Handbook of positive psychology* (pp. 257–276). New York, NY: Oxford University Press.

Stajkovic, A. D., & Luthans, F. (1998). Social cognitive theory and self-efficacy: Going beyond traditional motivational and behavioral approaches. *Organizational Dynamics*, *26*, 62–74.

Sutcliffe, K. M., & Vogus, T. J. (2003). Organizing for resilience. In K. S. Cameron, J. E. Dutton & R. E. Quinn (Eds.), *Positive organizational scholarship* (pp. 94–110). San Francisco, CA: Berrett-Koehler.

Tugade, M. M., & Fredrickson, B. L. (2004). Resilient individuals use positive emotions to bounce back from negative emotional experiences. *Journal of Personality and Social Psychology*, *86*, 320–333.

Van Maanen, J., & Schein, E. H. (1979). Toward a theory of organizational socialization. In B. M Staw (Ed.), *Research in organizational behaviour* (Vol. 1, pp. 209–264). Greenwich, CT: JAI Press.

Walumbwa, F. O., Peterson, S. J., Avolio, B. J., & Hartnell, C. A. (2010). An investigation of the relationships among leader and follower psychological capital, service climate and job performance. *Personnel Psychology*, *63*, 937–963.

Wanous, J. P., & Reichers, A. E. (2000). New employee orientation programs. *Human Resource Management Review*, *10*, 435–451.

Wright, T. A. (2010). More than meets the eye: The role of employee well-being in organizational research. In A. Linley, S. Harrington & N. Garcea (Eds.), *Oxford handbook of positive psychology and work*. New York, NY: Oxford University Press.

Wright, T. A., & Bonett, D. G. (2007). Job satisfaction and psychological well-being as nonadditive predictors of workplace turnover. *Journal of Management*, *33*, 141–160.

Wright, T. A., & Cropanzano, R. (1999). Psychological well-being and job satisfaction as predictors of job performance. *Journal of Occupational Health Psychology*, *5*, 84–94.

Xanthopoulou, D., Bakker, A. B., Demerouti, E., & Schaufeli, W. B. (2009). Work engagement and financial returns: A diary study on the role of job and personal resources. *Journal of Occupational and Organizational Psychology*, *82*, 183–200.

WORK ENGAGEMENT AND THE POSITIVE POWER OF MEANINGFUL WORK

Simon L. Albrecht

People prosper when they are engaged in meaningful work and organizations prosper when their employees are similarly engaged.

– Steger and Dik (2010, p. 139)

Positive psychology has emerged as an extremely popular, influential, and powerful paradigm within the science and practice of contemporary psychology. An internet search of the term "positive psychology" will yield around 37 million hits (April, 2013).

Positive psychology was originally aimed at counterbalancing a perceived overemphasis on understanding and working with the negative, dysfunctional, or "deficit" dimensions of human functioning (Seligman & Csikszentmihalyi, 2000). The deficit focus of traditional psychology has been characterized in terms of the "4 Ds" – damage, disease, disorder, and dysfunction (Bakker & Schaufeli, 2008). Positive psychology, in contrast, has as its focus the positive spectrum of human experience (Gable & Haidt, 2005; Seligman & Csikszentmihalyi, 2000), and concerns itself with constructs such as happiness, well-being, flourishing, optimal functioning, and flow (Linley, Joseph, Harrington, & Wood, 2006).

Seligman's (2002) book on authentic happiness served as an important catalyst which sparked and popularized much of the contemporary interest

Advances in Positive Organizational Psychology, Volume 1, 237–260
ISSN: 2046-410X/doi:10.1108/S2046-410X(2013)0000001013

in positive psychology. Seligman argued there are three distinct forms of a happy life. The first, the "pleasant life," is based in hedonic principles, and derives from the pursuit and experience of positive emotions. The second form, the "good life," derives from the pursuit, experience, and enjoyment of the things that people value and are good at. Seligman characterized the "good life" in terms of engagement and flow. The third form of happy life, the "meaningful life," provides for the highest and most lasting form of happiness. A meaningful life, according to Seligman, derives from the pursuit and experience of doing the things one values and believes in. In contrast to the hedonism associated with the "pleasant life," meaningfulness is associated with "eudemonia," a form of happiness achieved by living virtuously, engaging in meaningful activities and attaining goals that have intrinsic merit (Ryan & Deci, 2001; Ryff & Singer, 2008). Although Seligman (2011) has in recent times extended the three forms of the happy life to include relationships and achievement, the eudemonic elements associated with engagement, meaning, purpose, and achievement remain recognized as core dimensions of happiness and well-being.

POSITIVE PSYCHOLOGY AND WORK

The application of positive psychology to the context of work has attracted enormous interest within both academic and practitioner domains over the past decade (e.g., Keyes & Haidt, 2003; Linley, Harrington, & Garcea, 2010; Luthans, 2002). From a practitioner perspective, there has been a proliferation of organizational development, human resource, talent management, leadership development, team development and coaching programs, initiatives, and interventions that have positive psychological principles at their core. The Gallup organization, for instance, has administered the Clifton Strengths Finder in thousands of organizations across the globe, aiming to help people learn about and build upon their talents and strengths to enhance all facets of their working experience (see Clifton & Harter, 2003).

Within the academic domain there has similarly been a proliferation of academic books, reviews, research papers, commentaries, and conferences devoted to the topic of positive psychology at work (e.g., Cameron, Dutton, & Quinn, 2003; Linley et al., 2010). Positive organizational scholarship (POS; Cameron et al., 2003) and positive organizational behavior (POB; Luthans, 2002; Wright, 2003) have emerged as two distinct but related streams within the work-related positive psychology literature. Bakker and Derks (2010, p. 200) noted that POS is primarily concerned with "the workplace and the accomplishment of work-related outcomes" and POB is primarily concerned with "individual psychological states and human strengths that influence employee performance." Irrespective of the degree of overlap between the two streams (for commentary see Hackman, 2009; Luthans & Avolio, 2009; Roberts, 2006), both streams have emerged to support and progress "more focused theory building, research, and effective application of positive traits, states, organizations, and behaviors" (Luthans & Youssef, 2007, p. 322).

MEANINGFUL WORK

Meaningful work is fundamental to POS, and more generally to positive psychology (Cartwright & Holmes, 2006). Cartwright and Holmes argued that organizations need to address and understand the deeper needs of employees in order to retain them and keep them motivated, engaged, and performing. Understanding how to create, experience, manage, and maintain meaningful work provides powerful capability for achieving optimum and sustainable work outcomes for individuals and organizations (Steger & Dik, 2010).

Despite claims in support of the importance and utility of meaningful work there is no universally agreed definition as to its core characteristics or dimensions. Hackman and Oldham (1980) recognized meaningfulness as an important psychological condition at work, reflected in the extent to which people invest themselves in their job role and tasks. Kahn (1990) argued that the psychological state of meaningfulness refers to people feeling worthwhile, useful, and valuable, that they make a difference, and are not taken for granted in their work-related activities and experience. Irrespective of the numerous alternative definitions of meaningful work that have been offered (e.g., Cardador & Rupp, 2011; May, Gilson, & Harter, 2004; Spreitzer, 1995; Steger & Dik, 2010), notions of importance, purpose, and contribution are common to most. For the present purposes, meaningful work is defined as a positive psychological state whereby people feel they make a positive, important, and useful contribution to a worthwhile purpose through the execution of their work.

When thinking about the nature of meaningful work it is necessary to conceptually and empirically differentiate the construct from its antecedents, consequences, and correlates. It is also important to embed an understanding of meaningful work within reputable models, theories, and frameworks. For example, drawing from Self Determination Theory

(Deci & Ryan, 2000; Ryan & Deci, 2000), it will be important to establish whether people have a need for meaningful work, the factors that help satisfaction of that need, and the motivational and other consequences which result from the satisfaction of the need.

Although Steger and Dik (2010) argued that "empirical support lags behind the claims thus far made in the field about work as meaning" (p. 139), researchers have shown that meaningfulness is positively linked to psychological well-being (Zika & Chamberlain, 1992), positive mood (King, Hicks, Krull, & Del Gaiso, 2006), psychological benefits (Britt, Adler, & Bartone, 2001), and greater organizational commitment, intrinsic work satisfaction, and job involvement (Milliman, Czaplewski, & Ferguson, 2003). Nevertheless, additional research on the conceptualization, measurement, and modeling of meaningful work is needed (Steger & Dik, 2010).

WORK ENGAGEMENT

The past decade has witnessed a very considerable amount of academic and practitioner interest in the idea of work engagement (see Albrecht, 2010a; Bakker, Albrecht, & Leiter, 2011; Bakker & Leiter, 2010; Macey & Schneider, 2008). Macey, Schneider, Barbera, and Young (2009) commented that "rarely has a term ... resonated as strongly with business executives as employee engagement has in recent years" (p. xv).

Schaufeli, Salanova, González-Romá, and Bakker (2002), in what is the most widely cited scholarly definition of engagement, proposed that engagement is "a positive, fulfilling, work-related state of mind that is characterized by vigor, dedication, and absorption." Even though alternative conceptualizations and measures have been advanced (e.g., May et al., 2004; Rich, LePine, & Crawford, 2010), researchers have consistently shown engagement to be positively associated with attitudinal and well-being related outcomes such as commitment (Hallberg & Schaufeli, 2006) and health (Halbesleben, 2010), as well as with "bottom line" outcomes such as job performance (Bakker & Bal, 2010; Halbesleben & Wheeler, 2008), client satisfaction (Salanova, Agut, & Peiro, 2005), and financial returns (Xanthopoulou, Bakker, Demerouti, & Schaufeli, 2009a).

A broad range of theories has been invoked to explain the emergence and maintenance of employee engagement (e.g., Conservation of Resources Theory, Hobfoll, 1989; Self Determination Theory, Deci & Ryan, 2000; Social Exchange Theory, Blau, 1964; Role Theory, Kahn, 1990; Broaden and Build Theory of Positive Emotions, Fredrickson, 2001; the Job Demands–Resources (JD–R) model, Bakker & Demerouti, 2007, 2008).

The JD–R model remains the most widely cited and widely researched model of engagement. The JD–R model shows how job resources (e.g., autonomy, feedback, supervisor support) and personal resources (e.g., self-efficacy, optimism, resilience) directly influence work engagement, which in turn influences outcomes such as in-role performance, extra-role performance, creativity, and financial outcomes. Additionally, the JD–R model predicts that job resources become more salient and gain motivational potential when employees experience high levels of job demands (Bakker, 2010).

Despite the growing consensus around the JD–R model as a very useful framework for understanding work engagement, unresolved issues remain and there are numerous areas which warrant future research (see Albrecht, 2010b; Bakker et al., 2011). For example, despite the significant advances in understanding which organizational, job, and personal resources influence engagement, more remains to be learned about the psychological mechanisms that explain how and why the provision or experience of job resources results in increased engagement. The psychological processes assumed to underlie the associations have not been fully explored and have not been widely tested.

A number of theoretical perspectives and psychological processes such as felt obligation, satisfaction of needs for meaningfulness, and positive mood, can serve to explain how the provision of job resources can result in employee experiences of work engagement. Saks (2006), for example, invoked social exchange theory to explain how job resources such as feedback, autonomy, and organizational support, result in engagement. Saks argued that the amount of cognitive, emotional, and physical resources that an individual is prepared to devote to the performance of his or her work roles "is contingent on the economic and socio-emotional resources received from the organization" (p. 603). In other words, social exchange theory contends that favorable treatment or resourcing from one party establishes in another party a felt obligation to return or reciprocate such favorable treatment (Armeli, Eisenberger, Fasolo, & Lynch, 1998; Eisenberger, Cummings, Armeli, & Lynch, 1997). Saks, however, did not explicitly operationalize and test relevant social exchange constructs such as felt obligation or reciprocity in his research. Similarly, while engagement researchers (e.g., Bakker, 2009; Salanova, Schaufeli, Xanthopoulou, & Bakker, 2010) have invoked Fredrickson's (2001) broaden and build theory of positive emotions and Hobfoll's (1989) conservation of resources theory to explain the emergence of engagement, very few explicit tests of these theoretical explanations have been conducted within engagement-related research. Although researchers continue to work on identifying the psychological mechanisms, such as positive affect, that explain how personal and job resources lead to engagement (e.g., Salanova, Llorens, & Schaufeli, 2011), additional research is warranted. The present chapter primarily focuses on satisfaction of the need for meaningful work as a potential explanatory construct while also considering the potential mediating influence of felt obligation and positive affect.

May et al. (2004) and Van den Broeck, Vansteenkiste, De Witte, and Lens (2008) are among the few researchers who have focused on the psychological processes which explain how job resources result in the experience of work engagement. Van den Broeck and her colleagues reported that the satisfaction of three basic psychological needs, as suggested by Self Determination Theory (Ryan & Deci, 2000), partially mediated the influence of job resources on engagement (vigor) and the influence of job demands on emotional exhaustion. Van den Broeck et al. concluded that basic psychological needs represent "an overarching mechanism fuelling both employee motivation and energy and, hence, explaining the emergence of both work engagement and burnout" (p. 289).

Van den Broeck, Vansteenkiste, De Witte, Soenens, and Lens (2010) noted that the literature on basic need satisfaction has been hampered by the use of ad hoc measures that do not contain items that tap explicitly into the satisfaction of basic needs "as such" (p. 984). Van den Broeck et al. argued that many previously developed need satisfaction items better capture antecedents of need satisfaction as opposed to need satisfaction per se. However, in contrast to their assertion that their items reflect the "psychological experience of need satisfaction itself" (p. 283), similar criticisms can be leveled against the items developed by Van den Broeck et al. Items such as "I feel like I can pretty much be myself at work," "People at work care about me," and "I don't feel very competent at work" do not explicitly assess needs, nor the extent to which needs are satisfied. Van den Broeck et al.'s items appear to more strongly reflect antecedent job resources such as social support (e.g., "People at work care about me") or personal resources such as self-efficacy (e.g., "I don't feel very competent at work"). Valid measures of need satisfaction need to explicitly assess psychological needs and the extent to which such psychological needs are satisfied.

POSITIVE PSYCHOLOGY, MEANINGFUL WORK, AND ENGAGEMENT

Despite the obvious conceptual overlap between work engagement and a positive psychological approach to work, until recently, the POS and engagement literatures have, to a large extent, traveled along separate paths. Bakker and Demerouti (2008) and Bakker and Derks (2010) are among the not so many researchers and engagement scholars who have explicitly linked the construct of engagement to POS or POB. Chapters from Linley et al.'s (2010) recent handbook of "positive psychology and work" (e.g., Harter & Blacksmith, 2010; Stairs & Galpin, 2010) and chapters from the present edited volume also evidence efforts to advance clearer connections between the construct of engagement and POS.

The construct of meaningful work provides an obvious means by which connections between positive psychological scholarship and engagement might be further strengthened. The construct is of central importance to both disciplines. With respect to positive psychology, and as previously noted, Seligman (2002) identified the "meaningful life" as the highest form of happiness. With respect to engagement, Kahn (1990), who initiated much of the subsequent theory and research on engagement, argued that meaningful work is a necessary prerequisite to the experience of work engagement. More recently, Stairs and Galpin (2010) claimed that the "research is clear that people who are in jobs that are personally meaningful are more engaged than those who are not" (pp. 161–162). It needs to be noted, however, that Stairs and Galpin did not provide or reference empirical evidence in support of their claim and contrary to their claim, and despite a clear logic and clear conceptual links between the constructs, there is limited empirical evidence to suggest meaningful work is associated with engagement. Additional research is needed to establish the relationship between meaningful work and engagement. Furthermore, and as noted by Steger and Dik (2010) despite "the intuitive appeal of the claim that viewing work as a meaningful and socially valuable part of one's life, there is a need for continued effort in developing a theory of work as meaning" (pp. 132–133).

MEANINGFULNESS AS A PSYCHOLOGICAL PROCESS MEDIATING JOB RESOURCES AND WORK ENGAGEMENT

Kahn (1990) argued that the psychological experience of meaningfulness mediates the influence of job resources on work engagement. Kahn argued that autonomy, for instance, results in a sense of individual ownership over work, which then leads to the experience of psychological meaningfulness. Kahn also identified feeling valued, mutual respect, appreciation, rewarding interpersonal interactions with coworkers and clients, and feedback on performance as important "conditions" for the experience of meaningful work. Kahn proposed that the experience of meaningfulness, in turn, influences employee personal engagement or disengagement at work. Kahn's qualitative findings were corroborated in a follow-up empirical study by May et al. (2004). Of the three psychological states examined by May and colleagues (meaningfulness, safety, and availability), meaningfulness had by far the strongest positive association with engagement ($\beta = .73$, $\beta = .17$, $\beta = .01$, respectively).

Beyond the work of Kahn (1990) and May et al. (2004), alternative literatures also suggest that the psychological experience of meaningful work might mediate the influence of organizational, job, and personal resources on motivational outcomes such as engagement. The very significant body of research on job design (Hackman & Oldham, 1980) and psychological empowerment (Spreitzer, 1995; Thomas & Velthouse, 1990) suggests that jobs with enriched job characteristics result in a stronger sense of meaning, which in turn leads to positive outcomes such as job satisfaction and motivation. In the job characteristics model (JCM; Hackman & Oldham, 1980), for example, meaningful work is conceptualized as a critical psychological state mediating the influence of skill variety, task identity, and task significance on outcomes. Humphrey, Nahrgang, and Morgeson (2007), in their meta-analysis of job characteristics research, identified experienced meaningfulness as the most important or "most critical" (p. 1341) psychological state, mediating the relationship between job characteristics and outcomes. Indeed, Humphrey et al. suggested their results justify modification to the JCM such that experienced meaningfulness should be modeled as the primary mediator of the influence of motivational characteristics on work outcomes. Johns, Xie, and Fang (1992, p. 667) arrived at similar conclusions and argued that experienced meaning was a "particularly encompassing psychological state," serving as a mediator for all five of the motivational characteristics.

SATISFACTION OF NEED FOR MEANINGFUL WORK AS A MEDIATOR

Beyond the direct experience of meaningfulness, and consistent with need-based motivational theories (e.g., Herzberg, 1959; Maslow, 1943; McClelland, 1961), the *satisfaction of the need* for meaningfulness is theoretically motivational and therefore likely to be strongly associated with engagement. As previously noted, Van den Broek et al. (2008, 2010) referenced Self Determination Theory (Deci & Ryan, 2000) in an attempt to explain how job resources, through the satisfaction of needs for autonomy, belongingness, and competence, result in engagement. Also, as previously noted, there has been limited empirical research that has focused on satisfaction of the need for meaningfulness. Albrecht and Su (2012) are among the few researchers who have examined the mediating influence of the satisfaction of the need for meaningful work in the relationship between job resources and employee engagement. Albrecht and Su, using structural equation modeling on data drawn from a sample of Chinese telecommunications workers, found that performance feedback (as a job resource) was associated with engagement through fulfilling employees' need for meaningful work. No support, however, was found for satisfaction of meaningful work mediating the influence of autonomy or colleague support on engagement. Albrecht and Su concluded that further research is required to better understand how different job resources influence engagement through different psychological processes across different cultural contexts. The research summarized in the Research Preview (below) extends the Albrecht and Su study and provides additional empirical evidence in support of their proposed modeling within an English speaking sample.

Fig. 1 shows an extension of the JD–R model (Bakker, 2010; Bakker & Demerouti, 2007, 2008) that explicitly models the satisfaction of the need for meaningful work mediating the relationship between job and personal resources and engagement. Fig. 1 shows how job resources (e.g., autonomy,

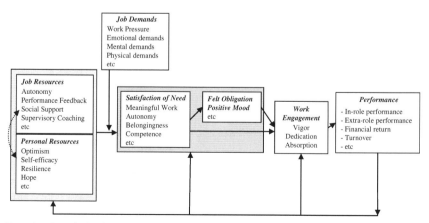

Fig. 1. Psychological Mediators in the Job Demands–Resources model (after Bakker, 2010; Bakker & Demerouti, 2007, 2008).

colleague support, performance feedback) and personal resources (e.g., self-efficacy) lead to the satisfaction of psychological needs (e.g., need for meaningfulness, autonomy, competence, belonging) that in turn lead to felt obligation and positive mood and to work engagement. Engagement, in turn, leads to desirable downstream performance outcomes. Consistent with research findings (e.g., Xanthopoulou et al., 2009a) reciprocal relationships are also modeled.

MEASURING MEANINGFUL WORK AND THE SATISFACTION OF NEED FOR MEANINGFUL WORK

Meaningful work has been measured in a number of ways. Oldham, Hackman, and Stepina (1978), for instance, measured experienced meaningfulness with four items: "most of the things I have to do in this job seem useless or trivial" (R); "the work I do on this job is very meaningful to me"; "most people on this job feel the work is useless or trivial" (R); and "most people on this job find the work very meaningful." Oldham and his colleagues reported an alpha reliability of $\alpha = .71$ for the four-item scale. May et al. (2004) measured psychological meaningfulness with six items drawn from Spreitzer's (1995) and May's (2003, unpublished) work: "the work I do on this job is very important to me," "my job activities are personally meaningful to me"; "the work I do on this job is worthwhile," "my job activities are significant to me"; "the work I do on this job is meaningful to me"; and "I feel that the work I do on this job is valuable." May et al. (2004) reported an alpha of $\alpha = .90$ for the six-item scale.

As previously noted, existing measures of need satisfaction have been criticized for not explicitly measuring need satisfaction per se (Van den Broeck et al., 2008). Also as previously noted, despite Van den Broeck et al. arguing that the items they developed reflect the "psychological experience of need satisfaction itself" (p. 283), a close inspection of their items suggests otherwise. To redress this situation, Albrecht and Su (2012) developed items specifically focused on the satisfaction of need for meaningful work. Albrecht and Su drafted four need satisfaction questions that were prefaced with: "At your work, to what extent are these psychological needs being satisfied?" The four items, translated into Chinese, were: "Feeling you are achieving something important through your work," "Feeling that your work helps make a positive difference to others," "Feeling that your work is meaningful," and "Feeling that through your work you make a worthwhile contribution." To prompt respondents to report on their level of satisfaction of the need, they were asked to respond on a 5-point Likert scale, ranging from 1 "not at all satisfied" to 5 "very highly satisfied." Respondents also had an option to indicate "not applicable/not a need." Albrecht and Su reported an alpha reliability of $\alpha = .85$ for the four-item scale and evidenced convergent and discriminant validity.

An additional consideration with respect to the measurement and modeling of need satisfaction centers on the issue of whether needs are best modeled as first-order factors or, alternatively, as part of a higher-order need satisfaction factor. Van den Broeck et al. (2008) modeled need satisfaction as a composite higher-order construct constituted of satisfaction with autonomy, belongingness, and competence. However, on theoretical grounds, the influence of a range of different resources on a range of different needs might usefully be examined. Consistent with this view, Van den Broeck et al. (2010) argued that task autonomy will more likely be strongly related to satisfaction of the autonomy need than to the satisfaction of belongingness or competence needs, whereas skill utilization and coworker support will more likely be strongly related to competence and relatedness need satisfaction, respectively. Additional needs such as the need for meaningful work (Kahn, 1990), need for achievement, and need for power (McClelland, 1965) might also usefully be examined within the JD–R context because of their previous application in motivational theories.

RESEARCH PREVIEW

Job resources and employee engagement: The mediating role of job meaningfulness, felt obligation, and positive mood

Work engagement has attracted growing attention in management and academic circles. The JD–R model (Bakker & Demerouti, 2008) shows how job resources influence work engagement. However, the psychological processes that underpin these relationships have not been fully established. The present research aimed to assess the potential mediating effects of satisfaction of need for meaningful work, felt obligation, and positive mood on the relationships between job resources and engagement. Drawing from the POS literature, needs theory (e.g., Deci & Ryan, 2000), social exchange theory (Blau, 1964), and the motivational processes implicit in the JD–R model (Bakker & Demerouti, 2007), the proposed relations are modeled below in Fig. A.

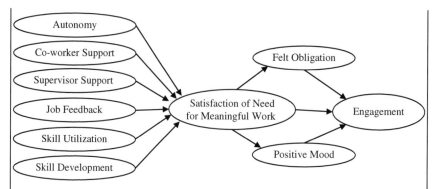

Fig. A.   Proposed Model.

Method

Participants, required to be working full-time for a minimum of six months in an organization of 20 or more employees, were recruited using a snowball sampling strategy. Participants ranged in age from 18 to 65 years and worked in a diversity of roles in a range of industries and sectors. The online survey process resulted in 384 useable cases being available for analyses. The items measuring satisfaction of the need for meaningful work are described in the body of the chapter. All additional measures were sourced or adapted from previously published studies. For example, the measure for felt obligation was adapted from Eisenberger, Armeli, Rexwinkle, Lynch, and Rhoades (2001) and the measure for positive mood was adapted from Warr (1990). Engagement was measured with items drawn from the UWES-9 (Schaufeli, Bakker, & Salanova, 2006), and measures of job resources were adapted from scales previously used in the engagement literature (e.g., Bakker, Demerouti, & Schaufeli, 2003; Bakker, Demerouti, Taris, Schaufeli, & Schreurs, 2003; Bakker, Demerouti, & Verbeke, 2004).

Results

Confirmatory factor analysis provided evidence to support the convergent and discriminant validity of the measures. The overall measurement model yielded acceptable fit statistics ($\chi^2/\mathrm{df} = 2.256$, GFI = .91, NFI = .91, TLI = .94, CFI = .95, RMSEA = .057) and all items loaded .72 (standardized loadings) or higher on their designated factor. Although structural equation modeling of the proposed model (see Fig. A) yielded generally acceptable fit indices ($\chi^2/df = 2.435$, GFI = .84, NFI = .90, TLI = .93, CFI = .94, RMSEA = .061), 4 of the 11 proposed structural paths were not significant. Autonomy, coworker support, and supervisor support were not significantly associated with satisfaction of the need for meaningful work, and felt obligation was not significantly associated with engagement. Respecification of the model (see Fig. B), based on an examination of the parameter estimates and the AMOS modification indices (see Anderson & Gerbing, 1988), yielded a theoretically defensible and good fitting model ($\chi^2/df = 2.418$, GFI = .85, NFI = .91, TLI = .94, CFI = .95, RMSEA = .061).

Fig. B shows positive mood and satisfaction of the need for meaningful work having a significant direct effect on engagement. Satisfaction of the need for meaningful work also had direct effects on positive mood and felt obligation.

Autonomy was found to have a strong direct effect on skill utilization and a significant indirect effect on satisfaction of the need for meaningful work through its influence on skill utilization. Skill utilization had significant direct associations with satisfaction of the need for meaningful work and with positive mood. Furthermore, and beyond the significant direct effects modeled in Fig. B, autonomy, supervisor support, skill development, skill utilization, and satisfaction of need for meaningful work, all had significant indirect effects on engagement. Autonomy, skill development, and skill utilization had significant indirect effects on felt obligation; and autonomy, supervisor

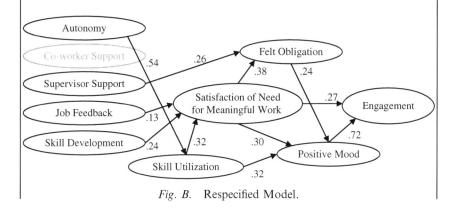

Fig. B. Respecified Model.

support, skill development, and skill utilization had significant indirect effects on positive mood. Felt obligation, although not having a significant direct effect on engagement, had a significant indirect effect on engagement through its influence on positive mood. Overall, the model explained 79% of the variance in engagement, 44% of the variance in positive mood, 27% of the variance in felt obligation, 30% of the variance in satisfaction of the need for meaningful work, and 29% of the variance in skill utilization.

Discussion

The theoretically proposed mediated relationships, explaining how job resources result in engagement, to a large extent were supported. Satisfaction of the need for meaningful work and positive mood were shown to have significant direct effects on engagement and also to mediate the influence of job resources on engagement. While felt obligation, as a social exchange related construct, did not directly influence engagement, the effects of various job resources on positive mood were found to be mediated by felt obligation. Interestingly, autonomy, rather than having a direct effect on need for meaningful work was found to have a strong direct effect on skill utilization and a significant indirect effect on satisfaction of need for meaningful work through its influence on skill utilization. Skill utilization emerged as an important predictor of satisfaction of the need for meaningful work and of positive mood. Skill utilization might therefore warrant additional attention as a job resource within JD–R related research and practice. Supervisor support, consistent with the social support literature (Eisenberger et al., 2001), had a social exchange related direct influence on felt obligation as well as significant indirect effects on positive mood and engagement.

Overall, despite meaningful work previously being identified as a central variable in the context of job design (Humphrey et al., 2007) there has been limited research on satisfaction of the need for meaningful work as a central explanatory mechanism accounting for how job resources result in employee engagement. The present research goes some considerable way toward highlighting the important role that meaningful work, positive mood, and felt obligation play in the motivational processes associated with employee engagement.

INTERVENTIONS TO DEVELOP MEANINGFULNESS AT WORK

Within the broad suite of positive psychological interventions being applied in organizational contexts, organizations have become increasingly interested in how to develop employee engagement (Bakker et al., 2011). Although many anecdotal and practitioner case-study accounts of how to develop engagement have been published (e.g., Buckingham & Coffman, 1999), Schaufeli and Salanova (2010) recently argued that there is limited published evidence suggesting that interventions to improve work engagement are effective. Certainly, given what is known from the accumulated organizational development literature, it is very likely there will never be a simple "magic pill" or "silver bullet" (Schneider, 1996, p. 10) which can be applied to develop, embed, and sustain engagement in organizational settings. In contrast, sustained and committed efforts using some combination of individual, job, and organizational level interventions will be needed. Meaningful work potentially provides a useful integrating lens by which such interventions can be designed, implemented, and evaluated.

At the level of the organization, the development and communication of clear and compelling purpose and vision statements potentially provide the foundation for employees experiencing their work to be meaningful and engaging. Organizational purpose statements define the reason an organization exists and organizational vision statements describe an "idealized picture of the future based around organizational values" (Rafferty & Griffin, 2004, p. 332). Purpose and vision provide for shared mental models (Cannon-Bowers, Salas, & Converse, 1990) and, being motivational in nature (Griffin, Parker, & Mason, 2010; Shamir, House, & Arthur, 1993), also provide the context for the initiation, direction, intensity, and maintenance of goal-directed effort (Kanfer, 1991), coordinated goal-focused decision-making, and for meaningful goal-focused interactions. In terms of Self Determination Theory (Deci & Ryan, 2000), purpose and vision enable employees to satisfy their needs for belongingness, competence, achievement, and control. Without a clearly defined and shared purpose and direction, satisfaction of such employee needs is unlikely to be attainable. It is therefore incumbent on all levels of leadership and management to ensure that employees have opportunities to understand and internalize their organization's purpose and to become connected to a shared and compelling vision. Effective organizational purpose and vision statements, ideally being participatively set, brief, clear, future oriented, stable, challenging, and inspiring (Baum, Locke, & Kirkpatrick, 1998) will help satisfy employees' need for meaningful and engaging work. Similarly, given that meaningful work is a basic value that people associate with work (Ros, Schwartz, & Surkiss, 1999), all levels of leadership and management need to recognize and actively endorse meaningful work and employee engagement as core organizational values (George & Brief, 1992). Increasingly, the literature makes clear that transformational and empowering leaders are key resources for the development of employee engagement (Albrecht & Andreeta, 2011; Tims, Bakker, & Xanthopoulou, 2011). Ongoing training and development interventions to support leadership and management effectiveness in these domains (e.g., multi-rater leadership feedback processes) are also warranted. More generally, Gruman and Saks (2011) recently argued that human resource management (HRM) practices and processes, such as performance management systems, need to be designed to promote employee engagement and to recognize individual needs, goals, and desires as important parts of goal setting and performance management processes.

With respect to job level interventions aimed at developing meaningful work and work engagement, the JCM (Hackman & Oldham, 1980) and the JD–R model (Bakker & Demerouti, 2007, 2008) suggest clear intervention strategies. Given that job characteristics and job resources have been shown to play an important role in the experience of meaningful work and of work engagement (May et al., 2004), the redesign of jobs can be undertaken in order to better satisfy employee needs for meaningful work and to promote engagement. For example, developing supervisor or colleague support and redesigning work processes to enhance feedback and autonomy will very likely increase the experience of meaningfulness and engagement (Bakker, 2010; Humphrey et al., 2007). More generally, job-enrichment initiatives (e.g., enabling workers to interface and negotiate more directly with clients or customers) have been shown to result in increased satisfaction of meaningfulness and engagement at work (Grant et al., 2007). Such job-enrichment practices potentially create positive challenges for employees and greater opportunities for workers to see the impact of their work, thereby increasing their motivation and engagement.

Finally, in terms of individual level interventions, training and development programs aimed at increasing the meaningfulness, positivity, and engagement that employees experience at work should be implemented. Beyond generic strengths-based positive psychology interventions that have been shown to be applicable in organizational contexts (see Clifton & Harter, 2003; Schaufeli & Salanova, 2010), the person–job fit, person–organization fit, and psychological contract literatures provide useful insights to inform such programs and interventions. More specifically, employees might usefully be encouraged and trained to engage in job crafting (Wrzesniewski & Dutton, 2001). Job crafting enables employees to more effectively focus on changing the characteristics of their jobs and their relationships with others "to revise the meaning of the work and the social environment at work" (Bakker, 2010, p. 238). Similarly, training and development activities focused on helping individuals identify their personal vision and purpose (George & Brief, 1992), and to match their personal vision and purpose with the organizational vision and purpose, will provide a firm platform to enhance individual meaning and engagement at work (Bindl & Parker, 2010). Interventions aimed at building personal resources such as positivity and psychological capital (e.g., efficacy beliefs, optimism, hope, and resiliency) will also be useful in increasing engagement at work (Sweetman & Luthans, 2010; Xanthopoulou, Bakker, Demerouti, & Schaufeli, 2009b). Ongoing research aimed at determining how best to adapt the increasingly available generic positive psychology interventions to different organizational contexts will also likely prove helpful.

Importantly, whichever strategies are used to enhance the experience of meaningful work, felt obligation, positivity, and engagement in organizational contexts, there is a clear and ongoing need to systematically evaluate the effectiveness of such interventions across a range of different contexts. Conventional evaluation taxonomies (Kirkpatrick & Kirkpatrick, 2006) assessing the impact of interventions at the level of reaction, learning, behavior, outcomes, and return on investments, might usefully be employed.

FUTURE RESEARCH

Additional research in a number of areas is needed to further establish the psychological processes that explain why and how organizational, job, and personal resources result in positive motivational individual, team, and organizational outcomes. As previously noted, additional research could usefully be devoted toward understanding which needs are most salient to, or best "matched" (De Jonge & Dormann, 2006) with, which resources. Similarly, researchers could usefully devote further attention toward identifying how psychological variables mediate the influence of organizational, job, and personal demands on an extended suite of motivational and health outcomes. Britt et al. (2001), for example, showed that experiencing work as meaningful had a positive association with perceived ability to deal with stress. More research could usefully be conducted in this area.

The inclusion of additional organizational level variables (e.g., senior leadership, vision clarity, organizational climate) will likely help advance our understanding of the determinants of meaningfulness and engagement at work (Albrecht, 2010b). Sivanathan, Arnold, Turner, and Barling (2004), for example, noted that transformational leadership has been found to be positively associated with congruence of values between leaders and followers (Jung & Avolio, 2000) and with employees believing in the higher purpose of work (Sparks & Schenk, 2001). Such findings have clear implications for leaders, leadership development, and employees' experiences of meaningfulness and engagement at work.

Additional research could usefully be conducted on the individual difference variables that influence the extent to which individuals experience meaning and engagement at work. Hardiness, as a personality trait, for example has been shown to be positively associated with the tendency to find meaning in work (Britt et al., 2001). Self-efficacy, attributional style, positivity, conscientiousness, and locus of control could all plausibly influence the extent to which employees perceive meaningfulness in their work and explain positive mood, felt obligation, and engagement. Steger and Dik (2010), on this issue, noted that "we need to better understand who is most likely to experience meaningful work ..., the basic personality, cognitive, and interpersonal styles of people who approach work as meaning ... [and the] extent ... work as meaning [is] a stable trait that varies little over time and across situations, as opposed to a malleable values-based characteristic that is amenable to change efforts" (p. 139).

Further research could also usefully be conducted on additional psychological variables likely to mediate the influence of demands and resources on work engagement. For example, research on the mediating influence of theoretically derived constructs such as positive mood, self-efficacy, psychological capital (Luthans & Youssef, 2007), and psychological empowerment (Spreitzer, 1995) could usefully be conducted. Such further research should best be framed within longitudinal designs to more confidently assess the causal, reciprocal, and dynamic relationships among the constructs considered (see Salanova et al., 2010).

CONCLUSION

There has been widespread academic and practitioner interest in understanding the newly emerged positive psychological construct of engagement. While job resources have been found to significantly influence engagement, the motivational processes implicit in the JD–R model have yet to be fully explored. Drawing from need-based motivational theories (e.g., Deci & Ryan, 2000) and social exchange theory (Blau, 1964), the case was here made that the degree of satisfaction regarding the meaningfulness of work can be important to understanding, generating, and managing work engagement. The issues, theories, measures, and models herein described, and the broader positive role of meaningful work, should be the subject of on-going empirical investigation within the domain of POS.

REFERENCES

Albrecht, S. L. (Ed.). (2010a). *The handbook of employee engagement: Perspectives, issues, research and practice.* Cheltenham, UK: Edward Elgar Publishers.

Albrecht, S. L. (2010b). Employee engagement: Ten key research questions. In S. L. Albrecht (Ed.), *The handbook of employee engagement: Perspectives, issues, research and practice* (pp. 3–19). Cheltenham, UK: Edward Elgar Publishers.

Albrecht, S. L., & Andreeta, M. (2011). The influence of empowering leadership, empowerment and engagement on affective commitment and turnover intentions in community health service workers: Test of a model. *Leadership in Health Services, 24*(3), 228–237.

Albrecht, S. L., & Su, J. M. (2012). Job resources and employee engagement in a Chinese context: The mediating role of job meaningfulness, felt obligation and positive mood. *International Journal of Business and Emerging Markets, 4,* 277–292.

Anderson, J. C., & Gerbing, D. W. (1988). Structural equation modelling in practice: A review and recommended two-step approach. *Psychological Bulletin, 103,* 411–423.

Armeli, S., Eisenberger, R., Fasolo, P., & Lynch, P. (1998). Perceived organizational support and police performance: The moderating influence of socioemotional needs. *Journal of Applied Psychology, 83,* 288–297.

Bakker, A. B. (2009). Building engagement in the workplace. In R. J. Burke & C. L. Cooper (Eds.), *The peak performing organization* (pp. 50–72). Oxon, UK: Routledge.

Bakker, A. B. (2010). Engagement and 'job crafting': Engaged employees create their own great place to work. In S. Albrecht (Ed.), *The handbook of employee engagement: Perspectives, issues, research and practice* (pp. 229–244). Cheltenham, UK: Edward-Elgar.

Bakker, A. B, Albrecht, S. L., & Leiter, M. P. (2011). Key questions regarding work engagement. *European Journal of Work and Organizational Psychology, 20,* 4–28.

Bakker, A. B., & Bal, P. M. (2010). Weekly work engagement and performance: A study among starting teachers. *Journal of Occupational and Organizational Psychology, 83,* 189–206.

Bakker, A. B., & Demerouti, E. (2007). The job demands-resources model: State of the art. *Journal of Managerial Psychology, 22,* 309–328.

Bakker, A. B., & Demerouti, E. (2008). Towards a model of work engagement. *Career Development International, 13,* 209–223.

Bakker, A. B., Demerouti, E., & Schaufeli, W. B. (2003). Dual processes at work in a call centre: An application of the job demands-resources model. *European Journal of Work and Organizational Psychology, 12,* 393–417.

Bakker, A. B., Demerouti, E., Taris, T. W., Schaufeli, W. B., & Schreurs, P. (2003). A multi-group analysis of the job demands–resources model in four home care organizations. *International Journal of Stress Management, 10*, 16–38.

Bakker, A. B., Demerouti, E., & Verbeke, W. (2004). Using the job demands-resources model to predict burnout and performance. *Human Resource Management, 43*, 83–104.

Bakker, A. B., & Derks, D. (2010). Positive occupational health psychology. In S. Leka & J. Houdmont (Eds.), *Occupational health psychology* (pp. 194–224). Oxford: Wiley-Blackwell.

Bakker, A. B., & Leiter, M. P. (Eds.). (2010). *Work engagement: A handbook of essential theory and research.* New York, NY: Psychology Press.

Bakker, A. B., & Schaufeli, W. B. (2008). Positive organizational behavior: Engaged employees in flourishing organizations. *Journal of Organizational Behavior, 29*, 147–154.

Baum, J. R., Locke, E. A., & Kirkpatrick, S. A. (1998). A longitudinal study of the relation of vision and vision communication to venture growth in entrepreneurial firms. *Journal of Applied Psychology, 83*, 43–54.

Bindl, U., & Parker, S. K. (2010). Feeling good and performing well? Psychological engagement and positive behaviours at work. In S. Albrecht (Ed.), *The handbook of employee engagement: Perspectives, issues, research and practice* (pp. 385–398). Cheltenham, UK: Edward-Elgar.

Blau, P. M. (1964). *Exchange and power in social life.* New York, NY: Wiley.

Britt, T. W., Adler, A. B., & Bartone, P. T. (2001). Deriving benefits from stressful events: The role of engagement in meaningful work and hardiness. *Journal of Occupational Health Psychology, 6*, 53–63.

Buckingham, M., & Coffman, C. (1999). *First, break all the rules.* New York, NY: Simon & Schuster.

Cameron, K. S., Dutton, J. E., & Quinn, R. E. (Eds.). (2003). *Positive organizational scholarship: Foundations of a new discipline.* San Francisco, CA: Berrett-Kohler.

Cannon-Bowers, J. A., Salas, E., & Converse, S. A. (1990). Cognitive psychology and team training: Training shared mental models and complex systems. *Human Factors Society Bulletin, 33*, 1–4.

Cardador, M. T., & Rupp, D. E. (2011). Organizational culture, multiple needs, and the meaningfulness of work. In N. M. Ashkanasy, C. P. M. Wilderom & M. F. Peterson (Eds.), *Handbook of organizational culture and climate* (2nd ed., pp. 158–180). Thousand Oaks, CA: Sage.

Cartwright, S., & Holmes, N. (2006). The meaning of work: The challenge of regaining employee engagement and reducing cynicism. *Human Resource Management Review, 16*, 199–208.

Clifton, D. O., & Harter, J. K. (2003). Investing in strengths. In K. S. Cameron, J. E. Dutton & R. E. Quinn (Eds.), *Positive organizational scholarship: Foundations of a new discipline.* San Francisco, CA: Berrett-Koehler.

Deci, E. L., & Ryan, R. M. (2000). The 'what' and 'why' of goal pursuits: Human needs and the self-determination of behavior. *Psychological Inquiry, 11*, 227–268.

De Jonge, J., & Dormann, C. (2006). Stressors, resources, and strain at work: A longitudinal test of the triple-match principle. *Journal of Applied Psychology, 91*, 1359–1374.

Eisenberger, R., Armeli, S., Rexwinkel, B., Lynch, P. D., & Rhoades, L. (2001). Reciprocation of perceived organisational support. *Journal of Applied Psychology, 86*, 42–51.

Eisenberger, R., Cummings, J., Armeli, S., & Lynch, P. (1997). Perceived organizational support, discretionary treatment, and job satisfaction. *Journal of Applied Psychology, 82,* 812–820.

Fredrickson, B. (2001). The role of positive emotions in positive psychology: The broaden and build theory of positive emotions. *American Psychologist, 56,* 218–226.

Gable, S. L., & Haidt, J. (2005). What (and why) is positive psychology? *Review of General Psychology, 9,* 103–110.

George, J. M., & Brief, A. P. (1992). Feeling good-doing good: A conceptual analysis of the mood at work-organizational spontaneity relationship. *Psychological Bulletin, 112,* 310–329.

Grant, A. M., Campbell, E. M., Chen, G., Cottone, K., Lapedis, D., & Lee, K. (2007). Impact and the art of motivation maintenance: The effects of contact with beneficiaries on persistence behavior. *Organizational Behavior and Human Decision Processes, 103,* 53–67.

Griffin, M. A., Parker, S. K., & Mason, C. M. (2010). Leader vision and the development of adaptive and proactive performance: A longitudinal study. *Journal of Applied Psychology, 95,* 174–182.

Gruman, J. A., & Saks, A. M. (2011). Performance management and employee engagement. *Human Resource Management Review, 21,* 123–136.

Hackman, J. R. (2009). The perils of positivity. *Journal of Organizational Behavior, 30,* 309–319.

Hackman, J. R., & Oldham, G. R. (1980). *Work redesign.* Reading, MA: Addison-Wesley.

Halbesleben, J. R. B. (2010). A meta-analysis of work engagement: Relationships with burnout, demands, resources and consequences. In A. B. Bakker & M. P. Leiter (Eds.), *Work engagement: Recent developments in theory and research* (pp. 102–117). New York, NY: Psychology Press.

Halbesleben, J. R. B., & Wheeler, A. R. (2008). The relative roles of engagement and embeddedness in predicting job performance and intention to leave. *Work & Stress, 22,* 242–256.

Hallberg, U. E., & Schaufeli, W. B. (2006). "Same same" but different? Can work engagement be discriminated from job involvement and organizational commitment? *European Psychologist, 11,* 119–127.

Harter, J. K., & Blacksmith, N. (2010). Employee engagement and the psychology of joining, staying in and leaving organizations. In P. A. Linley, S. Harrington & N. Garcea (Eds.), *Oxford handbook of positive psychology and work* (pp. 121–130). Oxford: Oxford University Press.

Herzberg, F. (1959). *The motivation to work.* New York, NY: Wiley.

Hobfoll, S. E. (1989). Conservation of resources: A new attempt at conceptualizing stress. *American Psychologist, 44,* 513–524.

Humphrey, S. E., Nahrgang, J. D., & Morgeson, F. P. (2007). Integrating motivational, social, and contextual work design features: A meta-analytic summary and theoretical extension of the work design literature. *Journal of Applied Psychology, 92,* 1332–1356.

Johns, G., Xie, J. L., & Fang, Y. (1992). Mediating and moderating effects in job design. *Journal of Management, 18,* 657–676.

Jung, D. I., & Avolio, B. J. (2000). Opening the black box: An experimental investigation of the mediating effects of trust and value congruence on transformational and transactional leadership. *Journal of Organizational Behavior, 21,* 949–964.

Kahn, W. A. (1990). Psychological conditions of personal engagement and disengagement at work. *Academy of Management Journal, 33*, 692–724.

Kanfer, R. (1991). Motivation theory and industrial and organizational psychology. In M. D. Dunnette & L. M. Hough (Eds.), *Handbook of industrial and organizational psychology* (Vol. 1, pp. 76–170). Palo Alto, CA: Consulting Psychologists Press.

Keyes, C. L. M., & Haidt, J. (Eds.). (2003). *Flourishing: Positive psychology and the life well lived*. Washington, DC: American Psychological Association.

King, L. A., Hicks, J. A., Krull, J., & Del Gaiso, A. K. (2006). Positive affect and the experience of meaning in life. *Journal of Personality and Social Psychology, 90*, 179–196.

Kirkpatrick, D. L., & Kirkpatrick, J. D. (2006). *Evaluating training programs: The four levels* (3rd ed.). San Francisco, CA: Berrett-Koehler Publishers, Inc.

Linley, P. A., Harrington, S., & Garcea, N. (2010). *Oxford handbook of positive psychology and work*. Oxford, UK: Oxford University Press.

Linley, P. A., Joseph, S., Harrington, S., & Wood, A. M. (2006). Positive psychology: Past, present, and (possible) future. *Journal of Positive Psychology, 1*, 3–16.

Luthans, F. (2002). The need for and meaning of positive organizational behavior. *Journal of Organizational Behavior, 6*, 695–706.

Luthans, F., & Avolio, B. J. (2009). The 'point' of positive organizational behavior. *Journal of Organizational Behavior, 30*, 291–307.

Luthans, F., & Youssef, C. M. (2007). Emerging positive organizational behavior. *Journal of Management, 33*, 321–349.

Macey, W. H., & Schneider, B. (2008). The meaning of employee engagement. *Industrial and Organizational Psychology: Perspectives on Science and Practice, 1*, 3–30.

Macey, W. H., Schneider, B., Barbera, K. M., & Young, S. A. (2009). *Employee engagement: Tools for analysis, practice, and competitive advantage*. Malden, MA: Wiley.

Maslow, A. (1943). A theory of human motivation. *Psychological Review, 50*, 370–396.

May, D. R., Gilson, R. L., & Harter, L. M. (2004). The psychological conditions of meaningfulness, safety and availability and the engagement of the human spirit at work. *Journal of Occupational and Organizational Psychology, 77*, 11–37.

McClelland, D. C. (1961). *The achieving society*. New York, NY: Van Nostrand.

McClelland, D. C. (1965). Toward a theory of motive acquisition. *American Psychologist, 20*, 321–333.

Milliman, J. F., Czaplewski, A. J., & Ferguson, J. M. (2003). Workplace spirituality and employee work attitudes: An exploratory empirical assessment. *Journal of Organizational Change Management, 16*, 426–447.

Oldham, G. R., Hackman, J. R., & Stepina, L. P. (1978). *Norms for the job diagnostic survey*. Technical Report No. 16. Yale University Press, New Haven, CT.

Rafferty, A. E., & Griffin, M. A. (2004). Dimensions of transformational leadership: Conceptual and empirical extensions. *Leadership Quarterly, 15*, 329–354.

Rich, B. L., LePine, J. A., & Crawford, E. R. (2010). Job engagement: Antecedents and effects on job performance. *Academy of Management Journal, 53*, 617–635.

Roberts, L. M. (2006). Shifting the lens on organizational life: The added value of positive scholarship. *Academy of Management Review, 31*, 292–305.

Ros, M., Schwartz, S. H., & Surkiss, S. (1999). Basic individual values, work values, and the meaning of work. *Applied Psychology: An International Review, 48*, 49–71.

Ryan, R. M., & Deci, E. L. (2000). Self-determination theory and the facilitation of intrinsic motivation, social development, and well-being. *American Psychologist, 55*, 68–78.

Ryan, R. M., & Deci, E. L. (2001). On happiness and human potentials: A review of research on hedonic and eudemonic well-being. *Annual Review of Psychology*, *52*, 141–166.

Ryff, C. D., & Singer, B. H. (2008). Know thyself and become what you are: A eudemonic approach to psychological well-being. *Journal of Happiness Studies*, *9*, 13–39.

Saks, A. M. (2006). Antecedents and consequences of employee engagement. *Journal of Managerial Psychology*, *21*, 600–619.

Salanova, M., Agut, S., & Peiro, J. M. (2005). Linking organizational resources and work engagement to employee performance and customer loyalty: The mediation of service climate. *Journal of Applied Psychology*, *90*, 1217–1227.

Salanova, M., Llorens, S., & Schaufeli, W. B. (2011). "Yes, I can, I feel good, and I just do it!" On gain cycles and spirals of efficacy beliefs, affect, and engagement. *Applied Psychology: An International Review*, *60*, 255–285.

Salanova, M., Schaufeli, W. B., Xanthopoulou, D., & Bakker, A. B. (2010). The gain spiral of resources and work engagement: Sustaining a positive work life. In A. B. Bakker & M. P. Leiter (Eds.), *Work engagement: Recent developments in theory and research* (pp. 118–131). New York, NY: Psychology Press.

Schaufeli, W. B., Bakker, A. B., & Salanova, M. (2006). The measurement of work engagement with a short questionnaire: A cross-national study. *Educational and Psychological Measurement*, *66*, 701–716.

Schaufeli, W. B., & Salanova, M. (2010). How to improve work engagement? In S. Albrecht (Ed.), *The handbook of employee engagement: Perspectives, issues, research and practice* (pp. 399–415). Cheltenham, UK: Edward-Elgar.

Schaufeli, W. B., Salanova, M., González-Romá, V., & Bakker, A. B. (2002). The measurement of engagement and burnout: A two sample confirmatory factor analytic approach. *Journal of Happiness Studies*, *3*, 71–92.

Schneider, B. (1996). Creating a climate and culture for sustainable organizational change. *Organizational Development Journal*, *24*, 6–15.

Seligman, M. E. P. (2002). *Authentic happiness: Using the new positive psychology to realize your potential for lasting fulfillment*. New York, NY: Free Press.

Seligman, M. E. P. (2011). *Flourish: A visionary new understanding of happiness and well-being*. New York, NY: Free Press.

Seligman, M. E. P., & Csikszentmihalyi, M. (2000). Positive psychology: An introduction. *American Psychologist*, *55*, 5–14.

Shamir, B., House, R. J., & Arthur, M. B. (1993). The motivational effects of charismatic leadership: A self-concept based theory. *Organization Science*, *4*, 577–594.

Sivanathan, N., Arnold, K. A., Turner, N., & Barling, J. (2004). Leading well: Transformational leadership and well-being. In P. A. Linley & S. Joseph (Eds.), *Positive psychology in practice* (pp. 241–255). Hoboken, NJ: Wiley.

Sparks, J. R., & Schenk, J. A. (2001). Explaining the effects of transformational leadership: an investigation of the effects of higher-orders motives in multilevel marketing organization. *Journal of Organizational Behavior*, *22*, 849–886.

Spreitzer, G. M. (1995). Psychological empowerment in the workplace: Construct definition, measurement, and validation. *Academy of Management Journal*, *38*, 429–459.

Stairs, M., & Galpin, M. (2010). Positive engagement: From employee engagement to workplace happiness. In P. A. Linley, S. Harrington & N. Garcea (Eds.), *Oxford handbook of positive psychology and work* (pp. 143–154). Oxford: Oxford University Press.

Steger, M. F., & Dik, B. J. (2010). Work as meaning: Individual and organizational benefits of engaging in meaningful work. In P. A. Linley, S. Harrington & N. Garcea (Eds.), *Oxford handbook of positive psychology and work* (pp. 131–142). Oxford: Oxford University Press.

Sweetman, D., & Luthans, F. (2010). The power of positive psychology: Psychological capital and work engagement. In A. B. Bakker & M. P. Leiter (Eds.), *Work engagement: Recent developments in theory and research* (pp. 54–68). New York, NY: Psychology Press.

Thomas, K. W., & Velthouse, B. A. (1990). Cognitive elements of empowerment: An 'interpretive' model of intrinsic task motivation. *Academy of Management Review, 15*(4), 666–681.

Tims, M., Bakker, A. B., & Xanthopoulou, D. (2011). Do transformational leaders enhance their followers' daily work engagement? *Leadership Quarterly, 22*, 121–131.

Van den Broeck, A., Vansteenkiste, M., De Witte, H., & Lens, W. (2008). Explaining the relationships between job characteristics, burnout, and engagement: The role of basic psychological need satisfaction. *Work & Stress, 22*, 277–294.

Van den Broeck, A., Vansteenkiste, M., De Witte, H., Soenens, B., & Lens, W. (2010). Capturing autonomy, competence, and relatedness at work: Construction and initial validation of the Work-related Basic Need Satisfaction scale. *Journal of Occupational and Organizational Psychology, 83*, 981–1002.

Warr, P. B. (1990). The measurement of well-being and other aspects of mental health. *Journal of Occupational Psychology, 63*, 193–210.

Wright, T. A. (2003). Positive organizational behavior: An idea whose time has truly come. *Journal of Organizational Behavior, 24*, 437–442.

Wrzesniewski, A., & Dutton, J. E. (2001). Crafting a job: Revisioning employees as active crafters of their work. *Academy of Management Review, 26*, 179–201.

Xanthopoulou, D., Bakker, A. B., Demerouti, E., & Schaufeli, W. B. (2009a). Reciprocal relationships between job resources, personal resources, and work engagement. *Journal of Vocational Behavior, 74*, 235–244.

Xanthopoulou, D., Bakker, A. B., Demerouti, E., & Schaufeli, W. B. (2009b). Work engagement and financial returns: A diary study on the role of job and personal resources. *Journal of Occupational and Organizational Psychology, 82*, 183–200.

Zika, S., & Chamberlain, K. (1992). On the relation between meaning in life and psychological well-being. *British Journal of Psychology, 83*, 133–145.

WHO IS PROACTIVE AND WHY? UNPACKING INDIVIDUAL DIFFERENCES IN EMPLOYEE PROACTIVITY

Chia-Huei Wu, Sharon K. Parker and Uta K. Bindl

Proactive behavior refers to self-initiated and future-oriented action that aims to bring about change (Parker, Williams, & Turner, 2006). Individuals can behave proactively in a variety of domains, such as in regard to their careers, improving their work environment, and influencing organizational strategy. Proactivity has been recognized as particularly critical in complex and uncertain work environments because it allows individuals to master situations in advance and to act on one's own initiative without the need for closer supervision (Griffin, Neal, & Parker, 2007). Supporting its benefits, recent meta-analytic evidence suggests that proactivity is mainly beneficial (Thomas, Whitman, & Viswesvaran, 2010).

Researchers have identified dispositional and situational antecedents of employee proactivity, as well as tried to understand the underlying motivational mechanisms linking antecedents and outcomes (Parker, Bindl, & Strauss, 2010). Review articles (e.g., Bindl & Parker, 2010; Wu & Parker, 2011) have shown that proactive behavior is predicted by certain dispositional characteristics, such as proactive personality, and by situational features, such as job autonomy, transformational leadership, and supportive organizational climate. Interactions between personal and environmental

Advances in Positive Organizational Psychology, Volume 1, 261–280
Copyright © 2013 by Emerald Group Publishing Limited
All rights of reproduction in any form reserved
ISSN: 2046-410X/doi:10.1108/S2046-410X(2013)0000001014

factors in shaping proactive behavior have also been identified (e.g., Griffin, Parker, & Mason, 2010; McAllister, Kamdar, Morrison, & Turban, 2007), suggesting that proactive behavior is determined by combinations of personal and situational forces.

Nevertheless, compared to research on situational antecedents of proactive behavior, dispositional antecedents to proactive behaviors have been less systematically investigated. One reason for why research has mostly focused on understanding situational antecedents to proactivity could be that these are more amenable to intervention than are stable dispositional characteristics (Geller, 2002). While we agree it is important to investigate how context influences proactivity, understanding what type of person will typically engage in proactive behaviors will provide additional insights. Proactive behaviors should be shaped by dispositional characteristics because these behaviors are by definition not required in a given job description and are thus typically not tied to formal reward and punishment systems in the organization (Van Dyne & LePine, 1998). Our goal in this chapter is to advance understanding of the role of personality traits for proactive behaviors at work.

Personality traits have been classified in different ways. Most typically, personality traits have been classified according to their content, notably via the Big Five personality framework (John, Naumann, & Soto, 2008). This type of classification is referred to as content classification. However, personality traits can also be classified according to how they influence behavior. An example of a functional classification approach is Buss and Finn's (1987) differentiation of personality into cognitive, affective, and instrumental traits. We focus particularly on the functional classification to review how personality traits can influence proactive behavior. Our approach offers a different perspective to the question of "who" is proactive, and also helps to integrate past findings on the role of personality traits in shaping proactive behaviors.

In the following sections, we first introduce the concept of proactive behavior at work and its features. We then discuss the functional classification of personality traits proposed by Buss and Finn (1987) and review the existing literature accordingly. Finally, we identify directions for further research.

PROACTIVITY IN THE WORKPLACE

Scholars have argued that different forms of proactive behaviors (e.g., career initiative, feedback seeking, and taking charge) all involve employees' self-initiated and future-focused efforts to bring about change in a situation (Parker et al., 2006). There are at least three important elements that define proactivity: future-focus, change-orientation, and self-initiation (Frese & Fay, 2001; Parker et al., 2006). First, proactive behavior is future-focused, which means that this action is targeted at anticipated problems or at opportunities with a long-term focus. Second, proactive behavior is change-oriented, involving not just reacting to a situation but being prepared to change that situation in order to bring about a different future. Third, and underpinning the prior two elements, proactive behavior is self-initiated, which means that employees initiate a proactive goal without being told to, or without requiring explicit instructions from supervisors. Accordingly, proactivity has also been conceived of as a process in which employees generate and implement, under their own direction, a proactive goal to bring about a different future (Bindl, Parker, Totterdell, & Hagger-Johnson, 2012; Frese & Fay, 2001; Grant & Ashford, 2008).

Although there are different forms of proactive behavior across many situations, Parker and Collins (2010) differentiated three overarching categories of proactive behavior according to their goals. First, employees can proactively aim to achieve a better fit between the person and the environment. This form of proactivity is referred to as "proactive person-environment fit behavior," and includes behaviors such as feedback inquiry, feedback monitoring (Ashford, Blatt, & VandeWalle, 2003), job change negotiation (Ashford & Black, 1996), and career initiative (Seibert, Kraimer, & Crant, 2001). Second, employees can proactively set out to improve the internal organizational environment, which Parker and Collins (2010) summarize as "proactive work behavior." This form of proactivity includes behaviors such as taking charge (Morrison & Phelps, 1999), voice (LePine & Van Dyne, 1998), individual innovation (Scott & Bruce, 1994), and problem prevention (Frese & Fay, 2001). Third, employees can be proactive in improving the fit of their organization with its wider environment, so-called "proactive strategic behavior." Example behaviors of this form of proactivity include strategic scanning (Parker & Collins, 2010), issue selling credibility (Dutton & Ashford, 1993), and issue selling willingness (Ashford, Rothbard, Piderit, & Dutton, 1998).

In contrast to the differentiation of proactive behavior based on individuals' specific goals, Griffin et al. (2007) differentiated proactive behavior based on the level in the organization to which an individual directs his/her proactive efforts. In brief, they specified the extent to which individuals engage in self-starting, future-oriented behavior relevant to: their individual work situations or roles (individual task proactivity); to a team's situation or the way the team works (team member proactivity); and to their organization and/or the way the organization works (organization member proactivity). Although different types of proactivity have their own meanings, they are also positively and moderately related to each other, suggesting that different forms of proactive behavior share the same common base of proactivity, and supporting the conceptualization of proactive behavior as one overarching concept.

Three common motivational mechanisms in triggering proactive behavior have been proposed by Parker et al. (2010). In order to enact proactive behavior individuals will consider whether they feel capable of being proactive (a "can do" pathway), whether they have some sense that they want to bring about a different future (a "reason-to" pathway), and whether they experience positive affect that fosters their proactive actions (an "energized-to" pathway). These mechanisms have been supported in empirical studies with different forms of proactive behavior (e.g., Bindl et al., 2012; Den Hartog & Belschak, 2007; Parker et al., 2006), suggesting that different forms of proactive behavior have common motivational mechanisms. A systematic model of how more distal, dispositional characteristics can motivate different types of proactivity at work is currently missing, and we propose next that a functional classification of personality traits can help generate such a framework.

A FUNCTIONAL CLASSIFICATION OF PERSONALITY TRAITS

In contrast to content classifications of personality traits (e.g., the "Big Five" framework), Buss and Finn (1987) draw on three aspects of behavior – cognitive, affective, and instrumental (James, 1890) – to classify personality traits. The cognitive aspect concerns the function of reflecting information processing in thinking and understanding; the affective aspect concerns the function of expressing emotional responses; and the instrumental aspect concerns the function of interacting with the environment (Elizur & Sagie, 1999; Levy & Guttman, 1975). Corresponding to these aspects, Buss and Finn (1987) identified that cognitive traits involve behavior that has a large component of thoughts, imagination, and information processing (e.g., *openness to experience* is a cognitive trait because it is associated with an increased tendency to consider unconventional or unfamiliar ideas); affective traits involve behaviors that have a strong emotional component (*neuroticism* is an affective trait due to its association with increased experience and expression of negative, distressing emotions); and instrumental traits involve behaviors that have an impact on the environment (e.g., *assertiveness* is an instrumental trait because it is associated with an increased tendency to speak up, lead others, and force others to accept one's opinions).

This functional classification framework suggests potential psychological mechanisms (i.e., cognitive, affective, or enactive) via which a specific trait can contribute to proactive behavior. For instance, extraversion as a broad personality trait has been found to be positively related to various forms of proactive behavior, such as information seeking (Tidwell & Sias, 2005), feedback seeking/relationship building (Wanberg & Kammeyer-Mueller, 2000), personal initiative (Fay & Frese, 2001), and voice (LePine & Van Dyne, 2001). This is likely because people high in extraversion are more comfortable and skilled in communicating ideas to others and are more action-oriented in regard to influencing the environment (LePine & Van Dyne, 2001). However, two facets of extraversion, *assertiveness* and *excitement*, should influence proactivity mainly via different mechanisms, according to Buss and Finn's (1987) classification. Assertiveness, an instrumental trait, likely facilitates proactive behavior through its effect on changing the environment, such as persuading others to build networks, and accumulating social capital for implementing proactive ideas (Thompson, 2005). In contrast, excitement, as an affective trait, is more likely to contribute to proactive behaviors via the role of positive feelings, which Bindl et al. (2012) identified as especially important for envisioning proactive goals and for energizing proactive action. This example shows how a functional classification can help to understand why certain personality traits can contribute to proactive behavior, not only because of their content, but also because of their potential mechanisms associated with instrumental, affective, and cognitive aspects of behavior.

While a functional classification of personality traits appears to facilitate understanding the role of personality traits in shaping proactive behaviors, different contents within the same functional classifications should additionally matter. For instance, positive affectivity and negative affectivity are both affective traits; however, they have been differentially linked with proactive behaviors (e.g., Den Hartog & Belschak, 2007). Consequentially, we will present in our review a combination of functions (cognitive, affective, and instrumental) and content of personality traits in discussing their associations with proactive behaviors.

PERSONALITY TRAITS AS INFLUENCING FACTORS OF EMPLOYEE PROACTIVITY

In this section, we draw on Buss and Finn's (1987) framework to review existing findings on the role of personality traits in shaping proactive behaviors. In brief, we suggest that cognitive traits will contribute to proactivity at work because these traits enhance the likelihood that an individual will recognize opportunities and will generate ideas for the future, both aspects that are akin to proactivity; affective traits will contribute to proactivity because these traits increase the experience of energy to purse more challenging goals; and finally, instrumental traits likely contribute to proactivity at work because these traits imply a strong tendency of mastering the environment, likely activating proactive behavior. We will proceed to review each of these traits, in turn. Fig. 1 provides a schematic overview of reviewed personality traits and their proposed influencing mechanisms on proactive behaviors at work.

Cognitive Traits

We expect cognitive traits to take on an important role in triggering proactive behavior because, according to a goal-regulatory perspective (see Parker et al., 2010), effective proactive behavior derives from envisioning a different future, as well as planning and reflecting on past outcomes – all activities that likely require cognitive effort. As Frese and Fay (2001)

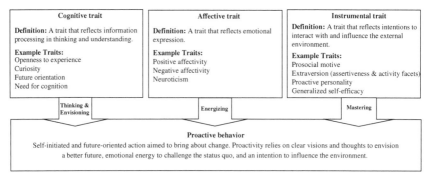

Fig. 1. A Schematic Model of Personality Traits, and Their Proposed Influences on Proactive Behavior.

indicated, proactive behavior is not the application of a standard procedure; rather, an individual must actively consider new methods or pathways to approach a future-oriented goal. Therefore, we suggest that cognitive traits that can lead an individual to generate more new ideas and envision a different future will positively contribute to proactive behavior. Here, we review four such cognitive traits – *openness to experience, curiosity, future orientation,* and *need for cognition* – that have been previously found to relate to proactive behavior.

Openness to Experience
Openness to experience can be viewed as a cognitive trait because people high in openness to experience tend to appreciate new experiences and explore unfamiliar situations (Costa & McCrae, 1992). One would expect openness to experience to relate positively to proactivity, and studies support this. Openness to experience has been found to positively correlate with feedback seeking and positive framing; two kinds of proactive socialization behavior for newcomers (Wanberg & Kammeyer-Mueller, 2000). Fay and Frese (2000) showed that psychologically conservative individuals, who are high in authoritarianism and rejection attitude of foreigners (and likely low on openness to experience), are less likely to engage in personal initiative. Fay and Frese (2001) also reported that individuals high in readiness to change, or "the preference for jobs that allow the change of routines and readiness to participate in qualification" (p. 114), are more likely to report personal initiative.

At the same time, however, studies have reported nonsignificant relationships between openness to experience and proactive behavior, including personal initiative (Fay & Frese, 2001), voice (LePine & Van Dyne, 2001), and task, relational and performance information seeking (Tidwell & Sias, 2005). These inconsistent findings can be explained by Bateman and Crant's (1993) argument that openness to experience also implies tolerance with others' thoughts, which might incline people against change-oriented proactivity. In other words, considering openness to experience as a single whole dimension may be overly crude because specific facets related to proactivity are grouped with nonrelevant facets. This lack of specificity could explain the unreliable relationship of openness to experience with proactivity.

Supporting this possibility, when studies consider facets of openness to experience, only three facets (i.e., facets of actions, ideas, and values) have been found to be positively related to proactive behavior. Facet of actions means willingness to try different activities and preference for novelty over the familiar or routine; facet of ideas means curiosity and willingness to consider unconventional ideas; and facet of values means readiness to reexamine values (social, political, or religious). LePine and VanDyne (2001) found that the facet of actions was positively related to voice behavior. Major, Turner, and Fletcher (2006) found that the facet of ideas and the facet of values predicted motivation to learn, which in turn, was associated with greater engagement in personal development activities. These findings highlight that we need to focus on specific facets of openness to experiences to fully understand how this trait shapes proactive behavior.

Curiosity

Curiosity is "an appetitive state involving the recognition, pursuit, and intense desire to investigate novel information and experiences that demand one's attention" (Kashdan & Steger, 2007, p. 159). We thus expect that curiosity will contribute to proactive behavior because it leads individuals to identify and exploit opportunities, especially in novel situations. Supporting this view, Kashdan and Steger (2007) reported that trait curiosity fosters proactive behaviors and proactive goal-directed efforts. Howell and Shea (2001) also reported that employees who are high in intellectual curiosity are more likely to engage in environmental scanning, which then triggers more championing behavior in innovation (e.g., conviction in innovation, building involvement and support, and persisting in the face of adversary). Similarly, Harrison, Sluss, and Ashforth (2011) found that curiosity can lead an individual to positively frame the external environment, which then enhances proactive behavior (i.e., taking charge).

Future Orientation

Future orientation is defined as the degree to which one is thoughtful about his/her future in motivation (goal setting), planning, and evaluation (Nurmi, 1991). Future orientation is a cognitive trait that has been theorized to positively contribute to proactive behavior. This perspective coincides with recent conceptualizations of proactivity as a goal-regulatory process that comprises elements such as envisioning (thinking ahead to bring about a better future), planning (developing plans for how to implement proactive ideas), action directed toward future impact (manifestation of anticipation and planning into concrete proactive behaviors), as well as reflection (monitoring and evaluating outcomes of proactive action; Bindl et al., 2012;

Frese & Fay, 2001; Grant & Ashford, 2008). All four phases of proactive goal regulation are influenced by a strong future orientation, which leads a person to think ahead, plan in advance, and take actions for the future. As such, it is not surprising that future-orientation can contribute to proactive behavior. Empirically, Parker and Collins (2010) have found that consideration of future consequences were positively related with three broad higher-order sets of proactive behaviors (i.e., proactive work behaviors, proactive strategic behaviors, and proactive person-environment fit behaviors).

Need for Cognition
Need for cognition is another cognitive trait that has been recently examined in proactivity literature (Wu, Parker, & de Jong, in press). Need for cognition is a personality variable reflecting "the tendency for an individual to engage in and enjoy thinking" (Cacioppo & Petty, 1982, p. 116). Need for cognition is expected to contribute to proactive behavior because deliberate and active thinking is needed when planning and enacting proactive actions. This thinking process has been discussed by Frese and Fay (2001), who argued that deliberate cognitive engagement is crucial to identify opportunities and find alternative ways to bring about changes. In this vein, need for cognition has been shown to be positively associated with individual innovation behavior (Wu et al., in press), with the latter being strongly related to proactive behaviors like taking charge and voice (Parker & Collins, 2010).

Affective Traits

We propose that affective traits will additionally influence proactive behavior because affect has been identified as a powerful activator of behavior (Carver & White, 1994; Elliot & Thrash, 2002). Affective traits comprise an individual's typical evaluative feelings across time and situations. In this vein, individuals who are high in *positive affectivity* tend to frequently experience positive emotions, such as enthusiasm and alertness, whereas people who are high in *negative affectivity* tend to frequently experience negative emotions, such as nervousness and distress. Both of these two traits have been associated with individuals' performance at work (Kaplan, Bradley, Luchman, & Haynes, 2009), as well as with proactive behavior more specifically (see Bindl & Parker, 2012), as we will review next.

Positive Affectivity
To date, ample evidence suggests that positive affective experience, activated positive affective in particular (Bindl et al., 2012), promotes positive ways of behaving at work (Forgas & George, 2001; Staw, Sutton, Pelled, 1994). Conceptually, these associations should prevail because positive affect facilitates individuals' focus on positive outcomes of their behaviors (Mayer, Gaschke, Braverman, & Evans, 1992) and generates high expectancy judgments for outcomes (Wegener & Petty, 1996).

We propose that positive affect should be particularly relevant for activating proactive behaviors. This is because proactivity is self-initiated, or generated by employees' themselves (Frese & Fay, 2001; Parker et al., 2010), and represents more internalized rather than externalized goals (Ryan & Deci, 2000). With weaker external forces on proactive behavior, there is more scope for internal influences, such as affect. For example, positive affective experience increases individuals' tendency to choose generative behaviors (Seo, Feldman, Barrett, & Bartunek, 2004). Additionally, because proactive behaviors are change-oriented and self-initiated, they likely require effortful and complex self-regulation processes (Muraven & Baumeister, 2000). As such, positive affectivity provides feelings of energy (Shraga & Shirom, 2009) and thus facilitates engagement and persistence in activities (Tsai, Chen, & Liu, 2007).

In support of these arguments, evidence suggests that positive affectivity is associated with higher levels of self-reported personal initiative (Den Hartog & Belschak, 2007) and improved proactive socialization behaviors among newcomers (Ashforth, Sluss, & Saks, 2007). Similarly, LePine and Van Dyne (2001) reported that indicators of positive affectivity in extraversion (positive emotions, excitement seeking) predict voice. Altogether, there is consistent evidence of a positive link between positive affectivity and proactive behaviors at work.

Negative Affectivity
Negative affect can negatively influence proactive behaviors to the extent that it may elicit negative outcome expectancies (Johnson & Tversky, 1983) and that it generates an orientation toward avoiding negative outcomes rather than approaching positive ones (Seo, Feldman Barrett, & Bartunek, 2004). Supporting this view, Ashforth et al. (2007) found negative affectivity had a negative correlation with proactive socialization behaviors among newcomers. Grant, Parker, and Collins (2009) similarly reported a negative correlation between negative affectivity and voice. In addition to purely affective experience-related measures, neuroticism (a trait from the Big Five

framework discussed earlier) is an indicator for negative affectivity that has been widely examined in the proactivity literature. Neuroticism is the tendency to experience negative, distressing emotions, such as fearfulness, social anxiety, poor inhibition of impulses, and helplessness (Costa & McCrae, 1987). Neuroticism has been found to be negatively associated with proactive behaviors, such as voicing suggestions for organizational improvement (LePine & Van Dyne, 2001) and actively seeking information on one's performance (Tidwell & Sias, 2005).

However, negative affectivity could also promote proactive behaviors to the extent that it signals a discrepancy between an actual situation and a desired situation, thereby stimulating individuals to engage in self-initiated and change-oriented behaviors in order to reduce the perceived discrepancy (Carver & Scheier, 1982). Supporting this view, Den Hartog and Belschak (2007) reported partial evidence of a positive relationship between negative affectivity and personal initiative. However, studies by Griffin et al. (2007) and Strauss, Griffin, and Rafferty (2009) did not find a significant relationship between neuroticism and proactive behavior with respect to completing individual tasks, being a team member, and being an organization member. Neuroticism did not predict newcomer's proactive behavior, including information seeking, feedback seeking, relationship building, and positive framing (Wanberg & Kammeyer-Mueller, 2000). These mixed findings on negative affective traits may highlight the need for further investigations on the role of negative affect in proactivity.

One possible explanation for the incoherent findings on negative affectivity with proactivity is that activation levels in negative affective traits could additionally matter in shaping proactive behaviors. Most studies to date have drawn on the PANAS scale of affectivity (Watson, Clark, & Tellegen, 1988), using items such as feeling *enthused, interested,* and *determined* for positive affectivity, and feeling *scared, afraid,* and *upset* for negative affectivity. The PANAS scale did not cover all types of affect in the circumplex model of affect (Russell, 1980) but rather included only the more activated quadrants, or high-activated positive and high-activated negative affect (Tellegen, Watson, & Clark, 1999).

To date, only Bindl and colleagues (2012) differentiated affect into four quadrants of the affective circumplex model with the combinations of high versus low activation and positive versus negative valence and examined the impact of each affect category on different stages in a proactive goal process (i.e., envisioning, planning, enacting, and reflecting). They found that high-activated positive mood was positively associated with all elements of the proactive process, and low-activated negative feelings of depressive and sad moods positively predicted employees' envisioning of proactive goals. These findings suggest that activation levels of affect should additionally be taken into account when investigating how affective traits influence proactive behaviors.

Instrumental Traits

By definition, proactive behavior aims to bring about change in the environment (Parker et al., 2006). Therefore, instrumental personality traits that are associated with tendencies to influence the environment through action can positively contribute to proactive behavior. We identify proactive personality (Bateman & Crant, 1993) and generalized self-efficacy (Morrison & Phelps, 1999) as two instrumental traits for which there is solid evidence of a link with proactivity. We also review evidence on prosocial motives (Grant & Berg, 2011), and specific facets of extraversion (LePine & Van Dyne, 2001) as instrumental traits for which there is some, but not consistent, evidence. We elaborate these findings in more detail.

Proactive Personality
Proactive personality describes a stable tendency to "scan for opportunities, show initiative, take action, and persevere until they reach closure by bringing about change" (Bateman & Crant, 1993, p. 105). As such, proactive personality represents an instrumental trait that is aimed at mastering the environment and has been positively linked to multiple forms of proactive behavior. For example, meta-analytic evidence suggests that proactive personality is positively linked to voice, taking charge, creativity, networking, and career initiative, amongst others (Fuller & Marler, 2009).

Generalized Self-Efficacy
Self-efficacy represents individual beliefs to be able to perform a goal-directed behavior in a specific situation (Bandura, 1994). Although self-efficacy involves cognitive elements of behavior with respect to self-perception, we also regard it as an instrumental trait because it emphasizes the ability of certain behaviors to influence the environment (Morrison & Phelps, 1999). In line with our view, Frese and Fay (2001) similarly proposed that self-efficacy is an intermediate variable that can transfer an individual's behavioral tendency into concrete behaviors, indicating the instrumental function of generalized self-efficacy in triggering behaviors to influence the external environment. Although Bandura (1994) and Frese and

Fay (2001) conceptualized self-efficacy as a state construct, it has also been regarded as a trait concept and has been shown to have a positive effect on promoting proactive behaviors such as personal initiative (Fay & Frese, 2001; Speier & Frese, 1997), as well as taking charge at work (Morrison & Phelps, 1999). Therefore, at the trait level, we consider self-efficacy as an instrumental trait that can contribute to proactive behavior.

Prosocial Motive
Prosocial motive refers to an individual's desire to have a positive impact on other people or social collectives (Grant & Berg, 2011). Prosocial motives at work have been theorized as a strong reason to engage in proactive behaviors (Wu & Parker, 2011) because different forms of proactive behavior at work have in common an emphasis on bringing about positive and constructive change. From this perspective, prosocial motive can be regarded as an instrumental trait, albeit with a more prosocial-oriented emphasis in influencing the environment. Supporting this view, prosocial motive has been found positively related to personal initiative (De Dreu & Nauta, 2009), as well as general initiative and voice (Grant & Mayer, 2009). The positive relationship between prosocial motive and proactive behavior can also be inferred from the duty or other-centered facet of conscientious-ness (Moon, 2001). Because the facet of duty reflects the extent to which an individual is concerned about the organization, high levels of prosocial motives were expected (and found) to be positively related to taking charge (Moon, Kamdar, Mayer, & Takeuchi, 2008). However, in Grant et al.'s (2009) study, high levels of prosocial motives did not have a direct positive association with voice and anticipatory helping behavior, suggesting the need for further studies to provide a cogent conclusion.

Extraversion (The Activity and Assertiveness Facets)
Extraversion, as a broad personality trait, describes the quantity and intensity of energy directed outward into the social world (Costa & McCrae, 1992). Extraversion can be regarded as an instrumental trait due to the extent that extraverted individuals tend to seek to interact with other individuals. Nevertheless, extraversion can additionally be regarded as an affective trait because it contains some facets (excitement seeking and positive emotions) that relate to positive affect (Costa & McCrae, 1992). Hence, when discussing the role of extraversion on proactive behavior, it is relevant to differentiate its different facets. However, most of studies only use the overall extraversion trait as a broad variable and show that extraversion is positively related to proactive behaviors, such as feedback

seeking and relationship building among newcomers (Wanberg & Kammeyer-Mueller, 2000), information seeking (Tidwell & Sias, 2005), and voice (LePine & Van Dyne, 2001).

In a more fine-grained fashion, studies by Major et al. (2006) and LePine and Van Dyne (2001) suggest two specific instrumental facets of overall extraversion that can contribute to proactive behavior: the activity facet, reflecting pace of living (e.g., a sense of urgency; a need to keep busy; and to maintain a rapid tempo); and the assertiveness facet, reflecting social ascendancy and forcefulness of expression (e.g., to be dominant and forceful; to have a tendency to speak up; Costa & McCrae, 1992). The activity facet has been positively associated with a motivation to learn as well as with developmental activity (Major et al., 2006), and the activity and assertiveness facets have been positively associated with voice (LePine & Van Dyne, 2001). However, more studies will be needed to provide a solid conclusion.

SUMMARY AND FUTURE RESEARCH

In our review, we suggested that the proactivity literature to date has tended to be rather disparate in its approach of considering disposition as an influencing factor of employee proactivity. By far the dominant approach has been to focus on the concept of proactive personality (Bateman & Crant, 1993) to acknowledge there are individual differences that shape proactive behaviors. Other researchers have used the Big Five personality framework to understand why people differ in proactive behavior, and yet others have identified personality traits in terms of motives that are relevant to proactivity. Although this research has provided compelling arguments for why individual personality constructs are important for understanding proactive behaviors at work, there is a need for integrating the existing findings in an overall conceptual framework. We suggest that the functional classification of personality traits (Buss & Finn, 1987) provides such a framework. Consistent with this reasoning, our review suggests that cognitive, affective, and instrumental traits can all contribute to proactive behavior. That is, proactivity research collectively suggests that proactive behavior is shaped by clear visions and thoughts about a better future, emotional energy to challenge the status quo, and an intention to influence environment, respectively.

To develop this possible integrating framework even further, we further suggest that the functional classification of personality can be linked to the three motivational mechanisms for proactive behavior proposed by Parker et al. (2010; i.e., can do, reason-to, and energized-to motivation). Most studies we reviewed suggest the direction of the relationship between a personality trait and proactive behavior without examining potential psychological processes that take place. Conceptually, according to the functional classification of personality traits, cognitive traits should be linked to the *reason-to* pathway because they are helpful to develop a proactive goal that guides subsequent proactive behaviors (e.g., Bindl et al., 2012), as well as the *can do* pathway, because with clearer goals that result from deep thinking and imagination, an individual should be more likely to have higher confidence to engage in proactive, goal-directed behavior (Grant & Ashford, 2008). Affective traits, especially positive affectivity, can be directly linked to the *energized-to* pathway given that these traits reflect an individual's typical affective experience across time and situations, likely affecting more fluctuant affective experiences. Finally, instrumental traits can be linked to the *reason-to* pathway because a higher tendency in mastering the environment directly provides a motive to enact behavior to influence the environment, as well as to the *can do* pathway, because individuals with a higher tendency of mastering the environment are also more likely to perceive themselves as having more capability to enact behaviors to influence environment. Empirical studies are now needed to test these and related speculations. In sum, we suggest that unpacking the psychological mechanisms that take place as personality shape proactive behaviors is an important topic for the future.

Additionally, a functional classification of personality traits can contribute to the investigation of the interaction effect between personality traits and situational factors in shaping an individual's proactive behavior. Based on the functional classification, a given personality trait has its own particular function in shaping proactive behaviors. As such, situational factors that have similar functions may moderate the impact of that personality trait on proactive behavior because they might enhance or replace the functions a personality trait has. Adopting this perspective, Wu et al. (in press) focused on the interaction effect of need for cognition (a cognitive trait) and work design variables (i.e., job autonomy and time pressure) in shaping individual innovation behavior. The researchers proposed that the functions of need for cognition in triggering individual innovation behavior, such as generating new ideas (Nair & Ramnarayan, 2000) and having stronger ownership of one's ideas due to the effortful thinking (Cacioppo, Petty, Kao, & Rodriguez, 1986), can be substituted with the situational influences of higher job autonomy and higher time pressure because these two work design factors drive similar behavioral functions (Wu & Parker, 2011). For example, autonomy has been shown to promote both idea generation and ownership (see Parker et al., 2006). In line with these predictions, the authors found that need for cognition had a positive effect on individual innovation behavior when job autonomy or time pressure was low to moderate, but no effect when job autonomy was high. This study therefore illustrates how a functional approach to personality traits can guide an understanding of the interactions between trait and situation in shaping proactive behavior.

A final contribution of considering a functional approach to personality traits for understanding proactivity concerns interactions between, and configurations of, personality traits. The fact that personality traits have different functions implies that these functions might work together in various synergistic and/or complementary ways. For example, it might be that having a strong focus on changing the environment (proactive personality) drives ineffective or unwise proactivity if the individual lacks a strong cognitive orientation toward thinking (e.g., need for cognition). Likewise, if an individual has a high need for cognition and thereby generates proactive ideas, yet at the same time is highly neurotic in his/her affective orientation, then the individual might generate proactive goals yet fail to achieve the goal because their negative affectivity inhibits their ability to deal with challenges or overcome obstacles. These speculative combinations of personality characteristics have not been considered, yet the functional classification of personality lends itself to such considerations as proactive behavior involves thinking, affective energizing, and acting.

CONCLUSION

Proactivity is undoubtedly shaped by personality. Exactly what types of personality, and how personality plays out, has had little attention. Drawing on the functional classification of personality traits proposed by Buss and Finn (1987), we suggested that personality traits, in addition to their content, also imply different functions (i.e., cognitive, affective, and instrumental) that differentially influence proactive behavior. We now recommend future studies that simultaneously consider both content and function, that investigate the underlying mechanisms of traits in shaping proactivity, and that theorize and test the person–environment interactions and person–person interaction effects implied by the functional classification of personality traits.

REFERENCES

Ashford, S. J., & Black, J. S. (1996). Proactivity during organizational entry: The role of desire for control. *Journal of Applied Psychology, 81*, 199–214.

Ashford, S. J., Blatt, R., & VandeWalle, D. (2003). Reflections on the looking glass: A review of research on feedback-seeking behavior in organizations. *Journal of Management, 29*, 773–799.

Ashford, S. J., Rothbard, N. P., Piderit, S. K., & Dutton, J. E. (1998). Out on a limb: The role of context and impression management in selling gender-equity issues. *Administrative Science Quarterly, 43*, 23–57.

Ashforth, B. E., Sluss, D. M., & Saks, A. M. (2007). Socialization tactics, proactive behavior, and newcomer learning: Integrating socialization models. *Journal Of Vocational Behavior, 70*, 447–462.

Bandura, A. (1994). Self-efficacy. In V. S. Ramachaudra (Ed.), *Encyclopedia of human behaviour* (Vol. 4, pp. 71–81). New York, NY: Academic Press.

Bateman, T. S., & Crant, J. M. (1993). The proactive component of organizational behavior: A measure and correlates. *Journal of Organizational Behavior, 14*, 103–118.

Bindl, U. K., & Parker, S. K. (2010). Proactive work behaviour: Forward-thinking and change-oriented action in organizations. In S. Zedeck (Ed.), *APA handbook of industrial and organizational psychology* (pp. 567–598). Washington, DC: American Psychological Association.

Bindl, U. K., & Parker, S. K. (2012). Affect and employee proactivity: A goal-regulatory perspective. In N. Ashkanasy, C. Härtel & W. Zerbe (Eds.), *Research on emotion in organizations* (Vol. 8, pp. 225–254). Bingley, UK: Emerald.

Bindl, U. K., Parker, S. K., Totterdell, P., & Hagger-Johnson, G. (2012). The fuel of the self-starter: How mood influences proactivity. *Journal of Applied Psychology, 97*, 134–150.

Buss, A. H., & Finn, S. E. (1987). Classification of personality traits. *Journal of Personality and Social Psychology, 52*, 432–444.

Cacioppo, J. T., & Petty, R. E. (1982). The need for cognition. *Journal of Personality and Social Psychology, 42*, 116–131.

Cacioppo, J. T., Petty, R. E., Kao, C. F., & Rodriguez, R. (1986). Central and peripheral routes to persuasion: An individual difference perspective. *Journal of Personality and Social Psychology, 51*, 1032–1043.

Carver, C. S., & Scheier, M. F. (1982). Control theory: A useful conceptual framework for personality-social, clinical, and health psychology. *Psychological Bulletin, 92*, 111–135.

Carver, C. S., & White, T. L. (1994). Behavioral inhibition, behavioral activation, and affective responses to impending reward and punishment: The BIS/BAS Scales. *Journal of Personality and Social Psychology, 67*, 319–333.

Costa, P. T., Jr., & McCrae, R. R. (1987). Neuroticism, somatic complaints, and disease: Is the bark worse than the bite? *Journal of Personality, 55*, 299–316.

Costa, P. T., Jr., & McCrae, R. R. (1992). *Revised NEO personality inventory (NEO PI-R) and NEO five factor inventory: Professional manual.* Odessa, FL: Psychological Assessment Resources.

De Dreu, C. K. W., & Nauta, A. (2009). Self-interest and other-orientation in organizational behavior: Implications for job performance, prosocial behavior, and personal initiative. *Journal of Applied Psychology, 94*, 913–926.

Den Hartog, D. N., & Belschak, F. D. (2007). Personal initiative, commitment and affect at work. *Journal of Occupational and Organizational Psychology, 80*, 601–622.

Dutton, J. E., & Ashford, S. J. (1993). Selling issues to top management. *Academy of Management Review, 18*, 397–428.

Elizur, D., & Sagie, A. (1999). Facets of personal values: A structural analysis of life and work values. *Applied Psychology: An International Review, 48*, 73–87.

Elliot, A. J., & Thrash, T. M. (2002). Approach-avoidance motivation in personality: Approach and avoidance temperaments and goals. *Journal of Personality and Social Psychology, 5*, 804–818.

Fay, D., & Frese, M. (2000). Conservatives' approach to work: Less prepared for future work demands? *Journal of Applied Social Psychology, 30*, 171–195.

Fay, D., & Frese, M. (2001). The concept of personal initiative: An overview of validity studies. *Human Performance, 14*, 97–124.

Forgas, J. P., & George, J. M. (2001). Affective influences on judgments and behavior in organizations: An information processing perspective. *Organizational Behavior and Human Decision Processes, 86*, 3–34.

Frese, M., & Fay, D. (2001). Personal initiative (PI): An active performance concept for work in the 21st century. In B. M. Staw & R. M. Sutton (Eds.), *Research in organizational behavior* (Vol. 23, pp. 133–187). Amsterdam: Elsevier Science.

Fuller, J. B., & Marler, L. E. (2009). Change driven by nature: A meta-analytic review of the proactive personality literature. *Journal of Vocational Behavior, 75*, 329–345.

Geller, E. S. (2002). Organizational behavior management and industrial/organizational psychology: Achieving synergy by valuing differences. *Journal of Organizational Behavior Management, 22*, 111–130.

Grant, A. M., & Ashford, S. J. (2008). The dynamics of proactivity at work. *Research in Organizational Behavior, 28*, 3–34.

Grant, A. M., & Berg, J. M. (2011). Prosocial motivation at work: When, why, and how making a difference makes a difference. In K. Cameron & G. Spreitzer (Eds.), *The Oxford handbook of positive organizational scholarship* (pp. 28–44). New York, NY: Oxford University Press.

Grant, A. M., & Mayer, D. M. (2009). Good soldiers and good actors: Prosocial and impression management motives as interactive predictors of affiliative citizenship behaviors. *Journal of Applied Psychology, 94*, 900–912.

Grant, A. M., Parker, S. K., & Collins, C. G. (2009). Getting credit for proactive behavior: Supervisor reactions depend on what you value and how you feel. *Personnel Psychology, 62*, 31–55.

Griffin, M. A., Neal, A., & Parker, S. K. (2007). A new model of work role performance: Positive behavior in uncertain and interdependent contexts. *Academy of Management Journal, 50*, 327–347.

Griffin, M. A., Parker, S. K., & Mason, C. M. (2010). Leader vision and the development of adaptive and proactive performance: A longitudinal study. *Journal of Applied Psychology, 95*, 174–182.

Harrison, S. H., Sluss, D. M., & Ashforth, B. E. (2011). Curiosity adapted the cat: The role of trait curiosity in newcomer adaptation. *Journal of Applied Psychology, 1*, 211–220.

Howell, J. M., & Shea, C. M. (2001). Individual differences, environmental scanning, innovation framing, and champion behavior: Key predictors of project performance. *Journal of Product Innovation Management, 18*, 15–27.

James, W. (1890). *The principles of psychology* (Vol. 1). New York, NY: Holt.

John, O. P., Naumann, L. P., & Soto, C. J. (2008). Paradigm shift to the integrative Big Five trait taxonomy: History, measurement, and conceptual issues. In L. Pervin & O. P. John (Eds.), *Handbook of personality: Theory and research* (pp. 114–158). New York, NY: Guilford.

Johnson, E. J., & Tversky, A. (1983). Affect, generalization, and the perception of risk. *Journal of Personality and Social Psychology, 45,* 20–31.

Kaplan, S., Bradley, J. C., Luchman, J. N., & Haynes, D. (2009). On the role of positive and negative affectivity in job performance: A meta-analytic investigation. *Journal of Applied Psychology, 94,* 162–176.

Kashdan, T. B., & Steger, M. F. (2007). Curiosity and pathways to well-being and meaning in life: Traits, states, and everyday behaviors. *Motivation and Emotion, 31,* 159–173.

LePine, J. A., & Van Dyne, L. (1998). Predicting voice behavior in work groups. *Journal of Applied Psychology, 83,* 853–868.

LePine, J. A., & Van Dyne, L. (2001). Voice and cooperative behavior as contrasting forms of contextual performance: Evidence of differential relationships with big five personality characteristics and cognitive ability. *Journal of Applied Psychology, 86,* 326–336.

Levy, S., & Guttman, L. (1975). On the multivariate structure of wellbeing. *Social Indicators Research, 2,* 361–388.

Major, D. A., Turner, J. E., & Fletcher, T. D. (2006). Linking proactive personality and the Big Five to motivation to learn and development activity. *Journal of Applied Psychology, 91,* 927–935.

Mayer, J. D., Gaschke, Y. N., Braverman, D. L., & Evans, T. W. (1992). Mood-congruent judgment is a general effect. *Journal of Personality and Social Psychology, 63,* 119–132.

McAllister, D. J., Kamdar, D., Morrison, E. W., & Turban, D. B. (2007). Disentangling role perceptions: How perceived role breadth, discretion, instrumentality, and efficacy relate to helping and taking charge. *Journal of Applied Psychology, 92,* 1200–1211.

Moon, H. (2001). The two faces of conscientiousness: Duty and achievement striving in escalation of commitment dilemmas. *Journal of Applied Psychology, 86,* 533–540.

Moon, H., Kamdar, D., Mayer, D. M., & Takeuchi, R. (2008). Me or we? The role of personality and justice as other-centered antecedents to innovative citizenship behaviors within organizations. *Journal of Applied Psychology, 93,* 84–94.

Morrison, E. W., & Phelps, C. C. (1999). Taking charge at work: Extrarole efforts to initiate workplace change. *Academy of Management Journal, 42,* 403–419.

Muraven, M., & Baumeister, R. F. (2000). Self-regulation and depletion of limited resources: Does self-control resemble a muscle? *Psychological Bulletin, 126,* 247–259.

Nair, K. U., & Ramnarayan, S. (2000). Individual differences in need for cognition and complex problem solving. *Journal of Research in Personality, 34,* 305–328.

Nurmi, J.-E. (1991). How do adolescents see their future? A review of the development of future orientation and planning. *Developmental Review, 11,* 1–59.

Parker, S. K., Bindl, U. K., & Strauss, K. (2010). Making things happen: A model of proactive motivation. *Journal of Management, 36,* 827–856.

Parker, S. K., & Collins, C. G. (2010). Taking stock: Integrating and differentiating multiple proactive behaviors. *Journal of Management, 36,* 633–662.

Parker, S. K., Williams, H. M., & Turner, N. (2006). Modeling the antecedents of proactive behavior at work. *Journal of Applied Psychology, 91,* 636–652.

Russell, J. A. (1980). A circumplex model of affect. *Journal of Personality and Social Psychology, 39,* 1161–1178.

Ryan, R. M., & Deci, E. L. (2000). Self-determination theory and the facilitation of intrinsic motivation, social development, and well-being. *American Psychologist*, *55*, 68–78.

Scott, S. G., & Bruce, R. A. (1994). Determinants of innovative behavior: A path model of individual innovation in the workplace. *Academy of Management Journal*, *37*, 580–607.

Seibert, S. E., Kraimer, M. L., & Crant, J. M. (2001). What do proactive people do? A longitudinal model linking proactive personality and career success. *Personnel Psychology*, *54*, 845–874.

Seo, M. G., Feldman Barrett, L. F., & Bartunek, J. M. (2004). The role of affective experience in work motivation. *Academy of Management Review*, *29*, 423–439.

Shraga, O., & Shirom, A. (2009). The construct validity of vigor and its antecedents: A qualitative study. *Human Relations*, *62*, 271–291.

Speier, C., & Frese, M. (1997). Generalized self-efficacy as a mediator and moderator between control and complexity at work and personal initiative: A longitudinal study in East Germany. *Human Performance*, *10*, 171–192.

Staw, B. M., Sutton, R. I., & Pelled, L. H. (1994). Employee positive emotion and favorable outcomes at the workplace. *Organization Science*, *5*, 51–71.

Strauss, K., Griffin, M. A., & Rafferty, A. E. (2009). Proactivity directed toward the team and organization: The role of leadership, commitment, and role-breadth self-efficacy. *British Journal of Management*, *20*, 279–291.

Tellegen, A., Watson, D., & Clark, L. A. (1999). On the dimensional and hierarchical structure of affect. *Psychological Science*, *10*, 297–303.

Thomas, J. P., Whitman, D. S., & Viswesvaran, C. (2010). Employee proactivity in organizations: A comparative meta-analysis of emergent proactive constructs. *Journal of Occupational and Organizational Psychology*, *83*, 275–300.

Thompson, J. A. (2005). Proactive personality and job performance: A social capital perspective. *Journal of Applied Psychology*, *90*, 1011–1017.

Tidwell, M., & Sias, P. (2005). Personality and information seeking: Understanding how traits influence information-seeking behaviors. *Journal of Business Communication*, *42*, 51–77.

Tsai, W. C., Chen, C. C., & Liu, H. L. (2007). Test of a model linking employee positive moods and task performance. *Journal of Applied Psychology*, *92*, 1570–1583.

Wanberg, C. R., & Kammeyer-Mueller, J. D. (2000). Predictors and outcomes of proactivity in the socialization process. *Journal of Applied Psychology*, *85*, 373–385.

Watson, D., Clark, L. A., & Tellegen, A. (1988). Development and validation of brief measures of positive and negative affect: the PANAS scales. *Journal of Personality and Social Psychology*, *54*, 1063–1070.

Wegener, D. T., & Petty, R. E. (1996). Effects of mood on persuasion processes: Enhancing, reducing, and biasing scrutiny of attitude-relevant information. In L. L. Martin & A. Tesser (Eds.), *Striving and feeling: Interactions among goals, affect, and self-regulation* (pp. 329–362). Mahwah, NJ: Lawrence Erlbaum Associates.

Wu, C. H., & Parker, S. K. (2011). Proactivity in the work place: Looking back and looking forward. In K. Cameron & G. Spreitzer (Eds.), *The Oxford handbook of positive organizational scholarship* (pp. 84–96). New York, NY: Oxford University Press.

Wu, C. H., Parker, S. K., & de Jong, J. P. J. (in press). Need for cognition as an antecedent of individual innovation behavior. *Journal of Management*.

JOB CRAFTING AND CULTIVATING POSITIVE MEANING AND IDENTITY IN WORK

Amy Wrzesniewski, Nicholas LoBuglio,
Jane E. Dutton and Justin M. Berg

INTRODUCTION

The design of a job is deeply consequential for employees' psychological experiences at work. Jobs are collections of tasks and relationships that are grouped together and assigned to an individual (Ilgen & Hollenbeck, 1992), and scholars have long been interested in the way these elements come together to constitute the experience of a job (Griffin, 1987; Hackman & Oldham, 1980). Research in this area has traditionally built on a core assumption that managers design jobs in a top-down fashion for employees, which places employees in the relatively passive role of being the recipients of the jobs they hold.

More recently, "job crafting" has emerged as a theoretical approach that expands perspectives on job design to include proactive changes that employees make to their own jobs (Wrzesniewski & Dutton, 2001). Job crafting is defined as "the physical and cognitive changes individuals make in the task or relational boundaries of their work" (Wrzesniewski & Dutton, 2001, p. 179). By altering task and relational boundaries, employees can change the social and task components of their jobs and experience different

Advances in Positive Organizational Psychology, Volume 1, 281–302
ISSN: 2046-410X/doi:10.1108/S2046-410X(2013)0000001015

kinds of meaning of the work and themselves. From the most routine to the most complex jobs, and from the lowest to the highest tiers of an organization (Berg, Wrzesniewski, & Dutton, 2010), we argue that employees have some degree of latitude in how they craft their jobs. Thus, the potential for job crafting to alter the ways in which employees define the meaning of their work and their work identities is relevant across a broad range of job situations. Further, others have found that job crafting has positive effects on employees' degree of psychological well-being (Berg, Grant, & Johnson, 2010) and work engagement and performance (Tims, Bakker, & Derks, 2012), suggesting that job crafting matters for a number of key individual and organizational outcomes.

Job crafting offers two important contributions to positive organizational psychology. First, the process of job crafting puts the proactive, agentic behaviors of employees center-stage, conceptualizing and empirically exploring the creative and motivational bases of employees altering their jobs to improve their experience of work. Second, job crafting adds to our understanding of positive organizational psychology through its focus on the range of generative outcomes of job crafting – including the experience of positive meaning and sense of self, engagement, commitment, turnover, and performance. As the field of positive organizational psychology seeks to better understand employees' optimal functioning at work, job crafting helps to illuminate the job-related actions that employees engage in to move themselves toward more optimal functioning.

The purpose of this chapter is to briefly review the job crafting literature to date and to open up new theoretical opportunities for understanding how job crafting can help employees cultivate a positive sense of meaning and identity in their work. While Wrzesniewski and Dutton (2001) theorized that job crafting often has important implications for employees' sense of meaning and identity in their work, the original job crafting theory does not specify that job crafting is necessarily positive or negative for employees' sense of meaning or identity. As a result, we have little theory to explain the mechanisms through which job crafting is likely to cultivate a more *positive* sense of meaning and identity for employees on the job. Thus, in this chapter, we elaborate job crafting theory to guide future research on the links between job crafting and the cultivation of positive meaning and identity in work over time. In other words, this chapter reviews the "old" and introduces some "new" – all with an appreciation of the importance of job crafting to the blossoming domain of positive organizational psychology (Donaldson & Ko, 2010) and positive organizational scholarship (Cameron, Dutton, & Quinn, 2003; Cameron & Spreitzer, 2012) more broadly.

JOB CRAFTING IN BRIEF

Job crafting involves creating or initiating change to the job, as opposed to reacting or responding to change in the job (Grant & Ashford, 2008; Griffin, Neal, & Parker, 2007). In essence, job crafting is the process of employees proactively changing the boundaries that comprise their jobs. Boundaries have been defined as "mental fences" (Zerubavel, 1991, p. 2) that people use to order and define limits around "physical, temporal, emotional, cognitive, and/or relational" entities (Ashforth, Kreiner, & Fugate, 2000, p. 474; Lamont & Molnar, 2002). Job crafters shape the boundaries that define their jobs in three main ways. First, job crafters may change the physical or temporal boundaries around the bundle of tasks that they consider to be their job. We refer to this as "task crafting," and it consists of adding or dropping tasks, adjusting the time or effort spent on various tasks, and redesigning aspects of tasks (e.g., a teacher who spends time learning new classroom technology to fulfill his passion for IT). Second, job crafters may redefine the relational boundaries that define the interpersonal interactions involved in performing their jobs. We refer to this as "relational crafting," and it consists of creating and/or sustaining relationships with others at work, spending more time with preferred individuals, and reducing or completely avoiding contact with others (e.g., a marketing analyst forming a relationship with someone in sales to better understand the impact of his work on salespeople). Third, job crafters may reframe the cognitive boundaries that ascribe meaning or purpose to the tasks and relationships that comprise their jobs. We refer to this as "cognitive crafting," and it consists of employees' efforts to perceive and interpret their tasks, relationships, or job as a whole in ways that change the significance of their work (e.g., a custodian who thinks of his job as enabling education by providing clean, distraction-free classrooms for students).

The three types of job crafting are not mutually exclusive, and job crafters may exercise any combination of the three. For example, in joining a new social media group at a financial services firm, an employee may add tasks like planning learning events for members, thus altering relationships by meeting and collaborating with new colleagues, and begin to see her job differently because it allows her to pursue her passion for social marketing. The different types of crafting may occur quickly (Petrou, Demerouti, Peeters, & Schaufeli, 2012) or unfold gradually over long periods of time.

The following example provides a more in-depth look at the form and effects of job crafting on the work of an employee, which we refer to throughout the chapter.

Diane is an internal audit manager at a large manufacturing organization. Having joined the company 15 years ago, she now oversees a group of 30 Certified Public Accountants (CPAs) that conduct periodic audits of the organization's functions. While Diane is no longer poring over the business records herself, she decides when and where many of the audits are conducted. She monitors the progress of her teams and intervenes when they meet resistance from managers in other divisions. A lifelong fan of mystery and crime novels, it was the detective nature of audit work that drew Diane to the field when she was an undergraduate. She spent many years travelling the world, visiting the company's production plants, and investigating the large asset purchases that showed up on the bottom line back at headquarters. However, Diane can easily recall an important turning point in her career. When the accounting firm Arthur Andersen was indicted in 2002 for its handling of the audits at Enron, she was horrified by the financial losses incurred by thousands of innocent employees. Since that time, Diane has considered her division the most important protector of the company's future. Internal audit is an important mechanism for uncovering improprieties, and for acting as a deterrent to anyone who might consider engaging in them. Whether accidental or not, she has no intention of letting the actions of a few employees cause harm to the rest of the company. This cognitive crafting has fundamentally altered Diane's experience of her job. Her work identity, while still encompassing the detective role, has broadened to include the role of defender of the people in the organization. She feels connected to her coworkers, even those she has never met, and has infused her work with a positive meaning it did not have before.

When Diane started at the company, she was one of only two women in the audit division. Shortly after earning her CPA, Diane joined the local division of the National Society of Accountants in her city, and for the past six years has been leading its outreach efforts. Several times each month, she speaks at schools, ranging from middle school math to community college business classes. Sharing her personal stories and the opportunities she sees in accounting, Diane's goal is to get young people, especially young women, interested in the field. Over the years she has convinced her supervisors to see the visits not just as something meaningful for her, but as a way to build the firm's community reputation. By adding these tasks and relationships to her job, Diane has crafted her work to fulfill her desire to inspire the next generation of accountants. She feels a connection to the future of the profession, and through these changes to the task, relational, and cognitive boundaries of her job, her work and her identity as an accountant and organization member have taken on new meaning.

We provide the example of Diane to illustrate some of the many ways job crafters change the boundaries of their jobs and to describe the nature of the impact of job crafting on the employee and possibly on others. In the next section, we move from examples to data to consider what job crafting researchers have found in studies of this behavior in a range of settings.

OVERVIEW OF JOB CRAFTING RESEARCH

Following the introduction of the job crafting model in 2001, empirical research has examined its prevalence and role in employees' work lives and its impact on organizations in which job crafting happens. Most of this research has focused on how job crafting transforms employees' performance and experience of their work. While very little of this work has directly considered the impact of job crafting on work meaning and identity, we highlight where we believe the research implications for meaning and identity are important and promising.

Most empirical job crafting research to date has focused on its relationship with individual job attitudes and performance. For example, in the first empirical study of job crafting, Ghitulescu (2006) surveyed engineers on autonomous teams in a manufacturing organization and special education teachers in a number of schools. She developed a job crafting scale and found that job crafting enhances individual job satisfaction and commitment levels, while increasing individual performance and decreasing absenteeism (Ghitulescu, 2006). In a study of outside salespeople for a large consumer products company, Lyons (2008) found that over three-quarters of the salespeople engaged in some form of job crafting, which was in turn positively correlated with quality of self-image, perceived control, and readiness to change. Lyons' study suggests that identity, operationalized as one's self-image, is related in important ways to job crafting activities. Utilizing a diary method to measure the daily experiences of engineers, Ko (2012) examined the role of flow experiences (Nakamura & Csikszentmihalyi, 2002) during job crafting episodes and their effects on employees. She found that employees reported positive emotions after episodes of job crafting, which was partially explained by flow experiences that occurred during job crafting.

While most research on job crafting has maintained a focus on the individual, Leana, Appelbaum, and Shevchuk (2009) introduced the concept of "collaborative crafting" to describe the group task crafting efforts of early childcare teachers. Working together to customize how work was organized and enacted, educators who collaboratively crafted their jobs were rated by external evaluators as providing a higher quality of care. This effect was especially strong for inexperienced teachers. Additionally, collaborative crafting resulted in higher individual organizational commitment and job satisfaction.

In a qualitative study of employees in a variety of jobs, Berg, Grant, and Johnson (2010) investigated how employees craft their jobs in response to having unanswered occupational callings – that is, feeling drawn to pursue an occupation other than the one in which they work. They found that employees who incorporated the tasks of their unanswered callings into their current jobs experienced the sort of pleasant psychological states of enjoyment and meaning that they associated with pursuing their unanswered callings. However, when employees came up short of their crafting intentions, they reported experiencing long-term regret if they did not view their current occupation as a calling but only intermittent regret if they did, which joins other qualitative work Berg, Wrzesniewski, and Dutton (2010) in highlighting the key role that time may play in determining the effects of job crafting. In this vein, Wrzesniewski and colleagues (2012) conducted a field quasi-experiment in a Fortune 500 technology company in which they compared the effects of engaging in job crafting versus engaging in job crafting in concert with skills development on employee happiness. They found that engaging in job crafting leads to short-term (6-week) boosts in happiness, while increases in happiness from job crafting in concert with skill development take longer to realize but have greater and longer-lasting effects (at least 6 months) than job crafting alone.

Tims, Bakker, and Derks (2012) have recently developed a scale to measure job crafting, using the framework of the job demands-resources model (Bakker & Demerouti, 2007; Demerouti, Bakker, Nachreiner, & Schaufeli, 2001). Their scale measures job crafting by assessing the degree to which employees report increasing social job resources, increasing structural job resources, increasing challenging job demands, and decreasing hindering job demands. In testing their scale, they also found that self-reports of job crafting correlate positively with colleagues' ratings of work engagement, employability, and performance. In other studies employing the job demand-resources model, Bakker and colleagues have linked job resources to reduced turnover intentions and higher levels of employee performance and engagement (Bakker, Demerouti, & Schaufeli, 2003; Bakker, Demerouti, & Verbeke, 2004; Bakker, Hakanen, Demerouti, & Xanthopoulou, 2007).

While these empirical studies have built important knowledge on some of the key antecedents and outcomes of job crafting for employees and their organizations, little theory or research has directly examined job crafting as a mechanism for employees to cultivate a positive sense of meaning and identity in work over time. Yet, these two outcomes may be at the center of why employees job craft and how job crafting can benefit them over time. Jobs as designed by managers tend to be "one-size-fits-all" and not customized to meet the particular needs, motives, and preferences of individual employees (cf. Hornung et al., 2010; Rousseau, Ho, & Greenberg, 2006). Typically, a job design is communicated to employees via a written job description, which is usually a static list of tasks, responsibilities, and reporting relationships, with all employees in the same job receiving the same list. In essence, job designs are traditionally seen and used as a means of top-down standardization and control – even job titles themselves have been construed as a means of bureaucratic control (Baron & Bielby, 1986; Strang & Baron, 1990). However, employees often have a fundamental desire to find positive meaning in their work (Rosso, Dekas, & Wrzesniewski, 2010) and construct a positive identity within their organizations (Dutton, Roberts, & Bednar, 2010), but traditional job designs are unlikely to come preloaded with much opportunity for either of these highly personalized pursuits. By bringing a job crafting perspective to bear, job designs are no longer construed as a static source of constraint and top-down control, but rather, a starting place – or a partially blank canvas – from which employees can alter the content of their jobs in ways that cultivate a positive sense of meaning and identity in their work. In so doing, employees may move from a "one-size-fits-all" job description to an individualized enactment of the job that serves as a source of positive meaning and identity expression, both of which are conducive to psychological strengthening and flourishing (Dutton et al., 2010; Rosso et al., 2010). In the sections that follow, we elaborate theory on job crafting to highlight the mechanisms that may link job crafting to the cultivation of positive meaning and identity in work.[1]

JOB CRAFTING AND POSITIVE MEANING OF WORK

Job crafting alters the meaning of work (Wrzesniewski & Dutton, 2001). As Wrzesniewski and Dutton note, "Job crafting changes the meaning of the work by changing job tasks or relationships in ways that allow employees to reframe the purpose of the job and experience the work differently

(Tausky, 1995)" (p. 186). We define positive meanings of work as the associations, frames, or elements of work in use by employees that define work as representing a valued, constructive activity. For example, a landscaper who forms an association between her efforts on the job and the beautification of outdoor spaces has found positive meaning in her work (conversely, a landscaper who associates her efforts with damage to the environment through use of chemicals and pesticides has not). Likewise, an editor who defines the elements of his work involving critique and revision as valuable for the ways they improve the quality of discourse has found positive meaning in elements of his work.

We differentiate between the meaning of the work and the meaningfulness of work; as Rosso and colleagues (2010) point out (see also Pratt & Ashforth, 2003), the meaning of work concerns what it is that work signifies or represents, while the meaningfulness of work refers to how much purpose or significance work has. Research on job crafting refers to changes of both types, in which *what* the work means can change, as well as *how much* the work means to the employee (Wrzesniewski & Dutton, 2001). The organizational behavior literature on the meaning of work tends to use both concepts interchangeably, usually referring to meaningfulness even when using the term "meaning of work" (Rosso et al., 2010). We primarily consider changes to the meaning of work that result from job crafting, rather than changes in meaningfulness alone, as meaningfulness by definition follows meaning, in that changes to the meaning of the work likely affect how much meaningfulness employees experience from it. Thus, a lens on employees' sense of the meaning of their work offers a more fundamental perspective on their experience of work than a lens on meaningfulness alone.

In short, the meaning of work is at the core of employees' experiences of their jobs. Whether employees believe that their work contributes to making the world a better place, or that it allows them to interact with people in ways that create important innovations, or that the work provides an opportunity to earn a living in order to support a family or various causes, work meanings act as lenses through which employees understand and respond to their work (Wrzesniewski, McCauley, Rozin, & Schwartz, 1997).

Job crafting and the meaning of work are intimately connected with each other.[2] As employees introduce changes to the task and relational components of their jobs, the emphasis of their activities and interactions shifts in ways that can have profound impacts on their experience of the work and their understanding of the meaning of it. In our earlier example,

Diane incorporated regular speaker visits and public engagements into her job. She did so in order to increase the potential for accounting to inspire a new generation of employees, because she feels passionately about this work. While Diane may have felt that accounting work was inspiring prior to changing the focus of her job, her ability to see the connection between her work activities, interactions, and relationships and the desire she had to promote the accounting profession grew directly as a result of her job crafting. Thus, the elements, associations, and frames she created in her job as a result of job crafting fundamentally changed the meaning of her work. Rather than thinking about being a champion for accounting while she carried out her prescribed job duties, Diane redrew the boundaries of the job to fully realize the meaning she aspired to in her work. In this way, her job crafting activities changed the meaning of her work while making it more meaningful.

The Self as a Source of Work Meaning

Research on meaning of work enumerates a broad set of sources of meaning in work, as well as pathways through which the meaning of work can change (Rosso et al., 2010). Ranging from the values, motivations, and beliefs that define the self to the role of spirituality in life, a variety of meaning sources have been identified in an effort to understand what employees draw upon in their experiences to compose work meaning. Rosso and colleagues (2010) identify four major sources of meaning in work. The first is the self, and encompasses the values, motivations, and beliefs that employees draw on to understand the meaning of their work. In general, research in this area suggests that when work aligns with these self-attributes, it becomes more meaningful. Thus, job crafting that helps employees to shape their tasks and interactions in ways that allow for more expression of their values, motivations, or beliefs is likely to have a direct impact on the positive meaning of their work by creating a sense of alignment between the self and the work. In the case of Diane's job crafting in her accounting role, it was partly her ability to bring her motivation and passion to the fore as an advocate for the profession that guided her job crafting and changed the meaning of her work so that she saw her work as an accountant as taking on more valued and constructive activities. Thus, job crafting creates opportunities for employees to experience the meaning of their work differently by aligning the job with their values, motivations, and beliefs.

Others as a Source of Work Meaning

The second source of meaning involves other people, both on and off the job, including coworkers, managers, and leaders, communities to which the employee belongs, and family. Research in this domain suggests that the ways in which employees experience membership in, communication with, social cues from, and contributions to these various groups and individuals in their work, affects the meaning of work. The implications for relational job crafting are powerful when employees view their jobs in terms of the role that other people play in their work (e.g., Grant, 2007, 2008). By reshaping with whom one is connected at or through work, whether in actual interaction or just in how employees think about their connections to these others, the meaning of the work is likely to change. For example, Wrzesniewski, Dutton, and Debebe (2003) describe the relational crafting undertaken by hospital cleaners who choose to interact with, care for, and provide comfort to patients and their families, even though this work is not part of their jobs. They note the impact that these interactions can have on transforming the meaning of their work in positive ways. Through changing the relational boundaries of the job to include interactions with these groups, these cleaners had a positive impact on the meaning of their work by tying it more explicitly to caring for others, thereby creating meaningful opportunities to benefit others (Grant, 2007).

Context as a Source of Work Meaning

The third source of meaning involves the context of the work itself, including the design of job tasks, the organizational mission within which the job happens, one's financial circumstances, and the role of nonwork domains, including the national culture that shapes narratives of work. While context may be seen as a constraint on job crafting, employees' contexts may also provide them with resources to use in crafting their jobs to cultivate positive meaning (e.g., Berg, Wrzesniewski, & Dutton, 2010). This source of meaning runs the gamut from rather direct and concrete aspects of the work to much more diffuse sources. The impact of job crafting on the design of the job is clear; task crafting involves making direct changes to work tasks, which has a direct impact on work meaning. Beyond task crafting, an employee can also craft aspects of the job to help the organization focus on activities or causes that the employee believes in deeply, possibly changing the employee's experience of the mission of the organizations as a result. For example, Diane's advocacy work helped to position her organization and its involvement in the cause of changing the accounting profession in ways that, while not changing the mission of the firm, changed aspects of its focus that likely created positive changes in the meaning of her work. Thus, job crafting helps employees transform the meaning of their work by altering aspects of the context in which work happens, creating opportunities to introduce elements to the design of the job or the mission of the firm that facilitate positive meanings of work.

Spirituality as a Source of Work Meaning

The fourth and final source of meaning identified by Rosso and colleagues involves spiritual life and the sense of having a sacred or spiritual calling (Rosso et al., 2010). In general, research in this area suggests that when individuals frame their work as a service to or expression of religious or spiritual aims, the work is infused with religious or spiritual meaning that employees experience as deeply important. In addition, individuals who believe that their occupation is a vocation that expresses the will of a religious entity experience what scholars would define as a sacred calling (Hardy, 1990; Weiss, Skelley, Haughey, & Hall, 2004). The connection between spiritual or religious meanings of work and cognitive crafting is clear – for job crafters who frame the execution of whatever work they are doing as a gesture toward (or deriving from) sacred sources, the work itself is likely to take on different, and positive meaning. For example, a banker who believes that his occupation was chosen by the religious entity in which he believes and that his work is a contribution to that entity (either literally or figuratively) has subscribed to a belief system that creates powerful implications for the cognitive crafting of the work. In effect, the work is a direct service to the religious entity, which ties the work to a focus and source of ultimate positive meaning.

Here, we have highlighted the sources of some of the positive meanings that can result from job crafting, and suggest that job crafting that produces these meanings is likely to deepen the meaningfulness of work as well. Along with a positive meaning of work, the quest for a positive work identity is likely to drive employees' job crafting, and possibly be the outcome of it. Below, we discuss the ways in which job crafting may cultivate positive work identities.

JOB CRAFTING AND POSITIVE WORK IDENTITIES

Job crafting is a potent mechanism for altering how one defines who one is at work (Wrzesniewski & Dutton, 2001). One important form of work identity is a person's organizational identity. An individual's organizational identity captures who one is and who one is becoming at work (Ashforth & Mael, 1989). Other possible work-related identities include one's professional identity, role identity, job identity, or team identity.

For purposes of building understanding about job crafting and identity, we focus on how job crafting affects various forms of positive organizational identities. By positive organizational identities, we mean the set of self-conceptions that are part of individuals' self-definitions as organizational members that are experienced as beneficial or valuable in some way (Roberts & Dutton, 2009). The belief that individuals desire to construct positive identities is a pervasive and enduring assumption of most identity research in sociology and psychology (Gecas, 1982). With the advent of positive organizational psychology and positive organizational scholarship more generally, there is interest in more precisely understanding how and what kinds of positive identities are possible in work contexts (Roberts & Creary, 2012; Roberts & Dutton, 2009).

Past research suggests there are at least four different ways that an individual's organizational identity (or any other work identity) can be positive, each focusing on a different feature of identity; specifically, its content, evaluation, development, and structure (Dutton et al., 2010). In the sections below we explore how job crafting is an important process through which individuals construct different kinds of positive organizational identities by altering the task, relational, and cognitive boundaries of their work.

Job Crafting and a Virtuous Organizational Identity

When individuals define themselves as organizational members who have attributes associated with people of good character then the kinds of qualities that are part of their identity content (e.g., wisdom, care, courage) make their organizational identity positive. We call this kind of positive identity virtuous because the self-attributes are qualities that are associated with virtue (Weaver, 2006) or moral character (e.g., Aquino & Reed, 2002). In this case, individual organizational identity is positive simply because individuals have infused their self-definition with qualities that philosophers have long associated with a good life (Aristotle, 1984; MacIntyre, 1981). In fact, there is striking consistency across religious and philosophical traditions about the kinds of qualities that define a person who is of good character (Peterson & Seligman, 2004).

Members can use various forms of job crafting to create virtuous organizational identities. In Diane's case, she uses two job crafting moves that help her to see herself as a more virtuous employee. The cognitive crafting that allowed her to see herself as a defender of the firm's honesty and fair practices infused her self-definition as organization member as a person who has integrity and is morally just. In addition, when she relationally altered her job through taking on more volunteer outreach to women in the community, she infused her self-definition with qualities such as courage and humanity. In both cases, altering the way she sees and acts in her job provides the seedcorn for transforming how she sees herself as an organization member. In this case, her self-definition moves in the direction of a more moral organizational identity, which is positive because of the inherent goodness this self-definition implies. Thus, job crafting is a means by which organizational members can become more virtuous organizational selves by thinking and acting in ways that evidence good, moral character.

Job Crafting and an Esteemed Organizational Identity

A basic assumption of most identity theories is that individuals want to be regarded as persons of significance and worth (Gecas, 1982). A second form of positive organizational identity captures the positivity that arises because one's social group (in this case one's work organization) is evaluated positively by the self or others (Dutton et al., 2010). If an organization is esteemed by the self and others, then individuals can bask in this reflected glory (Cialdini et al., 1976) and through a process of organizational identification, infuse these valued attributes into their self-definitions (Dutton, Dukerich, & Harquail, 1994).

Job crafting affords employees with numerous ways to infuse the self with positive meaning through connecting themselves with sources of positive regard for the organization. For example, an employee could alter the task and relational boundaries to allow immediate contact with customers who have positive impressions of the organization, perhaps because the organization has had a beneficial impact on their personal or work lives (Grant, 2007). Crafting one's job to allow one to experience others' positive regard for the organization can also be a collective crafting endeavor. Schoolteachers who craft their jobs as a group to alter opportunities to learn how parents appreciate the school are evidencing collective job crafting (Leana et al., 2009). They are using collective job crafting as a means for defining their organizations more positively by collecting feedback that suggests their organizations (and hence themselves as members) are doing good work, and therefore are valued and esteemed people.

Job Crafting and a Progressive Organizational Identity

A third form of positive identity focuses on the dynamic nature of social identities and how an individual's identity content changes over time. A progressive identity captures the idea that individuals can define themselves positively by seeing themselves as changing or evolving toward a desired self (Dutton et al., 2010). This form of positive identity is rooted in theories of human development that suggest it is desirable for individuals to progress and adapt toward a more evolved and desired self (e.g., Erikson, 1968; Levinson, 1986). When applied to an organizational member's sense of self, a progressive organizational identity allows a member to define oneself as evolving, changing, or growing toward a more desired or imagined self.

A recent study of how organizations shape the ways employees see themselves as growing provided numerous examples of employees crafting their work so that that they could grow themselves (and their self-conceptions) in a desired direction (Sonenshein, Dutton, Grant, Spreitzer, & Sutcliffe, 2013). Sonenshein et al. describe how in a social service agency providing a range of programs for elderly citizens, members of the administrative and support staff routinely altered the relational and task boundaries of their jobs so they could have more contact with seniors and provide help if needed. In one instance of this help-giving, a maintenance worker described himself as a "nurse" in recounting the help he gave to an elderly man in desperate need of care. By crafting his job to help someone in desperate need, this employee was able to define his identity in the organization in different and positive terms. Several members of this organization crafted their jobs to allow them to become the helping selves that the organization valued and desired. Thus, job crafting can be a pathway through which employees experiment with initiating job changes that allow them to grow toward having the qualities and characteristics they most desire.

Job Crafting and a Complementary Organizational Identity

A fourth way an individual's identity can be positive focuses not on the content, evaluation, or progression of one's self-definition, but instead on the relationship between the different aspects of one's identity (Dutton et al., 2010). Researchers suggest that it is beneficial for individuals to maximize the compatibility between their various role and social identities (Thoits, 1991). Accordingly, a more complementary organizational identity is one where individuals experience greater compatibility and consistency between who one sees oneself to be as a member of the organization and as a member of other social groups and roles.

A recent job crafting move by one of this chapter's authors illustrates the potency of this kind of proactive job change as a means for constructing an organizational self that is psychologically beneficial. Jane was invited to give a talk to an alumni group of her university about her research. Because both of her daughters are now living in the town where her work is located, they were able to attend. For the first time in 30 years she asked her daughters to attend her talk (the small job crafting move). During the public discussion of the research, both daughters made comments and added ideas, with the audience's recognition that they were related to the speaker. During this exchange, Jane experienced a powerful sense of integration between her role and membership as professor in the local university and her role as mother. For that moment, and lasting for some time afterwards, joy and contentment arose from the experienced compatibility between sometimes highly conflicted role identities and from the satisfaction of being able to authentically connect the two selves that represent mother and university faculty member. Indeed, researchers have noted the positive identity benefits of this kind of connection and integration of aspects of the self (Rothbard & Ramarajan, 2009).

Across the four positive meanings and four positive identities discussed above we can see the variety of ways that employees can use job crafting as a means for constructing work meanings and identities that are valued, significant, changing, and structured in ways that yield psychological and social benefits, thereby moving beyond Wrzesniewski and Dutton's (2001) conclusion that job crafting changes work meanings and identities in general. By delineating the different kinds of positive meanings and identities that job crafting may produce, future research can more fruitfully examine which particular forms of job crafting are likely to bring about these different meanings and identities. Further, we can begin to imagine how different organizational contexts affect the kinds of positive meanings and identities employees construct because of how the context limits or enables job crafting. However, questions remain about the nature of the causal links between these positive meanings and identities and job crafting – namely, when are these meanings and identities motivational drivers of job crafting, and when are they outcomes of job crafting? In the section that follows, we address this question in an effort to provide further guidance for future research in this area.

THREE PATHWAYS TO POSITIVE MEANING AND IDENTITY THROUGH JOB CRAFTING

We propose that the four sources of positive work meanings and four types of positive work identities discussed above can be motivational drivers of job crafting, outcomes of it, or both, depending on how employees view the meaning of their work and themselves at the outset of job crafting. To capture the key ways in which the temporal relationship between these positive outcomes and job crafting may differ between employees, we characterize three different archetypal types of job crafters to highlight pathways through which job crafting may link to one or more of these meanings or identities.

The Alignment Crafter

Alignment crafters seek to align their jobs with a preconceived positive view of their work meaning or identity. In other words, they engage in job crafting to fix a misalignment between their current job and its implications for their work meaning or identity and what they want and expect their work meaning or identity to be. As Bakker and his colleagues report, employees' ability to sense or create alignment between the demands of their jobs and the resources they have to meet these demands has positive implications for their engagement at work (Bakker et al., 2003, 2004, 2007). These findings are suggestive of the benefits employees reap when they experience or create alignment in their work. For example, an auto mechanic who sees himself as having an esteemed organizational identity but does not have opportunities to realize this identity in his work could seek direct interaction with customers in order to get it. In this way, the quest for a certain positive work meaning and/or identity that employees' jobs currently do not enable is what drives them to job craft. As a result of this orientation, these employees may only accrue the psychological benefits of experiencing a positive work meaning or identity if they succeed in crafting their jobs to facilitate their desired meaning or identity, otherwise they may experience frustration (Barlas & Yasarcan, 2006) or disappointment (Bell, 1985) as they fail to meet their crafting intentions.

The Aspirational Crafter

While alignment crafters have a preconceived vision of a positive work meaning or identity that is not fulfilled by their current job, aspirational crafters craft their jobs in order to develop their work and self into a desired future state that they do not currently experience. For example, an attorney who desires more emphasis on meaning in her work that is based in service to the community may put more time and energy into her existing pro bono cases while pursuing new ones, thus developing an identity in her work that did not exist before. In this way, aspirational crafters operate by recognizing opportunities to job craft in order to develop new work meanings and aspects of identity that they wish to create, while alignment crafters create new opportunities within the job to pursue the positive meaning or identity they do not currently experience at work. For this reason, alignment crafting may take longer to unfold than aspirational crafting, but alignment crafters may stand to benefit more in the long run because creating new opportunities may enable greater change over time than just exploiting existing opportunities. The actions that aspirational crafters take to realize desired "future work selves" (Strauss, Griffin, & Parker, 2012) and to create or experience more of the kinds of meanings they want from their work ((Berg, Grant, & Johnson, 2010)) help to seed the conditions in their jobs that allow for growth and development.

The Accidental Crafter

Accidental crafting occurs when employees unintentionally discover a positive meaning or identity through job crafting. For example, a hospital cleaner who helps a patient fetch an item from across the room may discover that this task allows him to experience a more virtuous organizational identity. In this way, accidental crafting involves unintentionally discovering opportunities for cultivating one or more positive meanings or identities within the job that employees did not consider before engaging in job crafting. While the positive work meanings and identities are drivers of both alignment and aspirational crafting, the positive meanings and identities are solely outcomes – not drivers – of accidental crafting. Because accidental crafters unlock opportunities for completely new types of positive meaning and identity, they may be well positioned to experience relatively quick and intense boosts in psychological flourishing as a result of their crafting as compared to alignment and aspirational crafters, whose job crafting is more intentional.

Taken together, these three archetypal pathways provide a preliminary framework for understanding how, over time, job crafting may be driven by the aforementioned positive meanings and identities (alignment and aspirational crafting), as well as how job crafting may drive the discovery of these meanings and identities (accidental crafting). By painting a picture of how and why employees might engage in job crafting to seek alignment, meet aspirational aims, or simply by accident, we hope to enliven the ways researchers think about and study job crafting. In the future, research on job crafting should more fully consider how this activity is rooted in a motivated and creative space in employees' lives, in which they are proactively seeking and designing into their work those elements that enable them to experience the meaning of their work and selves as enduringly positive (or encountering them by accident). We hope this framework will help guide future research on the temporal dynamics between job crafting and important psychological outcomes such as positive meanings and identities.

CONCLUSION

Recalling the purpose of this volume, researchers in positive organizational psychology seek to understand the strengths and virtues that enable individuals and organizations to thrive (Bakker & Schaufeli, 2008). Job crafting offers an important contribution to this field by envisioning employees not as passive recipients of job characteristics, but as active participants in the construction of the meaning of their work and themselves. In this chapter, we proposed a set of sources of positive work meanings and types of positive work identities that are likely to be a part of the job crafting process, as well as three archetypal pathways through which these meanings and identities may drive – and be driven by – job crafting over time. In so doing, we hope we opened up new questions and lines of research about the ways in which job crafting can strengthen employees and the organizations in which they work.

NOTES

1. While job crafting may negatively affect employees' sense of meaning and identity in their work, we focus in this chapter on the ways in which job crafting may be positive for work meaning and identity.

2. While the kind of meaning employees make of their work is likely to have implications for how they enact and craft their jobs, here we focus more on the impact of job crafting on job meaning.

REFERENCES

Aquino, K., & Reed, A. (2002). The self-importance of moral identity. *Journal of Personality and Social Psychology, 83*, 1423–1436.

Aristotle, X. (1984). *The complete works of Aristotle*. Princeton, NJ: Princeton University Press.

Ashforth, B. E., Kreiner, G. E., & Fugate, M. (2000). All in a day's work: Boundaries and micro role transitions at work. *Academy of Management Review, 23*, 472–491.

Ashforth, B. E., & Mael, F. (1989). Social identity theory and the organization. *Academy of Management Review, 14*, 20–39.

Bakker, A., Demerouti, E., & Schaufeli, W. (2003). Dual processes at work in a call centre: An application of the job demands–resources model. *European Journal of Work and Organizational Psychology, 12*, 393–417.

Bakker, A. B., & Demerouti, E. (2007). The job demands-resources model: State of the art. *Journal of Managerial Psychology, 22*, 309–328.

Bakker, A. B., Demerouti, E., & Verbeke, W. (2004). Using the job demands-resources model to predict burnout and performance. *Human Resource Management, 43*, 83–104.

Bakker, A. B., Hakanen, J. J., Demerouti, E., & Xanthopoulou, D. (2007). Job resources boost work engagement, particularly when job demands are high. *Journal of Educational Psychology, 99*, 274.

Bakker, A. B., & Schaufeli, W. B. (2008). Positive organizational behavior: Engaged employees in flourishing organizations. *Journal of Organizational Behavior, 29*, 147–154.

Barlas, Y., & Yasarcan, H. (2006). Goal setting, evaluation, learning and revision: A dynamic modeling approach. *Evaluation and Program Planning, 29*, 79–87.

Baron, J. N., & Bielby, W. T. (1986). The proliferation of job titles in organizations. *Administrative Science Quarterly, 31*, 561–586.

Bell, D. E. (1985). Disappointment in decision making under uncertainty. *Operations Research, 33*, 1–27.

Berg, J. M., Grant, A. M., & Johnson, V. (2010). When callings are calling: Crafting work and leisure in pursuit of unanswered occupational callings. *Organization Science, 21*, 973–994.

Berg, J. M., Wrzesniewski, A., & Dutton, J. E. (2010). Perceiving and responding to challenges in job crafting at different ranks: When proactivity requires adaptivity. *Journal of Organizational Behavior, 31*, 158–186.

Cameron, K. S., Dutton, J. E., & Quinn, R. E. (2003). *Positive organizational scholarship*. San Francisco, CA: Berrett-Koehler Publishers.

Cameron, K. S., & Spreitzer, G. M. (2012). *Oxford handbook of positive organizational scholarship*. New York, NY: Oxford University Press.

Cialdini, R. B., Borden, R. J., Thorne, A., Walker, M. R., Freeman, S., & Sloan, L. R. (1976). Basking in reflected glory: Three (football) field studies. *Journal of Personality and Social Psychology*, *34*, 366–375.

Demerouti, E., Bakker, A. B., Nachreiner, F., & Schaufeli, W. B. (2001). The job demands-resources model of burnout. *Journal of Applied Psychology*, *86*, 499–512.

Donaldson, S. I., & Ko, I. (2010). Positive organizational psychology, behavior, and scholarship: A review of the emerging literature and evidence base. *Journal of Positive Psychology*, *5*, 177–191.

Dutton, J. E., Dukerich, J. M., & Harquail, C. V. (1994). Organizational images and member identification. *Administrative Science Quarterly*, *39*, 239–263.

Dutton, J. E., Roberts, L. M., & Bednar, J. (2010). Pathways to positive identity construction at work: Four types of positive identity and the building of social resources. *Academy of Management Review*, *35*, 265–293.

Erikson, E. H. (1968). *Identity: Youth and crisis*. New York, NY: Norton.

Gecas, V. (1982). The self-concept. *Annual Review of Sociology*, *8*, 1–33.

Ghitulescu, B. E. (2006). *Shaping tasks and relationships at work: Examining the antecedents and consequences of employee job crafting*. University of Pittsburgh.

Grant, A. M. (2007). Relational job design and the motivation to make a prosocial difference. *The Academy of Management Review ARCHIVE*, *32*, 393–417.

Grant, A. M. (2008). Does intrinsic motivation fuel the prosocial fire? Motivational synergy in predicting persistence, performance, and productivity. *Journal of Applied Psychology*, *93*, 48–58.

Grant, A. M., & Ashford, S. J. (2008). The dynamics of proactivity at work. *Research in Organizational Behavior*, *28*, 3–34.

Griffin, M. A., Neal, A., & Parker, S. K. (2007). A new model of work role performance: Positive behavior in uncertain and interdependent contexts. *Academy of Management Journal*, *50*, 327–347.

Griffin, R. W. (1987). Toward an integrated theory of task design. *Research in Organizational Behavior*, *9*, 79–120.

Hackman, J. R., & Oldham, G. R. (1980). *Work redesign*. Reading, MA: Addison-Wesley.

Hardy, L. (1990). *The fabric of this world: Inquiries into calling, career choice and the design of human work*. Grand Rapids, MI: Wm B Eerdmans Publishing Co.

Hornung, S., Rousseau, D. M., Glaser, J. R., Angerer, P., & Weigl, M. (2010). Beyond top-down and bottom-up work redesign: Customizing job content through idiosyncratic deals. *Journal of Organizational Behavior*, *31*, 187–215.

Ilgen, D. R., & Hollenbeck, J. R. (1992). The structure of work: Job design and roles. In M. Dunnette & L. Hough (Eds.), *Handbook of industrial and organizational psychology* (pp. 165–207). Palo Alto, CA: Consulting Psychologists Press.

Ko, I. (2012). *Crafting a job: Creating optimal experiences at work*. Claremont, CA: The Claremeont Graduate University.

Lamont, M., & Molnar, V. (2002). The study of boundaries in the social sciences. *Annual Review of Sociology*, *28*, 167–195.

Leana, C., Appelbaum, E., & Shevchuk, I. (2009). Work process and quality of care in early childhood education: The role of job crafting. *Academy of Management Journal*, *52*, 1169–1192.

Levinson, D. J. (1986). A conception of adult development. *American Psychologist, 41*, 3–13.

Lyons, P. (2008). The crafting of jobs and individual differences. *Journal of Business and Psychology, 23*, 25–36.

MacIntyre, A. (1981). *After virtue.* South Bend, IN: Notre Dame Press.

Nakamura, J., & Csikszentmihalyi, M. (2002). The concept of flow. In C. R. Snyder & S. J. Lopez (Eds.), *Handbook of positive psychology* (pp. 89–105). New York, NY: Oxford University Press.

Peterson, C., & Seligman, M. E. P. (2004). *Character strengths and virtues: A classification and handbook.* New York, NY: Oxford University Press.

Petrou, P., Demerouti, E., Peeters, M. C. W., & Schaufeli, W. B. (2012). Crafting a job on a daily basis: Contextual correlates and the link to work engagement. *Journal of Organizational Behavior, 33*, 1120–1141.

Pratt, M., & Ashforth, B. (2003). Fostering meaningfulness in working and at work. In K. S. Cameron, J. E. Dutton & R. E. Quinn (Eds.), *Positive organizational scholarship: Foundations of a new discipline* (pp. 309–327). San Francisco, CA: Berrett-Koehler.

Roberts, L. M., & Creary, S. J. (2012). Positive identity construction: Insights from classical and contemporary theoretical perspectives. In K. S. Cameron & G. M. Spreitzer (Eds.), *Oxford handbook of positive organizational scholarship* (pp. 70–83). Oxford University Press.

Roberts, L. M., & Dutton, J. E. (2009). *Exploring positive identities and organizations: Building a theoretical and research foundation.* New York, NY: Routledge.

Rosso, B. D., Dekas, K. H., & Wrzesniewski, A. (2010). On the meaning of work: A theoretical integration and review. *Research in Organizational Behavior, 30*, 91–127.

Rothbard, N., & Ramarajan, L. (2009). Checking your identities at the door? Positive relationships between nonwork and work identities. In L. M. Roberts & J. E. Dutton (Eds.), *Exploring positive identities and organizations: Building a theoretical and research foundation* (pp. 125–149). New York, NY: Routledge.

Rousseau, D. M., Ho, V. T., & Greenberg, J. (2006). I-deals: Idiosyncratic terms in employment relationships. *Academy of Management Review, 31*, 977–994.

Sonenshein, S. J., Dutton, J. E., Grant, A. M., Spreitzer, G. M., & Sutcliffe, K. M. (2013). Growing at work: Employees' interpretations of progressive self-change at work. *Organization Science, 24*(2), 552–570.

Strang, D., & Baron, J. N. (1990). Categorical imperatives: The structure of job titles in California state agencies. *American Sociological Review, 55*, 479–495.

Strauss, K., Griffin, M. A., & Parker, S. K. (2012). Future work selves: How salient hoped-for identities motivate proactive career behaviors. *Journal of Applied Psychology, 97*, 580–598.

Tausky, C. (1995). The meanings of work. *Research in the Sociology of Work, 5*, 15–27.

Thoits, P. A. (1991). On merging identity theory and stress research. *Social Psychology Quarterly, 54*, 101–112.

Tims, M., Bakker, A. B., & Derks, D. (2012). Development and validation of the job crafting scale. *Journal of Vocational Behavior, 80*, 173–186.

Weaver, G. (2006). Virtue in organizations: Moral identity as a foundation for moral agency. *Organization Studies, 27*, 341–368.

Weiss, J. W., Skelley, M. F., Haughey, J. C., & Hall, D. T. (2004). Calling, new careers and spirituality: A reflective perspective for organizational leaders and professionals. In M. L. Pava & P. Primeaux (Eds.), *Spiritual intelligence at work: Meaning, metaphor and morals* (pp. 175–201). Amsterdam: Elsevier.

Wrzesniewski, A., Berg, J. M., Grant, A. M., Kurkoski, J., & Welle, B. (2012). *Job crafting in motion: Achieving sustainable gains in happiness and performance*. Working Paper.

Wrzesniewski, A., & Dutton, J. E. (2001). Crafting a job: Revisioning employees as active crafters of their work. *Academy of Management Review, 26*, 179–201.

Wrzesniewski, A., Dutton, J. E., & Debebe, G. (2003). Interpersonal sensemaking and the meaning of work. *Research in Organizational Behavior, 25*, 93–135.

Wrzesniewski, A., McCauley, C., Rozin, P., & Schwartz, B. (1997). Jobs, careers, and callings: People's relations to their work. *Journal of Research in Personality, 31*, 21–33.

Zerubavel, E. (1991). *The fine line*. New York, NY: Free Press.

WORK–FAMILY ENRICHMENT: A SYSTEMATIC REVIEW OF ANTECEDENTS, OUTCOMES, AND MECHANISMS

Tori L. Crain and Leslie B. Hammer

The majority of literature on the work–family interface has focused on the conflict associated with enactment in both work and family roles (Eby, Casper, Lockwood, Bordeaux, & Brinley, 2005). However, a growing body of research suggests that work and family also have beneficial effects on one another (e.g., McNall, Nicklin, & Masuda, 2010b). This phenomenon has been referred to as work–family enrichment, or the degree to which experiences in the work role improve the quality of life in the family role, and vice versa (Greenhaus & Powell, 2006).

To date, there has not been a systematic review conducted on the antecedents and outcomes associated with enrichment. This is partially due to the initial focus on constructs, theory, and measurement in the literature (for a review, see Zimmerman & Hammer, 2010). More recently, however, scholars have moved toward an examination of the antecedents and outcomes of enrichment, partially summarized in two meta-analyses (i.e., McNall et al., 2010b; Michel, Clark, & Jaramillo, 2011). While these meta-analyses are warranted, we felt there was still a need to collectively integrate the accumulating body of research on enrichment, as well as update the

Advances in Positive Organizational Psychology, Volume 1, 303–328
ISSN: 2046-410X/doi:10.1108/S2046-410X(2013)0000001016

existing reviews. Furthermore, we review past literature which has included enrichment as a mediating mechanism, in addition to those studies which have utilized a positive spillover–crossover model. We believe that this will help move the field forward in both conceptualization of the construct and in understanding the role that enrichment plays in the broader scholarly work–family literature. Such a review is necessary for informing continued research by facilitating the development of more complex models regarding enrichment processes.

The basis for our conceptualization of enrichment is in positive organizational psychology and, more specifically, the positive psychology movement with a focus on happiness and well-being (e.g., Seligman & Csikszentmihalyi, 2000). Consistent with positive organizational psychology is the study of work engagement, defined as a positive, fulfilling, work-related state of mind that is characterized by vigor, dedication, and absorption (Schaufeli & Bakker, 2004). The trend in both organizational research and practice has been to understand ways of improving employee engagement in the workplace. We argue that as part of supporting this movement, it is critical for both practitioners and scientists to develop a better understanding of the underlying mechanisms related to enrichment.

HISTORY AND THEORY OF ENRICHMENT

While based on ideas initially introduced in the 1970s (e.g., Sieber, 1974), the concept of work–family enrichment was first proposed by Greenhaus and Powell in 2006. This framework asserts that enrichment is experienced either through an instrumental path or an affective path. Enrichment occurs by means of the instrumental path when individuals have the belief that engagement in one role has directly increased their ability to perform in the other role. According to Greenhaus and Powell (2006), role experiences offer five categories of resources that may be acquired by an individual: skills and perspectives (e.g., interpersonal skills), psychological and physical resources (e.g., self-efficacy), social-capital resources (e.g., networking, information), flexibility (e.g., flexible work arrangements), and material resources (e.g., money). Enrichment occurs by way of the affective pathway when an increase in resources in one role enhances mood, spilling over, and permitting for increased functioning in the other role. In this way, a parent who plays with children before work, developing a good mood, may then bring those emotions into the workplace. This, in turn, may increase their ability to interact positively with coworkers, thus improving performance.

Work–family enrichment should be distinguished from the concept of work–family balance, which Greenhaus and Allen (2011) define as the feeling of being effective and satisfied with work and family. Greenhaus, Ziegert, and Allen (2012) further elaborate on the concept of work–family balance, and its relationship to work–family support and work–family interference/conflict (i.e., engagement in one role is made more difficult by engagement in the other role). However, the relationship between work–family enrichment and work–family balance was not examined in the latter study and thus is not clear.

Research on the benefits of engaging in both work and family roles has led to the development of multiple constructs with similar meaning. The transfer of affect, skills, behaviors, and values between work and family domains has been termed work–family positive spillover (Hanson, Hammer, & Colton, 2006). Alternatively, enrichment refers to the degree to which experiences in one role improve the quality of life in the other role, through the transfer of resources or positive affect from one role to the other (Carlson, Kacmar, Wayne, & Grzywacz, 2006). Facilitation refers to the extent to which involvement in one life domain provides developmental (e.g., skills), affective (e.g., moods), capital (e.g., income), or efficiency (e.g., focus, attention) gains that contribute to enhanced system functioning in the other domain (Wayne, Grzywacz, Carlson, & Kacmar, 2007). Although operationalized slightly differently, these constructs are closely related (Masuda, McNall, Allen, & Nicklin, 2012).

Wayne (2009) has suggested that work–family enrichment is an extension of positive spillover, and work–family facilitation an extension of work–family enrichment. In this way, the gains transferred from role to role, through the positive spillover process, can result in enhanced individual functioning in the receiving domain, or enrichment, and can subsequently result in enhanced system functioning in the receiving domain, or facilitation. Since the majority of research has captured the positive spillover and enrichment processes by focusing on individual outcomes and enhanced individual functioning in the receiving domain, we have chosen to use the term work–family enrichment.

In accordance with models of work–family conflict, the antecedents and consequences of enrichment have been generally thought to be domain specific. As such, work antecedents should be the primary predictors of work-to-family enrichment (WFE) and family antecedents should be the primary predictors of family-to-work enrichment (FWE) (Greenhaus & Powell, 2006). Alternatively, others (Siu et al., 2010) have argued that certain antecedents may be predictive of both WFE and FWE. For example, positive affect may spill over from the family domain and enhance performance in the work domain, thereby improving affect at work. Consequently, this affect could then enrich family life, providing evidence for feedback loops. A similar domain-specific assumption has been previously made in the literature regarding outcomes, such that consequences of enrichment should be related to the receiving domain. However, Voydanoff (2005a) and others have argued that an individual may attribute their enhanced performance in the receiving role to the resources generated in the originating role. Consequently, this increases satisfaction and other outcomes associated with the originating role.

REVIEW OF WORK–FAMILY ENRICHMENT STUDIES

Tables 1 and 2 contain 86 studies that have directly measured work–family enrichment, or a related construct. To find studies, we searched databases such as PsycINFO, EBSCO, JSTOR, and Google Scholar. Search terms included work–family enrichment, work–family positive spillover, work–family facilitation, and work–family enhancement. We included only those quantitative studies that have demonstrated significant statistical relationships with work–family enrichment or a related construct. Thus, this review should not be considered comprehensive, but does represent a more thorough examination of work–family enrichment than has been provided in the scholarly literature to date. Specifically, we add to Michel et al.'s (2011) findings by reviewing nonwork, work, and personal characteristics antecedents beyond personality. We also review relationships between enrichment and nonwork, work, and health and well-being outcomes not covered by McNall et al. (2010b). It should be noted that while we are referring to antecedents and outcomes, a majority of the existing research is cross-sectional and, therefore, directionality is only inferred.

Antecedents of Work–Family Enrichment

As shown in Table 1, antecedents of work–family enrichment can be broadly grouped into the categories of nonwork-related variables, work-related

Table 1. Antecedents of Work–Family Enrichment.

Antecedent	Direction	Relationship	Supporting Studies
Nonwork-Related Antecedents			
Age of child	FWE	+	Lu, Siu, Spector, and Shi (2009)
Child care role quality	FWE	+	Brockwood (2002)
Emotion–work satisfaction	FWE	+	Stevens, Minnotte, Mannon, and Kiger (2007)
Family cohesion	FWE	+	Stevens et al. (2007)
Family involvement	FWE	+	Allis and O'Driscoll (2008)
	WFE	–	Aryee, Srinivas, and Tan (2005)
Family role quality	FWE	+	Pedersen, Minnote, Kiger, and Mannon (2009)
Family salience	FWE	+	Carlson et al. (2006)
	WFE	+	Carlson et al. (2006)
Family mutuality	FWE	+	Carlson et al. (2006)
	WFE	+	Carlson et al. (2006)
Friend demands	WFE	+	Voydanoff (2004a)
Household rewards	FWE	+	Voydanoff (2005b)
Home time demands	WFE	+	van Steenbergen, Ellemers, and Mooijaart (2009)
Household demands	FWE	–	Voydanoff (2005b)
Involvement in community	FWE	+	Kirchmeyer (1992)
Negative relationship consequences	WFE	–	van Steenbergen et al. (2009)
Overload at home	FWE	–	Rotondo and Kincaid (2008)
Parental status	FWE	+	Zimmerman (2009)
	FWE	+	Innstrand, Langballe, Espnes, Aasland, and Falkum (2010a)
Parenting involvement	FWE	+	Kirchmeyer (1992)
Parenting time commitment	FWE	–	Kirchmeyer (1992)
Partner's ability to leave work to care for children	FWE	+	Pedersen et al. (2009)
Partner chore hours	FWE	+	Rotondo and Kincaid (2008)
Personal growth	WFE	+	Grzywacz and Butler (2005)
Positive affective response to family	FWE	+	Yanchus, Eby, Lance, and Drollinger (2010)
Relationship satisfaction	FWE	+	Stevens et al. (2007)

Table 1. (*Continued*)

Antecedent	Direction	Relationship	Supporting Studies
Relationship with family	FWE	+	Carlson et al. (2006)
	WFE	+	Carlson et al. (2006)
Satisfaction with housework	FWE	+	Stevens et al. (2007)
Sense of community	FWE	+	Voydanoff (2004a, 2005b)
Sports, recreation, and fitness	FWE	+	Hecht and Boies (2009)
Support from children	FWE	+	Wadsworth and Owens (2007)
Support from family	FWE	+	Aryee et al. (2005); Baral and Bhargava (2011); Bhargava and Baral (2009); Karatepe and Bekteshi (2008); Siu et al. (2010)
Support from spouse	FWE	+	Cinamon and Rich (2010); Lu et al. (2009); Voydanoff (2005b)
	WFE	+	Cinamon and Rich (2010); Lu et al. (2009)
Support from friends	WFE	+	Voydanoff (2004b); Wadsworth and Owens (2007)
Support from family and friends	FWE	+	van Steenbergen et al. (2009)
	WFE	+	van Steenbergen et al. (2009)
Unsafe neighborhood	FWE	+	Voydanoff (2005a)
Volunteer status	FWE	–	Hecht and Boies (2009)

Work-Related Antecedents

Achievement striving	WFE	+	Proost, De Witte, De Witte, and Schreurs (2010)
Autonomy	FWE	+	Carlson et al. (2006); Voydanoff (2004b)
	WFE	+	Carlson et al. (2006); Grzywacz and Butler (2005); Karimi and Nouri (2009); Siu et al. (2010)
Burnout	FWE	–	Innstrand, Langballe, Espnes, Falkum, and Aasland (2008)
	WFE	–	Innstrand et al. (2008)
Congruence	WFE	–	Chen, Powell, and Greenhaus (2009)
	WFE	+	Chen et al. (2009)
Developmental experiences	FWE	+	Carlson et al. (2006)
	WFE	+	Carlson et al. (2006)
Effort–reward imbalance ratio	FWE	–	Franche et al. (2006)

Table 1. (*Continued*)

Antecedent	Direction	Relationship	Supporting Studies
Family-friendly coworkers	FWE	+	Lu et al. (2009)
	WFE	+	Lu et al. (2009)
Family-supportive supervisor behaviors	FWE	+	Hammer, Kossek, Yragui, Bodner, and Hanson (2009); Odle-Dusseau, Britt, and Greene-Shortridge (2012)
	WFE	+	Hammer et al. (2009); Lu et al. (2009); Odle-Dusseau et al. (2012)
Income adequacy	WFE	+	Zimmerman (2009)
Job characteristics	WFE	+	Baral and Bhargava (2011); Bhargava and Baral (2009); Taylor, Delcampo, and Blancero (2009)
Job control	WFE	+	Butler, Grzywacz, Bass, and Linney (2005)
Job demands	FWE	−	Butler et al. (2005)
	WFE	+	Mustapha, Ahmad, Uli, and Idris (2011b); Voydanoff (2004a)
	WFE	−	Butler et al. (2005); Karimi and Nouri (2009)
Job involvement	WFE	+	Aryee et al. (2005)
Job performance-based self-esteem	WFE	−	Innstrand et al. (2010b)
Job resources	FWE	+	Hakanen, Peeters, and Perhoniemi (2011)
	WFE	+	Hakanen et al. (2011)
Job role quality	WFE	+	Brockwood (2002)
Job salience	FWE	+	Carlson et al. (2006)
	WFE	+	Carlson et al. (2006)
Leader–member exchange	WFE	+	Culbertson, Huffman, and Alden-Anderson (2010)
Organizational citizenship behavior	WFE	+	Kwan and Mao (2011)
Organizational support	WFE	+	McNall, Masuda, Shanock, and Nicklin (2011); Wadsworth and Owens (2007)
Perceived career advancement	FWE	+	King, Botsford, and Huffman (2009)
Positive affective responses to work	WFE	+	Yanchus et al. (2010)
Relationship management	FWE	+	Seery, Corrigall, and Harpel. (2008)
	WFE	+	Seery et al. (2008)
Relationship with supervisor	FWE	+	Carlson et al. (2006)
	WFE	+	Carlson et al. (2006)

Table 1. (*Continued*)

Antecedent	Direction	Relationship	Supporting Studies
Schedule flexibility	WFE	+	Carlson, Grzywacz, and Kacmar (2010); McNall, Masuda, and Nicklin (2010a)
Segmentation of work domain from family domain	WFE	−	Powell and Greenhaus (2010)
Skill development	WFE	+	Kwan, Mao, and Zhang (2010)
Skill level	WFE	+	Butler et al. (2005); Grzywacz and Butler (2005)
Social skills	WFE	+	Grzywacz and Butler (2005)
Substantive complexity	WFE	+	Grzywacz and Butler (2005)
Support from coworker	WFE	+	Wadsworth and Owens (2007)
Support from supervisor	FWE	+	Bhargava and Baral (2009); van Steenbergen et al. (2009)
	WFE	+	Baral and Bhargava (2011); Bhargava and Baral (2009); Siu et al. (2010); Cinamon and Rich (2010); Taylor et al. (2009); Wadsworth and Owens (2007); van Steenbergen et al. (2009)
Surface acting	WFE	−	Seery et al. (2008)
Supportive culture	FWE	+	Pedersen et al. (2009)
Team resources	FWE	+	Hunter, Perry, Carlson, and Smith (2010)
	WFE	+	Hunter et al. (2010)
Work engagement	FWE	+	Siu et al. (2010)
	WFE	+	Siu et al. (2010)
Work pride	WFE	+	Voydanoff (2004b)
Work–life balance policies	WFE	+	Baral and Bhargava (2011)
Work–family climate	WFE	+	Taylor et al. (2009)
Work–family culture	WFE	+	Baral and Bhargava (2011)
Work social support	FWE	+	Karatepe and Bekteshi (2008)
	WFE	+	Karatepe and Bekteshi (2008)

Personal Characteristics Antecedents

Advice seeking	WFE	+	Rotondo and Kincaid (2008)
Agreeableness	FWE	+	Wayne, Musisca, and Fleeson (2004)
Conscientiousness	FWE	+	Wayne et al. (2004)
Core self-evaluations	FWE	+	Bhargava and Baral (2009)

Table 1. (*Continued*)

Antecedent	Direction	Relationship	Supporting Studies
	WFE	+	McNall et al. (2011); Westring and Ryan (2010)
Direct action coping	FWE	+	Rotondo and Kincaid (2008)
Extraversion	FWE	+	Wayne et al. (2004)
	WFE	+	Grzywacz and Butler (2005); Rotondo and Kincaid (2008); Wayne et al. (2004)
Femininity	WFE	+	Powell and Greenhaus (2010)
Internal locus of control	N/A	+	Andreassi and Thompson (2007)
Neuroticism	FWE	–	Aryee et al. (2005)
	WFE	–	Wayne et al. (2004)
Openness to experience	WFE	+	Wayne et al. (2004)
Positive Affect	FWE	+	Michel and Clark (2009)
	WFE	+	Michel and Clark (2009)
Positive thinking	FWE	+	Rotondo and Kincaid (2008)
	WFE	+	Rotondo and Kincaid (2008)
Secure attachment style	FWE	+	Sumer and Knight (2001)
	WFE	+	Sumer and Knight (2001)

Note: FWE, family-to-work enrichment; WFE, work-to-family enrichment. All relationships shown are significant at $p < .05$.

variables, and personal characteristics. Most of this research has focused on identifying work and nonwork antecedents, while less attention has been paid to individual differences. We identified 54 antecedents related to FWE and 60 antecedents related to WFE.

Nonwork antecedents include family, community, and recreation constructs, although family variables have been examined the most. In line with Greenhaus and Powell's (2006) proposition that the primary antecedents of enrichment should come from the originating domain, nonwork antecedents are examined in relation to FWE more than WFE. While many different nonwork constructs have been addressed, social support from different sources has received the majority of the attention (e.g., Aryee et al., 2005) and is positively related to enrichment.

Various work-related variables have been associated with enrichment. Autonomy and supervisor support have been examined with the greatest frequency. As a whole, the literature primarily supports a relationship between work-related antecedents and WFE, rather than FWE. However, a few studies have found evidence for work-related antecedents being associated with FWE. For example, multiple studies have provided evidence for the positive link between autonomy (e.g., Carlson et al., 2006) and family supportive supervisor behaviors (e.g., Hammer et al., 2009) with both directions of enrichment. A number of studies have also found negative associations between job demands and both directions of enrichment (e.g., Butler et al., 2005), although two studies found a positive relationship between demands and WFE (Mustapha et al., 2011b; Voydanoff, 2004a). This may be the result of work demands reflecting work engagement, which could in turn contribute positively to enrichment (Voydanoff, 2004a).

According to our review of the scholarly work, personal characteristics also seem to influence both directions of enrichment. A recent meta-analysis conducted by Michel et al. (2011) examined the effects of personality on enrichment and found extraversion, agreeableness, conscientiousness, and openness to experience to be positively related to the overall construct of work–family enrichment, encompassing both WFE and FWE. However, as our review shows, other personal characteristics such as core self-evaluations (e.g., McNall et al., 2011) and attachment style (Sumer & Knight, 2001) have also been positively related to both directions of enrichment separately.

Outcomes of Work–Family Enrichment

To date, only one meta-analysis has been conducted on the outcomes of the positive side of the work–family interface (McNall et al., 2010b). This review examined six consequences, job satisfaction, affective commitment, turnover intentions, family satisfaction, life satisfaction, and physical/mental health, associated with enrichment. The current review of outcomes, as shown in Table 2, aims to build on this prior work by identifying additional studies that have examined these relationships. In line with McNall et al. (2010b), we propose that outcomes of enrichment can be broadly grouped into nonwork-related outcomes, work-related outcomes, and health and well-being outcomes. We identified 38 outcomes associated with FWE and 34 associated with WFE.

The majority of research on nonwork-related consequences of enrichment has focused on family (e.g., Hanson et al., 2006) and life satisfaction (e.g., Gareis et al., 2009), as both are related to WFE and FWE. Interestingly, our

Table 2. Outcomes of Work–Family Enrichment.

Outcome	Direction	Relationship	Supporting Studies
Nonwork-Related Outcomes			
Family effort	FWE	+	Wayne et al. (2004)
	WFE	−	Wayne et al. (2004)
Family performance	WFE	+	Carlson et al. (2010)
Family satisfaction	FWE	+	Bhargava and Baral (2009); Boyar and Mosley (2007); Carlson et al. (2006); Carlson, Grzywacz, and Zivnuska (2009); Haar and Bardoel (2008); Hanson et al. (2006); Hill (2005); Hunter et al. (2010); Jaga and Bagraim (2011); Wayne et al. (2004)
	WFE	+	Brockwood (2002); Carlson et al. (2006); Carlson et al. (2010); Hanson et al. (2006)
Home commitment	FWE	+	van Steenbergen, Ellemers, and Mooijaart (2007)
	WFE	+/−	van Steenbergen et al. (2007)
Home performance	FWE	+	van Steenbergen et al. (2007)
	WFE	+/−	van Steenbergen et al. (2007)
Home resources	FWE	+	Hakanen et al. (2011)
Life satisfaction	FWE	+	Gareis, Barnett, Ertel, and Berkman (2009); Hill (2005); Lu et al. (2009)
	WFE	+	Gareis et al. (2009); Hill (2005); Karatepe and Bekteshi (2008); Lu et al. (2009); Masuda et al. (2012)
Marital risk	FWE	−	Voydanoff (2005a)
Marital satisfaction	FWE	+	Hakanen et al. (2011); Hill (2005); Voydanoff (2005a)
Need for autonomy satisfaction	WFE	+	Roche and Haar (2010)
Need for relatedness satisfaction	FWE	+	Roche and Haar (2010)
Need for competence satisfaction	FWE	+	Roche and Haar (2010)
Partner relationship quality	FWE	+	Gareis et al. (2009)
	WFE	−	Gareis et al. (2009)
Positive family well-being	FWE	+	Allis and O'Driscoll (2008)

Table 2. (*Continued*)

Outcome	Direction	Relationship	Supporting Studies
Work-Related Outcomes			
Career satisfaction	FWE	+	Gordon, Whelan-Berry, and Hamilton (2007); Lu et al. (2009)
	WFE	+	Gordon et al. (2007); Jaga and Bagraim (2011); Lu et al. (2009)
Job exhaustion	WFE	−	Kinnunen, Feldt, Geurts, and Pulkkinen (2006)
Job performance	FWE	+	Carlson, Witt, Zivnuska, Kacmar, and Grzywacz (2008); Karatepe and Bekteshi (2008); Karatepe and Kilic (2009); van Steenbergen et al. (2007); van Steenbergen and Ellemers (2009)
	WFE	+	Carlson et al. (2010); Carlson, Ferguson, Kacmar, Grzywacz, and Whitten (2011a); Carlson, Zivnuska, Kacmar, Ferguson, and Whitten (2011b); Karatepe and Bekteshi (2008); van Steenbergen et al. (2007); van Steenbergen and Ellemers (2009)
Job behavior search	WFE	−	van Steenbergen et al. (2007)
Job effort	FWE	+	Wayne et al. (2004)
	WFE	+	Wayne et al. (2004)
Job satisfaction	FWE	+	Balmforth and Gardner (2006); Bhargava and Baral (2009); Boz, Martinez, and Munduate (2009); Brockwood (2002); Carlson et al. (2006); Hanson et al. (2006); Lu et al. (2009); Voydanoff (2005a)
	WFE	+	Balmforth and Gardner (2006); Bhargava and Baral (2009); Boyar and Mosley (2007); Carlson et al. (2006); Carlson et al. (2009); Carlson et al. (2010); Carlson et al. (2011b); Gordon et al. (2007); Hanson et al. (2006); Hill (2005); Jaga and Bagraim (2011); Karatepe and Kilic (2009); Lourel, Ford, Gamassou, Gueguen, and Hartmann (2009); Lu et al. (2009); Masuda et al. (2012); McNall et al. (2010a); Voydanoff (2005a); Wayne et al. (2004); Wayne, Randel, and Stevens (2006)
Job stress	FWE	−	Voydanoff (2005a)
	WFE	−	Voydanoff (2005a)

Table 2. (*Continued*)

Outcome	Direction	Relationship	Supporting Studies
Organizational citizenship behavior	FWE	+	Bhargava and Baral (2009)
	WFE	+	Balmforth and Gardner (2006); Bhargava and Baral (2009)
Organizational commitment	FWE	−	Hill (2005)
	FWE	+	Balmforth and Gardner (2006); Bhargava and Baral (2009); Gordon et al. (2007); Karatepe and Kilic (2009); Karatepe and Magaji (2008); Lu et al. (2009); Wayne et al. (2006); van Steenbergen et al. (2007)
	WFE	+	Balmforth and Gardner (2006); Bhargava and Baral (2009); Carlson et al. (2009); Gordon et al. (2007); Lu et al. (2009); Odle-Dusseau et al. (2012); van Steenbergen et al. (2007)
Organizational support performance	WFE	+	Odle-Dusseau et al. (2012)
Positive work well-being	FWE	+	Allis and O'Driscoll (2008)
Psychological contract fairness	WFE	+	Taylor et al. (2009)
Turnover intentions	FWE	+	Gordon et al. (2007)
	FWE	−	Balmforth and Gardner (2006)
	WFE	−	Amah (2009); Balmforth and Gardner (2006); Carlson et al. (2009); Haar and Bardoel (2008); McNall et al. (2010a); Mustapha et al. (2011b); Odle-Dusseau et al. (2012)
Work satisfaction	FWE	−	van Steenbergen et al. (2007)
	WFE	+	van Steenbergen et al. (2007)

Health and Well-Being Outcomes

Outcome	Direction	Relationship	Supporting Studies
Affect balance	FWE	+	Gareis et al. (2009)
	WFE	+	Gareis et al. (2009)
BMI	FWE	−	van Steenbergen and Ellemers (2009)
Burnout	FWE	−	Cinamon and Rich (2010); Innstrand et al. (2008)

Table 2. (*Continued*)

Outcome	Direction	Relationship	Supporting Studies
Cholesterol	WFE	−	van Steenbergen and Ellemers (2009)
Chronic health problems	FWE	−	Grzywacz (2000)
Depression	FWE	−	Franche et al. (2006); Grzywacz and Bass (2003); Hammer, Cullen, Neal, Sinclair, and Shafiro (2005)
	WFE	−	van Steenbergen et al. (2007)
	WFE	+	Hammer et al. (2005)
Individual stress	WFE	−	Hill (2005)
Mental health	FWE	+	Gareis et al. (2009); Grzywacz (2000); Hanson et al. (2006); Stoddard. and Madsen (2007)
	WFE	+	Gareis et al. (2009); Grzywacz (2000); Hanson et al. (2006); Stoddard. and Madsen (2007)
Negative well-being	FWE	−	Grzywacz (2000)
Overall health	FWE	+	Stoddard and Madsen (2007)
	WFE	+	Stoddard and Madsen (2007)
Personal distress	WFE	−	Schneewind, Reeb, and Kupsch (2010)
Physical health	WFE	+	Grzywacz (2000)
Poor physical stamina	WFE	−	van Steenbergen and Ellemers (2009)
Positive mood	FWE	+	Carlson et al. (2011b); Carlson, Hunter, Ferguson, and Whitten (in press)
	WFE	+	Carlson et al. (2011b); Carlson et al. (in press)
Positive psychological well-being	FWE	+	Carlson et al. (2006); Grzywacz (2000)
	WFE	+	Carlson et al. (2006)
Problem drinking	FWE	−	Grzywacz and Marks (2000); Grzywacz and Bass (2003)
	WFE	+	Grzywacz and Marks (2000)
Psychological distress	FWE	−	Carlson et al. (in press); Haar and Bardoel (2008)
	WFE	−	Carlson et al. (in press); Haar and Bardoel (2008); Kinnunen et al. (2006)
Sickness absence	FWE	−	van Steenbergen and Ellemers (2009)
	WFE	−	van Steenbergen and Ellemers (2009)
Sleep quality	FWE	−	Williams, Franche, Ibrahim, Mustard, and Layton (2006)

Table 2. (*Continued*)

Outcome	Direction	Relationship	Supporting Studies
Husbands' depression	FWE	−	Hammer et al. (2005)
Wives' depression	WFE	−	Hammer et al. (2005)
Vigor	FWE	+	Cinamon and Rich (2010)

Note: FWE, family-to-work enrichment; WFE, work-to-family enrichment. All relationships shown are significant at $p < .05$.

review suggests that more support has been found for the association between family satisfaction and FWE, rather than WFE. These findings are in line with Voydanoff's (2005a) argument that an individual may attribute their enhanced performance in the receiving role to the resources generated in the originating role. However, Carlson et al. (in press) pursued this very hypothesis but did not find evidence for FWE having a significantly stronger impact on family satisfaction than WFE.

In all, eight of the studies examining work-related outcomes found a positive relationship between job performance and both directions of enrichment. Consistent with prior research (McNall et al., 2010b), job satisfaction and organizational commitment are positively related with both directions of enrichment, although Hill (2005) found a negative relationship between FWE and organizational commitment. Mixed results, however, are demonstrated concerning the relationship between FWE and turnover intentions, as Gordon et al. (2007) found a positive relationship, while Balmorth and Gardner (2006) found a negative relationship. Additionally, six studies showed a negative relationship between WFE and turnover intentions. Our conclusions are contrary to those of the McNall et al. (2010b) meta-analysis that suggested there was no relationship between WFE and turnover intentions. We found five additional studies that were not represented in the meta-analysis and therefore have drawn alternative conclusions. The multiple findings suggesting that work outcomes are related to FWE are similarly motivated by Voydanoff's (2005a) argument and Carlson et al.'s (in press) findings indicating a stronger relationship between WFE and job satisfaction, than FWE and job satisfaction. Individuals may attribute their success in the receiving domain to the resources generated in the originating domain, thus decreasing outcomes such as turnover intentions.

Research on the health and well-being outcomes of enrichment has examined various aspects of physical and psychological health. For example, FWE has been positively associated with sleep quality (Williams et al., 2006) and negatively associated with chronic health problems (Grzywacz, 2000). Furthermore, as mental health outcomes have been positively linked with both directions of enrichment (e.g., Gareis et al., 2009), psychological distress has been negatively associated with WFE (Haar & Bardoel, 2008). These results are in line with McNall et al.'s (2010b) prior findings that both directions of enrichment are positively associated with physical and mental health.

MODELS INCLUDING WORK–FAMILY ENRICHMENT AS A MEDIATING MECHANISM

As suggested by Greenhaus and Powell (2006), two streams of research have grown out of the early work on the benefits of engaging in both work and family roles. These include first, those studies that have linked work-domain variables with family-domain variables, and second, those studies that have directly measured work–family enrichment and related constructs with self-report scales. The following section will focus on this second line of research. These studies are grouped by antecedent.

Various studies have determined the relationship between workplace constructs and outcomes via work–family enrichment, with enrichment mediating the relationship between satisfaction in both the work and family domains and outcomes in the corresponding opposite domain. For example, Carlson et al. (2010) found that WFE fully mediated the job satisfaction–family performance relationship and partially mediated the family satisfaction–job performance relationship.

Workplace demands and resources have also been examined in mediation models of work–family enrichment (e.g., Mustapha et al., 2011b). In a Malaysian sample of single mothers, job demands were found to be positively related to WFE, which in turn was positively related to one's intention to stay, resulting in partial mediation (Mustapha et al., 2011b). Alternatively, in a three-year longitudinal study, job resources had a positive effect on work engagement through WFE, indicating partial mediation (Hakanen et al., 2011). Additionally, reciprocal effects were found for the effect of WFE on work engagement. WFE has also been found to mediate the relationships between job characteristics and job satisfaction, affective commitment, and organizational citizenship behavior (Baral & Bhargava, 2010). Taylor et al. (2009) determined that WFE mediated the relationship between job characteristics and psychological contract fairness. In a recent study by Hunter et al. (2010), WFE partially mediated the association between team resources and project satisfaction, while FWE mediated the association between team resources and family satisfaction, for a group of graduate and undergraduate students. Another workplace resource, flexible work arrangements, has been positively associated with WFE, which in turn was positively related to both job satisfaction and negatively related to turnover intentions, resulting in mediation (McNall et al., 2010a). WFE also partially mediates the relationship between a family–friendly work environment and intention to stay, in a sample of single mothers (Mustapha, Ahmad, Uli, & Idris, 2011a).

Some evidence points to the availability of supervisor support as an antecedent in studies where work–family enrichment is tested as a mediator. Baral and Bhargava (2010) found WFE to mediate the relationship between supervisor support and affective commitment. A study by Taylor et al. (2009) suggests that supervisor support is related to WFE, which was subsequently associated with psychological contract fairness. Recently, Odle-Dusseau et al. (2012) found WFE to mediate the relationships between family-supportive supervisor behaviors and organizational commitment, intention to leave, and organizational support performance, the dimension of job performance that is marked by the extent to which one provides support for coworkers and others in the organization.

Work–family climate or culture may also play a role in mediation models of work–family enrichment. Gordon et al. (2007) found partial mediation results for the association between work–family culture and job satisfaction, career satisfaction, and organizational commitment via WFE. Findings from the study by Taylor et al. (2009) indicate that WFE mediates the relationship between work climate for family and psychological contract fairness.

Other scholarly work that has examined work–family enrichment as a linking mechanism has included nonwork or family antecedents. For example, having children less than 18 years of age at home is negatively related to FWE, which is in turn negatively related to depression, resulting in mediation effects (Franche et al., 2006). The relationship between psychological involvement in family and personal benefit activities and positive well-being is mediated by FWE (Allis & O'Driscoll, 2008). WFE has also been found to partially mediate the relationship between one's community participation and affective community resources and job stress relationships (Voydanoff, 2005a). This same study additionally found

partial mediation for FWE with the association between affective community resources and marital satisfaction and marital risk relationships.

In all, few studies have tested the mediating role of work–family enrichment. Those that have explored this relationship have primarily included
workplace resources as antecedents, although nonwork variables have also
been examined. Job satisfaction is the major outcome variable studied in
addition to organizational commitment and well-being.

It is evident that further research is necessary to determine the role of
work–family enrichment in linking work and family attitudes and behaviors
in positive ways. Surprisingly, the majority of the existing studies measured
only one direction of the relationship (i.e., WFE, as opposed to FWE) as a
mediator. WFE and FWE are separate constructs and may differentially
relate to work and family antecedents and outcomes in unique ways, as has
been suggested by others (e.g., Grzywacz, 2000), thus emphasizing the
importance of future work to investigate both directions of the construct.

Research is needed examining on the mediating effects of work–family
enrichment in the relationship between social support and strain outcomes,
as studies including these constructs are scarce, yet reveal promising results.
Two studies have thus far incorporated supervisor support antecedents in
work–family mediation models (Baral & Bhargava, 2010; Taylor et al.,
2009), while one study has included family-specific supervisor support as an
antecedent (Odle-Dusseau et al., 2012). This suggests that organizations
may look to enhance both general supervisor support, as well as family-
specific supervisor support, as a cost-effective means for enriching the work–
life interface and subsequent employee work attitudes and behaviors.

The preliminary research reviewed above also indicates that a few
different well-being factors are affected in mediation models with enrichment. However, recent meta-analytic evidence points to a number of health
and well-being outcomes that are related to enrichment (McNall et al.,
2010b) and are apt for studying in future mediation models.

SPILLOVER–CROSSOVER MODELS

Although enrichment research has primarily investigated work–family
enrichment on individual-level outcomes, a few studies have examined the
effects of enrichment-related constructs using a crossover paradigm (e.g.,
Hammer et al., 2005). More recently, a spillover–crossover perspective has
been proposed, whereby work–family conflict that is experienced by one
individual is transferred and experienced by another individual in the
same social environment (Bakker, Demerouti, & Burke, 2009; Bakker,

Demerouti, & Dollard, 2008). This framework can be extended to the transmission of positive experiences.

Crossover represents a complementary level of analysis to work–family enrichment research, in that it allows for an understanding of how experiences are transmitted on the inter-individual level. Crossover is a dyadic contagion process whereby one person's experience affects the experience of another person in the same social environment, and was originally proposed to explain the contagion of stressors or strain within the spousal dyad (Bolger, DeLongis, Kessler, & Wethington, 1989). Westman (2001) proposes that crossover can occur by means of a direct effect, resulting from empathic reactions, or an indirect effect, resulting from the two individuals' interactions with each other. In addition, individuals can be subjected to the same common stressors present in a shared environment, although this does not constitute a crossover process.

Work–family researchers have argued that the definition and investigation of crossover should be broadened to include the crossover of positive experiences or positive feelings (e.g., Westman, 2001). Demerouti (2012) found evidence for a positive spillover–crossover model between spousal dyads. Specifically, a partner's work resources were found to spill over to their own individual energy, as mediated by their work–self facilitation. Work–self and family–self facilitation are new constructs representing the degree to which an individual's engagement in work contributes to enhanced functioning while engaging in personal interests (Demerouti, 2012). In turn, that partner's energy was found to cross over to their partner's home resources, and subsequently spill over to their own individual energy levels through family–self facilitation. This work has helped to explicate the process by which positive experiences can cross over between partners. Further research is needed on utilizing a spillover–crossover perspective, in order to better understand how work–family enrichment can be transferred between individuals.

CONCLUSIONS

We have reviewed the empirical research on predictors, outcomes, and mechanisms linking work and family attitudes and behaviors via work–family enrichment. A total of 86 studies are represented in Tables 1 and 2, most of which have publication dates after 2000. The significant increase in research on work–family enrichment parallels that of the positive psychology movement and more specifically, that of positive organizational psychology. We believe that it is important for organizational practitioners and scholars to develop structures and systems that support the increase in work–family enrichment, given the significant individual and organizational outcomes associated with both WFE and FWE. Additionally, focusing on work–family enrichment demonstrates a move away from the traditional disease model in occupational health and organizational psychology, to a more positive health perspective that represents positive organizational psychology.

ACKNOWLEDGMENT

The authors wish to thank Carlos H. Rodriguez for his assistance with this chapter.

REFERENCES

Allis, P., & O'Driscoll, M. (2008). Positive effects of nonwork-to-work facilitation on well-being in work, family, and personal domains. *Journal of Managerial Psychology, 23*, 273–291.

Amah, O. E. (2009). The direct and interactive roles of work family conflict and work family facilitation in voluntary turnover. *International Journal of Human Sciences, 6*, 812–826.

Andreassi, J. K., & Thompson, C. A. (2007). Dispositional and situational sources of control: Relative impact on work-family conflict and positive spillover. *Journal of Managerial Psychology, 22*, 722–740.

Aryee, S., Srinivas, E. S., & Tan, H. H. (2005). Rhythms of life: Antecedents and outcomes of work-family balance in employed parents. *Journal of Applied Psychology, 90*, 132–146.

Bakker, A. B., Demerouti, E., & Burke, R. (2009). Workaholism and relationship quality: A spillover-crossover perspective. *Journal of Occupational Health Psychology, 14*, 23–33.

Bakker, A. B., Demerouti, E., & Dollard, M. F. (2008). How job demands affect partners' experience of exhaustion: Integrating work-family conflict and crossover theory. *Journal of Applied Psychology, 93*, 901–911.

Balmforth, K., & Gardner, D. (2006). Conflict and facilitation between work and family: Realizing the outcomes for organizations. *New Zealand Journal of Psychology, 35*, 69–76.

Baral, R., & Bhargava, S. (2010). Work-family enrichment as a mediator between organizational interventions for work-life balance and job outcomes. *Journal of Managerial Psychology, 25*, 274–300.

Baral, R., & Bhargava, S. (2011). Examining the moderating influence of gender on the relationships between work-family antecedents and work-family enrichment. *Gender in Management: An International Journal, 26*, 122–147.

Bhargava, S., & Baral, R. (2009). Antecedents and consequences of work-family enrichment among Indian managers. *Psychological Studies, 54*, 213–225.

Bolger, N., DeLongis, A., Kessler, R. C., & Wethington, E. (1989). The contagion of stress across multiple roles. *Journal of Marriage and Family, 51*, 175–183.

Boyar, S. L., & Mosley, D. C. (2007). The relationship between core self-evaluations and work and family satisfaction: The mediating role of work-family conflict and facilitation. *Journal of Vocational Behavior, 71,* 265–281.

Boz, M., Martinez, I., & Munduate, L. (2009). Breaking negative consequences of relationship conflicts at work: The moderating role of work family enrichment and supervisor support. *Revista de Psigologia del Trabajo y de las Organizaciones, 25,* 113–121.

Brockwood, K. J. (2002). *An examination of positive work-family spillover among dual-earner couples in the sandwiched generation.* Unpublished doctoral dissertation. Portland State University.

Butler, A. B., Grzywacz, J. G., Bass, B. L., & Linney, K. D. (2005). Extending the demands-control model: A daily diary study of job characteristics, work-family conflict and work-family facilitation. *Journal of Occupational Health Psychology, 78,* 155–169.

Carlson, D. S., Ferguson, M., Kacmar, K. M., Grzywacz, J. G., & Whitten, D. (2011a). Pay it forward: The positive crossover effects of supervisor work-family enrichment. *Journal of Management, 37,* 770–789.

Carlson, D., Zivnuska, S., Kacmar, K. M., Ferguson, M., & Whitten, D. (2011b). Work-family enrichment and job performance: A constructive replication of affective events theory. *Journal of Occupational Health Psychology, 16,* 297–312.

Carlson, D. S., Grzywacz, J. G., & Kacmar, K. M. (2010). The relationship of schedule flexibility and outcomes via the work-family interface. *Journal of Managerial Psychology, 25,* 330–355.

Carlson, D. S., Grzywacz, J. G., & Zivnuska, S. (2009). Is work-family balance more than conflict and enrichment? *Human Relations, 62,* 1459–1486.

Carlson, D. S., Hunter, E. M., Ferguson, M., & Whitten, D. (in press). Work-family enrichment and satisfaction: Mediating processes and relative impact of originating and receiving domains. *Journal of Management.*

Carlson, D. S., Kacmar, K. M., Wayne, J. H., & Grzywacz, J. G. (2006). Measuring the positive side of the work-family interface: Development and validation of a work-family enrichment scale. *Journal of Vocational Behavior, 68,* 131–164.

Carlson, D. S., Witt, L. A., Zivnuska, S., Kacmar, M., & Grzywacz, J. G. (2008). Supervisor appraisal as the link between family-work balance and contextual performance. *Journal of Business Psychology, 23,* 37–49.

Chen, Z., Powell, G. N., & Greenhaus, J. H. (2009). Work-to-family conflict, positive spillover, and boundary management: a person-environment fit approach. *Journal of Vocational Behavior, 74,* 82–93.

Cinamon, R. G., & Rich, Y. (2010). Work family relations: Antecedents and outcomes. *Journal of Career Assessment, 18,* 59–70.

Culbertson, S. S., Huffman, A. H., & Alden-Anderson, R. (2010). Leader-member exchange and work-family interactions: The mediating role of self-reported challenge- and hindrance-related stress. *The Journal of Psychology: Interdisciplinary and Applied, 144,* 15–36.

Demerouti, E. (2012). The spillover and crossover of resources among partners: The role of work-self and family-self facilitation. *Journal of Occupational Health Psychology, 17,* 184–195.

Eby, L. T., Casper, W. J., Lockwood, A., Bordeaux, C., & Brinley, A. (2005). Work and family research in IO/OB: Content analysis and review of the literature (1980–2002). *Journal of Vocational Behavior, 66,* 124–197.

Franche, R. L., Williams, A., Ibrahim, S., Grace, S. L., Mustard, C., Minore, B., & Stewart, D. E. (2006). Path analysis of work conditions and work-family spillover as modifiable workplace factors associated with depressive symptomology. *Stress and Health, 22*, 91–103.

Gareis, K. C., Barnett, R. C., Ertel, K. A., & Berkman, L. F. (2009). Work-family enrichment and conflict: Additive effects, buffering, or balance? *Journal of Marriage and Family, 71*, 696–707.

Gordon, J. R., Whelan-Berry, K. S., & Hamilton, E. H. (2007). The relationship among work-family conflict and enhancement, organizational work-family culture, and work outcomes for older working women. *Journal of Occupational Health Psychology, 12*, 350–364.

Greenhaus, J. H., & Allen, T. D. (2011). Work-family balance: A review and extension of the literature. In J. C. Quick & L. E. Tetrick (Eds.), *Handbook of occupational health psychology* (2nd ed., pp. 165–183). Washington, DC: American Psychological Association.

Greenhaus, J. H., & Powell, G. N. (2006). When work and family are allies: A theory of work-family enrichment. *Academy of Management Review, 31*, 72–92.

Greenhaus, J. H., Ziegert, J. C., & Allen, T. D. (2012). When family-supportive supervision matters: Relations between multiple sources of support and work–family balance. *Journal of Vocational Behavior, 80*, 266–275.

Grzywacz, J. G. (2000). Work-family positive spillover and health during midlife: Is managing conflict everything? *American Journal of Health Promotion, 14*, 236–243.

Grzywacz, J. G., & Bass, B. L. (2003). Work, family, and mental health: Testing different models of work-family fit. *Journal of Marriage and Family, 65*, 248–262.

Grzywacz, J. G., & Butler, A. B. (2005). The impact of job characteristics on work-family facilitation: Testing a theory and distinguishing a construct. *Journal of Occupational Health Psychology, 10*, 97–109.

Grzywacz, J. G., & Marks, N. F. (2000). Family, work, work-family positive spillover, and problem drinking during midlife. *Journal of Marriage and Family, 62*, 336–348.

Haar, J. M., & Bardoel, E. A. (2008). Positive spillover from the work-family interface: A study of Australian employees. *Asia Pacific Journal of Human Resource, 46*, 275–287.

Hakanen, J. J., Peeters, M. C. W., & Perhoniemi, R. (2011). Enrichment processes and gain spirals at work and at home: A 3-year cross-lagged panel study. *Journal of Occupational and Organizational Psychology, 84*, 8–30.

Hammer, L. B., Cullen, J. C., Neal, M. B., Sinclair, R. R., & Shafiro, M. V. (2005). The longitudinal effects of work-family conflict and positive spillover on depressive symptoms among dual-earner couples. *Journal of Occupational Health Psychology, 10*, 138–154.

Hammer, L. B., Kossek, E. E., Yragui, N. L., Bodner, T. E., & Hanson, G. C. (2009). Development and validation of the multidimensional measure of family supportive supervisor behaviors (FSSB). *Journal of Management, 35*, 837–856.

Hanson, G. C., Hammer, L. B., & Colton, C. L. (2006). Development and validation of a multidimensional scale of perceived work-family positive spillover. *Journal of Occupational Health Psychology, 11*, 249–265.

Hecht, T. D., & Boies, K. (2009). Structure and correlates of spillover from nonwork to work: An examination of nonwork activities, well-being, and work outcomes. *Journal of Occupational Health Psychology, 14*, 414–426.

Hill, J. E. (2005). Work-family facilitation and conflict, working fathers and mothers, work-family stressors and support. *Journal of Family Issues, 26*, 793–819.

Hunter, E. M., Perry, S. J., Carlson, D. S., & Smith, S. A. (2010). Linking team resources to work-family enrichment and satisfaction. *Journal of Vocational Behavior, 77,* 304–312.

Innstrand, S. T., Langballe, E. M., Espnes, G. A., Aasland, O. G., & Falkum, E. (2010a). Work-home conflict and facilitation across four different family structures in Norway. *Community, Work & Family, 13,* 231–249.

Innstrand, S. T., Langballe, E. M., Espnes, G. A., Falkum, E., & Aasland, O. G. (2008). Positive and negative work-family interaction and burnout: A longitudinal study of the reciprocal relations. *Work & Stress, 22,* 1–15.

Innstrand, S. T., Langballe, E. M., Falkum, E., Espnes, G. A., Aasland, O. G., & Falkum, E. (2010b). Personality vulnerability and work-home interaction: The effect of job performance-based self-esteem on work/home conflict and facilitation. *Scandinavian Journal of Psychology, 51,* 480–487.

Jaga, A., & Bagraim, J. (2011). The relationship between work-family enrichment and work-family satisfaction outcomes. *South African Journal of Psychology, 41,* 52–62.

Karatepe, O. M., & Bekteshi, L. (2008). Antecedents and outcomes of work-family facilitation and family-work facilitation among frontline hotel employees. *International Journal of Hospitality Management, 27,* 517–528.

Karatepe, O. M., & Kilic, H. (2009). The effects of two directions of conflict and facilitation on frontline employees' job outcomes. *The Service Industries Journal, 29,* 977–993.

Karatepe, O. M., & Magaji, A. B. (2008). Work-family conflict and facilitation in the hotel industry: A study in Nigeria. *Cornell Hospitality Quarterly, 49,* 395–412.

Karimi, L., & Nouri, A. (2009). Do work demands and resources predict work-to-family conflict and facilitation? A study of Iranian male employees. *Journal of Family and Economic Issues, 30,* 193–202.

King, E. B., Botsford, W. E., & Huffman, A. H. (2009). Work, family, and organizational advancement: Does balance support the perceived advancement of mothers? *Sex Roles, 61,* 879–891.

Kinnunen, U., Feldt, T., Geurts, S., & Pulkkinen, L. (2006). Types of work-family interface: Well-being correlates of negative and positive spillover between work and family. *Scandinavian Journal of Psychology, 47,* 149–162.

Kirchmeyer, C. (1992). Perceptions of nonwork-to-work spillover: Challenging the common view of conflict-ridden relationships. *Basic and Applied Social Psychology, 13,* 231–249.

Kwan, H. K., & Mao, Y. (2011). The role of citizenship behavior in personal learning and work-family enrichment. *Frontiers of Business Research in China, 5,* 96–120.

Kwan, H. K., Mao, Y., & Zhang, H. (2010). The impact of role modeling on protégés personal learning and work-to-family enrichment. *Journal of Vocational Behavior, 77,* 313–322.

Lourel, M., Ford, M. T., Gamassou, C. E., Gueguen, N., & Hartmann, A. (2009). Negative and positive spillover between work and home. *Journal of Managerial Psychology, 24,* 438–449.

Lu, J. F., Siu, O. L., Spector, P. E., & Shi, K. (2009). Antecedents and outcomes of a fourfold taxonomy of work-family balance in Chinese employed parents. *Journal of Occupational Health Psychology, 14,* 182–192.

Masuda, A. D., McNall, L. A., Allen, T. D., & Nicklin, J. M. (2012). Examining the constructs of work-to-family enrichment and positive spillover. *Journal of Vocational Behavior, 80,* 197–210.

McNall, L. A., Masuda, A. A., & Nicklin, J. M. (2010a). Flexible work arrangements, job satisfaction, and turnover intentions: The mediating role of work-to-family enrichment. *Journal of Psychology, 144,* 61–81.

McNall, L. A., Masuda, A. D., Shanock, L. R., & Nicklin, J. M. (2011). Interaction of core self-evaluations and perceived organizational support on work-to-family enrichment. *The Journal of Psychology, 145*, 133–149.

McNall, L. A., Nicklin, J. M., & Masuda, A. (2010b). A meta-analytic review of the consequences associated with work-family enrichment. *Journal of Business Psychology, 25*, 381–396.

Michel, J. S., & Clark, M. A. (2009). Has it been affect all along? A test of work-to-family and family-to-work models of conflict, enrichment, and satisfaction. *Personality and Individual Differences, 47*, 163–168.

Michel, J. S., Clark, M. A., & Jaramillo, D. (2011). The role of the Five Factor model of personality in the perceptions of negative and positive forms of work-nonwork spillover: A meta-analytic review. *Journal of Vocational Behavior, 79*, 191–203.

Mustapha, N., Ahmad, A., Uli, J., & Idris, K. (2011a). Antecedents of intention to stay with the mediating effects of work-family factors among single mothers. *European Journal of Social Sciences, 22*, 262–279.

Mustapha, N., Ahmad, A., Uli, J., & Idris, K. (2011b). Work-family facilitation and family satisfaction as mediators in the relationship between job demands and intention to stay. *Asian Social Science, 7*, 142–153.

Odle-Dusseau, H. N., Britt, T. W., & Greene-Shortridge, T. M. (2012). Organizational work family resources as predictors of job performance and attitudes: The process of work-family conflict and enrichment. *Journal of Occupational Health Psychology, 17*, 28–40.

Pedersen, D. E., Minnote, K. L., Kiger, G., & Mannon, S. E. (2009). Workplace policy and environment, family role quality, and positive family-to-work spillover. *Journal of Family and Economic Issues, 30*, 80–89.

Powell, G. N., & Greenhaus, J. H. (2010). Sex, gender, and the work-to-family interface: Exploring negative and positive interdependencies. *Academy of Management Journal, 53*, 513–534.

Proost, K., De Witte, H., De Witte, K., & Schreurs, B. (2010). Work–family conflict and facilitation: the combined influence of the job demand–control model and achievement striving. *European Journal of Work and Organizational Psychology, 19*, 615–628.

Roche, M., & Haar, J. M. (2010). Work-family interface predicting needs satisfaction: The benefits for senior management. *Journal of Social & Behavioural Research in Business, 1*, 12–23.

Rotondo, D. M., & Kincaid, J. F. (2008). Conflict, facilitation, and individual coping styles across the work and family domains. *Journal of Managerial Psychology, 23*, 484–506.

Schaufeli, W. B., & Bakker, A. B. (2004). Job demands, job resources and their relationship with burnout and engagement: A multi-sample study. *Journal of Organizational Behavior, 25*, 293–315.

Schneewind, K. A., Reeb, C., & Kupsch, M. (2010). Bidirectional work-family spillover and work-family balance: How are they related to personal distress and global stress? *Family Science, 1*, 123–134.

Seery, B. L., Corrigall, E. A., & Harpel., T. (2008). Job-related emotional labor and its relationship to work-family conflict and facilitation. *Journal of Family Economic Issues, 29*, 461–477.

Seligman, M. E. P., & Csikszentmihalyi, M. (2000). Positive psychology: An introduction. *American Psychologist, 55*, 5–14.

Sieber, S. D. (1974). Toward a theory of role accumulation. *American Sociological Review, 39,* 467–478.

Siu, O., Lu, J., Brough, P., Lu, C., Bakker, A. B., Kalliath, T., & Shi, K. (2010). Role resources and work-family enrichment: the role of work engagement. *Journal of Vocational Behavior, 77,* 470–480.

Stevens, D. P., Minnotte, K. L., Mannon, S. E., & Kiger, G. (2007). Examining the "neglected side of the work-family interface": Antecedents of positive and negative family-to-work spillover. *Journal of Family Issues, 28,* 242–262.

Stoddard., M., & Madsen, S. R. (2007). Toward an understanding of the link between work-family enrichment and individual health. *Journal of Behavioral and Applied Management, 9,* 2–15.

Sumer, H. C., & Knight, P. A. (2001). How do people with different attachment styles balance work and family? A personality perspective on work-family linkage. *Journal of Applied Psychology, 86,* 653–663.

Taylor, B. L., Delcampo, R. G., & Blancero, D. M. (2009). Work-family conflict/facilitation and the role of workplace supports for U.S. Hispanic professionals. *Journal of Organizational Behavior, 30,* 643–664.

van Steenbergen, E. F., & Ellemers, N. (2009). Is managing the work-family interface worthwhile? Benefits for employee health and performance. *Journal of Organizational Behavior, 30,* 617–642.

van Steenbergen, E. F., Ellemers, N., & Mooijaart, A. (2007). How work and family can facilitate each other: Distinct types of work-family facilitation and outcomes for women and men. *Journal of Occupational Health Psychology, 12,* 279–300.

van Steenbergen, E. F., Ellemers, N., & Mooijaart, A. (2009). Combining work and family: How family supportive work environments and work supportive home environments can reduce work-family conflict and enhance facilitation. In D. R. Crane & E. J. Hill (Eds.), *Handbook of families & work: Interdisciplinary perspectives.* New York, NY: University Press of America.

Voydanoff, P. (2004a). Implications of work and community demands and resources for work-to-family conflict and facilitation. *Journal of Occupational Health Psychology, 9,* 275–285.

Voydanoff, P. (2004b). The effects of work demands and resources on work-to-family conflict and facilitation. *Journal of Marriage and Family, 66,* 398–412.

Voydanoff, P. (2005a). Social integration, work-family conflict and facilitation, and job and marital quality. *Journal of Marriage and Family, 67,* 666–679.

Voydanoff, P. (2005b). The differential salience of family and community demands and resources for family-to-work conflict and facilitation. *Journal of Family and Economic Issues, 26,* 395–417.

Wadsworth, L. L., & Owens, B. P. (2007). The effects of social support on work-family enhancement and work-family conflict in the public sector. *Public Administration Review, 67,* 75–87.

Wayne, J. H. (2009). Reducing conceptual confusion: Clarifying the positive side of work and family. In D. R. Crane & E. J. Hill (Eds.), *Handbook of families and work: Interdisciplinary perspectives* (pp. 105–140). New York, NY: University Press of America.

Wayne, J. H., Grzywacz, J. G., Carlson, D. S., & Kacmar, K. M. (2007). Work-family facilitation: A theoretical explanation and model of primary antecedents and consequences. *Human Resource Management Review, 17,* 63–76.

Wayne, J. H., Musisca, N., & Fleeson, W. (2004). Considering the role of personality in the work-family experience: Relationships of the big five to work-family conflict and facilitation. *Journal of Vocational Behavior, 64*, 108–130.

Wayne, J. H., Randel, A. E., & Stevens, J. (2006). The role of identity and work–family support in work–family enrichment and its work-related consequences. *Journal of Vocational Behavior, 69*, 445–461.

Westman, M. (2001). Stress and strain crossover. *Human Relations, 54*, 717–751.

Westring, A. F., & Ryan, A. M. (2010). Personality and inter-role conflict and enrichment: Investigating the mediating role of support. *Human Relations, 63*, 1815–1834.

Williams, A., Franche, R. L., Ibrahim, S., Mustard, C. A., & Layton, F. R. (2006). Examining the relationship between work-family spillover and sleep quality. *Journal of Occupational Health Psychology, 11*, 27–31.

Yanchus, N. J., Eby, L. T., Lance, C. E., & Drollinger, S. (2010). The impact of emotional labor on work-family outcomes. *Journal of Vocational Behavior, 76*, 105–117.

Zimmerman, K. L. (2009). *Operationalizing the antecedents of work-family positive spillover: A longitudinal study.* Unpublished doctoral dissertation. Portland State University.

Zimmerman, K. L., & Hammer, L. B. (2010). Positive Spillover: Where have we been and where are we going? In J. Houdmont & S. Leka (Eds.), *Contemporary occupational health psychology: Global perspectives on research, education, and practice* (Vol. I, pp. 272–295). Chichester, UK: Wiley-Blackwell.

CAPTURING THE MOMENT IN THE WORKPLACE: TWO METHODS TO STUDY MOMENTARY SUBJECTIVE WELL-BEING

Wido G. M. Oerlemans and Arnold B. Bakker

Employees may experience all kinds of emotional ups and downs during a regular workday. Consider a woman in a traffic jam on her way to work. She may be annoyed because of it. Yet, later at work, she may experience enthusiasm as a result of the positive feedback she receives from her boss. After work, she may spend the evening with friends, watch TV, exercise, or instead continue to work because of a deadline that is due the next morning. Importantly, everyday changes in momentary affective experiences at work and elsewhere appear to affect important outcomes, including job satisfaction (Judge & Ilies, 2004), employee well-being (Demerouti, Bakker, Geurts, & Taris, 2009; Fuller et al., 2003; Gross, Meier, & Semmer, 2013), organizational citizenship behavior (Dalal, Lam, Weiss, Welch, & Hulin, 2009), and job performance (Bakker & Oerlemans, 2011; Beal, Weiss, Barros, & MacDermid, 2005; Xanthopoulou, Bakker, Demerouti, & Schaufeli, 2009).

In the current chapter, we will describe two research methods – the Experience Sampling Method (ESM) and the Day Reconstruction Method (DRM) – that organizational psychologists can use to capture the momentary affective experiences of individuals in reaction to their everyday

Advances in Positive Organizational Psychology, Volume 1, 329–346
ISSN: 2046-410X/doi:10.1108/S2046-410X(2013)0000001017

working life. We will argue that these momentary affective experiences are important in advancing knowledge and practice within the field of organizational psychology, especially in terms of employee well-being and employee performance. Moreover, we describe the practical challenges involved in conducting empirical studies based on an ESM or DRM design.

STUDYING MOMENTARY SUBJECTIVE WELL-BEING

Subjective Well-Being (SWB) refers to how a person evaluates his or her life (Diener, Sandvik, & Pavot, 1991). This appraisal may take the form of cognitions – when a person makes a conscious evaluative judgment about his or her satisfaction with (working) life; or take the form of affect, when people experience negative or positive emotions in response to everyday life. In this chapter, we concentrate on the latter form of SWB – momentary affective experiences (Russell, 1980, 2003) in everyday working life, which we also refer to as momentary SWB.

The momentary SWB of employees has a considerable impact on both personal and organizational outcomes (e.g., Ilies, Schwind, & Heller, 2007), which we will discuss below. However, first, we address the question what kind of methodologies we can use as organizational psychologists to accurately capture and study (changes in) momentary affective experiences in the everyday lives of employees, as well as their consequences. Momentary affective experiences are usually organized around specific episodes that occur in people's everyday life. For instance, it is well known that autobiographical memory is structured hierarchically, with specific events nested within broader episodes (Conway & Pleydell-Pierce, 2000). Thus, when individuals are asked to describe a recent workday that is still fresh in their memory, it is likely that they will describe their day by "reconstructing" their daily events, behaviors, and affective states into meaningful episodes that happened in a "natural" chronological order. For example, as an academic, you may remember getting up, having breakfast, and commuting to work. After getting into the office, you started off by answering e-mails from students and colleagues, after which you attended the weekly meeting of your research group. Thereafter, you had lunch with your colleagues and in the afternoon you continued working on a paper. At the end of your workday, you commuted back home, prepared a meal, ate dinner (perhaps together with your family), and spent the evening by doing some household chores and watching TV before going to bed.

The boundaries between episodes appear to be important in terms of the consolidation and encoding of our affective experiences into our memory (Kurby & Zacks, 2008). Thus, at the end of a specific episode, individuals update their memory in terms of activities, social interactions, or other objects that were present during a particular episode (Beal & Weiss, 2013; Swallow, Zacks, & Abrams, 2009). In other words, the time at the end of an episode and the start time of the next episode represent an important moment where people actually evaluate and decide what to take away from their experience.

Based on this knowledge, we argue that there are at least two fruitful ways for organizational psychologists to (re)capture the flow of episodes and momentary SWB as experienced during the workday: the ESM (Csikszentmihalyi, Larson, & Prescott, 1977), which asks individuals to report on their SWB "in the moment"; and the DRM (Kahneman, Krueger, Schkade, Schwarz, & Stone, 2004), where individuals report on their momentary SWB after chronologically reconstructing the various episodes of the preceding day.

Experience Sampling Method

ESM refers to a method of data collection in which participants respond to repeated signals over the course of time, while functioning within their natural setting (Scollon, Kim-Prieto, & Diener, 2009). Although ESM as a method is not new (Brandstaetter, 1983; Csikszentmihalyi et al., 1977), recent technological advances have facilitated the use of ESM as a research technique. Today, handheld devices (e.g., personal digital assistants (PDAs), or smartphones) can be preprogrammed to signal employees at various moments, asking them to report on their affective experiences "in the moment." In addition, the software in handheld devices allows for a direct transfer to statistical software packages for immediate analysis. Also, the software may enable participants to receive personalized feedback on their handheld devices, depending on the way in which they respond to the questions asked.

There are various ways in which ESM may be used (Reis & Gable, 2000; Wheeler & Reis, 1991). First, "interval contingent sampling" refers to data collection in which participants complete self-reports after a designated interval for a preset time period (e.g., hourly reports, daily reports). Second, "event-contingent sampling" occurs when participants complete self-reports when a predesignated event occurs (e.g., reporting after every social interaction; Cote & Moskowitz, 1998). Third, "signal-contingent sampling" refers to participants responding to various questions (e.g., affective states) when prompted by a randomly timed signal. Of course, the kind of ESM technique that is used depends on the research questions under study.

When studying intra-individual changes in SWB, it is important to ask employees not only about their momentary affective states, but also about the elements in the environment (e.g., quality and quantity of activities, events, interpersonal interactions, and so on) that may affect employees' affective experiences. In this sense, Stone, Shiffman, and DeVries (1999) have coined the term "Ecological Momentary Assessment" (EMA) to study both affective experiences *as well as* elements in the environment potentially related to those momentary affective experiences with the ESM.

Day Reconstruction Method

An alternative and less intrusive way to capture momentary emotional states is the DRM (Kahneman et al., 2004). Kahneman and his colleagues argued that by carefully reconstructing one's day into episodes, individuals are able to call upon their episodic memory to accurately remember their affective experiences during each episode. To this end, the DRM asks individuals to reconstruct in chronological order all episodes of the day. A particular episode is operationalized by the time an activity began and ended, the domain where such an activity took place (e.g., at home or at work), and also social interactions that may have occurred during such episodes. After carefully reconstructing all episodes of a particular day, participants are asked to indicate their affective experiences for each episode. Affective experiences may contain a range of positive and/or negative affective states like feelings of happiness, excitement, satisfaction, stress, anger, fatigue, or depression.

As alluded to before, people appear to encode and store their affective experiences into their memory when one episode ends and another episode starts (Kurby & Zacks, 2008). The DRM therefore facilitates access to encoded affective experiences by asking individuals about specific episodes – including begin and end times – that occurred during the preceding day. The DRM is susceptible to recall bias, as it uses chronological reconstruction to recall into memory the momentary SWB during episodes that occurred during the previous day. To investigate the accuracy of affective experiences as reported with the DRM, Dockray et al. (2010) compared an ESM with a DRM during similar time points of the day. In this study, 94 women aged 21–54 years completed an ESM and DRM diary for two days. Via ESM, the participants reported on their "current" feelings during six fixed time points (after getting up, at 10:00, 12:00, 15:00, 17:00, and before going to bed) on a scale from 1 (not at all) to 5 (very much). Feelings analyzed were happy, tired, stressed, frustrated, and angry. Note that only happiness was considered as a positive emotional state whereas all other states investigated were negative. At the end of a 24-hour cycle, participants completed a DRM diary, where they were asked to reconstruct all episodes of the last 24 hours. Each episode was defined in terms of onset and duration, location, social situation, and activity. After reconstructing their day, participants were asked to report on the same positive and negative states as reported in the ESM. The affective states as reported with the ESM during particular hours of the day were then compared to the affective states as reported with the DRM on the same hours of the day. Dockray and colleagues concluded that, after adjustment for attenuation, the mean correlations between affective states reported with ESM and DRM ranged from .58 to .78 on workdays, and from .67 to .90 on nonwork days. Interestingly, momentary happiness showed the highest between-method correlation, ranging from .71 on a workday to .90 on nonwork days. Although the overlap between ESM versus DRM is not perfect, it shows that the DRM is able to (re)capture fluctuations in momentary affective states to a reasonable extent. In addition, the DRM provides rich information on the actual episodes that occur in the everyday life of individuals.

CAUSES AND CONSEQUENCES OF MOMENTARY SWB

Why should organizational psychologists be interested in studying momentary SWB? We argue that there are at least four reasons for doing so. First, a growing body of research shows that the level of SWB fluctuates significantly on a within-person level. For example, Bakker, Oerlemans, Demerouti, and Sonnentag (2013) used a DRM design to study intra-individual, daily fluctuations in SWB (i.e., happiness, vigor, state of being recovered) among 85 employees over the course of nine workdays. Interestingly, results showed that 59% of the variance in happiness,

66% of the variance in vigor, and 88% of the variance in recovery before sleep (i.e., a combination of feeling relaxed and recovered) could be attributed to fluctuations on a within-person and day level. Another example is the ESM study of Ilies and Judge (2002), where 27 employees completed momentary job satisfaction measures at four different times during the day for a period of four weeks, resulting in a total of 1907 observations. Results showed that the within-individual variance for daily job satisfaction was 36%.

Second, fluctuations in momentary SWB can be attributed to very specific events, activities, social interactions, or other "momentary" indicators that vary within individuals, on a day-to-day basis. For instance, the DRM study of Bakker et al. (2013) showed that continuing work-related activities during off-job time at night had a negative effect on daily happiness, whereas engaging in exercise had a positive effect on daily SWB (i.e., happiness, vigor, and recovery before sleep). In a similar vein, Dimotakis, Scott, and Koopman (2010) followed 60 full-time employees over the course of 10 workdays with an ESM. The participants completed measures of interpersonal interaction characteristics and affective states at three randomly signaled hours within three two-hour time blocks (9:30–11:30 am; 12:00–2:00 pm; and 2:30–4:30 pm), as well as a measure of job satisfaction at the end of each workday. Dimokakis and his colleagues showed that momentary positive interactions in the workplace had a positive effect on daily positive affect at work, whereas momentary negative interactions in the workplace were positively related to daily negative affect at work.

Intra-individual changes in SWB have also been linked to *time-based variations*. For example, some studies have indicated that people experience greater pleasant affect later in the day versus in the morning, and on weekends versus on workdays (e.g., Dockray et al., 2010; Egloff, Tausch, Kohlmann, & Krohne, 1995; Larsen & Kasimatis, 1990). Moreover, intra-individual changes in momentary SWB also depend on *physiological changes within individuals* across time. For example, using ESM, Ilies, Dimotakis, and Watson (2010) followed 67 employees over 10 working days by signaling people four times a day to fill out their positive affect and negative affect while simultaneously monitoring employees' blood pressure and heart rate levels. The results showed – among other things – that momentary experienced negative affect within employees related significantly to momentary blood pressure. In addition, both momentary positive and negative affects related significantly and positively to momentary elevations in heart rate.

A third reason why organizational psychologists should be interested in momentary SWB is that fluctuations in momentary SWB predict important personal and organizational outcomes. For example, Dimotakis et al. (2010) showed in their study that the direct effects of positive and negative daily workplace interactions on daily job satisfaction were mediated by the positive and negative affective states that people experienced that day in the workplace. Thus, momentary fluctuations in affective states can explain why daily interactions at work affect daily job satisfaction. Moreover, following 42 employees over the course of five consecutive workdays with a diary booklet, Xanthopoulou et al. (2009) showed that daily fluctuations in employee work engagement (i.e., a positive affective/motivational state that is characterized by vigor, dedication, and absorption) predicted daily financial returns in fast food restaurants. Specifically, on days where employees experienced more work engagement (i.e., beyond their general level of work engagement), financial returns were significantly higher compared to days where employees felt less engaged. Another example is the study of Binnewies, Sonnentag, and Mojza (2009), where 92 employees from public service organizations were followed over the course of one workweek. On pocket computers, employees answered two daily surveys (before work and after work). Results showed that the momentary state of being recovered in the morning (i.e., feeling physically and mentally refreshed and energetic) was a significant predictor of daily task performance.

Fourth and finally, individual differences *between* employees can affect the way in which daily, or even momentary events, activities, and social interactions at work have an impact on momentary SWB and its consequences on the intra-individual level (*within* employees). In Bakker et al.'s (2013) DRM study, employees also filled out a questionnaire assessing their enduring level of workaholism (i.e., a strong inner drive to work excessively hard; Taris, Schaufeli, & Verhoeven, 2005). Results revealed that spending time on daily work-related activities during nonwork hours at night had a stronger negative relationship with daily SWB (i.e., happiness, vigor, recovery) for employees who scored high (vs. low) on workaholism. In contrast, spending more time on daily physical activities had a more positive impact on daily SWB for employees who scored high (vs. low) on workaholism. These findings imply that particularly workaholics experience negative consequences from working during nonwork time, and instead benefit more from other activities after work such as physical exercise. One other example from outside the organizational research domain is the study of Oerlemans, Bakker, and Veenhoven (2011) who used the DRM to follow 438 retired elderly across 16 days. In addition to the DRM, participants also filled out a personality questionnaire (the Ten Item Personality Index (TIPI); Gosling, Rentfrow, & Swann, 2003). The findings demonstrated that elderly who were high on extraversion experienced more happiness when engaging in social activities compared to individuals who scored low on extraversion. In addition, highly extraverted individuals spent more of their daytime on social activities. Thus, it seems useful to combine research methods that can assess between-person differences (i.e., in enduring SWB, or trait personality) with ESM or DRM to better understand how within-person processes may work out differently across time depending on more stable characteristics that vary between persons.

In sum, based on the above findings, we argue that the ESM and the DRM (or similar diary methods) are useful tools for organizational psychologists that help to shed light on intra-individual changes in SWB, as well as their causes and consequences.

ESM OR DRM

Organizational psychologists should be aware of the pros and cons when considering to perform a study based on either an ESM or a DRM. We therefore discuss some of the most important considerations in this section.

Labor Intensive

One major consideration is that both methods are rather labor intensive for the participants. Consider that a typical ESM study lasts about one to two weeks. During that time, participants are signaled multiple times a day at which they have to fill out various questions on a handheld device. Let's consider a study where employees have to answer 10 questions for five times a day. The total number of questions to be answered over a two-week time period would then be 700 ($10 \times 5 \times 14$). Even when participants are able to respond quickly to the ESM signal – for instance answering all the questions in two minutes – it will take participants about 140 minutes ($2 \times 5 \times 14$) to answer all questions. With the DRM, participants are usually approached only once per day. However, participants first have to reconstruct the episodes (e.g., in terms of activities, social interactions, and affective experiences) of the preceding (or previous) day in chronological order, and then indicate their affective experiences during each reported episode. Depending on the exact number of activities and affective experiences reported, it may take participants about 15 minutes per day to fill out a diary based on the DRM. Then, the total time involved when using a DRM design for two weeks would be about 210 minutes (15 × 14). Note, however, that shorter time periods may also suffice and thus reduce the total number of questions asked, and the time needed to fill out each questionnaire.

Disruptive Nature

A second consideration relates to the disruptive nature of ESM versus DRM in the daily life of participants. When using the ESM, participants respond to an automated signal which is in most cases a beeping sound. This alarm disrupts one's activities and conversations at work, and may annoy participants and others who are present when the signal beeps. There may also be instances where respondents are not likely to reply to the ESM signal, or during which it is impossible to do so. For example, at meetings, the signal can be considered disruptive and the device is likely to be turned off. Moreover, when working in a high volume setting (e.g., industrial workers in factories), beeping sounds may not be heard by all of the participants, although vibrating devices or visual signals could circumvent this problem. Also, participating in an ESM study could be outright dangerous for some groups of employees, for instance, when driving a truck or when working as an air traffic controller. When using a DRM, participants have more autonomy to decide a time and a place that suit them most during which they can fill out their diary. This prevents most of the annoyances involved in having to respond to automated signals right away as with ESM.

"Real Time" versus "Recalled" Affective Experiences

A third consideration involves the time lag involved in capturing momentary affective experiences. An advantage ESM has over DRM is that it can assess true "in vivo" behavior and emotional experiences of employees multiple times during the day, with hardly any time lag. Instead, the DRM uses episodic recall to assess affective experiences. However, it appears that the DRM captures affective experiences rather well as compared to the ESM method (Dockray et al., 2010). Moreover, one important advantage of the DRM is that participants reconstruct all of their activities, social interactions, and affective experiences of the day. This might be advantageous over using an ESM, as researchers can get a full overview on what kind of episodes have unfolded in chronological order, as well as affective experiences of employees during each episode.

Group Size

There appear to be differences in the sample size when comparing ESM to DRM based studies. ESM studies typically involve only small sample sizes of about 20 to 100 employees (e.g., Bono, Foldes, Vinson, & Muros, 2007; Fullagar & Kelloway, 2010; Ilies, & Judge, 2002). Compared to ESM, DRM studies appear to have attracted somewhat larger groups of participants. For example, Kahneman et al. (2004) included 909 employed women over the course of one workday; Oerlemans et al. (2011) were able to include 438 retired seniors who reconstructed one day per month for over two years. Finally, Knabe, Rätzel, Schöb, and Weimann (2010) included 171 employed and 177 unemployed individuals using a combination of DRM and survey methods. Group size may be important depending on the type of research questions. Consider that as organizational psychologists, we would like to examine differences in the daily within-person fluctuations in job satisfaction of employees working in two different organizations. It would be important to include a large sample of employees of both organizations to accurately answer this research question. A small subsample of motivated and conscientious employees from both organizations would not be enough, although the fine-grained within-person fluctuations can still be analyzed with small group sizes.

CHALLENGES INVOLVED IN MOTIVATING PARTICIPANTS

How can we motivate employees to participate in either ESM or DRM studies? One classic way to motivate individuals to participate in such lengthier studies is to *offer money* or *gifts*. Monetary incentives have been shown to significantly improve compliance (Lynn, 2001). However, we should be cautious when deciding on the amount of compensation. Stone, Kessler, and Haythornwaite (1991) reported that an incentive of $250 resulted in overall poor quality of data, showing that more money may not always result in data that is better usable.

A second way to motivate participants is to *develop innovative designs* that are (more) attractive and intuitive for participants. For instance, at the Erasmus University in Rotterdam, we initiated a research project called "Happiness Indicator" (in Dutch: Gelukswijzer), which includes a "Happiness diary" that is based on a DRM design. Going beyond traditional paper-and-pencil questionnaires, we have developed a web-based DRM diary that individuals fill out online. In the online happiness diary, participants reflect on their preceding day by reconstructing in chronological order from half hour to half hour their activities and social interactions from the time they got up until the time they went to bed. To facilitate data collection, participants are presented with a visual timeline and a predefined activity bar to report their time spent on each of their activities during the preceding day (see Fig. 1). Upon completion of the timeline, participants are presented a second screen to report on their happiness during each of the reported activities (see Fig. 2). Since its launch in 2010, the Happiness Indicator has attracted over 40,000 participants, who together reported well over 200,000 episodes and happiness scores.

One example of an attractive design to acquire data on a large scale with an ESM is the "track your happiness" research project initiated by Matt Killingsworth at Harvard University (www.trackyourhappiness.org). Participants can download an iPhone application after first responding to a survey that includes questions about sociodemographic background.

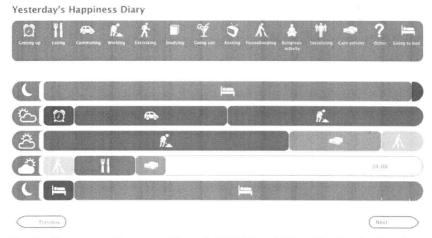

Fig. 1. Yesterday's Happiness Diary: A DRM-Based Diary Used in the Happiness Indicator Project – Showing Main Activity Category Bar and Timeline.

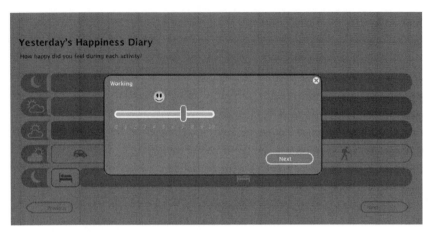

Fig. 2.   Yesterday's Happiness Diary: A DRM-Based Diary Used in the Happiness
Indicator Project – Showing Happiness Scale per Activity Type.

Next, participants can indicate how many times they want to be notified
during the day. Each notification involves questions about how people are
feeling, where they are, and what kind of activity they are doing. Whereas
this is no different from any other ESM approach, the iPhone application
makes it very easy for participants to fill out all of the questions asked. At
the start of 2011, the database already included 5,000 people reporting on
close to 250,000 activities and momentary affective experiences (see
Killingsworth & Gilbert, 2010).

A third way of motivating employees to participate is by *including online
feedback.* For instance, Bakker and colleagues have developed Internet
applications – based on the Job Demands–Resources Model (e.g., Bakker &
Demerouti, 2007) called the "Job Demands–Resources Monitor" and the
"Engagement App." Employees who fill in an online questionnaire receive
personalized feedback on their computer or smartphone about their most
important job demands and resources. For example, the feedback includes
histograms of the specific demands and resources identified as important for
work engagement, and participants' scores are compared with a benchmark
(comparison group). In addition, the feedback mode is interactive, such that
participants can click on the histograms and receive written feedback about
the meaning of their scores on the demands and resources. In a similar way,
feedback about work engagement has been included in these web-based
tools. The PDF report that can be generated after filling out the Job

Demands–Resources Monitor can be used as input for interviews with human resources managers and personal coaches – to discuss how personal working conditions can be optimized. In this way, it becomes more beneficial for employees to participate in studies. Also, the feedback itself may be used to optimize the working environment.

The Happiness Indicator we have developed at the Erasmus University in Rotterdam, as well as the "track your happiness" project initiated by Matt Killingsworth also include various personal feedback modules. In both projects, participants receive personalized feedback on how their happiness varies, depending on what they do, where they are, time of day, and various other factors that are collected with either the DRM or ESM. Moreover, in the Happiness Indicator, participants can also compare their happiness during activities with other participants who have similar backgrounds (e.g., in terms of age, gender, educational level, and marital status), using a dynamic benchmark. The website also includes survey questions about enduring work-related well-being, personality, and monthly happiness. When filling out personality and enduring work-related well-being questionnaires, individual scores of participants are compared with scores of a representative national (Dutch) sample. Standard deviations (SD) of the national sample are used to provide participants with feedback on their individual score. For example, the individual score could be very low (-2 SD), low (-1 SD), normal (mean), high ($+1$ SD), or very high ($+2$ SD) as compared with the national sample. Based on this comparison, participants receive personalized and automated feedback in the form of histograms and text messages.

Importantly, personalized feedback may also be an effective starting point for intervention studies, aimed at developing, embedding, and sustaining positive work-related well-being and behavior in organizational settings (e.g., Bakker, Oerlemans, & Ten Brummelhuis, in press).

ANALYZING ESM AND DRM DATA WITH HIERARCHICAL LINEAR MODELING

How should organizational psychologists analyze the data that have been collected with the ESM or DRM? Importantly, data based on the DRM and ESM are by definition hierarchically structured; activities or experiences are nested within specific days, and days are nested within persons (e.g., Larson & Delespaul, 1992). Therefore, it is important to use statistical software such as Hierarchical Linear Modeling (HLM) that can handle nested data. There are various reasons for doing so.

First of all, HLM tends to handle missing data rather well (for details, read Snijders & Bosker, 1999), which is especially important in follow-up research where some participants are likely to fail to respond to some of the signals (ESM) or sometimes forget to reconstruct their day (DRM). Second, HLM can model time. This is important, as we know that momentary affective experiences are (also) dependent on time. For instance, people usually experience more positive affective states at the end of the day as compared to the beginning of the day (Rusting & Larsen, 1998). Moreover, people appear to experience higher positive affective states during the weekend (i.e., the so-called "weekend peak effect") and during off-job time compared to workdays (Egloff et al., 1995). Moreover, momentary affective states experienced during a previous moment or activity are likely to spill over to the next moment or activity (Larsen, 1987). HLM can take into account both time variables and lagged effects of affective states experienced during previous moments.

Third, HLM takes the dependency of the hierarchical structure of the ESM or DRM data into account (Reis & Gable, 2000). Put differently, ordinary multiple regression analysis is based on the assumption of independent observations. However, as events are nested within persons, and persons are nested within groups (e.g., organizations), there is a clear hierarchical structure that violates this assumption. HLM analysis takes such dependencies into account. Fourth, the technique allows the simultaneous estimation of within-person and between-person effects, and possible "cross-level" interactions between variables on each of the two levels (Reis & Gable, 2000). This makes it possible to analyze whether episodes on the event-level are experienced differently, depending on factors that reside at the between-person level. For example, in the DRM study of Bakker et al. (2013), HLM analyses were used to examine the cross-level interaction effect of a variable that resides on the between-person level (i.e., workaholism) on the within-person relationship between the daily time spent on off-job activities and daily SWB.

Various software programs are capable of handling nested data. For instance, SPSS 16.0 and higher (now PASW Statistics) is capable of handling HLM analyses. Another popular HLM software program is called Multi Level for Windows (MLWin; Rasbash, Browne, Healy, Cameron, & Charlton, 2000). In addition, software programs such as Mplus (Muthén & Muthén, 1998) are capable of performing HLM analyses. One advantage of

Mplus is that it also produces model fit indices that are commonly reported in Structural Equation Modeling (SEM).

CONCLUSION

This chapter outlined two research methods – the Experience Sampling Method (ESM) and the Day Reconstruction Method (DRM) – as useful tools for organizational psychologists to study changes in momentary SWB in everyday working life. We showed that momentary affective states fluctuate significantly within persons, depending on the chronological flow of events and social interactions people experience during the days. In turn, fluctuations in momentary affective experiences are predictive of important personal and organizational outcomes, including daily SWB and daily performance. We wrote this chapter to inspire organizational psychologists to start using ESM and DRM next to more traditional research methods. It is fascinating that both methods provide a very realistic picture (or better: a movie) of how people experience and react to real-life situations. It is our hope that organizational psychologists will use ESM and DRM methods in order to better understand which kind of psychological processes help individuals to become happier and more productive in their everyday work lives.

REFERENCES

Bakker, A. B., & Demerouti, E. (2007). The job demands resources model: State of the art. *Journal of Managerial Psychology*, *22*, 209–328.

Bakker, A. B., & Oerlemans, W. G. M. (2011). Subjective well-being in organizations. In K. S. Cameron & G. M. Spreitzer (Eds.), *The Oxford handbook of positive organizational scholarship* (pp. 178–189). New York, NY: Oxford University Press.

Bakker, A. B., Oerlemans, W. G. M., Demerouti, E., & Sonnentag, S. (2013). Workaholism and daily recovery: A day reconstruction study of leisure activities. *Journal of Organizational Behavior*, *34*, 87–107.

Bakker, A.B., Oerlemans, W.G.M., & Ten Brummelhuis, L. (2013). Becoming fully engaged in the workplace: What individuals and organizations can do to foster work engagement. In C. Cooper & R. Burke (Eds.), *The fulfilling workplace: The organization's role in achieving individual and organizational health* (pp. 55–70). Surrey, UK: Gower.

Beal, D. J., & Weiss, H. M. (2013). The episodic structure of life at work. In A. B. Bakker & K. Daniels (Eds.), *A day in the life of a happy worker* (pp. 8–24). Hove, UK: Psychology Press.

Beal, D. J., Weiss, H. M., Barros, E., & MacDermid, S. M. (2005). An episodic process model of affective influences on performance. *Journal of Applied Psychology, 90,* 1054–1068.

Binnewies, C., Sonnentag, S., & Mojza, E. J. (2009). Daily performance at work: Feeling recovered in the morning as a predictor of day-level job performance. *Journal of Organizational Behavior, 30,* 67–93.

Bono, J. E., Foldes, H. J., Vinson, G., & Muros, J. P. (2007). Workplace emotions: The role of supervision and leadership. *Journal of Applied Psychology, 92,* 1357–1367.

Brandstaetter, H. (1983). Emotional responses to other persons in everyday life situations. *Journal of Personality and Social Psychology, 45,* 871–883.

Cote, S., & Moskowitz, D. S. (1998). On the dynamic covariation between interpersonal behavior and affect: Prediction from neuroticism, extraversion, and agreeableness. *Journal of Personality and Social Psychology, 75,* 1032–1046.

Csikszentmihalyi, M., Larson, R. J., & Prescott, S. (1977). The ecology of adolescent activity and experience. *Journal of Youth and Adolescence, 6,* 281–294.

Dalal, R. S., Lam, H., Weiss, H. M., Welch, E. R., & Hulin, C. L. (2009). A within-person approach to work behavior and performance: concurrent and lagged citizenship-counterproductivity associations, and dynamic relationships with affect and overall job performance. *Academy of Management Journal, 52,* 1051–1066.

Demerouti, E., Bakker, A. B., Geurts, S. A. E., & Taris, T. W. (2009). Daily recovery from work-related effort during non-work time. In S. Sonnentag, P. L. Perrewé & D. C. Ganster (Eds.), *Current perspectives on job-stress recovery: Research in occupational stress and well being* (Vol. 7, pp. 85–123). Bingley, UK: JAI Press.

Diener, E., Sandvik, E., & Pavot, W. (1991). Happiness is the frequency, not the intensity, of positive versus negative affect. In F. Strack, M. Argyle & N. Schwarz (Eds.), *Subjective well-being: An interdisciplinary perspective* (pp. 119–139). New York, NY: Pergamon.

Dimotakis, N., Scott, B. A., & Koopman, J. (2010). An experience sampling investigation of workplace interactions, affective states, and employee well being. *Journal of Organizational Behavior, 32,* 572–588.

Dockray, S., Grant, N., Stone, A. A., Kahneman, D., Wardle, J., & Steptoe, A. (2010). A comparison of affect ratings obtained with ecological momentary assessment and the day reconstruction method. *Social Indicator Research, 2,* 269–283.

Egloff, B., Tausch, A., Kohlmann, C., & Krohne, H. W. (1995). Relationships between time of day, day of the week, and positive mood: Exploring the role of mood measure. *Motivation and emotion, 19,* 99–100.

Fullagar, C. J., & Kelloway, E. K. (2010). Flow at work: An experience sampling approach. *Journal of occupational and organizational psychology, 82,* 595–615.

Fuller, J. A., Stanton, J. M., Fisher, G. G., Spitzmuller, C., Russell, S. S., & Smith, P. C. (2003). A lengthy look at the daily grind: Time series analyses of events, mood, stress, and satisfaction. *Journal of Applied Psychology, 88,* 1019–1033.

Gosling, D., Rentfrow, P. J., & Swann, W. B., Jr. (2003). A very brief measure of the big-five personality domains. *Journal of Research in Personality, 37,* 504–528.

Gross, S., Meier, L. L., & Semmer, N. K. (2013). Latent growth modeling applied to diary data: The trajectory of vigor across a working week as an illustrative example. In A. B. Bakker & K. Daniels (Eds.), *A day in the life of a happy worker* (pp. 114–131). New York, NY: Psychology Press.

Ilies, R., Dimotakis, N., & Watson, D. (2010). Mood, blood pressure, and heart rate at work: An experience-sampling study. *Journal of Occupational Health Psychology, 15,* 120–130.

Ilies, R., & Judge, T. A. (2002). Understanding the dynamic relationships among personality, mood, and job satisfaction: A field experience sampling study. *Organizational Behavior and Human Decision Processes, 89*, 1119–1139.

Ilies, R., Schwind, K., & Heller, D. (2007). Employee well-being: A multi-level model linking work and non-work domains. *European Journal of Work and Organizational Psychology, 16*, 326–341.

Judge, T. A., & Ilies, R. (2004). Affect and job satisfaction: A study of their relationship at work and at home. *Journal of Applied Psychology, 89*, 661–673.

Kahneman, D., Krueger, A. B., Schkade, D. A., Schwarz, N., & Stone, A. A. (2004). A survey method for characterizing daily life experience: The day reconstruction method. *Science, 3*, 1776–1780.

Killingsworth, M. A., & Gilbert, D. T. (2010). A wandering mind is an unhappy mind. *Science, 330*, 932.

Knabe, A., Rätzel, S., Schöb, R., & Weimann, J. (2010). Dissatisfied with life but having a good day: Time use and well being for the unemployed. *The Economic Journal, 120*, 867–889.

Kurby, C. A., & Zacks, J. M. (2008). Segmentation in the perception and memory of events. *Trends in Cognitive Sciences, 12*, 72–79.

Larsen, R. J. (1987). The stability of mood variability: A spectral analytic approach to daily mood assessments. *Journal of Personality and Social Psychology, 52*, 1195–1204.

Larsen, R. J., & Kasimatis, M. (1990). Individual differences in entrainment of mood to the weekly calendar. *Journal of Personality and Social Psychology, 58*, 164–171.

Larson, R., & Delespaul, P. A. E. G. (1992). Analyzing experience sampling data: A guidebook for the perplexed. In M. W. deVries (Ed.), *The experience of psychopathology: Investigating mental disorders in their natural settings* (pp. 58–78). New York, NY: Cambridge University Press.

Lynn, P. (2001). The impact of incentives on response rates to personal interview surveys: Role and perceptions of interviewers. *International Journal of Public Opinion Research, 13*, 326–336.

Muthén, L. K., & Muthén, B. O. (1998). *Mplus user's guide [computer software manual]*. Los Angeles, CA: Muthén & Muthén.

Oerlemans, W. G. M., Bakker, A. B., & Veenhoven, R. (2011). Finding the key to happy aging: A day reconstruction study of happiness. *Journal of Gerontology: Psychological Sciences, 66B*, 1–10.

Rasbash, J, Browne, W. J., Healy, M., Cameron, B., & Charlton, C. (2000). *The MLwin software package, version 1.10*. London: Institute of Education.

Reis, H. T., & Gable, S. L. (2000). Event-sampling and other methods for studying everyday experience. In H. T. Reis & C. M. Judd (Eds.), *Handbook of research methods in social and personality psychology* (pp. 190–222). New York, NY: Cambridge University Press.

Russell, J. A. (1980). A circumplex model of affect. *Journal of Personality and Social Psychology, 39*, 1161–1178.

Russell, J. A. (2003). Core affect and the psychological construction of emotion. *Psychological Review, 110*, 145–172.

Rusting, C. L., & Larsen, R. J. (1998). Diurnal patterns of unpleasant mood: Associations with neuroticism, depression, and anxiety. *Journal of Personality, 66*, 85–103.

Scollon, C. P., Kim-Prieto, C., & Diener, E. (2009). Experience sampling: Promises and pitfalls, strengths and weaknesses. *Social Indicator Research, 39*, 157–180.

Snijders, T. A. B., & Bosker, R. J. (1999). *Multilevel analysis: An introduction to basic and advanced multilevel modeling*. Thousand Oaks, CA: Sage Publications.

Stone, A. A., Kessler, R. C., & Haythornwaite, J. A. (1991). Measuring daily events and experiences: Decisions for the researcher. *Journal of Personality, 59*, 575–607.

Stone, A. A., Shiffman, S. S., & DeVries, M. W. (1999). Ecological momentary assessment. In D. Kahneman, E. Diener & N. Schwarz (Eds.), *Well-being: Foundations of a hedonic psychology* (pp. 26–39). New York, NY: Russell Sage Foundation.

Swallow, K. M., Zacks, J. M., & Abrams, R. A. (2009). Event boundaries in perception affect memory encoding and updating. *Journal of Experimental Psychology: General, 138*, 236–257.

Taris, T. W., Schaufeli, W. B., & Verhoeven, L. C. (2005). Workaholism in the Netherlands: Measurement and implications for job strain and work-nonwork conflict. *Applied Psychology: An International Review, 54*, 37–60.

Wheeler, L., & Reis, H. T. (1991). Self-recordings of everyday life events: Origins, types, and uses. *Journal of Personality, 59*, 339–354.

Xanthopoulou, D., Bakker, A. B., Demerouti, E., & Schaufeli, W. B. (2009). Work engagement and financial returns: A diary study on the role of job and personal resources. *Journal of Occupational and Organizational Psychology, 82*, 183–200.

ABOUT THE CONTRIBUTORS

Simon L. Albrecht is a registered psychologist and has a PhD and a master's degree in Organizational Psychology. Simon's PhD focused on identifying the dimensions, antecedents, and consequences of organizational trust. Simon is a Senior Lecturer within the Organizational Psychology program at Deakin University, Melbourne, Australia. Teaching, research, and practice interests are in the areas of work engagement, organizational development and change, leadership development, culture and climate, and organizational politics. Simon has published in numerous international journals, has numerous book chapters in print, and has presented at international conferences. In addition to his academic and research interests Simon also has considerable consultancy experience. He has previously been a director of a human resource consultancy engaged in delivering a broad range of organizational development activities and programs.

Arnold B. Bakker is Professor and Chair of the Department of Work & Organizational Psychology, Erasmus University Rotterdam, and Adjunct Professor at the Department of Sociology and Social Policy, Lingnan University, Hong Kong. He is president of the European Association of Work and Organizational Psychology, secretary-general of the Alliance of Organizational Psychology, and a Fellow of APS. Bakker's research focuses on positive organizational psychology (e.g., work engagement, JD-R model, happiness, flow, and performance). He publishes regularly in the major I/O journals, including *Journal of Applied Psychology*, *Journal of Organizational Behavior*, and *Journal of Occupational Health Psychology*. For more details, see http://www.arnoldbakker.com.

Charlotte P. Barner is Adjunct Professor and faculty advisor for the organizational dynamics concentration within the Annette Caldwell Simmons School Education and Human Development at Southern Methodist University's Master's of Liberal Studies program. Dr. Barner coleads the graduate school's study abroad programs in Ireland and India. Her doctorate is in human and organizational learning from The George Washington University. She has over 20 years of senior corporate leadership experience in human and organizational learning and development. Charlotte is an executive consultant, author, and speaker.

Robert W. Barner is Lecturer with the Graduate Program of Dispute Resolution & Conflict Management, within the Annette Caldwell Simmons School of Education & Human Development, at Southern Methodist University. Within this role he teaches courses in organizational dynamics, and directs study abroad programs in Ireland and India. Dr. Barner is the author of seven books, including five foreign language translations. He has published in many academic journals, and is also currently a reviewer for four academic journals.

Justin M. Berg is a PhD candidate in Management at The Wharton School, University of Pennsylvania. His research focuses on creativity, proactivity, and the meaning of work in organizations. His work has been published in *Organization Science, Academy of Management Review*, and the *Journal of Organizational Behavior*.

Uta K. Bindl is an Assistant Professor of Management and Organizations at the University of Western Australia's UWA Business School. Uta received her PhD in Work Psychology from the Institute of Work Psychology at the University of Sheffield. Uta's main research areas include positive work behaviors, particularly employee proactivity, as well as well-being and emotion regulation at work. Uta has to date published her research in leading outlets such as the *Journal of Applied Psychology*, the *Journal of Management*, and the *APA Handbook of Industrial and Organizational Psychology*.

Kim S. Cameron is William Russell Kelly Professor of Management and Organization in the Ross School of Business and Professor of Higher Education in the School of Education at the University of Michigan. He currently serves as Associate Dean in charge of Executive Education in the Ross School. Professor Cameron has served as Dean of the Weatherhead School of Management at Case Western Reserve University, Associate Dean in the Marriott School of Management at Brigham Young University, and as a Department Chair at the University of Michigan. He also served on the faculties of the University of Wisconsin-Madison and Ricks College. Dr. Cameron's work has been published in more than 120 academic articles and 14 scholarly books, and his current research focuses on the virtuousness of and in organizations and their relationships to organizational success. He is one of the cofounders of the Center for Positive Organizational Scholarship at the University of Michigan. Dr. Cameron received BS and MS degrees from Brigham Young University and MA and PhD degrees from Yale University. He served as a Fulbright Distinguished Scholar and was a recipient of the Organizational Behavior Teaching Society's Outstanding Educator Award and the Academy of Management OMT Division's Trailblazer Award. In addition to his faculty responsibilities, he consults with a variety of business, government, and educational organizations in North America, South America, Asia, Africa, and Europe on positive leadership, organizational culture change, and developing positive dynamics in organizations.

Tori L. Crain, MS is a graduate student in the Department of Psychology at Portland State University. She is currently receiving her PhD in industrial/organizational psychology with a minor in occupational health psychology. Her research interests include both positive and negative aspects of the work–family interface, in addition to the interplay between work, family, and sleep.

Hans De Witte is Full Professor in Work Psychology at the Faculty of Psychology and Educational Sciences of the KU Leuven, Belgium, where he is member of the Research Group Work, Organizational and Personnel Psychology (WOPP), and is appointed as Extraordinary Professor at the North-West University of South Africa (Vanderbijlpark Campus). His research includes the study of the psychological consequences of job insecurity, unemployment, temporary employment, and downsizing, as well as mobbing and job stress (e.g., burnout) versus well-being at work (e.g., work engagement). He has published in journals such as the *European Journal of Work and Organizational Psychology, Work & Stress, Journal of Occupational and Organizational Psychology*, and *Applied Psychology: An International Review*. He is member of the European Network of Work & Organizational Psychologists (ENOP) and of the executive board of the Scientific Committee Unemployment, Job Insecurity & Health of ICOH.

Maren Dollwet is an Organizational Behavior PhD Candidate at Claremont Graduate University in California. As part of her research, Maren has investigated constructs rooted in Positive Organizational Psychology (e.g., Positive Psychological Capital, hope in the workplace) and their contributions to theory and practice. Furthermore, Maren is very involved in research on multinational workplaces and international assignments. She has developed an assessment tool to measure and develop cross-cultural skills and her dissertation examines the effectiveness of various expatriate onboarding strategies to facilitate adjustment to international assignments for both expats and their spouses.

Stewart I. Donaldson is Professor of Psychology, Dean, and Director of the Claremont Evaluation Center at Claremont Graduate University, USA. He is the Chair of the International Positive Psychology Association's 2013 World Congress of Positive Psychology in Los Angeles, June 27–30. Donaldson's recent research focuses on positive organizational psychology and the design and evaluation of positive interventions. He serves on many editorial advisory boards and among his 10 books and numerous journal publications are *Applied Positive Psychology: Improving Everyday Life, Health, Schools, Work, and Society* (Routledge, 2011) and Positive Organizational Psychology, Behavior, and Scholarship: A Review of the Emerging Literature and Evidence Base (*Journal of Positive Psychology*, 2010). Donaldson has received early career achievement awards from the Western Psychological Association and the American Evaluation Association.

Adrienne Dougherty received her BA in Psychology with High Honors from California State University, Fullerton, where she was recipient of the National Institute of Health's Minority Access to Research Careers Fellowship. She is currently a second year doctoral student in Social Psychology at the University of Michigan working with Drs. Oscar Ybarra and Ethan Kross. She is also a recipient of a National Science Foundation Graduate Research Fellowship. Adrienne is broadly interested in emotions and emotion regulation. She is currently examining whether the effectiveness of different emotion regulation techniques depends on the type of discrete emotion people are trying to regulate. She is also examining the role that language plays in self-regulation.

Jane E. Dutton is the Robert L. Kahn Distinguished University Professor of Business Administration and Psychology. She is a cofounder of the Center for Positive Organizational Scholarship at the Ross School of Business, University of Michigan (http://www.centerforpos.org/). Her research focuses compassion at work, job crafting, positive identities, and high-quality connections in work organizations.

Taru Feldt is an Adjunct Professor and Vice Chair of the Department of Psychology, University of Jyväskylä, Finland. Feldt's research focuses mainly on occupational health psychology (e.g., job strain, work engagement, recovery, personal work goals). She currently leads research projects focusing on long-term development of occupational health and ethical culture of organizations. She publishes in the journals of occupational health (e.g., *Work & Stress*, *Anxiety Stress and Coping*) and business ethics (e.g., *Journal of Business Ethics*).

Barbara L. Fredrickson is Kenan Distinguished Professor of Psychology and Director of the Positive Emotions and Psychophysiology Lab (a.k.a. PEP Lab) at the University of North Carolina. She is a leading scholar studying positive emotions and human flourishing, and her research on positive emotions and lifestyle change is funded by the U.S. National Institutes of Health. Dr. Fredrickson has published more than 100 peer-reviewed articles and book chapters and with the publication of *Positivity* (2009, Crown) and *Love 2.0* (2013, Penguin) she has written about her research for general audiences as well. Dr. Fredrickson's contributions have been recognized with numerous honors, including the American Psychological Association's Templeton Prize in Positive Psychology and the Society of Experimental Psychology's Career Trajectory Award. Her work has influenced scholars and practitioners worldwide, within education, business, healthcare, the military, and beyond, and she is regularly invited to give keynotes nationally and internationally. She lives in Chapel Hill with her husband and two sons.

Marylène Gagné is a Professor at University of Western Australia School of Psychology. Marylène is a leading researcher in the area of work motivation, and her research examines the effects of work factors, such as job design, leadership, and compensation, on intrinsic and extrinsic work motivation. She also examines the effects of these different types of motivation on performance, well-being, and employee retention. She publishes her work in the *Journal of Organizational Behavior*, *Educational and Psychological Measurement*, and *Motivation and Emotion*. She is associate editor for the *European Journal of Work and Organizational Psychology* and serves on four other journal editorial boards.

Jamie A. Gruman is an Associate Professor in the Department of Business at the University of Guelph, and an Adjunct Professor in the Faculty of Applied Health Sciences at the University of Waterloo, both in Ontario, Canada. He is also a founding member and serves as Chair of the Board of Directors of the Canadian Positive Psychology Association. Dr. Gruman's research focuses largely on positive organizational psychology, and the on-boarding of new employees. His work has appeared in journals such as *The Journal of Vocational Behavior*, *Human Resource Management*, *Human Resource Management Review*, *The Journal of Managerial Psychology*, *Industrial and Organizational Psychology*, and books such as the *Handbook of Employee Engagement*, and the *Oxford Handbook of Organizational Socialization*.

Leslie B. Hammer is a Professor of Psychology in the Department of Psychology at Portland State University, Portland, Oregon. Her research focuses on ways in which organizations can help reduce work and family stress and improve positive spillover by facilitating both formal and informal workplace supports. She is the Director of the Center for Work-Family Stress, Safety, and Health, the Director of the Occupational Health Psychology graduate training program at Portland State University, and the Associate Director of the Oregon Healthy Workforce Center, one of four centers of excellence in Total Worker Health. She is a Past Founding President of the Society for Occupational Health Psychology and has published in the *Journal of Applied Psychology, Journal of Occupational Health Psychology, Journal of Management*, and other noted outlets.

Ulla Kinnunen is Professor of Psychology at the School of Social Sciences and Humanities in the University of Tampere, Finland. At present, her research interests focus on occupational well-being from the perspectives of stress, burnout, work engagement, and recovery. Kinnunen's work has appeared in scholarly journals, including *Journal of Occupational Health Psychology, Journal of Organizational Behavior, Work & Stress, Journal of Occupational and Organizational Psychology*, as well as numerous edited volumes. She serves as an Associate Editor of *Work & Stress* and on the editorial boards of the *Journal of Organizational Behavior* and the *Journal of Personnel Psychology*.

Ethan Kross is an Assistant Professor in the Psychology Department at the University of Michigan and the Director of the University of Michigan Emotion and Self-Control Laboratory. He is also a Faculty Associate at the University of Michigan's Research Center for Group Dynamics and Depression Research Center. His research examines the psychological processes that underlie self-control and has been funded by both federal (e.g., NSF, NIMH) and private (John Templeton) agencies. Kross publishes regularly in leading scientific journals (e.g., *Proceedings of the National Academy of Science, Psychological Science, Journal of Personality and Social Psychology, Biological Psychiatry*), and has his research disseminated to the public through various media outlets (CBS Evening News, *Science Magazine, The New York Times*, CNN).

David Seungjae Lee is a PhD student in Social Psychology at the University of Michigan. His research examines the role of social factors (e.g., social support, social network, interaction dynamics) in how people judge others, regulate emotions, and make decisions in their best interest.

Nicholas LoBuglio is a doctoral student in Management at the Wharton School of the University of Pennsylvania. His research focuses on group cultures, relationships at work, and emotional experiences. He received his BA from the University of North Carolina at Chapel Hill.

Fred Luthans is University and George Holmes Distinguished Professor of Management at the University of Nebraska. A former President of the Academy of Management, he is currently editor of three journals and author of several books and numerous articles. His research at first focused on what he called O.B. Mod. (organizational behavior modification) and in recent years what he formulated and termed as "positive organizational behavior (POB)" and "psychological capital (PsyCap)." He has been actively doing teaching, research, and consulting in Europe, Southeast Asia, South Korea and especially China over the past 35 years.

Anne Mäkikangas, PhD, is an Adjunct Professor in Work Psychology. She works as academy research fellow in the University of Jyväskylä, Finland. She has experience in examining occupational well-being from personality, job stress, and positive psychology perspectives. In addition, she has expertise in research methodology. Mäkikangas's work has been published in a range of journals including *Psychological Assessment, Journal of Occupational and Organizational Psychology, European Journal of Work and Organizational Psychology*, and *Work & Stress*.

Saija Mauno completed her PhD in Psychology in 1999. At the moment she works as a full professor in University of Tampere, Finland and as an academy research fellow in University of Jyväskylä, Finland. Her research interests cover work–family interface, occupational well-being, changes in labor markets, and coping resources. She has published articles in several international journals, for example, *Work & Stress, Journal of Vocational Behavior, European Journal of Work and Organizational Psychology*.

Wido G. M. Oerlemans is a post-doctoral researcher at the Department of Work & Organizational Psychology, Erasmus University Rotterdam, The Netherlands. His research interests include daily lifestyle and happiness, the use of signature strengths, daily recovery from work, and occupational well-being. In addition, he uses research techniques such as experience sampling and the day reconstruction method to accurately capture subjective experiences in real time. He has published articles in several international journals, for example, *Journal of Happiness Studies, Journal of Organizational Behavior, Journal of Gerontology*, and *Psychology of Sports and Exercise*.

Sharon K. Parker is a Winthrop Professor at the UWA Business School, University of Western Australia. She is an Australian Research Council Future Fellow and also an Honorary Professor at the Institute of Work Psychology, University of Sheffield, where she was previously the Director. Professor Parker is an Associate Editor for the *Journal of Applied Psychology* and a past and present member of several other editorial boards. She is a representative-at-large for the Organizational Behavior Division of the Academy of Management, and is a member of the Society for Industrial and Organizational Psychology and the Academy of Management. Her research interests are focused on proactive behavior, work design, self-efficacy, and employee perspective taking. Professor Parker has published several books, including a Sage publication on job and work design, over 40 refereed journal articles (including publications in top tier journals such as *Journal of Applied Psychology* and *Academy of Management Journal*), 35 book chapters, and numerous technical and practitioner publications.

Alan M. Saks is Professor of Organizational Behavior and Human Resources Management at the University of Toronto. He conducts research on recruitment and applicant reactions, job search, transfer of training, employee engagement, and the socialization and on-boarding of newcomers. He is the author and coauthor of several textbooks including *Organizational Behavior: Understanding and Managing Life at Work*, *Managing Performance through Training and Development*, and *Research, Measurement, and Evaluation of Human Resources*.

Jeffrey Sanchez-Burks is an Associate Professor of Management and Organizations at the University of Michigan Ross School of Business and a Faculty Associate at the Research Center for Group Dynamics at the Institute for Social Research in Ann Arbor. He received his PhD in Social Psychology from the University of Michigan. Previously, he was on the faculty at the University of Southern California and has had visiting appointments at universities in Singapore, France, Turkey, and Russia. His research focuses on intercultural relations, strategic creativity, and social emotional intelligence. Sanchez-Burks serves on the editorial board of *Organization Science*, is an elected Fellow of the Society of Experimental Social Psychology, and is a member of the Association for Psychological Science, and the Academy of Management.

Tanya Vacharkulksemsuk is an advanced-level PhD candidate in Social Psychology at the University of North Carolina, Chapel Hill. Her research focuses on positive psychology and emotions, nonverbal behaviors, and interpersonal relationships in the workplace. She will begin a post-doctoral research fellowship at the University of California, Berkeley, Haas School of Business in Fall 2013, supported through the National Science Foundation.

Anja Van den Broeck is an Affiliated Lecturer at the Research Group Work, Organizational and Personnel Psychology at the KU Leuven and a Lecturer (equivalent of Assistant Professor) at the Human Relations Research Group of the University College Brussels (Belgium). She is specialized in work and motivation psychology. Her research focuses on the interplay between job design (i.e., job hindrances, challenges, and resources) and other management practices (e.g., reward policies and learning opportunities) and impaired (i.e., burnout) and optimal (i.e., work engagement) well-being and motivation (e.g., Self-Determination Theory). She has published in journals such as *Work & Stress, Journal of Vocation Behavior, Journal of Occupational and Organizational Psychology, European Journal of Work and Organizational Psychology*, and *Applied Psychology: An International Review*.

Joris Van Ruysseveldt is Assistant Professor at the Faculty of Psychology, Open University of the Netherlands, where he teaches courses in Work Psychology, Psychology of Organizational Change, HRM and Selection and Assessment. His research focuses on the interrelationships between organizational change, workplace learning and work-related stress, on organizational justice and employee well-being, and on positive organizational psychology (engagement, active learning, performance). He publishes in major journals, including *Work & Stress, Journal of Vocational Behavior, European Journal of Work and Organizational Psychology, International Journal of Stress Management*, and *Cognitive, Affective, & Behavioral Neuroscience*.

Els Vanbelle is a researcher of the Research Group Work, Organizational and Personnel Psychology in the Department of Psychology and Educational Sciences of the KU Leuven (Belgium) since September 2011. In November 2012, she started her PhD on job crafting under the supervision of Prof. Dr. Hans De Witte and Prof. Dr. Anja Van den Broeck. Her aim is to elaborate on a process model of job crafting, which is about altering one's job characteristics in order to optimize one's well-being and functioning. Her research on job crafting fits in with broader topics of her interest such as job-related well-being, job design, motivation, personal values and identity, the work–nonwork interface, and well-being in general.

Maarten Vansteenkiste obtained his PhD at the university of Leuven (2005) under supervision of Prof. Dr. W. Lens, Prof. Dr. E. Deci, and Prof. Dr. H. De Witte. After one year of post-doc studies, funded by the Flemish institute for research, he accepted a position as a Professor in Motivation and Developmental Psychology at Ghent University, Belgium. Through his research, he tries to expand Self-Determination Theory, a well-known and empirically validated motivation theory. He is especially interested in theoretically and empirically linking Self-determination Theory with other well-established motivation theories and has used SDT as a source of inspiration to study motivational dynamics in a variety of life domains, including education, parenting, well-being, ecology, work, and sport and exercise. He has published widely about these topics in diverse high quality journals. Currently, he is supervising several doctoral students, is an editorial board member of several journals, and he was awarded the Richard E. Snow Award for distinguished early career contributions to educational psychology (2009) by APA division 15.

Amy Wrzesniewski is Associate Professor of Organizational Behavior at the Yale School of Management, Yale University. She received her PhD from the University of Michigan. She has won the IBM Faculty Award for her research. Her research on the meaning of work has been published in a wide range of top academic journals and highlighted in several best-selling books and popular press outlets. Her current research involves studying how employees shape their tasks, interactions, and relationships with others in the workplace to change the meaning of the job.

Chia-Huei Wu is a PhD candidate at the UWA Business School, University of Western Australia. He holds a master's degree in Psychology from National Taiwan University and a master's degree in Philosophy from University of Sheffield. His research area covers organizational behavior, quality of life research, and indigenous Chinese psychology. He has published 46 journal articles, 6 book chapters, and 63 conference reports and has served as a reviewer for different international journals. His work has been published in outlets including *Journal of Applied Psychology*, *Journal of Management*, *Journal of Occupational and Organizational Psychology*, *Quality of Life Research*, *Personality and Individual Differences*, and *Social Indicators Research*, among others. He has also contributed chapters to books, including *The Oxford Handbook of Leadership and Organizations* and *The Oxford Handbook of Positive Organizational Scholarship*.

Oscar Ybarra is Professor of Psychology at the University of Michigan and Director of the Adaptive Social Cognition Lab. He is also a Faculty Associate at the Research Center for Group Dynamics, Faculty Associate at the Center for Culture, Mind & the Brain, Organizational Studies, and the Center for Entrepreneurship. He also holds a visiting professorship at Southwest University in Chongqing, China. Dr. Ybarra's research revolves around the social underpinnings of cognition and intelligence, how people navigate their web of relations with others, and how people balance connecting socially with the need to pursue and protect other valued goals. Dr. Ybarra's research has been published in the top journals in the field, and his work on social judgment has been used in presentations before congressional hearings on aging and fraud. His work on social interaction and mental exercising has received much media attention across the globe and in many outlets in the United States such as *Forbes, The New York Times, U.S. News & World Report, LA Times*, and the *Washington Post*.

Carolyn M. Youssef-Morgan is the Redding Chair of Business at Bellevue University, Nebraska, USA, a core faculty member in the PhD in Human Capital Management program, and a leading researcher, author, speaker, and consultant on positivity in the workplace. Besides coauthoring *Psychological Capital: Developing the Human Competitive Edge* (Oxford University Press, 2007) with Fred Luthans and Bruce Avolio, her research on psychological capital has been published in the *Journal of Management, Journal of World Business, Organizational Dynamics, International Journal of Human Resource Management*, and numerous recognized edited volumes such as the *Handbook of Positive Psychology* and the *Handbook of Positive Organizational Scholarship*. She also serves as a voting member on the U.S. Technical Advisory Group, designated by the Society for Human Resource Management (SHRM), the American National Standards Institute (ANSI), and the International Organization for Standardization (ISO) to create and represent the United States' view on global human resource standards.

Yufang Zhao is Professor and Associate Dean of the School of Psychology, Southwest University, China. She is a fellow of the Chinese Psychological Society and Chinese Social Psychology Society. Zhao's research focuses on social interaction and health psychology (e.g., intergroup threat, stereotype, mass behavior, and mental health). She publishes regularly in psychology journals, including *Psychological Science* (in China), *Scandinavian Journal of Psychology, Social Behavior and Personality*, and *Experimental Brain Research*.

AUTHOR INDEX

SUBJECT INDEX